Rethinking Peace and Conflict Studies

Series Editors
Oliver P. Richmond, University of Manchester, Manchester, UK
Annika Björkdahl, Department of Political Science, Lund University, Lund, Sweden
Gëzim Visoka, Dublin City University, Dublin, Ireland

This agenda-setting series of research monographs, now more than a decade old, provides an interdisciplinary forum aimed at advancing innovative new agendas for peace and conflict studies in International Relations. Many of the critical volumes the series has so far hosted have contributed to new avenues of analysis directly or indirectly related to the search for positive, emancipatory, and hybrid forms of peace. Constructive critiques of liberal peace, hybrid peace, everyday contributions to peace, the role of civil society and social movements, international actors and networks, as well as a range of different dimensions of peace (from peacebuilding, statebuilding, youth contributions, photography, and many case studies) have been explored so far. The series raises important political questions about what peace is, whose peace and peace for whom, as well as where peace takes place. In doing so, it offers new and interdisciplinary perspectives on the development of the international peace architecture, peace processes, UN peacebuilding, peacekeeping and mediation, statebuilding, and localised peace formation in practice and in theory. It examines their implications for the development of local peace agency and the connection between emancipatory forms of peace and global justice, which remain crucial in different conflict-affected regions around the world. This series' contributions offer both theoretical and empirical insights into many of the world's most intractable conflicts, also investigating increasingly significant evidence about blockages to peace.

This series is indexed by Scopus.

Rasmus Bellmer · Frank Möller

Peace, Complexity, Visuality

Ambiguities in Peace and Conflict

Rasmus Bellmer
Berghof Foundation
Berlin, Germany

Frank Möller
Tampere University
Tampere, Finland

ISSN 1759-3735   ISSN 2752-857X (electronic)
Rethinking Peace and Conflict Studies
ISBN 978-3-031-38217-8   ISBN 978-3-031-38218-5 (eBook)
https://doi.org/10.1007/978-3-031-38218-5

© The Editor(s) (if applicable) and The Author(s), under exclusive license to Springer Nature Switzerland AG 2023

This work is subject to copyright. All rights are solely and exclusively licensed by the Publisher, whether the whole or part of the material is concerned, specifically the rights of translation, reprinting, reuse of illustrations, recitation, broadcasting, reproduction on microfilms or in any other physical way, and transmission or information storage and retrieval, electronic adaptation, computer software, or by similar or dissimilar methodology now known or hereafter developed.
The use of general descriptive names, registered names, trademarks, service marks, etc. in this publication does not imply, even in the absence of a specific statement, that such names are exempt from the relevant protective laws and regulations and therefore free for general use.
The publisher, the authors, and the editors are safe to assume that the advice and information in this book are believed to be true and accurate at the date of publication. Neither the publisher nor the authors or the editors give a warranty, expressed or implied, with respect to the material contained herein or for any errors or omissions that may have been made. The publisher remains neutral with regard to jurisdictional claims in published maps and institutional affiliations.

Cover design by © MC Richmond

This Palgrave Macmillan imprint is published by the registered company Springer Nature Switzerland AG
The registered company address is: Gewerbestrasse 11, 6330 Cham, Switzerland

Preface

Once again, politics and the media are dominated by images of confrontation, polarization, armed aggression, material destruction and human suffering—all the sorry ingredients of modern warfare. War sidelines peace, war images sideline peace images.

However, we want to write about peace, suggesting that peace research needs to focus again on peace rather than dealing with peace in passing, implicitly or by implication only.

And we want to reflect upon complexity.

Finally, we want to say a couple of words about hope, impact and a feeling of senselessness that can easily emerge in a time such as ours—even among experienced peace researchers (who have seen it all before), let alone among students.

We need to talk about peace. Once the dynamics of the war machine start in the military, in politics and in the media, peace and its advocates find it difficult to get heard. The current militarization of international affairs affects not only foreign and security policy but also our whole society and our way of doing and thinking about basically anything.

Thus, we need to talk about peace and its many dimensions; we need to talk about peaceful change and how to achieve it; we need to talk about peace by peaceful means. This is the Nordic tradition in peace research. It is a strong tradition that we can build on rather than abandon in times of crisis.

There is abundant literature indicating that things are not as bad as they seem. When consulting the media currently, we easily forget that war is the exception, not the rule.

Douglas Fry's study *Beyond War: The Human Potential for Peace* documents human progress over time toward peaceful conflict resolution.

Rutger Bregman, in *Humankind: A Hopeful History*, presents much evidence undermining the belief that human beings are inherently violent.

Randall Collins's study *Violence: A Micro-sociological Theory* shows how difficult it actually is to make human beings exert violence on fellow human beings.

Going back in time, Lewis Coser's work on the constructive role of social conflict and Karl Deutsch's work on security community building still deserve attention, just as does the human security literature from the 1990s (and its current feminist reincarnation) emphasizing human beings as referent objects of peace and security rather than states, power or territory and exploring the causes of peace, not of war.

In the current situation, peaceful alternatives are neither particularly obvious nor particularly popular among those arguing for militarized security. We acknowledge that peace research right now finds it difficult to present a convincing answer to the recurrence of power politics.

However, there have always been ups and downs, trends in one direction and countertrends in the opposite direction—Rwanda, Yugoslavia, Syria, Yemen, etc.—reflecting political developments, historical experiences, ideological preferences, discursive constructions and, generally speaking, different ways of seeing things. Peace processes can be interrupted; peace is complex, and peace takes time. However, time alone doesn't make peace.

Indeed, the thirty years since the end of the Cold War are, historically speaking, a blink of an eye. During this time, there were attempts to establish peace on the basis of international cooperation, economic, political and even military integration, including among former enemies, the rule of law, interaction, communication and exchange of people and ideas.

These attempts always had to compete with a history of power politics that has now returned to the front stage and the front pages. Whether it stays there or not depends, to some extent, on us—as peace researchers and as citizens having to cope with the complexity of modern life, including the complexities of peace and war.

Studying peace and conflict equals studying complexity. In a complex system, the system's individual elements are all interconnected. Changes to one element will directly or indirectly affect other elements. They will always have more than one effect, and not always will they have the desired effect, no matter how well the changes had been prepared.

In complex situations, the known becomes the unknown, the expected becomes the unexpected, the predictable becomes the unpredictable, and the unknown, the unexpected and the unpredictable all become part of everyday experience. Side effects will always occur but can neither be predicted nor adequately prepared for.

Indeed, where there is complexity, there is also ambiguity; where there is ambiguity, there is never only one set of problems. Nor is there only one path toward resolution.

That's normal. In complex systems, it cannot be otherwise.

And because this is so, we need to be humble and patient: we will never achieve everything we set out to achieve and what we do achieve will take more time than we hoped it would.

However, we also need to be self-confident: peace research has, over the last decades, produced a wealth of knowledge that we can use to understand complexity and, by so doing, to contribute to the improvement of social relations—step by step.

Peace and conflict cannot be adequately understood without understanding their components; understanding the components, however, is insufficient for understanding the overall operation of peace and conflict, as the components interact with one another in diverse and often unpredictable ways.

This is why peace and conflict research can be frustrating—especially to those of us who look for and expect immediate social impact. A feeling of senselessness can easily emerge.

However, this is also why peace and conflict research can be immensely rewarding.

In *The War of the Saints*, Jorge Amado wrote that "no word spoken against violence and tyranny is entirely vain and useless: Somebody who hears it might just overcome fear and start to rebel" (p. 37).

Peace is a social concept. We *do* social concepts by analyzing them, applying them, changing them, developing them, thinking and talking about them—or ignoring them.

We believe that nothing we do in peace and conflict research—then, now and in future—is entirely in vain and useless, even if the effects of our work are sometimes hard to pin down. At any moment, somebody might listen to us, talk to us, read our texts and start working with us to create a more peaceful world.[1]

Berlin, Germany Rasmus Bellmer
Tampere, Finland Frank Möller

---

[1] This text originally appeared as "Notes on the Future of Peace Research" at https://www.imageandpeace.com/2022/04/28/notes-on-the-future-of-peace-research/ and is reproduced here in a slightly different version.

Acknowledgments

We are grateful to Kone Foundation for the generous funding we received for our project *Peace Videography* from 2020 to 2022. Without this funding, the present book would not have been written.

Chapter 10 has appeared as "Active Looking: Images in Peace Mediation" in *Peacebuilding* (December 2022) and is reproduced here with kind permission from Taylor and Francis (https://doi.org/10.1080/21647259.2022.2152971).

We would like to thank Ananda Kumar and Sarah Roughley at Palgrave Macmillan, the anonymous reviewer for Palgrave Macmillan, Melvin Lourdes and the production team and the series editors, Oliver Richmond, Annika Björkdahl and Gëzim Visoka.

Except as noted, we visited *Bosnia: Uncertain Paths to Peace* in February, March and April 2023.

May 2023

Rasmus Bellmer
Frank Möller

Contents

1	**Introduction: Ambiguities in Local and Global Contexts**	1
	Spaces of Possibility and New Openings	1
	The Book's Main Arguments	9
	Studying the Complexity and Ambiguity of the International	10
	Why Visuality?	12
	Why Bosnia?	14
	The Book's Structure	16
	References	20

Part I Complexity and Ambiguity

2	**Approaching Complexity in Peace and Conflict**	25
	Introduction	25
	Complexity in International Relations and Peace and Conflict Studies	30
	How to Cope with Complexity	38
	Photocomplexity	43
	Conclusion	47
	References	48
3	**Tolerance of Ambiguity**	53
	Introduction	53
	Ambiguities in Peace and Conflict Dynamics	55
	How to Cope with Ambiguity: Tolerance of Ambiguity	61

	Photoambiguity	67
	Conclusion	71
	References	73
Part II	**New Photographies and Visual Ambiguities**	
4	**The Crisis of Photojournalism and the Emergence of New Photographies**	81
	Introduction	81
	A Blurring of Boundaries	82
	Crisis of Photojournalism, Crisis of Confidence	85
	New Photographies	90
	Conclusion	101
	References	103
5	**Visual Ambiguities: Controlling the Meaning of Images in a Digital and Interactive World**	107
	Introduction	107
	Control of Meaning	110
	Digitization and Interaction	118
	Conclusion	126
	References	129
Part III	***Bosnia: Uncertain Paths to Peace***	
6	**Introducing *Bosnia: Uncertain Paths to Peace***	135
	Introduction	135
	The Photophilosophy of Bosnia: Uncertain Paths to Peace	139
	Visual Controversies	150
	Conclusion	154
	References	155
7	**Navigating *Bosnia: Uncertain Paths to Peace***	159
	Introduction	159
	Entering Bosnia: Uncertain Paths to Peace	162
	First Navigation	166
	Second Navigation	171
	Third Navigation	173
	Fourth Navigation	175
	Conclusion	178
	References	181

8	**The Grids: Architectural Space and Panel-to-Panel Transitions**	183
	Introduction	183
	Messiness, Anxiety and Apprehension	185
	Navigating the Grids	188
	Approaching the Grid Structure in Terms of Individual Images	195
	Approaching the Grid Structure as Sequential Art	199
	Conclusion	202
	References	205
9	**Interactivity and the Author-Audience Relationship**	209
	Introduction: Bosnia, 1993–1996	209
	Bosnia: Uncertain Paths to Peace and the Media Environment at the Time	213
	Interactivity and Interactive Documentation	217
	Interactivity and Narrative Openness	220
	Conclusion	228
	References	230

Part IV Leveraging Ambiguity for Peace

10	**Embracing Difference: Learning from Bosnia?**	235
	Introduction	235
	Learning from Bosnia?	237
	Embracing Difference, Transforming Conflict	246
	Conclusion	250
	References	251
11	**Exploring the Surround, Appreciating Complexity**	255
	Introduction	255
	Revisiting Images, Reordering Events	258
	Images and the Surround	261
	Photographic Inclusions and Appearances, Exclusions and Disappearances	266
	Conclusion	273
	References	275
12	**Active Looking: Images in Peace Mediation**	279
	Introduction	279
	Narratives in Mediation: Beyond Consensus-as-Sameness	281

	Active Listening	283
	Active Looking	286
	Conclusion	295
	References	297
13	**Concluding Reflections: Tolerance of Ambiguity and the Ambiguity of Tolerance**	303
	What Are the Limits of Tolerance?	305
	Is Our Case Study Well Chosen?	307
	Do We Establish New Binaries?	309
	References	314

Bibliography   315

Index   335

About the Authors

Rasmus Bellmer is based in Berlin and currently works for the Berghof Foundation. He holds a master's degree in Peace, Mediation and Conflict Research. From 2020 to 2022, he worked as a project researcher in the research project *Peace Videography*, funded by Kone Foundation, and was affiliated with the Tampere Peace Research Institute, Tampere University, Finland. His research was published in journals, such as *International Political Sociology*, *Peacebuilding* and *Journal of Peace Education*.

Frank Möller is a peace and conflict researcher residing in Tampere (Finland). He is affiliated with Tampere University as Docent in Peace and Conflict Research. From 2020 to 2022, he was in charge of the project *Peace Videography*, funded by Kone Foundation, and in 2023, he received a scholarship grant from the Gerda Henkel Foundation. He is the co-editor of *Art as a Political Witness* (2017) and the author of *Visual Peace: Images, Spectatorship and the Politics of Violence* (2013), *Peace Photography* (2019) and numerous journal articles and book chapters.

List of Figures

Fig. 1.1	Sarajevo Rose, Novo Sarajevo, 9 July 2022 (Photograph © Frank Möller)	2
Fig. 1.2	*Stolperstein* (commemorating the Department Store Nathan Israel), Berlin, 1 May 2023 (Photograph © Frank Möller)	2
Fig. 1.3	Pockmarked building, Sarajevo, 5 July 2022 (Photograph © Frank Möller)	4
Fig. 1.4	Sarajevo, 28 June 2018 (Photograph © Frank Möller)	11
Fig. 1.5	Sarajevo #1 (Photograph © Frank Möller)	20
Fig. 2.1	Sarajevo #2 (Photograph © Frank Möller)	48
Fig. 3.1	Sarajevo #3 (Photograph © Frank Möller)	73
Fig. 4.1	Sarajevo #4 (Photograph © Frank Möller)	102
Fig. 5.1	Sarajevo #5 (Photograph © Frank Möller)	128
Fig. 6.1	Dayton Accords (Dokumentationszentrum Flucht, Vertreibung, Versöhnung, Berlin)	145
Fig. 6.2	Sarajevo #6 (Photograph © Frank Möller)	155
Fig. 7.1	Sarajevo #7 (Photograph © Frank Möller)	180
Fig. 8.1	Trying to make sense of the suburbs grid, notes, February 2023	190
Fig. 8.2	Sarajevo #8 (Photograph © Frank Möller)	205
Fig. 9.1	Sarajevo #9 (Photograph © Frank Möller)	230
Fig. 10.1	Baščaršija (Photograph © Frank Möller)	239
Fig. 10.2	Bosnian coffee (Photograph © Frank Möller)	241
Fig. 10.3	Sebilj (Photograph © Frank Möller)	245
Fig. 10.4	Sarajevo #10 (Photograph © Frank Möller)	251

Fig. 11.1	Sarajevo #11 (Photograph © Frank Möller)	274
Fig. 12.1	Sarajevo #12 (Photograph © Frank Möller)	296
Fig. 13.1	Complexity grid (© Rasmus Bellmer and Frank Möller; photography © Frank Möller)	313

LIST OF TABLES

| Table 8.1 | Suburbs grid, Uniform Resource Locators (URLs) | 194 |
| Table 8.2 | Sarajevo grid, Uniform Resource Locators (URLs) plus key words from the Index page | 195 |

CHAPTER 1

Introduction: Ambiguities in Local and Global Contexts

SPACES OF POSSIBILITY AND NEW OPENINGS

Craters in the pavement filled in with red resin—no *Stolpersteine* (Berlin's famous *stumbling stones*, designed by the artist Gunter Demnig to commemorate people persecuted between 1933 and 1945, small yet distinct concrete blocks situated "in front of the last voluntarily chosen places of residence of the victims of the Nazis"[1]) but equally painful, discreet and inobtrusive reminders of what human beings are capable of doing in times of organized violence: the Sarajevo Roses (see Fig. 1.1), reminders of both artillery attacks during the siege of Sarajevo and the people wounded and killed between 1992 and 1996.

While the *Stolpersteine* reveal the identity and the fate of the people or institutions they honor (see Fig. 1.2), the Sarajevo Roses "contain no symbols or inscriptions that would indicate that they are memorials" (Ristic 2018: 179). Neither do they reveal who the victims were—the names, identity and ethnicity of the person(s) killed here remain hidden—nor who the perpetrators were. Resin, like human memory, tends to wither away. Attempts at preserving the Sarajevo Roses currently compete with attempts at replacing them (see Ristic 2018: 177–207).

[1] https://www.stolpersteine-berlin.de/en (accessed 20 April 2023).

© The Author(s), under exclusive license to Springer Nature Switzerland AG 2023
R. Bellmer and F. Möller, *Peace, Complexity, Visuality*, Rethinking Peace and Conflict Studies,
https://doi.org/10.1007/978-3-031-38218-5_1

1

Fig. 1.1 Sarajevo Rose, Novo Sarajevo, 9 July 2022 (Photograph © Frank Möller)

Fig. 1.2 *Stolperstein* (commemorating the Department Store Nathan Israel), Berlin, 1 May 2023 (Photograph © Frank Möller)

Mirjana Ristic explains that before and during the siege of Sarajevo, residents "did not divide themselves along ethnic lines" (2018: 182). The perpetrators did not discriminate either, attacking everyone who defended the idea of Sarajevo as a multiethnic and multicultural city or who merely dared to appear in public space. Private space was not safe, either. Today, the Sarajevo Roses

> prompt residents of and visitors to the city to see the layers of time in space and inquire about the present through the lens of the past. Not only are they able to reflect on the violence against the city and its residents during the siege, but also on the ongoing post-war reconstruction process. They invite passers-by to pause and contemplate the past and then move on, continue walking and turn towards the future. (p. 183)

Moving on after reflection and turning toward the future is one possible response to an encounter with a Sarajevo Rose. Pausing, contemplating, reflecting and returning (mentally, imaginatively, emotionally) to the past without being capable of leaving it behind is another possible response in a city, the memorial landscape of which is so strongly dedicated to the memory of the siege. This memory still figures prominently in the built environment, too (see Fig. 1.3)—an identity provider for those who survived the siege and "a means of maintaining … power" (p. 184). People suffering from traumatic memories cannot but remember and reenact the past. For other people, moving on toward the future or moving back toward the past are two possible options (among many others) the Roses offer. Rather than deciding which option is the better or more adequate one, we simply wish to note the coexistence of these options.

The Sarajevo Roses operate on observers without "giving reassuring answers and interpreting a particular version of history," Ristic explains (p. 182). Rather, "the silence of Roses engages the audience to actively construct their own versions of the past" (p. 182), thus interrogating hegemonic designations of meaning. The Roses "allow multiple versions of memory and history to coexist and thus they open up the possibility of reconciliation and re-establishment of Bosnian inter-ethnic unity" (p. 182). Simultaneously, the coexistence of multiple versions of memory and history may render reconciliation difficult; it may foster dialog about different memories, but it may also make such dialog difficult. Indeed, not everyone seems to appreciate the coexistence of multiple versions

Fig. 1.3 Pockmarked building, Sarajevo, 5 July 2022 (Photograph © Frank Möller)

of memory and history. The Sarajevo Roses have to compete with other memorials, including memorial plaques that are not only "more noticeable than Sarajevo Roses as they have been lifted from the ground to the viewer's eye level" (p. 185) but also "include inscriptions and say explicitly what they mean" (p. 186) and how they are supposed to be read. While the Sarajevo Roses serve memory, the memorial plaques also serve the politics of memory, conditioning spaces of possibility.

We will encounter the difference between, on the one hand, interpretive openness and narrative plurality and, on the other hand, binding designations of meaning and narrative closure often in this book. And while we certainly would not recommend interpretive openness as the *default* method to be applied to every problem we encounter, our argument—inspired and informed by complexity theory—is clearly one in favor of narrative plurality, appreciation of difference and tolerance of ambiguity. Bosnia and the capital city of Sarajevo, especially in their pre-war and pre-siege incarnation, offer inspiration, and while we do not think that their characteristic multiculturalism can be reestablished any time soon, we believe nevertheless that reflecting on it is of more than just historical relevance, because such reflection expands spaces of possibility beyond what is currently politically practiced, thus envisioning the step from what is to what might be. If it is true that where we are heading for depends to some extent on where we come from, then the traditional Bosnian way is one possible option with which to address questions pertaining to identity and difference, outlining paths to peace that other approaches block. It is an option with which to embrace and capitalize on difference. The traditional Bosnian way as it appears in the literature is an exercise in tolerance of ambiguity (within limits, of course) or at least an exercise in more tolerance of ambiguity than can be observed elsewhere—and this 'elsewhere' includes Bosnia and Herzegovina today.

We agree with John Law that the social world is a "kaleidoscope of impressions and textures" that cannot adequately be grasped in terms of "definite processes out there that are waiting to be discovered" (Law 2004: 6) and to be analyzed by experts applying methodological rigor in search of a definitive "single point of view" (p. 98). Such a single point of view fixes an issue once and for all, providing closure and consistency as well as "authorising a single account of out-thereness" (p. 122), which "necessarily disqualifies any of the possible alternatives" (p. 123). As Law notes, "events and processes are not simply complex in the sense that they are technically difficult to grasp (though this is certainly often the case). Rather, they are also complex because they *necessarily exceed our capacity to know them*" (p. 6; italics in original). We would like to add that even if we know events and processes (or parts thereof), we sometimes do not have the words to articulate our knowledge. There is indeed a "need for assemblages that mediate and produce entities that cannot be refracted into words" (p. 122). Hence, our focus is on visuality.

In the Euro-North American tradition, knowledge, adequate planning and programming are seen to guarantee the achievement of desired outcomes. In peacebuilding, for example, analysis of the sources of a conflict in combination with assessments of needs is integrated into strategies that will then be applied step-by-step. At the end, the conflict will have been resolved and peace will have been built—except that in many cases, the conflict will *not* have been resolved and peace will *not* have been built. This is so among other things because the operating mechanisms of the necessarily complex systems in which peacebuilding interferes are intrinsically uncertain; despite peacebuilders' best efforts, their "ability to fully know complex systems is inherently limited" (de Coning 2018: 309). From a complexity point of view,

> given the emergent behavior of complex systems, even if one independent variable seems to explain some aspect of system behavior today, this provides no guarantee that it will continue to have the same effect in future, let alone in another context altogether. (Beaumont and de Coning 2022: 6)

Thus, results from one case study can neither be unproblematically extrapolated to other case studies nor applied without modification to the same case at a different time. Likewise, peacebuilders possess limited abilities to anticipate and integrate into peacebuilding, how peacebuilding affects complex systems and how complex systems affect peacebuilding: "the dynamic, non-linear and emergent behaviour of complex social systems can, at times rapidly, evolve in unpredictable ways, especially when they are under conflict-affected pressure" (de Coning 2018: 309). Peacebuilding, thus, fails, although peacebuilders are, within the limits of their knowledge, adequately prepared.

In this tradition, it is inconceivable, unbearable and intolerable that something cannot be completely understood; that agreement on that which is not (yet) clear cannot or should not be reached; that "continuously iterative processes" should replace "predefined steps in a determined-design programme cycle" (de Coning 2018: 309); and that there may be "coherence without consistency" (Law 2004: 139), the one, as Law explains, embracing difference, the other making difference impossible:

> The word "consistency" bears a heavy weight because it draws on the particular demands of logic or discourse. It is intolerant of difference or multiplicity. These are easily turned into signs of inconsistency or incompatibility. ... But coherence – or non-coherence – is more permissive. Indeed more than that. Non-coherence may be what keeps the system held together. (p. 99)

Images are non-coherent in the sense that they always carry with them a multitude or plurality of meanings. "*In the midst of representational singularity there is multiplicity.* But this is not seen" (literally and figuratively) in the Euro-North American tradition (p. 137; italics in original). We might add that if it *is* seen, this multiplicity is regularly Othered by means of texts stipulating and controlling meaning—or relegated to the arts or the personal (p. 98). Non-coherent images are discursively given meaning that is alleged to be consistent (transforming plurality into singularity and complex stories into linear, one-dimensional ones) and thus both integrated into already existing discursive formations and invalidated as potential sources of alternative knowledge production—including knowledge that recognizes the non-coherence of the social world and tries to capitalize on it in order to improve living conditions. In this tradition, it is indeed unusual, to say the least, to think in, and inspired by, images (see Mitchell 1994). Consequently, "[t]he multiple or the fractional, the elusive, the vague, the partial and the fluid" that images signify "are being displaced into Otherness" (Law 2004: 137). Indeed, Euro-North American thinking denies multiplicity as an organizing principle. It is obsessed with ordering the world in dualistic categories such as self/other, we/they, the social/the natural, subject/object, inclusion/exclusion, word/image, human/non-human and active/passive—either-or rather than as-well-as. And while this is hardly a new observation, it is one of the book's recurrent themes that visuality may help us appreciate attitudes and politics based on as-well-as rather than either-or thus expanding spaces of possibility in a non-coherent world.

Fundamentally, the notion of inside/outside—the sovereign nation-state operating within an anarchic environment—"continues to inform our understanding of how and where effective and progressive political practice can be advanced" (Walker 1993: 13). Regarding the post-Yugoslav environment, David Campbell specifies that the application of the norm of sovereignty combined with "territorial and cultural alignment" to Bosnia where "restoration of sovereignty, revisiting the status quo ante, could not be the goal" (Campbell 1998: 165–166)—indeed, "Bosnia ha[d] never existed, since the medieval kingdom, as an independent state" (Glenny 1996: 144)—proved fatal: superimposing the concept of national and cultural identity on a population that was not only characterized by the absence of such an identity but that defined itself precisely in terms of such an absence, i.e., in terms of multiculturalism, ethnic and religious plurality (until nationalist politicians gained the upper hand in the early 1990s) and the Bosnian way (see Markowitz 2010 and Chapter 10 of the present book), was a recipe for disaster, as observers noted already at the time (see Glenny 1996: 138–152).

Many fine books have been written about Bosnia and Herzegovina after the Balkan Wars of the 1990s and the siege of Sarajevo—including scholarly books, journalistic accounts, memoirs, novels, graphic novels and comics, and photographic monographs. We will refer to many of them throughout the book. In this introduction, we would like to emphasize Campbell's *National Deconstruction*, published in 1998. Campbell concludes his book with "reflection on 'the multiethnic Bosnia that existed' and the manner in which it can still aid judgments about the political possibilities"—despite "ethnic partition in place, nationalist parties victorious, populations increasingly homogenized, and ethnic cleansing still in operation" (p. 210). "Drawing attention to Bosnian identity" (p. 218)—understood in terms of "complex histories and hybrid identities" (p. 209), "radical interdependence" (p. 212) and "similarities and differences [that] were not determined prior to their interaction" (p. 213)—"is," as Campbell explains, "not to engage in nostalgia for the politics of multiculturalism. It is to appreciate how even in the face of overwhelming odds, the logic of nationalism and the nation-state cannot eradicate the heterogeneous condition that problematizes it" (p. 218). Campbell's book thus considers "those strategies that might have problematized closure and might still foster new openings" (p. 219). As an exercise in "thinking otherwise" (Danchev 2009: 4), the book is still important, just as is Fred Ritchin and Gilles Peress's photojournalistic project *Bosnia: Uncertain Paths to Peace*—an exercise in showing otherwise—which we will discuss in Part III. Binding designations of meaning ascribed to visual images cannot eradicate images' plurality of meanings and visual connotations, which can, when (re)discovered and (re)vitalized, provide new openings. As we wrote elsewhere:

> We want to suggest thinking about images of peace in terms of their relation to the complexity of social life. Helpful questions might be: Does an image tell us anything new? Does it display a perspective that is commonly underrepresented in (visual) discourse? Do we gain a better understanding of social relations … one that reflects [their] complex dynamics? Does it render the complex dynamics behind a certain social conflict more visible? Does it challenge the tendency to simplification underlying much published photojournalistic work? Does it help us understand that in complex situations, there is never just one cause and there is never just one path to resolution?[2]

---

[2] https://www.imageandpeace.com/2022/03/14/ways-of-showing-peace-iii-peace-images-and-complexity/.

The Ritchin–Peress project documents not only Bosnia's uncertain paths to peace but also the post-siege predicament the citizens of Sarajevo found themselves in. We would like to suggest in this book that it also contributes to peacebuilding or at least enables viewers to diversify their perspectives on both Bosnia and peacebuilding. It does so not although but *because* it positions itself to some extent outside the above tradition (not only photographically), embracing "culture … as a space of multiple voices and forces" (Couldry 2000: 4) thus exploring "a common space of intellectual and political commitment … that works *with* difference and not by *reducing* difference" (Couldry 2000: 21–22; italics in original). This is our commitment as well, not only a commitment for cultural studies for which Nick Couldry speaks in the above quotation. Conflict resolution scholar Sara Cobb suggests in her work on the mediation of conflict narratives that reducing complexity by silencing the narratives of the Other leads to a "flattening of the Other," a "narrative form of dehumanization" (2013: 50). Cobb thus requests narratives that have a humanizing effect "through the process of revealing or unveiling the complexity of the people, as persons, as human beings" (p. 200), thus complexifying narratives. Images, too, can complexify how we see ourselves and others. As we wrote elsewhere, while "there will certainly be different views on whether an image contributes to a complexification of our understanding of social reality," this image might start "a conversation and a discussion – an exchange of ideas from which new perspectives [can] emerge including peaceful ones transforming, perhaps, images *of* peace into images *for* peace."[3] While we do not present a case study on Bosnia or Sarajevo based on long-term ethnographic research on location in this book, we nevertheless hope that what we have to say is more than merely an illustration of the argument that we develop with regard to complexity, ambiguity and visuality.

The Book's Main Arguments

Studying international relations equals studying ambiguity. The international system is complex, and where there is complexity, there is also ambiguity; where there is ambiguity, there is neither only one problem-set nor only one path toward resolution. In ambiguous situations, different

---

[3] https://www.imageandpeace.com/2022/03/14/ways-of-showing-peace-iii-peace-images-and-complexity/.

permissible interpretations compete with one another. Complexity, thus, is as much about ambiguity as it is about difference.

To appropriately describe, think about and theorize international relations, including peace and conflict dynamics, means grappling with complexity, ambiguity and difference while simultaneously acknowledging the limits of one's endeavors. "Tensions, ambiguities, juxtapositions, incongruities, gaps, voids, and contradictions adequately capture the world as a messy place; its components are out-of-sync." This confusion "has to be captured both visually and analytically aiming not at reduction of complexity but at adequate representation and analysis of it as a condition for the possibility of adequate political responses" to it (Möller 2020: 3). This book asserts not only that we cannot avoid ambiguities but also that we can learn to become tolerant of ambiguities and deal with them in a constructive manner, improving the quality of social relations. We argue for living with ambiguities rather than by reducing them to simple but ultimately misleading interpretations.

By exploring the concept of tolerance of ambiguity, we hope to contribute to and envision new ways of thinking about and engaging in a world full of ambiguities. Crucially, in a world saturated not only with ambiguities but also with visual images, it is mandatory to think ambiguity and visuality together. We do this in the context of post-war Bosnia and post-siege Sarajevo (see Fig. 1.4). We argue that we can capitalize on the tolerance of ambiguity-enhancing potentialities inherent in visual images—their non-coherence—and thus increase our capability of tolerating ambiguities. To this end, we have to radicalize visual analysis and develop new ways of perspective-taking.

Studying the Complexity and Ambiguity of the International

There can be observed growing awareness of the complexity of social reality articulated in references to complexity in both everyday conversations and professional discussions revolving around international conflict. In our lives, we are frequently facing ambiguities, and ambiguities reflect uncertainty, nonlinearity and multi-causality. As a consequence, interventions into complex social systems do not guarantee a specific outcome, let alone the desired one, no matter how well-planned they are: the known becomes the unknown, the predictable becomes the unpredictable; and

Fig. 1.4 Sarajevo, 28 June 2018 (Photograph © Frank Möller)

both the unknown and the unpredictable become part of everyday experience. Side effects cannot always be predicted; they often appear as surprise effects for which actors cannot adequately prepare. Underappreciation of complexity explains, in part, the failure of many international interventions.

Awareness of the various actual and potential consequences of an action in a complex system helps us understand the multitude of interpretations that every event invites. Some of these interpretations are mutually supportive, while others are mutually exclusive or exist independent of one another. All of them, however, try to explain and understand a system's operating procedures in such a manner that it appears logical from the point of view of the interpreter, reflecting her own individual and collective experience, interests and identities. This is another way of saying that every interpretation appears permissible from the interpreter's point of view even if others disagree. Studying the narratives underlying international relations and peace and conflict dynamics, therefore, is equivalent to studying ambiguities. In ambiguous situations, several permissible interpretations compete with one another. Such narrative competition implies that our interpretations have to become more, not less, complex if we wish to approximate international dynamics and social reality.

In this book, we posit that ambiguities are inevitable: they cannot be avoided. Every action (including actions aimed at removing ambiguities) can, and will, have unintended effects. We contend that we need to actively engage with ambiguities to appropriately move in a world full of ambiguities, to properly conduct research and to navigate political decisions and actions. Thus, we introduce to international relations the concept of *tolerance of ambiguity* (TA) and propose that it is not only important to cope with ambiguities but also that visual images can help us learn how to do so. In the book, then, we engage with complexity and ambiguity through the TA-enhancing capabilities of visuality and visual images.

Why Visuality?

We live in a world that is saturated not only with ambiguities but also with images: photographs, films, videos, graffiti, paintings, memes, etc. The international system and its dynamics have been approached visually in several visual and aesthetic turns proclaimed over the last twenty years or so, but the connection with complexity and ambiguity has not yet been systematically explored, neither theoretically nor based on case studies. One of the most common approaches to visual images (save for images of art) is disambiguation, i.e., establishing *the* meaning of a given image, exploring how this meaning has come into being, and analyzing how the image and the meaning assigned to it operate in and on society (discourse analysis posing as visual analysis). In contrast, we suggest acknowledging and capitalizing on the plurality of meanings that all images necessarily carry with them and, by so doing, learning to cope with ambiguities beyond visuality as well. Thus, we treat images' non-coherence as a merit rather than a liability that has to be replaced by visual consistency.

Indeed, we feel that the visual turn in the discipline of International Relations is insufficiently radical and increasingly standardized. While standardization is not entirely a bad thing—it always reflects a certain degree of acceptance within the discipline—it also prevents visual analysis from taking full advantage of what visuality offers. Visual analysis in International Relations, often focusing on discourses revolving around images or meanings assigned to images, exhibits a certain uneasiness with regard to images, which, in turn, is characteristic of Western approaches to visuality. Images' very visible ambiguity, interpretive openness and plurality of meanings—their non-coherence—often make audiences feel uneasy about images. In contrast, we suggest that if we want to understand an ambiguous world, then we have to appreciate and reinvigorate images' ambiguities, complexify viewing patterns and rediscover discursively marginalized meanings.

Visual images transform neutral occurrences into events, conditioning what qualifies as an event and how we, literally and metaphorically, see these events. Our ways of seeing condition (how we understand and make sense of) the international: image-makers and image-interpreters determine how we see the world and what we make of what we see. Images condition what is and what is not political. From this, it follows that there is no such thing as an *un*political image: images determine what we think of as possible, conditioning spaces of possibility.

Such (actual and potential) spaces are always more variegated and harder to pin down than they appear when translated into language. Images' plurality of meanings tends to disappear from verbal descriptions. Intended and unintended visual connotations may support, alter, challenge, undermine, thwart or exist independently of the image's main message as it is discursively constructed. In photojournalism, for example, the ambiguous character of images is usually described as a liability to be fixed through verbal or written designations of meaning and descriptions of context. In contrast, we argue that images' non-coherence enables spaces where we can confront and learn to cope with complexity and ambiguity. From this, it follows that we are interested neither in identifying *the* meaning of an image nor in establishing a hierarchy of possible meanings derived, for example, from different degrees of credibility and plausibility. We regard images as a public space where we can confront our perspective with others' perspectives: we respect and actively look for ambiguities and ambivalences, gaps and omissions, the obvious and the less obvious, the central and the peripheral, the visible and the invisible. As a step toward "perspective-taking" (Wendt 1999: 333), we need—ideally—to look at images through the eyes of others as well. Since this is not always possible (and we should definitely refrain from speculating about what others see), we have to acknowledge—research pragmatically and research ethically—both that others may see different things when looking at what seems to be the same image and that they have good reasons for so doing. Such acknowledgment relativizes our own point of view and paves the way toward tolerance of visual ambiguities.

We certainly do not argue that visuality is always the best or even the only way of addressing complex social systems. Addressing such systems through images produces knowledge that other approaches fail to produce, but other approaches produce knowledge that visual analysis cannot generate. Thus, with Paul Beaumont and Cedric de Coning, we argue for methodological and epistemological pluralism when analyzing complex systems. Accepting such pluralism is an exercise in tolerance of ambiguity. Such pluralism may produce not only different but "contradictory findings" but this "ensures that scholars and policymakers are reminded of the limited nature of their knowledge." No approach can explain everything, but every approach can explain something. Methodological and epistemological pluralism indeed requires scholars to develop tolerance of ambiguity with regard to their and others' research outcomes, which is another way of saying that "scholars from different epistemologies" need to

> engage in a constructive dialogue that recognizes not only both the substantial differences between them, but also that the other approach has its distinct legitimate value ... Crucially, this implies recognizing and communicating *across* difference rather than striving to eliminate difference via grand plans to "unify," "integrate," or "synthesize" alternative approaches. (Beaumont and de Coning 2022: 7, all above quotations; italics in original)

Why Bosnia?

We follow Michael Shapiro's advice that "conceptualizations ... are best developed in the context of specific historical episodes" (2004: 35). However, why the Bosnian context? More than 25 years after the signing of the Dayton Peace Accords, uncertainty and insecurity prevail in Bosnia, the socio-economic development stagnates, many young and well-educated people emigrate, the formal and institutional arrangements agreed upon in Dayton, including Bosnia's territorial integrity, seem under threat, and the country's path toward European integration makes little progress. However, while the peace in Bosnia may be "paralyzed" and fragile (Bennett 2016), regression to violent forms of dealing with conflict has largely been avoided. This is an immense achievement, given the complexity and ambiguities of the current situation. Complexity and ambiguity can be captured visually.

While the discussion continues of photography's purpose, politics and overall relevance in conflict and post-conflict settings, there can be observed a certain emphasis in Bosnia on aftermath representations of trauma and the legacies of the past. While this emphasis is perfectly legitimate and understandable, it might also create memory bubbles within which current political discussions unfold and from which it is difficult to escape. However, during and after the war in the former Yugoslavia, Bosnia served as a laboratory for new photographic approaches to war and violent conflict: aftermath photography, forensic photography, participatory photography and post-conflict photography. This laboratory served as the visual and conceptual framework within which our visual data—Fred Ritchin, Gilles Peress and the *New York Times on the Web*'s interactive project *Bosnia: Uncertain Paths to Peace*—came into being. This project is still valid; it is, indeed, an important and underappreciated precursor to current forms of interactive documentaries. Interactive elements facilitating narrative pluralism anticipated by Ritchin and Peress have, in the meantime, been thoroughly integrated into documentary journalism, but IR can also learn from them. At the same time, the Ritchin–Peress project differs from many recent formats due to its explicit focus on *peace*. It is for this reason that it is particularly interesting from a peace and conflict perspective. Furthermore, the technical simplicity of the project—at least in comparison with current and future interactive formats—facilitates analysis without recourse to technological details and jargon, thus enabling communication of the research results to a non-specialized audience.

The current situation in Bosnia is complex and ambiguous. We sketch two possible responses to complex ambiguities—tolerance of ambiguity and disambiguation. While we prefer the former rather than the latter, we also explain that this should not be understood as a strict binary: tolerance of ambiguity in some parts of the system may coexist with disambiguation in other parts. We propose that visuality has tolerance of ambiguity-building potentialities and exemplify these potentialities by discussing *Bosnia: Uncertain Paths to Peace* in the book's third part. This project is still, in part, available on the Internet, thus facilitating readers' critical engagement with both the project and our argument. We suggest that this project, rather than presenting simple but ultimately misleading narratives, utilizes images' plurality of meanings and interpretive openness in such a manner that complexity and ambiguity become comprehensible. In accordance with complexity theory, however, we need to be careful when thinking about the current situation in Bosnia in light of a project developed more than 25 years ago in different circumstances.

Appreciating tolerance of ambiguity pushes IR toward a more complete understanding of the messiness of social conflict and enables more options for political action than would be available if intolerance of ambiguity ruled.

The Book's Structure

The book is subdivided into four parts: (I) Complexity and Ambiguity (Chapters 2 and 3); (II) New Photographies and Visual Ambiguities (Chapters 4 and 5); (III) *Bosnia: Uncertain Paths to Peace* (Chapters 6–9); and (IV) Leveraging Ambiguity for Peace (Chapters 10–13). As academic books are currently supposed to be written in such a manner that the individual chapters can be understood independently of the preceding and the following ones, redundancies cannot be entirely avoided.

In this book, we argue that studying international relations equals studying complexity and ambiguities. In Chapter 2, we take the first analytical step by exploring complexity in the context of international relations and peace and conflict studies. We understand complexity as a specific way of thinking, a frame of reference and discuss diverse literature from IR and peace and conflict research exploring what complexity means for our understanding of international relations. Thinking in terms of complexity offers a profound basis for a critique of existing approaches and practices—a critique from which possible alternatives and spaces of possibility can be derived. The chapter ends with brief remarks on the relationship between complexity and visual representation in terms of photocomplexity. In Chapter 3, we suggest accepting complexity and ambiguities rather than reducing them: if we scale down complexity, we will find it difficult to address the social world appropriately. Our analyses and our political decisions might fall short of our expectations. Thus, in this chapter, we engage with the question of how to deal with ambiguity without resorting to disambiguation and simplification (although some degree of simplification cannot be avoided when writing about anything). To this end, we look at complexity through the concept of tolerance of ambiguity (TA), discuss it in relation to IR theory, and suggest how to constructively deal with TA in the context of international relations. Essentially, attempts at disambiguation—reducing complexity—will also have effects that actors cannot anticipate. Becoming aware of the various consequences of an action in a complex system makes us recognize the multitude of possible and permissible interpretations that any event engenders. At the same time, we need to define some borders for what counts as permissible interpretation in order to avoid a politically dangerous and morally questionable *anything goes* approach to ambiguity. We conclude the chapter with reflections on the relationship between ambiguity and visual representation in terms of photoambiguity.

Opening the book's second part, Chapter 4 introduces selected new photographic approaches to war, genocide and violence, including mass civilian suffering that emerged in Bosnia and Herzegovina in the 1990s. These new approaches were inspired by the recognition that traditional photojournalistic work could not stop the violence, although it managed to raise international awareness and produce memorable photographs. The wars in ex-Yugoslavia revealed the simplicity of the conventional linkage between photographic documentation, awareness-raising and political responses that had informed photojournalism since its inception. In this chapter, we develop a typology of the new photographies emerging in Bosnia (and elsewhere) at that time. It is this visual environment within and beyond which Fred Ritchin and Gilles Peress developed their project *Bosnia: Uncertain Paths to Peace* (see Part III). It is this visual environment, too, within which IR and peace and conflict studies try to make sense of what happened in Bosnia. In chapter 5, we further develop our theoretical background concerning visual images, especially the word–image relationship, and explore how different approaches to this relationship affect the extent to which images can be controlled by means of words. An image's hidden ambiguity awaits rediscovery by curious observers who are not afraid of hegemonic photographic discourses, who want to reclaim photography's ambiguity and who wish to interact with images. Viewing, thus, becomes an essentially political act enabling viewers to understand and critically interrogate the politics of interpretation inherent in each single designation of meaning. In the digital world, viewers may contribute not only to the evolution of meaning assigned to an image but also, through active interaction, to the evolution of the image. Accepting the existence of ambiguities and explicitly leveraging them, we believe, will create a space to change how we think about ambiguity, control of meaning, difference of perspective and, ultimately, politics and society.

In Chapter 6, kicking off Part III, we introduce the online project *Bosnia: Uncertain Paths to Peace* created by Ritchin and Peress in cooperation with the *New York Times on the Web* in 1996. The most noteworthy feature of this interactive, multimedia project in our context is its high degree of interactivity, inevitably leading to a plurality of simultaneously existing narratives that are neither prescribed by the project's creators, hierarchically ordered, nor assessed in light of their truth value. The project challenges the authorial voice of its creators while allowing an unusual degree of audience participation and co-authorship, thus appealing to tolerance of ambiguity rather than to disambiguation. We present its main ideas, its practical implementation and its design. The project is an important precursor to current war photography, aiming to acknowledge the messiness of violent conflict rather than reducing it to simple, one-dimensional narratives. Narrative pluralism and the website's interactive design both challenge some of the foundations of photojournalistic practice and change the audience's viewing experience. The project acknowledges the creator's limited knowledge about the issue at hand and invites a variety of interpretations of the conflict to emerge.

In Chapter 7, we sketch different navigational approaches to *Bosnia: Uncertain Paths to Peace*. We show that different approaches connect us differently to the website and that which it represents—post-siege Sarajevo—thus diversifying our experience with both the website and the city. We perform a weak form of auto-ethnography and auto-navigation with recourse to our research notes. We add theoretical thoughts to our personal reflections because interacting with images is always a combination of personal reflection and learned knowledge. We will share with our readers our own personal experience when navigating the website and (self)critically explore what we have learned about both the website and our preconceptions. In Chapter 8, we analyze the project's grids—compilations of smaller images taken either in Sarajevo or in the city's suburbs—in light of different navigational approaches, focusing on individual images or on panel-to-panel transitions. In Chapter 9, we explore the project's interactive design. Digitization has indeed changed how image-makers and viewers interact both with each other and with visual material—a process that *Bosnia: Uncertain Paths to Peace* anticipated and actively sought by understanding meaning as the result of a conversation among the material presented on the website, the photographer, the picture editor and the audience. Indeed, the project assigned to the audience a degree of co-authorship and, thus, responsibility that went far beyond the role that photojournalism conventionally assigns to spectators. Instead of trying to capture complex, ambiguous and contradictory stories in the ostensibly authoritative voice of the photographer/journalist, it enables the emergence of a plurality of authors and voices co-constructing the story in its complexity, reflecting shifting roles, authorities and responsibilities.

Acknowledging the complexity of our social world, we believe that the search for sameness and identity underlying many domestic and international peacebuilding activities does not do justice to this ambiguous reality (Part IV). In Chapter 10, then, we address politics and society in terms of difference rather than sameness and identity. Western discourse deems difference problematic, a danger, a challenge, a barrier to constructive cohabitation and even a source for violence and war. However, social conflict offers many possibilities to deal with difference constructively: it can serve the improvement of social interaction among and between different social groups, provided that some basic techniques be applied and some fundamental characteristics of conflict be understood. In the chapter, we show why we consider embracing difference a relevant resource for peaceful change, first against the backdrop of the Bosnian and the Sarajevan context and then in regard to more general and (photo-) philosophical reflections.

In Chapter 11, we explore the *surround*—peripheral image components—as a place for alternative meaning-making and knowledge production. We criticize the standard approach to representability—inclusion in the frame (i.e., visibility) as a condition for the possibility of political debate—as too narrow and mechanical: what is *included* in the frame can nevertheless be *excluded* from perception, discourse and politics. We note that interpretive-hermeneutical approaches to image analysis may increase the invisibility of some image components by emphasizing others. Visibility and invisibility thus do not simply follow patterns of inclusion in and exclusion from the frame linked to an inside and an outside, respectively: analysis of the surround shows that the outside may be inside. What appears in the surround, while appearing there accidentally rather than intentionally, may increase our knowledge of both the scenario depicted and photography's role in and beyond it and, therefore, perform a critical function. Regarding the surround may lead us anywhere, thus offering alternatives to merely unimaginatively accepting or rejecting established designations of meaning. In Chapter 12, we explore the potential contributions of images to international peace mediation. Inspired by the concept of active listening and narrative approaches to mediation, we advance the notion of *active looking* in peace mediation: a visual-discursive mediation practice that includes images as a mode of expression and contribution to meaning-making processes, capitalizing on specific characteristics of images, especially as regards their relationship to verbal language, which we explore in terms of ineffability, approximation, elusiveness and commonalities. We propose active looking as both an approach to conflict mediation and a mediation skill derived from an understanding of conflict transformation that—instead of aiming at problem-solving based on sameness—appreciates openness, difference and ambiguity.

Concluding the book, Chapter 13 asks (in lieu of a summary): What are the limits of tolerance? Is our case study well chosen? Do we create new binaries strictly distinguishing tolerance of ambiguity from disambiguation and visual-narrative simplification from complexification? We conclude our conclusions with a visual complexity grid, reproducing the Sarajevo photographs that already appear at the end of each chapter (Sarajevo #1–Sarajevo #12). Chapter 8 offers some suggestions on how the grid may be read. We conclude the present chapter with the first of our Sarajevo photographs (see Fig. 1.5) to be introduced in the following chapter in terms of photocomplexity.

Fig. 1.5 Sarajevo #1 (Photograph © Frank Möller)

References

Beaumont, Paul, and Cedric de Coning. 2022. Coping with Complexity: Toward Epistemological Pluralism in Climate-Conflict Scholarship. *International Studies Review*. https://doi.org/10.1093/isr/viac055.

Bennett, Christopher. 2016. *Bosnia's Paralysed Peace*. London: Hurst & Company.
Campbell, David. 1998. *National Deconstruction: Violence, Identity, and Justice in Bosnia*. Minneapolis and London: University of Minnesota Press.
Cobb, Sara. 2013. *Speaking of Violence: The Politics and Poetics of Narrative in Conflict Resolution*. New York: Oxford University Press.
Couldry, Nick. 2000. *Inside Culture: Re-imagining the Method of Cultural Studies*. London: Sage.
Danchev, Alex. 2009. *On Art and War and Terror*. Edinburgh: Edinburgh University Press.
de Coning, Cedric. 2018. Adaptive Peacebuilding. *International Affairs* 94 (2): 301–317.
Glenny, Misha. 1996. *The Fall of Yugoslavia: The Third Balkan War*. London: Penguin.
Law, John. 2004. *After Method: Mess in Social Science Research*. London and New York: Routledge.
Markowitz, Fran. 2010. *Sarajevo: A Bosnian Kaleidoscope*. Urbana, Chicago, and Springfield: University of Illinois Press.
Mitchell, W.J.T. 1994. *Picture Theory: Essays on Verbal and Visual Representation*. Chicago and London: The University of Chicago Press.
Möller, Frank. 2020. Peace Aesthetics: A Patchwork. *Peace & Change: A Journal of Peace Research* 45 (1). https://doi.org/10.1111/pech.12385.
Ristic, Mirjana. 2018. *Architecture, Urban Space and War: The Destruction and Reconstruction of Sarajevo*. Houndmills: Palgrave Macmillan.
Shapiro, Michael J. 2004. *Methods and Nations: Cultural Governance and the Indigenous Subject*. New York and London: Routledge.
Walker, R.B.J. 1993. *Inside/Outside: International Relations as Political Theory*. Cambridge: Cambridge University Press.
Wendt, Alexander. 1999. *Social Theory of International Politics*. Cambridge: Cambridge University Press.

PART I

Complexity and Ambiguity

CHAPTER 2

Approaching Complexity in Peace and Conflict

INTRODUCTION

'Oh well, it is complex.' This utterance has become a frequently heard statement in academia, policy circles and communication between ordinary people regarding all kinds of conflicts, including international ones. In 1985, Jürgen Habermas wrote about what he called a new lack of clarity or comprehensibility—*Die neue Unübersichtlichkeit*, a term with which he addressed, among other things, the crisis of the welfare state and the end of utopian energy (Habermas 1985). The reference to sight or, more precisely, to our failure to grasp what appears to be in front of our eyes—*Unübersichtlichkeit*—escapes from most English translations but is noteworthy in our context: obstacles block our vision, we see only parts of reality, nothing is as it seems, everything appears blurred, confusing, difficult to see, recognize, survey, order. Internationally, however, the Cold War still seemed to offer some degree of predictability, reliability and assurance—obscene assurance, to be sure, as it was based on the threat of mutual annihilation. Furthermore, its complexity was rendered invisible by such simplifying terms as 'the West' and 'the East,' 'us' and 'them' or 'capitalism' and 'socialism,' often used without much reflection, seemingly ordering the world and promising both manageability and internal cohesion. Currently, internal divisions and polarizations compete with coherence, the world appears out of order, dystopian imaginations

© The Author(s), under exclusive license to Springer Nature Switzerland AG 2023
R. Bellmer and F. Möller, *Peace, Complexity, Visuality*, Rethinking Peace and Conflict Studies,
https://doi.org/10.1007/978-3-031-38218-5_2

triggered by climate change and war compete with utopian ones in terms of human progressiveness and peace, and what appears in front of our eyes seems to be even *unübersichtlicher*, more confusing, more irritating, still more difficult to grasp than before. Writing eight years after Habermas and, therefore, influenced by what seemed to be the end of the Cold War, R. B. J. Walker noted that "[r]itualized attitudes and postures have atrophied, scholarly literatures have been declared redundant and policy-making elites have been forced to regroup" (1993: 2). This could have been written today.

Referring to complexity is often meant to articulate a feeling or perception that it is increasingly difficult to develop a straightforward, unambiguous position regarding a given conflict, as both the conflict and its connections with other conflicts appear too multidimensional to invite simple answers or allow complete comprehension. A growing number of exceptions challenge attempts at generalization; clear-cut divisions in, for example, victim versus perpetrator or aggressor do not always work. Aiming to understand the causes of a conflict appears almost impossible, as decades or even centuries of history between conflicting parties render difficult identification of a conflict's starting point; the conflicting parties will most likely identify different events as causes for the dispute, and they will be quite adamant that their position is the correct one. As always, "the identification of a point of origin depends on where we think we are now" (Walker 1993: 27). Moreover, options and possibilities, while increasing, are interconnected in such a manner that outcomes become unpredictable, which makes it very challenging to find realistic pathways out of a conflict. Strategies for ending violence and creating a ground for peace seem unattainable. In short, feelings prevail that more has to be considered to be able to make a reasonable and justified decision about one's own position with regard to the conflict at stake. However, even then, the outcome of one's positioning does not always match expectations, and new information can challenge one's previous understanding of the conflict.

In many cases, reference to a conflict's complexity articulates a sense of being overwhelmed by the plethora of factors that need to be considered to express a competent opinion and make a qualified judgment. It can signal cognitive overload on the part of an individual caused by the perceived inability to consider all components of an issue that one might need to take into account to make a decision. The sentence that opened this chapter often follows a coping mechanism culminating, at least temporarily, in an end of thinking, constituting some sort of cognitive closure and analytical capitulation regarding the topic at hand. Shutting oneself off from more, possibly even conflicting, information can be a useful and necessary instrument to figure out a way to deal with the abundance of cognitive stimuli we are constantly confronted with (Coleman 2011: 61).

In other cases, the reference to complexity can express a feeling that the issue at stake is beyond our possibilities to achieve change for the better. It might represent the perception that a specific problem cannot possibly be solved or that it can be solved only at the prize of causing other, possibly even more severe problems that later generations will have to tackle with. Dilemmas, for example, offer equally unfavorable options. Or take the discussion revolving around some conflicts that continue to affect people's lives for several decades, so-called protracted conflicts. Referring to their complexity might not only offer a welcome excuse to not engage, or even abandon, ongoing initiatives, as those conflicts 'can't be solved anyways.' In some situations, it might even convey a rather condescending notion, as it reproduces the understanding of some conflicts as better than others—i.e., more conducive to resolution or transformation than others—as they allow room for rationality. As such, they can be overcome by rational people, as, for instance, Western Europeans tend to think of themselves, having achieved political integration after World War II based on rational decision-making and sober cost–benefit calculations. Here, persisting hatred and animosity seem to have been transformed into more benevolent forms of social interaction.

The complexity of intractable and long-standing conflicts in other areas of the world, in contrast, seems to confirm an underlying perception of these conflicts as impossible to solve, as they do not follow the principles of rationality elemental to Western thinking since the enlightenment, as these are allegedly fueled by negative emotions, greed or 'ancient hatred' as had been argued during both the Yugoslav wars of the 1990s and the 1994 genocide in Rwanda against the Tutsi in order to legitimize Western inactivity. In extreme cases, even the alleged character of the people involved may be blamed for their failure to deal with conflict rationally (with 'rationally' being defined by Western standards). This patronizing sentiment regarding the alleged insolvability of complex conflicts then allows policymakers to abandon these conflicts altogether and deny their own responsibility for both the conflicts' origins and their resolution or transformation. In all above scenarios, the reference to a conflict's complexity marks some sort of end of process, an end to thinking about the causes for violence and possible paths to peace, allowing oneself to not further engage with a conflict as it seems futile—a waste of time and resources—to do anything about it anyways. And it hardly matters whether a conflict is complex in fact or socially constructed as such (for a variety of reasons) because the consequences of factual and socially constructed complexity are similar. Thus, once a conflict is constructed as complex and once this understanding is widely shared, the conflict's alleged complexity becomes real in its consequences.

Our thinking in this book starts with the recognition of the complexity of social conflicts. We argue that both social systems and social conflicts possess a high degree of complexity. "Our world is becoming increasingly complex," writes Peter T. Coleman, arguing that "[d]ue in large part to physical, biological, and human cultural evolution, we are confronted with progressively more complex ecological, political, economic, and social problems. These problems place extreme demands on our capacity to comprehend and react adaptively" (Coleman 2006: 346). In parallel with factual complexification, our perception of complexity also increases due, in part, to a massive increase in information, communication and mobility. We, therefore, cannot avoid having to face complexity in our social environment. However, rather than reducing complexity to an empty signifier legitimizing inactivity and representing political and intellectual capitulation, we wish to suggest that we need to acknowledge and actively deal with complexity in order to transform social conflict and improve social relations between and among groups of people. We believe that thinking of possible actions to increase the likelihood of peaceful relations between conflicting parties requires us to understand the complexity underlying a given conflict as a first step toward resolution.

We approach complexity through ambiguities. We suggest that at the core of the frequent reference to complexity is increasing recognition that complex systems lead to ambiguities, i.e., that every system, every situation is open to diverse interpretations regarding its operating procedures and evaluations of its qualities. We suggest that the complexity of social interaction becomes visible through encounters with ambiguities and that the visualization of ambiguities can help us cope with complexity. Actions within, or aiming to influence, a system can be interpreted as positive, negative or irrelevant in a given context, depending on what we look at, what factors we consider for our judgments, how we understand the relationships among these factors, and where we locate them on a scale from irrelevant to important to non-negotiable. Not all factors are equally relevant, but different actors may (and are indeed likely to) assign to any of them different degrees of importance, reflecting the actors' experiences, interests and identities. While a specific take on an issue can make sense for an individual, different subject positions can lead to diverging ways of looking at and thinking about things, all of which appear reasonable and coherent from the point of view of those articulating them. Even if actors single out specific factors and pay attention only to them, this selection will inevitably influence other factors as well, thus changing the overall dynamics of the system and leading to new aspects open for interpretation. Therefore, "[o]urs is the age of interconnections, ambiguity, and uncertainty," write Amandine Orsini and several colleagues in a rather recent forum contribution (2019: 2). If we acknowledge complexity, we will also have to face ambiguities. We should not be afraid of them.

In a complex and ambiguous environment, clear-cut divisions do not work; we will always find exceptions to the rule, subject positions, experiences and stories that do not fit or even dispute our understanding and interpretation. Ambiguities, therefore, pose a challenge—a challenge to established ways of thinking, a challenge to taken-for-granted categories, heuristics and sense-making strategies. Coping with ambiguities is not easy but coping with them successfully is immensely rewarding. It certainly requires us to look at a given conflict from diverse angles and to consider more and more information before we can make a qualified decision, if ever.[1] For those of us who engage with international conflicts as researchers, practitioners or lay observers—"mediators of the moment" (Walker 1993: 1)—ambiguities make our work much more difficult than it would be without them. Trying to ignore them is an almost logical response: positioning oneself in an environment where ambiguities put our beliefs and convictions into question becomes a task that can be overwhelming and, at times, impossible. However, life without ambiguities would be similar to life without social conflict: immobile, stagnating, paralyzed, inactive, dull and devoid of change.

International intervention into systems that face conflicts—and intervention can here imply anything from peace operations and peacebuilding

---

[1] It is one of the ambiguities of digitization that, while it increases information immeasurably, it is precisely this increase in information that overwhelms us and makes it difficult to distinguish what is relevant in a given context from what is irrelevant, not to mention the facilitation of manipulation and deception enabled by digitization (see Jones 2022).

initiatives to research in and about conflict-affected societies including journalistic reporting—will, in all likelihood, have more than one effect; and the effect(s) it has may not be the intended one(s). Even if it does have the intended effect, intervention may have other effects as well, which may negatively affect the overall situation. No matter how hard we try to do the right thing, no matter how much information we process and no matter how many opinions we consult before we begin doing anything, we constantly run into ambiguous situations. Furthermore, rather than being fixed, situations constantly evolve; their component parts and the relationship among these parts also change, and consequently, the complexity of the overall situation changes as well. Thus, dealing with complexity and ambiguities is essential for researchers, practitioners and policymakers. How photojournalists represent complexity is equally important because it is mostly through journalistic reporting that we encounter international conflict. In this chapter, we set out the role of complexity in peace and conflict dynamics. We discuss selected literature on complexity and examine the role of complexity in conflict and peace processes. We argue that reducing conflicts' complexity, while seemingly rendering them manageable, is only one possible approach and neither always nor necessarily the best one.

Complexity in International Relations and Peace and Conflict Studies

In recent years, complexity thinking has gained traction in international relations (IR) (Korosteleva and Petrova 2022; Kavalski 2015; Clemens, Jr. 2001) and peace and conflict studies (Bächtold 2021; Brusset et al. 2016; Moe 2015). Approaching the international system and peace and conflict dynamics through a complexity lens is, however, certainly not a new idea. Indeed, "IR theorists have been looking at complexity at least since the late 1990s" (Orsini et al. 2019: 2).[2] For Emilian Kavalski, Complex International Relations (CIR), as he calls the "CT [complexity theory; the authors] approach to world politics" (Kavalski 2007: 441), constitute a profound challenge to conventional IR research, referred to

---

[2] Unfortunately, space limitations do not allow us to elaborate on the genealogy of research of international relations inspired by complexity thinking and how these approaches challenge established IR theories. For this see Bousquet and Curtis (2011) and Kavalski (2007).

as the "Fifth debate." In all their diversity, these approaches recognize "[c]omplexity [as] a structural condition of world politics" (Orsini et al. 2019: 5).

As Antoine Bousquet and Simon Curtis (2011: 45) clarify, "complexity is less a definitive theoretical corpus than a conceptual toolkit, even though there is a definite coherence and complementarity between all its elements." Likewise, David Byrne and Gillian Callaghan understand "the notion of complexity" as a "way of thinking" (2023: 114), a "frame of reference" that "implies new ways of framing problems, deploying methods and interpreting data" (2023: 7). Applied to a specific context, complexity theory often results in enumerations of possible approaches to complexity, all of which are interconnected. However, complexity theory does not necessarily tell actors how to deal with complexity precisely or how to establish policy priorities and translate them into policy (see Clemens, Jr. 2001). The complexity perspective, consequently, does not present "the one way for studying international life"; instead, it aims "(by acknowledging that there are many ways) to provide a conceptual framework within which IR theory can learn, adapt and interact" (Kavalski 2007: 444). Recommendations based on complexity thinking, thus, are always provisional; often they seem too vague to serve as clear policy guidelines, let alone generalizable ones.

In a scientific sense, complexity refers to a system in which "the elements are interconnected, and thus changes to one will directly affect some while indirectly affecting – even if to almost imperceptible degrees – others" (Brusset et al. 2016: 9). Such a system "has the ability to adapt, and ... demonstrates emergent properties, including self-organising behaviour" (de Coning 2016b: 20). In other words, a complex system—such as the international system—emerges as a result of the interconnectedness of the individual parts and "function[s] as an integrated whole that cannot be reduced to subsystems" (Jones and Hughes 2003: 491). It, therefore, gains characteristics that do not necessarily exist within the individual elements. Thus, a complex system can be more and less than its individual components (de Coning 2016b: 21); it cannot be understood without understanding its ingredients, but such understanding will not gain sufficient insights into the system's overall operating procedures (Cilliers 1998: viii). Approaching systems through a complexity lens thus "challenges the notion that by understanding the behaviour of each component part of a system the system can be understood as a whole" (Loode 2011: 70). This is one of the reasons why political interventions into the system, while taking place all the time, are hard to calculate in terms of an intention–outcome ratio: "it is very difficult if not impossible to say if and under what condition it [political steering; the authors] could and will be successful," notes Matthias Albert (2019: 10) with regard to such interventions.

A complex system is, thus, characterized by nonlinearity; "the outputs are not proportional to the inputs" (de Coning 2016b: 22). As a consequence, interventions in some elements result in dynamic and disproportionate effects, many of which can be unintended and nonpredictive. This nonlinear relationship between the different entities of a system and outside interventions is "an essential part, in fact a precondition, for emergence, self-regulation, and adaption in complex systems" (de Coning 2016b: 24). According to John Urry, complex systems

> have the ability to adapt and co-evolve as they organize through time. Such complex social interactions are likened to walking through a maze whose walls rearrange themselves as one walks through; new footsteps have to be taken in order to adjust to the walls of the maze that are adapting to each movement made through the maze. (2005: 3)

In contrast, in a complicated system such as a car, "[a]t no stage is another part going to take over the function of the missing part to keep the system working close to its previous levels" (Loode 2011: 70; see also Cilliers 1998: 3). While a complicated thing (such as a car) "can be taken apart into its bits and reassembled from those bits" (Byrne and Callaghan 2023: 12), complex systems cannot. Recognizing the complex nature of a system, therefore, challenges the principle of causality underlying how we frequently make sense of and theorize social processes (Chandler 2014: 22; Wendt 1999: 79–89). As Coleman explains,

> [t]hinking in straight lines is part of Western science and society's long tradition of linear causality, the focus on how X causes or leads to Y. This focus has helped us understand how many of the pieces of the conflict puzzle influence other pieces. But it does not seem to help us understand how the many pieces of more difficult conflicts come together, or what will happen when they do. (2011: 20)

Consequently, "in the social world," Byrne argues, "and in much of reality including biological reality, causation is complex. Outcomes are determined not by single causes but by multiple causes, and these causes may, and usually do, interact in a non-additive fashion" (1998: 20). However, Byrne and Callaghan do not abandon the notion of causality altogether. In a complex setting, the statement 'X determines Y,' rather than specifying what Y will look like *exactly*, establishes a space of possibilities within which Y will unfold—not a specific event but a relatively open space conditioning what can be done and what cannot be done in a given context (2023: 27).

From the above, it follows that "[a]n awareness of Complexity informs us that it is not possible to interfere in a complex system, and have only one effect" (de Coning 2016b: 33), let alone only the desired one. As a result, in a complex system, it is hardly ever possible to settle on one definite effect of an intervention, regardless of whether this intervention was intentional or not, human-made or not (de Coning 2020: 2). Due to a complex system's nonlinear and emergent character, then, the effects of an intervention might vary, and what effects can be observed and how they are interpreted can change from subject position to subject position. As always, interpretation can, but does not necessarily have to, be in accordance with a system's factual complexity; it can indeed evolve quite independently of it, transforming complexity into a speech act: to say that a thing is complex has real consequences, regardless of the thing's factual complexity (or lack thereof). Diverse perspectives always compete over social and discursive hegemony: the interpretation of a situation—the assigned meaning—depends on the perspective, it depends on what we look at and how we look at it (and how it looks back at us). As interpretations can change with new information available and old information reinterpreted or even forgotten, complexity also contains a temporal factor.

Regarding the connection to peace and conflict processes, complexity "becomes central to any efforts to understand how global systems (which encapsulate all of the sub-scales; regional, international, national, and local) generate violence of different kinds and how peacebuilders operate within such systems" (Millar 2019: 10). The past decades have shown that the international system acts in ways that cannot be projected with certainty, and future developments remain vague. Seemingly linear processes from A to B can be interrupted at any point. Gëzim Visoka thus proposes that "[a]ll peacebuilding interventions have been dominated by unplanned outcomes" (2016: 2). Critically, the exact arrangement of a system in a specific temporal and spatial setting does not necessarily depend on actors pushing for it. "Intent is not necessary. Systems function in ways unintended by any of the agents involved in those systems" (Millar 2019: 12). Situations that we could call (mal)functions of a system according to our moral evaluations do not need to be the objective of actors; they emerge because of the interrelationship between actors and factors in a nonlinear fashion. It is for this reason that "it need not be the end goal of any particular actor to have a system (either domestically or internationally) in which the privileges of some actors or groups are dependent on the marginalization or disempowerment of others" (Millar 2019: 12). However, the interconnected actions of a variety of actors operating in a complex system might nevertheless result in marginalization, disempowerment and even violence toward certain groups, violence in its different appearances.

In particular, critiques of the liberal peace paradigm in international peacebuilding emphasize that social systems such as societies engaged in violent conflict are nonlinear and complex (Chandler 2013). The limited success of peacebuilding initiatives in the past decades that leveraged the top-down liberal script (see Richmond 2006) forces the international community to realize that peacebuilding interventions in social systems do not guarantee the desired outcome, no matter how well-planned they are. Rather, developments on the ground are far from straightforward, and adjustments do not necessarily lead to a controllable outcome. Instead, they often even result in unpredicted—and frequently counterproductive—changes in other parts of the system. Therefore, researchers increasingly acknowledge the shortcomings of international interventions, blame the underappreciation of complexity for such shortcomings, and link these shortcomings to peacebuilding's underlying "modernist and liberal approaches" (Randazzo and Torrent 2021: 5) based on teleological, "progressivist accounts of history and development" (Randazzo 2017: 2). Elisa Randazzo and Ignasi Torrent, therefore, argue that "[c]omplexity, then, becomes a tool for critiquing simplistic peacebuilding praxis as well as for conceptually outlining what makes top-down peacebuilding unsuitable for its own given aims of restoring peace to war-torn societies" (2021: 5). Here, complexity-influenced thinking is strong in regard to criticizing established practices but much weaker with regard to outlining alternative practices. Knowing what does *not* work does not necessarily tell us what *does* work in complex systems.

Nonlinear thinking in critical scholarship is closely linked to the "local turn" in peacebuilding research and practice, characterized by a "shift from the formal sphere of government institutions and elite interactions to a sustained focus on the local or societal level" (Chandler 2013: 22).[3] This paradigmatic transformation is probably one of the most persuasive developments in recent years, influencing thinking in academic, policy and practitioner circles alike. Rather than "linear ends-based or goal-orientated interventions" (Chandler 2013: 19–20), the local turn postulates that peace remains illusory if interventions only address the elite level in a target country and, thus, directs its attention toward everyday interactions of the local population (see Mac Ginty 2021): "For the non-linear, societal or process-based approach it is the social milieus of everyday life that are crucial, not formal politics operating in the rarefied sphere of international-elite diplomacy and negotiation" (Chandler 2013: 23). From this perspective, it is the relationship between actors but also the relationship between actors and objects that define structures and outputs. These relationships, however, are hereby understood as uncertain by nature, and the outcomes thus take on a possibly unintended character (Randazzo and Torrent 2021: 4). The complexity perspective, therefore, introduces a "sensitiv[ity] to interdependencies and the uncertainty of the effects of the interactions between a varied range of actors" (Randazzo and Torrent 2021: 4).

Consequently, starting from the recognition of the complexity of violent conflicts and the nonlinearity of social relations, different approaches to studying peace and conflict dynamics have emerged as alternatives to the conventional but under-complex war–peace binary and its ramifications. The roles of failing/failures and adjustments/adaptations are rethought (Randazzo and Torrent 2021: 6; Paffenholz 2021) and concepts such as peace without peace (Bargués 2020) or resilience (Chandler 2014; de Coning 2016a; Kaufmann 2013; Bargués-Pedreny 2015, 2019; critical: Byrne and Callaghan 2023: 159) are suggested. Approaching conflicts through a complexity lens seems to allow us to think about processes in an interconnected manner. Rather than isolating specific aspects and elevating them to factors considered more important than others, be it the relationship between states and their high-level

---

[3] The discussion about the local turn does not go without critiques which we, however, cannot discuss in this chapter. Advancements of the concept that aim to overcome the local-international binary such as hybridity (Bargués-Pedreny and Randazzo 2018; Richmond 2015) cannot be discussed here, either.

representatives as in classical IR literature or local actors in critical peacebuilding approaches, complexity thinking enables us to link diverse actors and aspects across social and systemic levels (see Millar 2019, 2021a, 2021b) without necessarily assigning priority to any of them in terms of their relevance for the achievement of overarching goals, such as building peace. Complexity thinking "is conceived of as an analytical tool that enables us to reach a more comprehensive understanding of the behaviour of beings (actors) [...]" (Randazzo and Torrent 2021: 4).

Moreover, looking at complexity directly concerns our ability to 'understand' a conflict. It renders visible the incompleteness of what we can know. This perspective cannot but make us humble and modest. "Nonlinearity," suggests Coleman, "requires that interveners have humility; for changes are often unpredictable and uncontrollable" (2006: 340). The complex system lens reminds us that "[w]hen something is complex it cannot have one definitive problem-set" (de Coning 2016b: 34). Nor can it have one definitive set of solutions. Accordingly, an "explicit, reflexive awareness of the incompleteness of our understanding is … vital so that decisions are taken with a large degree of caution (and humility) while at the same time demanding that we think through the possible ramifications" (Hughes 2012: 116). Despite this limitation, "[p]eacebuilders are always attempting to build peace amidst a complex global system in which violence is an emergent process" (Millar 2019: 10). However, the complexity of a system is not merely a challenge to conventional peacebuilding strategies based on a linear input–output ratio; it also offers a new perspective on conflicts, their intractability and the prospects of peace. Wendell Jones and Scott Hughes write that "complex adaptive systems can produce truly novel, unexpected responses" (Jones and Hughes 2003: 491). As Danny Burns puts it (similar to Byrne and Callaghan quoted above), "[t]he notion that intervention A will lead to outcome B needs to be replaced by something more akin to: intervention A may open up a space for action in this location, which might have an effect on people and relationships elsewhere, which may open up spaces for further action" (2011: 104). In the same direction, Randazzo and Torrent argue that "[i]f complexity allows us to acknowledge the limits of knowing and affecting the world through purposeful action, this can usher in a position of epistemological uncertainty that ultimately disarms those actors who may have dogmatic and even manipulative tendencies" (2021: 15). The complexity lens, then, does not only complicate the situation for peacebuilders (and especially for dogmatic and manipulative ones). It also offers the possibility of leaving "conflict traps" (see Coleman 2011: 7) and entering pathways to peace.

While the literature on the complexity of conflicts is growing rapidly, the development in the field is at the same time highly controversial. This can hardly be otherwise, given the diversity of the discussion. To give just one example, Stefan Bächtold, in a recent paper, sets out how complexity-inspired peacebuilding both on the ground and in academia, advocating learning and adaptivity, can have diametral effects to those intended. Instead of improving peacebuilding activities and increasing inclusiveness, as supporters of the complexity approach frequently suggest, "complexity-inspired professional peacebuilding discourse insulates peacebuilders from being accountable to the populations they target" (2021: 506). Bächtold articulates a strong view on the impact of complexity-inspired thinking in peacebuilding: "Overall, the practical uptake of complexity theory and systems thinking in peacebuilding has potentially made interventions more exclusive than inclusive, by constituting peacebuilding interventions as non-objectionable and by denying the people targeted by peacebuilding to be considered subjects that interventions ought to be accountable to" (p. 517). For him, complexity thinking is just another attempt to change peacebuilding activities without disrupting the power structures and hierarchies that are "deeply engrained in peacebuilding interventions' practices, technical concepts, and discourses" (p. 517). In this line of thought, complexity-inspired approaches merely reproduce the power dynamics at play.

As this example shows, the introduction of complexity theory into peacebuilding research and practice can potentially lead to unintended, nonlinear consequences. Although they have emancipating potential, possibly harmful side effects cannot be excluded. Complexity-based peacebuilding must be aware of this danger, consistently interrogating its own performance. Thus, the application of complexity thinking in peacebuilding can lead to ambiguous results in practice (facts). And the nonlinear and emergent character causing unintended and unexpected secondary effects leads us to multiple, possibly contradictory interpretations of an action (discourse). We are facing ambiguities.

How to Cope with Complexity

Applying complexity thinking to social problems can be a part of the solution or a part of the problem. While the recognition that societies—particularly those engaged in violent conflict—are complex is increasingly shared across those actors working with them, individuals involved in conflicts in one way or another tend to simplify rather than try to grasp the complexity of the conflict (as we will show in detail in Chapter 12). Individuals do not always appreciate complexity, as they commonly have "the press for coherence" or a "need for closure" (Coleman 2011: 65). For Coleman, this is a normal cognitive function at the core of which "is the drive to reduce the tension, disorientation, and dissonance that come from complexity, incoherence, and contradiction" (2011: 65). Because complexity is cognitively demanding and difficult to sustain and navigate, individuals favor applying different strategies to address it. One approach is downplaying or ignoring the existence of complexity. Coleman describes this process as follows:

> Often, our initial reaction is to feel overwhelmed. We may feel anxious and despair of our ability to respond effectively. This motivates our attempts to deny or avoid a problem. We might fail to recognize it altogether, or acknowledge the issues while simultaneously refusing to engage them. (2011: 43)

This reaction usually results in more or less deliberate ignorance about the complexity of an issue, assuming that complexity disappears if ignored (which it may do if we reduce it to a speech act).

A second common approach to dealing with complex issues lies in the reduction of complexity (Coleman 2011: 43–44). For example, one possible mechanism is acknowledging the complexity of the overall conflict complex while trying to deal with selected component parts of the complex that seem to be more susceptible to resolution. As argued above, this approach is problematic from a complexity point of view. However, such a reduction is not necessarily negative and in line with an individual's strive for coherence, which is "a necessary and functional process that helps us interpret and respond to our world efficiently and (hopefully) effectively" (Coleman 2011: 63). Furthermore, we are constantly engaging with information and cognitive signals, not all of which are assessed individually but rather in clusters. Social categories and mental shortcuts serve an important role in reducing the information load that we must process to make conscious as well as unconscious decisions. Without simplification of our social reality, we would never be able to decide anything; always thinking through all possible options would result in paralysis.

However, subdividing a complex cluster in its ingredients and then dealing with the ingredients successively means—even if it were possible to identify all ingredients—treating a complex issue as if it were merely a complicated one (the sum of its parts, all of which can be dealt with individually without affecting the overall system and subsequently reassembled), underestimating the dynamics operating among the cluster components and overestimating one's capability of both influencing any of them and identifying all of them in the first place. In the short run, peacebuilding strategies aiming to improve individual conflict components may seem to work; in the long run, however, such strategies will face challenges emanating from the conflict complex's inherent ambiguities and contradictions.

In any case, simplification and (un)conscious mental shortcuts—biases—have real-life effects on our actions. In extreme cases, simplification allows for accommodating only one option, one interpretation of events and situations, often derived from and connected with binaries such as right versus wrong, good versus evil or perpetrator versus victim. It might also lead to accommodating only one specific understanding of both the roots of a conflict and the options available for peaceful development. In other words, simplifications narrow spaces of possibility (which is precisely their political function in conflicts instrumentalized to increase an ingroup's coherence).

In conflict, individuals nevertheless tend and are instructed to reduce complexity. For instance, Coleman argues that a conflict becomes intractable "when the many different components of a conflict collapse together into one mass, into one very simple 'us versus them' story that effectively resists change" (2011: 9). It is the reduction of complexity—Coleman calls it the "reduction of multidimensionality" (2006: 329)—that spirals a conflict toward more fundamental positions and makes it close to impossible to solve. Following Coleman, the image or perception that we have of an Other—may it be an individual or a group—is responsible for how we react to a social situation that is potentially destructive or harmful to the relationship we have with our counterpart.

This image depends on all sorts of aspects, including previous encounters. In Coleman's words,

> [s]uch multidimensionality and complexity in relationships mitigates against malignant social relations. For instance, if my friend harms me, our common goals and bonds should buffer my experience of the harm and constrain any overly aggressive response. Under these conditions, I am able to maintain a nuanced understanding of my friend, the act, and even myself (my role and responsibility in bringing about the act). (2006: 329)

According to Coleman, it is the complexity of our image of the Other (or the world more generally) that prevents us from reacting more strongly and forcefully in a conflict situation. However, the complexity of the image that we have of ourselves, too, is in danger to lose its complexity:

> as conflicts escalate and persist, we often see the character of the relations between distinct psychological elements (i.e., my beliefs, attitudes, and feelings toward my friend) and distinct social elements (i.e., group memberships, bonds, and goals) becoming more aligned and positively correlated so that they begin to trigger and mutually reinforce one another. (2006: 329)

Crucially, "[s]uch convergence can result in viewing one's group identity so that a negation of the other becomes a fundamental aspect of one's identity" (2006: 330).

Regarding the narratives people engage with during a violent conflict to make sense of the conflict and one's own social positions within it, Sara Cobb makes an important observation: over time, "as conflicts become protracted, narratives become, structurally, increasingly simple" (2013: 51). She contends that

> conflict narratives, over time, are drained of complexity as parties develop narrative "short cuts" – events in the main plot line become "dense" with meaning in that they stand as a semiotic marker for the entire set of contextualizing narratives that provided stability for that event. (2013: 51)

As a result,

> the subjectivity of the Other is truncated, and their intentions, motivations, or emotional experience is left out of the speaker's story. The flattening of the Other is a narrative form of dehumanization, for indeed, to be human is to be constructed as having intentions and emotions. (2013: 59)

Consequently, during such a process, long-lasting conflicts "tend to become increasingly difficult and complicated over time" while "simultaneously begin[ning] to seem incredibly simple" (Coleman 2011: 28). The conflict becomes increasingly complex but its narratives become increasingly simple. For example, a conflict's complexity can be explained away with reference to ostensible long-lasting patterns of enmity that then seem to justify the conflict's discursive simplification in terms of 'us' versus 'them.' Alternatively, the overall conflict may appear increasingly simple (addressed, for example, in terms of 'ancient hatreds,' which never explain much), while on the individual person-to-person level, things may be more complex. As the story of Zoran's return in Chapter 8 shows, simple constructions of social reality in terms of 'us' versus 'them' do not prevent the emergence of individual friendships across such group boundaries. Such border crossings, however, might not challenge or even undermine 'us'-versus-'them' constructions on the group level; it is more likely that they will be treated as 'exceptions confirming the rule.' Importantly, then, to the binaries that often inhibit conflict resolution, one more binary should be added: simplification versus complexification, as both may occur simultaneously on different levels.

Consequently, while the reduction of complexity is a natural and, in many cases, necessary and useful cognitive strategy, the process of narrowing down the complexity of a conflictual social situation is at the core of the intractability and insolvability of conflicts. In turn, maintaining a complex understanding of an issue and possibly even recovering some of the complexity that was lost during the process are promising venues for a more constructive handling of conflict situations. As Coleman argues, "[i]n our research, more complex approaches, in terms of how the participants thought about the issues, felt, and behaved, were in fact better" (2011: 57). He states that "developing more complex patterns of thinking, feeling, acting, and social organizing can mitigate this [the human drive toward consistency and coherence in their perception; the authors], resulting in more constructive responses to conflict" (p. 68).

Therefore, Coleman describes a third strategy to cope with complexity: "*actively engag[ing] with complexity*" (2011: 44, italics in original). He clarifies that engaging with complexity does not mean getting bogged down in detail. Being overwhelmed with complexity and nuances can be as much of a barrier to the constructive handling of complexity as its excessive reduction. "Either extreme – overwhelming complexity or oversimplified coherence – is problematic" (2011: 64). Coleman, however, sees one option as riskier or more likely to happen: "But in difficult, long-term conflicts, the tide pulls fiercely toward simplification of complex realities. This is what we must contend with" (2011: 64) while at the same time acknowledging that all engagements with the complex character of issues will require some sort of simplification when writing, talking or thinking about them.

All models—and language and thinking are models of reality, too—require simplification: "If we're to understand anything, we have to simplify, which means we have to make boundaries," writes Donella Meadows (2009: 97). For this reason, engaging with complexity "typically entails an iterative process of *differentiation* of the relevant aspects of and perspectives on the problem. *And then* an *integration* of this information within some coherent framework that makes it comprehensible and useful" (Coleman 2011: 44, italics in original). However, who decides what is relevant in a given conflict and what is not? Who decides which framework is coherent and which is not? In a similar vein—simplifying before complexifying—John Paul Lederach, while identifying "[c]omplexity emerg[ing] from multiplicity, interdependency, and simultaneity" as "*the* great challenge of peacebuilding" (2005: 33; italics in original), suggests "think[ing] about simplicity as a source of energy rather than as the choice of reductionism." However, his suggestion "to locate a core set of patterns and dynamics that generate the complexity" conflates a complex issue with a complicated one where components can be neatly separated from one another and treated in isolation before being reassembled for further treatment and where agreement can be achieved regarding the core set of patterns in a given conflict.

Dealing with a complex world saturated with ambiguities requires taking complexity seriously. It can certainly mean a balancing act of simplifying the complex nature of a situation without getting lost in the quicksand of detail. It can also mean having to do something that, from a complexity point of view, cannot be done successfully (e.g., disassembling and subsequently reassembling a conflict's constituent parts) but that is inevitable all the same because not doing it would result in paralysis. Currently, however, there seems to be a tendency to overly reduce complexity. As several scholars coming from a narrative tradition to conflict resolution contend, however, building peace requires what Cobb calls an "evolution of meaning" (2013: 24) or a "plot evolution" in the words of John M. Winslade and Gerald Monk (2006: 223). An appropriate representation of and thinking about a conflict requires an adequate degree of complexity to open pathways out of the "conflict trap" (Coleman 2011: n.p.) and to overcome the intractability of a conflict. Therefore, Coleman suggests that "[t]his growth of complexity, brought about by decoupling important issues"—without ignoring the ways they interact with one another—"can not only provide solutions for the specific issues at stake, but may also start a social process that lowers the intensity of the conflict and paves the way for the operation of other compensatory mechanisms" (2006: 243).

PHOTOCOMPLEXITY

Our choice of words above was not accidental:

> Actions within, or aiming to influence, a system can be interpreted as positive, negative or irrelevant in a given context, depending on what we *look* at.
>
> While a specific take on an issue can make sense for an individual, different subject positions can lead to diverging ways of *looking* at and thinking about things.
>
> Diverse perspectives always compete over social hegemony: the interpretation of a situation … depends on the perspective, it depends on what we *look* at and how we *look* at it (and how it *looks* back at us).
>
> *Looking* at complexity directly concerns our ability to "understand" a conflict. It *renders visible* the incompleteness of what we can know.

We see complexity. Viewing is a complex experience, and complexity is part of visuality. Nothing is as it seems: "It's not what you think"—seeing does not equal visualizing (Pylyshyn 2003). Visualizing is a visual communication process connecting what can be seen with what cannot be seen thus creating a whole out of fragments. We do this all the time, and some genres of image production depend on it (see Chapter 8). Not everything can be seen, however, and what can be seen often remains unobserved because written or verbal discourse directs our attention elsewhere. Thus, not only the visual is complex but the relationship between images and words (a major subject of what follows in this book, see especially Chapter 5) is also complex. Importantly, "[c]omplexity inherent in the visual and in its relation to the reality it (cl)aims to depict implies that different people interpret the same scene and the same image differently" (Bellmer and Möller 2022: 9). This is so not only because cropping (see Chapter 11) and captions may evoke different interpretations but also because the visual is in itself complex. Indeed, even a seemingly simple and obvious picture can be understood in many different ways, communicating different realities to different observers—depending on the socialization of the interpreters, visual memories that the interpreters bring with them to the viewing experience, the context within and the company with which such experience takes place, the form in which we encounter an image (looking at an image in an exhibition space is different from looking at the same image on the computer screen; regarding an image in a photojournalistic context is different from regarding the same image in an artistic one) and so on. What we *see* reflects who we *are*. Not least, it depends on what we *want* to see or what we *believe* to see (for the latter aspect, see Morris 2014).

Complexity theory may help us identify different layers of complexity—photocomplexity—inherent in images and viewing experiences. We find Byrne and Callaghan's approach to complexity referred to above—"a frame of reference" and "a general way of thinking"—particularly useful. Not only does it help us avoid becoming lost in Theory; it also helps us understand that complexity is neither *only* a function of the real (whatever that is) nor *only* a function of discursive constructions. Rather, it is an "ontological … way of thinking about what the world is made from, both in terms of the entities which constitute the world *and* the relationships among those entities" (Byrne and Callaghan 2023: 21; italics in original), alerting us that representations, including visual ones, are social constructions and that "such representations are also real in their consequences" (Byrne and Callaghan 2023: 118).

The photographer Jerry Thompson insists that lens-made pictures "are inextricably linked to the real world" (2003: 3). However, the image "is not a mere reproduction of what is out there in front of the photographer or the filmmaker" (Rancière 2009: 93–94), regardless of early photography's claim to be just that, photojournalism's insistence on truth and forensic photography's approach to image-based investigation as evidence (see Chapter 4). Thus, while photography's truth claims deserve some degree of skepticism, visual culture is nevertheless linked to the real world in the sense that emerging meanings assigned to an image or meaning-making processes have real consequences in this world, provided that the resulting meaning is shared by a significant number of people or a small number of people in significant positions. (It will change your life if you and your image are visually-discursively constructed as a terrorist, regardless of whether or not you *are* a terrorist.) This is why constructivist and poststructuralist approaches to visuality are so important: these approaches decouple processes of meaning-making (and their analyses) from the world as it *truly* is (because what the world *truly* is can neither be known nor represented) while insisting on real-world consequences of designations of meaning. Both ontologies—the photojournalistic one in terms of truth insisting that it is possible to know the world and to represent it visually, and the poststructuralist one denying this possibility and focusing on analysis of our accounts of the world and the real-life consequences of these accounts—are related to complexity and ambiguity, the one by inviting disambiguation, the other by insisting on ambiguity. We will encounter both approaches in this book. And while much of photojournalism is an exercise in disambiguation (see Chapter 4), we are not primarily concerned with photojournalism (conventionally understood) in this book, and disambiguation concerns us mainly as a negative reference point.

Furthermore, as we will show in Chapter 5, digitization has substantially changed visuality and increased its complexity. While the changeability and contingency of meaning assigned to a given image has long since been acknowledged in the literature, the image has been treated in itself as a rather stable visual point of reference. Mention *The Falling Soldier* and visually educated people of a certain generation will precisely know what image you are referring to; they will also think that they know what it looks like. While meanings changed (in the case of this particular image as a consequence of discussions about its authenticity), the image remained the same. Digitization, however, implies that not only meaning changes over time but also its visual point of reference, the image. In contrast to analog photography (from which most photo theory emerged and which it reflects), the digital photograph is based on creating discrete and malleable records of the visible that can and will be linked, transmitted, recontextualized, and fabricated. [...] As such, the digital photograph can be conceived of as a meta-image, a map of squares, each capable of being individually modified and, on the screen, able to serve as a pathway elsewhere. (Ritchin 2009: 141)

Such modification undermines the notion of the image as a stable reference point for discursive meaning-making. Thus, currently, meaning assigned to an image changes, but so does the image, further complexifying the relationship among the visual, designations of meaning and the real.

To add yet another layer of complexity, we include in this book photographs taken in the city of Sarajevo between 2018 and 2022 to illustrate our case study (Part III) and offer our readers a sense of place today (Sarajevo #1–Sarajevo #12). However, these images, appearing at the end of each chapter, are only loosely linked to the text that surrounds them. We expect our readers all the same to look for some connections that these images have to our case study; after all, we co-present images and written text in the same book. However, in lieu of precise instructions of how to read these images in the present context, we assign the task of meaning-making to our readers, expecting that different readers will come up with different interpretations. Ours is not a photojournalistic approach; fixing meaning to avoid confusion on the part of the reader/viewer and guaranteeing that the images are understood as intended is not our aim. However, confusion on the part of the reader/viewer is not our aim, either. Rather, we follow to some extent Robert Lyons and Scott Straus's approach—photographs without captions in the context of the 1994 genocide in Rwanda—about which we say elsewhere that it is "more appreciative of the approximate" (Möller 2010: 124)—and, thus, more appreciative of ambiguities—than are other photographic projects on the same subject:

there is no obvious connection between the text and the images, or more precisely, between the interviews and the photographs: the book presents Straus's interviews with people whose photographs have not been taken and photographs of people interviewed by Lyons during the photographic session; these [Lyons'] interviews, however, are not reproduced in the book. The book co-presents the verbal (transcribed interviews) and the visual (photographs) without claiming that there necessarily is any connection between the verbal and the visual. (p. 125)

According to Straus, their book is "a marriage of two separate projects of disparate origins, one written and academic, the other visual and aesthetic" (Lyons and Straus 2006: 16). Our book is not a marriage of two separate projects of disparate origins, and we need to clarify to some extent the relationship between the written and academic, and the visual and aesthetic. We will do so in Chapter 5.

Conclusion

In this chapter, we argued that complexity thinking has been applied to IR and peace and conflict studies both implicitly and explicitly for several decades and demonstrated that if we acknowledge the international system and international conflict as complex, we will inevitably face ambiguities. Acknowledging a system's complexity does not tell us how to deal with this complexity; acknowledging ambiguities inherent in complexity will not tell us how to respond to them, either. We proposed that dealing with complexity is necessary if we want to understand and engage with social conflicts. In line with different prominent strands of international theory, we suggested that ambiguities do not necessarily constitute an obstacle to peaceful development. In what follows, we suggest that our complex social reality requires us to respond to ambiguity not with simplification but with openness for diverse perspectives and interpretations. We, therefore, argue that to appropriately deal with social conflict, we need to learn to stand ambiguities.

In the following chapter, then, we will argue for accepting complexity rather than reducing it: with simplification comes a greater distance between the self and social reality. If we scale down complexity, we might not address the social world appropriately; our analyses and our political decisions might fall short of our expectations. We will engage with the question of how to deal with ambiguity without resorting to disambiguation and simplification. To this end, we will look at complexity through the concept of tolerance of ambiguity (TA), discuss it in relation to international theory and suggest how to constructively deal with TA in the context of peace and conflict. The practical application of complexity theory, while acknowledging complexity, will always also have to engage with limitations to complexity and permissible interpretations. Likewise, while opposing disambiguation, TA nevertheless requires some boundaries. It is this condition of tension that interests us. With Meadows, we argue that "[t]here is no single, legitimate boundary to draw around a system. We have to invent boundaries for clarity and sanity; and boundaries can produce problems when we forget that we've artificially created them" (Meadows 2009: 97). We will end the next chapter with brief remarks on photoambiguity. We conclude the present chapter with the second of our Sarajevo photographs (Fig. 2.1) introduced above in terms of photocomplexity.

Fig. 2.1 Sarajevo #2 (Photograph © Frank Möller)

References

Albert, Mathias. 2019. Luhmann and Systems Theory. *Oxford Research Encyclopedias, Politics,*. https://doi.org/10.1093/acrefore/9780190228637.013.7.

Bächtold, Stefan. 2021. Donor Love Will Tear Us Apart: How Complexity and Learning Marginalize Accountability in Peacebuilding Interventions. *International Political Sociology* 15 (4): 504–521.

Bargués-Pedreny, Pol. 2015. Realising the Post-modern Dream: Strengthening Post-conflict Resilience and the Promise of Peace. *Resilience* 3 (2): 113–132.

Bargués-Pedreny, Pol, and Elisa Randazzo. 2018. Hybrid Peace Revisited: An Opportunity for Considering Self-Governance? *Third World Quarterly* 39 (8): 1–18.

Bargués-Pedreny, Pol. 2019. Resilience Is "Always More" Than Our Practices: Limits, Critiques, and Skepticism About International Intervention. *Contemporary Security Policy* 41 (2): 1–24.

Bargués, Pol. 2020. Peacebuilding Without Peace? On How Pragmatism Complicates the Practice of International Intervention. *Review of International Studies* 46 (2): 237–255.

Bellmer, Rasmus, and Frank Möller. 2022. Active Looking: Images in Peace Mediation. *Peacebuilding* 11 (2). https://doi.org/10.1080/21647259.2022.2152971.

Bousquet, Antoine, and Simon Curtis. 2011. Beyond Models and Metaphors: Complexity Theory, Systems Thinking and International Relations. *Cambridge Review of International Affairs* 24 (1): 43–62.

Brusset, Emery, Cedric de Coning, and Bryn Hughes, eds. 2016. *Complexity Thinking for Peacebuilding Practice and Evaluation*. London: Palgrave Macmillan.

Burns, Danny. 2011. Facilitating Systemic Conflict Transformation Through Systemic Action Research. In *The Non-linearity of Peace Processes: Theory and Practice of Systemic Conflict Transformation*, ed. Daniela Körrpen, Norbert Ropers and Hans J. Giessmann, 97–110. Opladen & Farmington Hills, MI: Barbara Budrich Publishers.

Byrne, David. 1998. *Complexity Theory and the Social Sciences*. London and New York: Routledge.

Byrne, David, and Gillian Callaghan. 2023. *Complexity Theory and the Social Sciences: The State of the Art*. London and New York: Routledge.

Chandler, David. 2013. Peacebuilding and the Politics of Non-linearity: Rethinking 'Hidden' Agency and 'Resistance.' *Peacebuilding* 1 (1): 17–32.

Chandler, David. 2014. *Resilience: The Governance of Complexity*. New York: Routledge.

Cilliers, Paul. 1998. *Complexity and Postmodernism: Understanding Complex Systems*. London and New York: Routledge.

Clemens, Walter, Jr. 2001. *The Baltic Transformed: Complexity Theory and European Security*. Lanham: Rowman and Littlefield.

Cobb, Sara. 2013. *Speaking of Violence: The Politics and Poetics of Narrative in Conflict Resolution*. New York: Oxford University Press.

Coleman, Peter T. 2006. Conflict, Complexity, and Change: A Meta-Framework for Addressing Protracted, Intractable Conflicts—III. *Peace and Conflict: Journal of Peace Psychology* 12 (4): 325–348.

Coleman, Peter T. 2011. *The Five Percent: Finding Solutions to Seemingly Impossible Conflicts*. New York: Public Affairs.

de Coning, Cedric. 2016a. From Peacebuilding to Sustaining Peace: Implications of Complexity for Resilience and Sustainability. *Resilience* 4 (3): 166–181.

de Coning, Cedric. 2016b. Implications of Complexity for Peacebuilding Policies and Practices. In *Complexity Thinking for Peacebuilding Practice and Evaluation*, ed. Emery Brusset, Cedric de Coning, and Bryn Hughes, 19–48. London: Palgrave Macmillan.

de Coning, Cedric. 2020. Insights from Complexity Theory for Peace and Conflict Studies. In *The Palgrave Encyclopedia of Peace and Conflict Studies*, ed. Oliver Richmond and Gëzim Visoka, 1–10. Cham: Palgrave Macmillan. https://doi.org/10.1007/978-3-030-11795-5_134-1.

Habermas, Jürgen. 1985. *Die neue Unübersichtlichkeit. Kleine Politische Schriften V*. Frankfurt: Suhrkamp.

Hughes, Bryn. 2012. Peace Operations and the Political: A Pacific Reminder of What Really Matters. *Journal of International Peacekeeping* 16 (1–2): 99–118.

Jones, Marc Owen. 2022. *Digital Authoritarianism in the Middle East: Deception, Disinformation and Social Media*. London: Hurst & Co.

Jones, Wendell, and Scott H. Hughes. 2003. Complexity, Conflict Resolution, and How the Mind Works. *Conflict Resolution Quarterly* 20 (4): 485–494.

Kaufmann, Mareile. 2013. Emergent Self-Organisation in Emergencies: Resilience Rationales in Interconnected Societies. *Resilience* 1 (1): 53–68.

Kavalski, Emilian. 2007. The Fifth Debate and the Emergence of Complex International Relations Theory: Notes on the Application of Complexity Theory to the Study of International Life. *Cambridge Review of International Affairs* 20 (3): 435–454.

Kavalski, Emilian, ed. 2015. *World Politics at the Edge of Chaos: Reflections on Complexity and Global Life*. New York: State University of New York Press.

Korosteleva, Elena A., and Irina Petrova. 2022. What Makes Communities Resilient in Times of Complexity and Change? *Cambridge Review of International Affairs* 35 (2): 137–157.

Lederach, John Paul. 2005. *The Moral Imagination: The Art and Soul of Building Peace*. Oxford: Oxford University Press.

Loode, Serge. 2011. Peacebuilding in Complex Social Systems. *Journal of Peace, Conflict & Development* 18: 68–82.

Lyons, Robert, and Scott Straus. 2006. *Intimate Enemy: Images and Voices of the Rwandan Genocide*. New York: Zone Books.

Mac Ginty, Roger. 2021. *Everyday Peace: How so-Called Ordinary People Can Disrupt Violent Conflict*. Oxford: Oxford University Press.

Meadows, Donella H. 2009. *Thinking in Systems: A Primer*. London: Earthscan.

Millar, Gearoid. 2019. Toward a Trans-Scalar Peace System: Challenging Complex Global Conflict Systems. *Peacebuilding* 8 (3): 1–18.

Millar, Gearoid. 2021a. Ambition and Ambivalence: Reconsidering Positive Peace as a Trans-Scalar Peace System. *Journal of Peace Research* 58 (4): 640–654.

Millar, Gearoid. 2021b. Trans-Scalar Ethnographic Peace Research: Understanding the Invisible Drivers of Complex Conflict and Complex Peace. *Journal of Intervention and Statebuilding* 15 (3): 1–20.

Moe, Louise Wiuff. 2015. The Strange Wars of Liberal Peace: Hybridity, Complexity and the Governing Rationalities of Counterinsurgency in Somalia. *Peacebuilding* 4 (1): 1–19.

Möller, Frank. 2010. Rwanda Revisualized: Genocide, Photography, and the Era of the Witness. *Alternatives* 35 (2): 113–136.

Morris, Errol. 2014. *Believing Is Seeing (Observations on the Mysteries of Photography)*. New York: Penguin.

Orsini, Amandine, Philippe Le Prestre, Peter M. Haas, Malte Brosig, Philipp Pattberg, Oscar Widerberg, Laura Gomez-Mera, Jean-Frédéric. Morin, Neil E. Harrison, Robert Geyer, and David Chandler. 2019. Forum: Complex Systems and International Governance. *International Studies Review* 22 (4): 1008–1038.

Paffenholz, Thania. 2021. Perpetual Peacebuilding: A New Paradigm to Move Beyond the Linearity of Liberal Peacebuilding. *Journal of Intervention and Statebuilding* 15 (3): 367–385.

Pylyshyn, Zenon W. 2003. *Seeing and Visualizing: It's Not What You Think*. Cambridge and London: MIT Press.

Rancière, Jacques. 2009. *The Emancipated Spectator*, trans. Gregory Elliott. London: Verso.

Randazzo, Elisa. 2017. *Beyond Liberal Peacebuilding: A Critical Exploration of the Local Turn*. New York: Routledge.

Randazzo, Elisa, and Ignasi Torrent. 2021. Reframing Agency in Complexity-Sensitive Peacebuilding. *Security Dialogue* 52 (1): 3–20.

Richmond, Oliver P. 2006. The Problem of Peace: Understanding the 'Liberal Peace.' *Conflict, Security & Development* 6 (3): 291–314.

Richmond, Oliver P. 2015. The Dilemmas of a Hybrid Peace: Negative or Positive? *Cooperation and Conflict* 50 (1): 50–68.

Ritchin, Fred. 2009. *After Photography*. New York: Norton & Company.

Thompson, Jerry L. 2003. *Truth and Photography: Notes on Looking and Photographing*. Chicago: Ivan R. Dee.

Urry, John. 2005. The Complexity Turn. *Theory, Culture & Society* 22 (5): 1–14.

Visoka, Gëzim. 2016. *Peace Figuration after International Intervention: Intentions, Events and Consequences of Liberal Peacebuilding*. London and New York: Routledge.

Walker, R.B.J. 1993. *Inside/Outside: International Relations as Political Theory*. Cambridge: Cambridge University Press.

Wendt, Alexander. 1999. *Social Theory of International Politics*. Cambridge: Cambridge University Press.
Winslade, John M., and Gerald Monk. 2006. Does the Model Overarch the Narrative Stream? In *The Blackwell Handbook of Mediation: Bridging Theory, Research, and Practice*, ed. Margaret S. Herrman, 217–227. Malden: Blackwell Publishing.

CHAPTER 3

Tolerance of Ambiguity

INTRODUCTION

In the preceding chapter, we argued that systems such as the international system are not only complicated but complex. To say that a system is complex is another way of saying that it is more than the sum of its component parts; it cannot be adequately understood by analyzing these parts individually. Thus, when analyzing these parts individually (as research is bound to do), researchers must be aware of the limits of such analysis: systems cannot be disaggregated into their component parts and subsequently reassembled without losing essential elements of their operating procedures and dynamics. They develop logics and dynamics on their own that can neither be fully predicted nor completely comprehended. Attempts to influence a system will always have more than one effect, and these effects operate among the system's component parts in unpredictable ways, including ways that undermine what the influencer aspired to achieve by intervening in the system in the first place. We identified three principal ways of responding to a system's complexity: denying complexity, reducing complexity and trying to live with complexity (ideally, capitalizing on complexity to improve the living conditions of the subjects inhabiting the system). That systems are complex and that human beings will never completely understand them requires of everyone intervening in the system a high degree of caution,

© The Author(s), under exclusive license to Springer Nature Switzerland AG 2023
R. Bellmer and F. Möller, *Peace, Complexity, Visuality*, Rethinking Peace and Conflict Studies,
https://doi.org/10.1007/978-3-031-38218-5_3

empathy and modesty: we can never understand a system completely. Awareness is needed of the limits and (unintended) consequences of one's action and other actors' (factual but also possible, likely but also unlikely) reactions to one's action—and one's own reaction to others' reactions to one's original action, and so on. However, characterized by "uncountable chain reactions" (see Khanna 2022; our translation), a system cannot be limited to simple action–reaction dynamics because systems, as political agents, will develop their own actions and dynamics. Such awareness includes the willingness to permanently call into question the adequateness of one's actions and the presuppositions from which they are derived. In short, living and operating within a system requires permanent critical self-reflection.

In the present chapter, we continue this train of thought by arguing that systems are not only complex; complex systems always create ambiguities. Indeed, the more complex a system is, the more ambiguous both the system itself and interventions into it will be (see Juncos 2018: 566). While some research addresses ambiguity as decision-making under uncertainty and thus as a form of risk management (see Juncos 2018), we understand it in a rather basic sense, following the Oxford Dictionary's definition of ambiguity as "the state of having more than one possible meaning" and "the state of being difficult to understand or explain because of involving many different aspects."[1] This everyday take on ambiguity understands the concept in a much broader sense than merely referring to the multiple syntactic or lexical meanings of words, grammar or our whole language system, as is common in linguistics (see Winkler 2015).

Rather similar to our understanding of complexity, ambiguity, too, is a way of thinking, a frame of reference structuring thinking and acting. It is not a proper theory but, rather, a concept and like every concept, ambiguity, like complexity, is something we *do*. For example, we will regularly be in situations where several possible interpretations will coexist, where we can interpret and normatively judge an issue as positive, negative or irrelevant in a given context. Our value judgments depend on our personal situations and our previous individual and collective experiences with the topic at hand, but they also shift, depending on what elements and characteristics we include in our judgment process, especially when

---

[1] https://www.oxfordlearnersdictionaries.com/definition/english/ambiguity?q=ambiguity (accessed 6 October 2021).

we consider the complex nature of systems. Last but not least, systems have a temporal dimension marking the role of time and its relation to a system. As Paul Cilliers writes in regard to complex systems: "Not only do they evolve through time, but their past is co-responsible for their present behaviour. Any analysis of a complex system that ignores the dimension of time is incomplete, or at most a synchronic snapshot of a diachronic process" (1998: 4). Exploring ambiguities, too, necessitates a historical perspective to engage with their evolution or emergence (see Gallo 2012: 159) because ambiguities are not simply *there*: their there-ness comes from somewhere, it has a history.

Similar to the preceding chapter, in the present chapter, we will review parts of the literature on ambiguity and focus on the question of how to cope with ambiguity in a constructive manner, aiming to improve the living conditions of the subjects exposed to ambiguous situations or situations regarded as ambiguous. Just as we concluded Chapter 2 with short reflections on photocomplexity, we conclude this chapter with brief remarks on photoambiguity to be further developed in the following chapters but showing already here the importance of visuality in the context of ambiguity.

Ambiguities in Peace and Conflict Dynamics

Ambiguity can reference many things, including the coexistence of seemingly mutually exclusive character traits in an individual (see Short 2014 for the former French President Mitterrand) or unclear signals sent by policymakers in response to or in anticipation of a political challenge, often termed strategic ambiguity (see Zabotkina et al. 2021). Here, ambiguity appears as a politico-rhetorical device, the aim of which is to increase one's freedom of political action by being deliberately vague so that whatever one ultimately decides seems to coincide with the preceding utterance; a policy option enabling several options in the event but avoiding commitment to one specific option before the event; a decision-making option postponing decision-making but nevertheless determining a space of possibilities within which the decision can be expected to be made ultimately (for the current US policy on Taiwan, see, e.g., Willasey-Wilsey 2022). Silence can be both a deliberate political response to ambiguity and a deliberately ambiguous policy option, a part of strategic ambiguity "understood in a continuum with speech rather than in opposition to it" (Dingli and Cooke 2022: 4). Strategic ambiguity is a response to complexity; it constructs both a space and "a boundary of possibility … What will happen depends on a precise configuration of complex causes derived both from the internal characteristics of the system and from its whole environment, including systems with which it is interpenetrating and with which it shares subsystems" (Byrne and Callaghan 2023: 24). The precise configuration of such complex causes cannot be predicted. "Unproductive ambiguities" have been identified in decolonial discourses where such binaries as colonial/decolonial tend to obscure the continuation of the one in the other (see Dube 2022).

In his classic writing *Seven Types of Ambiguity*, William Empson defines ambiguity as "an indecision as to what you mean, an intention to mean several things, a probability that one or other or both of two things has been meant, and the fact that a statement has several meanings" (1949: 5–6). Ambiguity, thus, signifies linguistic vagueness, underspecificity or a lack of precision. This is not exactly what we are interested in. In the literature on international conflict, ambiguity has been engaged with as a resource, as something that can be leveraged to achieve specific outcomes. For example, discussions revolve around the relationship between ambiguity and peace agreements (Dingley 2005), norm ambiguity (Widmaier and Glanville 2015) and constructive ambiguity (Bryan 2016: 21–23; Golubović 2020; Dingley 2005; Zabotkina et al. 2021). We are not particularly interested in such rather technical discussions, either.

Instead, we take a step back and argue, quite generically and basically, that an increasing (sense of) complexity and encounters with ambiguous situations are crucial aspects of today's international sociopolitical environment—aspects to which actors have to respond but often do not know how. Confusion starts with such a basic term as conflict which often appears as something that has to be avoided or prevented. Conflict, however, is ambiguous in the sense that it can have a positive or a negative impact on society (or a combination of both: it can have a positive impact on one part of society and a negative impact on another part, or it can positively influence a specific policy area but negatively influence others). As such, conflict can improve social relations within and among groups of people or render such improvement difficult (see Coser 1956). Disambiguation of such complex terms and concepts as conflict and limitation of conflict to undesired (often violent) consequences which, therefore, must be avoided, limit spaces of possibility and prevent the constructive elements of social conflict from operating within and among groups.

Ambiguity, then, is more than just the clash of different perspectives or the mere refusal to make a clear statement. It implies constant negotiation between the parts of a system. It is, therefore, about discursive practices and rules of engagement that render some interpretations more legitimate than others and assign ontological superiority to some policies rather than others. Ambiguities are often experienced as a conflict, as an incompatibility of beliefs, needs, ideas or accounts. As has been observed a long time ago, however, "[t]here is a tendency in popular thinking to consider too many values as incompatible with each other" (Deutsch et al. 1957: 126)—and there is a tendency in political decision-making to exploit such thinking to further particular interests and to separate in-groups from out-groups.

We thus want to emphasize one important characteristic of ambiguity that Adam Sennet refers to as "multiple *permissible* interpretations" of an issue (2021; italics added) which can be evoked intentionally or unintentionally. Focusing on *permissible* interpretations counteracts accusations of "anything goes," i.e., lack of moral and other standards. However, even within the space of permissible interpretations, ambiguities prevail because in complex systems, there is more than one permissible interpretation on a regular basis. Definitions must be found for socially shared understandings of what counts as permissible in a given situation. Establishing what counts as permissible means establishing boundaries separating spaces of possibility from spaces of impossibility and "new configurations of what can be seen, what can be said and what can be thought" (Rancière 2009: 103) from configurations of what can*not* legitimately be seen, what can*not* be said and what can*not* be thought. Even within spaces of possibility, however, ambiguities abound. The frontier where spaces of possibility meet spaces of impossibility is a space for politics, not a border but a meeting-place or at least a place for constant (re)negotiation of what counts as permissible. In this sense, and in accordance with complexity theory, such spaces of possibility are always emergent: they are never fixed but in a permanent process of evolution (see Byrne and Callaghan 2023: 56–57).[2]

However, there can be observed a strong tendency to limit the number of permissible interpretations not only to a smaller number but also to

---

[2] The alternative formulation that spaces of possibility are always in the process of coming into being is problematic as it implies that once such spaces have come into being, the process stops.

merely one permissible and even thinkable option, one interpretation of events and situations, often legitimized with reference to an ostensible 'lack of alternatives.' We experience such a reduction of options and interpretations whenever we encounter clear-cut divisions based on binaries such as good versus evil, perpetrator versus victim, war versus peace, or truth versus lie, which are common responses to complexity and ambiguity, ordering the world in a seemingly easily comprehensible and manageable manner in relation to which individuals can position themselves. One specific position is assigned moral or ontological superiority to others. However, such rigid categories do not accurately describe a world that is full of ambiguous situations (Bauer 2018: 12), "marked by vague, incomplete, fragmented, multiple, probable, unstructured, uncertain, inconsistent, contrary, contradictory, or unclear meaning" (Norton 1975: 608). Such meaning is referenced by metaphors such as "[s]lippery, indistinct, elusive, complex, diffuse, messy, textured, vague, unspecific, confused, disordered, emotional, painful, pleasurable, hopeful, horrific, lost, redeemed, visionary, angelic, demonic, mundane, intuitive, sliding and unpredictable" all of which try "to open space for the indefinite" (Law 2004: 6). We frequently encounter ambiguous situations and, thus, the above metaphors, be it in interpersonal communication or in wider social interactions. Individual positions may make sense from the individual/personal perspective while others' points of view can appear misleading or simply 'wrong.'

Take, for example, Séverine Autesserre's account of professional peacemakers or, in her terminology, *Peace, Inc.*, the structures and people involved in international organizations' "conventional way to end wars" (2021: 5) and *Peaceland*, "the world of aid workers who spend their lives hopping from conflict zone to conflict zone" (2021: 6). Autesserre shows in great detail how peacebuilders' perceptions and consequently their interpretations of issues diverge depending on their role and location within a peace operation. She demonstrates how international intervenors tend to develop very different takes on their work and the overall conflict dynamics reflecting their everyday experiences and interactions. She highlights "different information and different priorities" (2014: 27) resulting from varying everyday experiences as the cause for the emergence of ambiguities. This is critical for the relationship between the different groups; it has a strong impact on the overarching approach to an intervention:

> Due to these various divisions, capital-based interveners often view their field-based colleagues as absorbed in unimportant local matters and unable to see the bigger picture .... Conversely, field-based peacebuilders frequently present their superiors in capital cities and headquarters as having only a theoretical and superficial knowledge of their areas of deployment. (2014: 27)

Everybody who witnesses a conversation between a peace activist and an academic peace researcher will observe a similar situation: the academic will accuse the activist of lack of theoretical knowledge while the activist will criticize the academic's insistence on theory as irrelevant on the ground and uninformed by local circumstances. These different perspectives do make sense individually; all of them seem permissible. Once they meet, tensions emerge. Such tensions can be constructive but often they are not, with individuals claiming to have better knowledge of and superior insights into a given conflict. Failure to communicate likely results. Different subject positions can lead to ambiguities, and rather than discussing the pros and cons of one's position, individuals often insist on the correctness of their own position, thus making the discursive negotiation of the overall conflict difficult. Egos play a role, of course. However, it is not only very hard but often totally pointless to try to prove that one's position is more legitimate, more adequate in the context or simply better than are others. For many people, it seems equally or even more difficult to accept that others' positions may be better suited indeed to explain a given situation as all positions are derived from individual trajectories, as a result of which individuals believe in the rightfulness and superiority of their positions because these positions are gained from individual experience and the memory of experience.

Peacebuilding is an attempt to respond constructively to a given conflict—an "external policy intervention with the intention of assisting post-conflict or conflict-prone states to build a sustainable peace on the basis of liberal institutional frameworks of constitutionalism, market freedoms, democracy and the rule of law" (Chandler 2017: 3). However, peacebuilders face numerous conflicts while going about their business. This cannot be otherwise given what we wrote in the preceding chapter about interventions in complex situations. These conflicts determine the relations between the peacebuilders and the societies into which they intervene—which are often neither "post-conflict" nor "conflict-prone" but are still in a state of conflict even if physical violence has stopped—but they also characterize the internal relations among the peacebuilders (see Autesserre above). When we engage in a conflict—as researchers, as lay observers or as journalists—we always become a part of the conflict, of which we often possess preconceived notions derived from our own experience and socialization, including information made available through the media and the Internet as two of the main institutions suggesting what notion is permissible in a given context. Journalists carefully cultivate the self-image of objective, disinterested observers (see Chapter 4), but as Joe Sacco notes, "journalists are not flies on the wall that are neither seen nor heard" (2012: xi). By their very presence, which "is almost always felt" (Sacco 2012: xi), journalists influence and often change the dynamics of the conflict they subsequently claim to cover objectively.

Conflicts are "messy, dynamic situations," "recreated every day" (Caspersen 2018: 43) by people engaging with them in a variety of constantly changing and mutually coexisting subject positions. Information 'directly from the ground' or provided by the media can always be interpreted in many different ways; theories can be applied to cases differently. Oftentimes, "when a conflict is analysed or when decisions about an actual or potential conflict are taken, the kind of reasoning that is followed is simplistic, linear, to say the least. Complexity is disregarded, let alone the need for systemic thinking" (Gallo 2012: 157). In our response—as a 'direct' party to the conflict, as a member of the international community, but even as an individual consuming information about the conflict—we tend to simplify. We assign the roles of the villain and the victim, we form our opinions on foreign policies and interventions, and vote for those parties that promise a specific approach to 'end' the conflict at stake. We blame those who suggest different routes of engagement and call them morally questionable or irresponsible, thus "assigning an inferior ontological status" to their interpretations (Berger and Luckmann 1967: 132). For that reason, acknowledging the ambiguous nature of conflicts and the international system requires us to reflect on our positions and interpretations, accepting that what we know is inherently limited. Just as we have observed in the preceding chapter with regard to complexity, recognizing ambiguities demands from us modesty and humility as well as openness for diverging perspectives and positions. Not doing so can have an actual impact on peoples' lives. As Giorgio Gallo argues, "[w]ithout a systemic and holistic framework, decisions may worsen the conflict, resulting in increased and prolonged suffering for the involved populations, and the analysis may lead to poor and misleading understanding of the conflict's dynamics and perspectives" (Gallo 2012: 157).

How to Cope with Ambiguity: Tolerance of Ambiguity

Acknowledging the existence of ambiguity in complex systems does not tell us how to deal with ambiguity. Acknowledgment is a necessary but not a sufficient step. It does not inform us about the degree of ambiguity in a situation, either; ambiguity is a matter of degrees, not one of existence versus non-existence, and it affects different component parts of a complex system differently. Nor does it tell us how to distinguish situations characterized by factual ambiguities from situations to which actors only assign ambiguity as a rhetorical strategy to achieve whatever they want to achieve. That something is claimed to be ambiguous need not mean that it is ambiguous in fact—but such claims have political consequences all the same.

The reverse, however, is more complicated and unsettling: a complex system does not lose its ambiguousness only because actors claim that it is not ambiguous, that things are actually quite simple, and that *this* is the correct reading of a situation while alternative readings are incorrect. Following speech act approaches to international relations, then, it may be possible to talk ambiguity *into* existence, but it is not equally possible to talk it *out of* existence because (some degree of) ambiguity always exists in complex systems, no matter how much actors (or speakers) try rhetorically to downplay it. Ignoring a system's ambiguity by claiming that the system is not ambiguous and acting accordingly has real consequences. For example, after decades of rhetorical and political neglect, nuclear weapons are still ambiguous, guaranteeing human survival (according to some) while simultaneously threatening it (according to others). Ignoring such ambiguity by strictly adhering to one interpretation is a risky strategy.

We encountered this problem in Chapter 2, where we argued that a system can be complex in fact or it can appear to be complex as a result of discursive constructions and, as such, independent of the 'real' complexity of the system. We argued that discursive constructions have political consequences and that a system that, as a result of such constructions, appears or is said to be complex *is* complex in a politically important way, determining spaces of possibility. Complexity theory helped us understand that not only *real* reality but also socially constructed reality has real consequences (Byrne and Callaghan 2023: 118). It also helped us understand the dangers inherent in social constructivism once we forget that a complex social system is not really interested in how we talk about it. It affects us and it has real consequences anyway. Systems are political actors, too, exhibiting agency. Ambiguity, too, has real consequences even if we rhetorically deny its existence. It also has real consequences if we construct it discursively.

Thomas Bauer (2018) is among those authors who elaborate on how individuals tend to cope with ambiguities once they (even subconsciously) acknowledge their existence. He suggests that two strategies are commonly applied. The first, and rather obvious, strategy that can be observed frequently is resorting to disambiguation, that is, reducing the variety of possible interpretations to a smaller number, *in extremis* to only one legitimate interpretation. This approach is frequently linked with an obsession with truth values, the negation of history and a striving for purity aiming to establish one binding meaning. Part of such reduction unfolds through language, reflecting that language is a necessarily limited and limiting system of signs and categorizations. Language is often applied strategically not only to make complex situations (appear) manageable but also to make a given interpretation seem more legitimate than others, culminating in claims that there are no alternatives. The consequences of this anti-discursive procedure are already visible today in increasing social polarizations and failures to communicate between the political elites and some parts of the citizenry as well as between different social groups within a society. The second strategy is that individuals and collectives end up in the contrary of one meaning and postulate *no* meaning. What Bauer calls "indifference" can lead to an acceptance of all meaning as equally valid thereby, according to Bauer, reducing the overall importance of an issue (2018: 28–30). In both scenarios, active engagement with ambiguities is avoided; both strategies allow individuals to not reflect on their own position and interpretation, as there seemingly is no challenge (of importance) to preconceived understandings of a situation. As always, however, there are more than two options.

At the end of the 1940s, Else Frenkel-Brunswick, following her research on the Authoritarian Personality, coined the term Tolerance of Ambiguity (TA). In her research, she observed that some subjects possessed the ability to recognize and deal with the coexistence of positive and negative characteristics in the same subject or object.[3] More specifically, children recognized both positive and negative qualities in their parents. Reducing their parents neither to positive nor to negative characteristics, these children seemed able to live with ambiguity (Frenkel-Brunswick 1949: 116; Müller-Christ and Weßling 2007: 185). The concept has raised much interest in the fields of psychology, social psychology and cognitive science. It has also been taken up in research on medical students (see Bentwich and Gilbey 2017; Geller 2013; Hancock and Mattick 2020) as well as organizations and leadership (McLain et al. 2015). The link to IR and peace and conflict dynamics has not yet been explored systematically although TA is likely to influence both an individual's and social groups' capability of dealing with conflict constructively and nonviolently.

Stanley Budner, in a frequently used definition of the concept, defines TA "as 'the tendency to perceive ambiguous situations as desirable'" whereas intolerance of ambiguity indicates the opposite, namely, "the tendency to perceive (i.e. interpret) ambiguous situations as sources of threat" (1962: 29; quotes within quotes in original without further references). TA thus signifies not merely acknowledgment of the existence of ambiguity; it also signifies value judgment regarding the desirability of ambiguity—an appreciation of ambiguity that can be linked to the appreciation of difference in earlier IR texts informed by critical social theory (see George and Campbell 1990), the commitment for cultural studies to work "*with* difference and not by *reducing* difference" (Couldry 2000: 21–22; italics in original) and the focus on compatibility in classical security community literature emphasizing *compatible* rather than *common* values. This literature has shown that a plurality of positions, including ambiguous ones, need not be a problem for a social relationship to evolve peacefully as long as these positions are not incompatible.[4] Even if they are incompatible, such incompatibility will be relevant only if it affects

---

[3] If you want to seem particularly clever, you can use the term agathokakological for something or someone composed of both good and evil, as the clever people at Merriam-Webster know. See *Merriam-Webster.com Dictionary*, Merriam-Webster, https://www.merriam-webster.com/dictionary/agathokakological (accessed 18 January 2023).

[4] Contrariwise, social constructivist approaches (Adler and Barnett 1998) and liberal universalism (as shown by Mouffe 2013: 19–42) emphasize *common* values, thus regarding a reduction of ambiguities and pluralism as a condition for peaceful change.

core functions of the relationship (Deutsch et al. 1957: 125–126); and even in this case, violence is not deemed inevitable. Indeed, there seems to be a tendency to underestimate how difficult it actually is for individuals and groups of people to resort to physical violence (see Collins 2008).

For several scholars of the international, looking at the international from different angles, a variety of positions, interpretations and perspectives does not seem to pose an obstacle to peaceful cohabitation. For example, advocates of the agonistic peace approach emphasize that multiple positions are not only desired—being the precondition for the existence of "the political" (Mouffe 2013: 2); such multitude is also at the very core of every society through the fundamental construction of an I/we and the respective you/they (Shinko 2008: 478). In this understanding, the "we/they opposition" (Mouffe 2013: 9) does not require transcendence; rather, institutions and mechanisms are needed to prevent antagonistic and violent forms of dealing with difference (Nagle 2014: 471; Strömbom 2019: 949). Indeed, "many us/them relations are merely a question of recognizing difference" (Mouffe 2013: 5). Providing a space where the struggle between a multitude of positions can take place so as to allow it to take an agonistic rather than an antagonistic form is crucial in this approach (Aggestam et al. 2015: 1738). Such a systemic and holistic approach requires acknowledgment of the complexity of a conflict—any conflict—and recognition of its inherent ambiguities as well as development of institutions capable of dealing with ambiguities non-antagonistically, as individuals may be overburdened.[5]

However, neither appreciation of ambiguity nor recognition of difference can be taken for granted. Many approaches to conflict resolution regard identity and sameness as the most promising sites for peaceful relations between individuals and groups. Consequently, as Sara Cobb explains, they understand the process of ending a violent conflict as "a 'shared' experience, as though the sameness of experience, the reduction of differences, would be the venue for the evolution of relationships" (2013: 235–236). (We referred to Cobb's work already in the preceding chapter and will return to it in Chapter 12) Similarly, peace mediation

---

[5] Likewise, the classical security community literature emphasizes the need for institutions capable of dealing constructively with an increase in communication among groups of people because communication may overwhelm individuals.

and other conflict resolution concepts have put "consensus, commonality, and unity rather than difference" (Brigg and Bleiker 2011: 23) at the core of their actions and, ultimately, of their thinking about peaceful relations. From a complexity point of view, such conflict resolution strategies are problematic and simplistic. However, they are also indicative of social practice. Travis Proulx and Michael Inzlicht describe ambiguity as a situation in which individuals and groups of people struggle to create meaning and to make sense of their environment and experiences—a violation of their expected relations, as they put it (2012: 320). They suggest that individuals usually resort to "palliative behaviors"—assimilation, accommodation, affirmation, abstraction and assembly—"aimed at preventing or diminishing an aversive sense of meaninglessness, rather than resolving meaning violations, per se" (2012: 318). Individuals are assumed to aim for cognitive closure (Kruglanski and Webster 1996; Holmes 2015) because vague and unclear meanings of situations can be perceived as a threat (Norton 1975: 608). Thus, keeping up a straightforward interpretation of a situation can require shutting oneself off to those aspects of reality that pose a danger to a clear assessment (Müller-Christ and Weßling 2007: 185). Therefore, "those who are intolerant of ambiguity are [commonly] described as having a tendency to resort to black-and-white solutions," thereby confirming the existing system of power and authority, whereas those who are tolerant of ambiguity perceive "ambiguous situations … as desirable, challenging and interesting" (Furnham and Marks 2013: 718), thereby (at least potentially) challenging the existing system or interrogating its appearance of or claim to naturalness. Intolerance of ambiguity, as Jamie Holmes (2015: unpaginated) notes, "marks the end of thinking, looking, and listening" while tolerance of ambiguity *invites* and *embraces* thinking, looking and listening.

Understood as an individual's cognitive style of information processing (Reis 1997: 12), many scholars follow Frenkel-Brunswick by describing TA as *an individual's broader personality trait* that "generalizes to the entire emotional and cognitive functioning of the individual, characterizing cognitive style, belief and attitude systems, interpersonal and social functioning, and problem solving behavior" (Furnham and Ribchester 1995: 180). Alternatively, other scholars argue that TA is rather observable *in relation to specific areas only* and thus not necessarily generalizable within an individual (Durrheim and Foster 1997; Müller-Christ and Weßling 2007: 189). Both understandings of TA as a "differential psychology conception of a stable, perhaps even biologically based trait" versus "a set of attitudes" (Furnham and Marks 2013: 725) have been associated with "processes as varying as creativity and organizational culture, authoritarianism and schizophrenia" (Furnham and Ribchester 1995: 196). Georg Müller-Christ and Gudrun Weßling (2007: 190) highlight that particularly a conceptualization of TA as relating to specific areas within an individual might promise that this is a transferable and learnable characteristic.

Analogous to the position that individual TA varies across issue areas, we want to suggest that groups of people also display different degrees of and attitudes toward TA depending on the policy areas they collectively face in a given situation.[6] The more importance they assign to a policy area, the less TA can be expected to be displayed. However, as the IR literature shows, contested issue areas can be *depoliticized* by first recognizing them and then removing them from the political agenda (at least temporarily), thus "depriv[ing] of political significance any incompatible values" (Deutsch et al. 1957: 46) that might otherwise block communication. Thus, ambiguity can be dealt with *pragmatically* (within the limits complex systems pose) rather than *ideologically*. But even if dealt with pragmatically, ambiguity does not disappear; it is depoliticized for the time being and conserved for later treatment. Furthermore, intolerance of ambiguity regarding the in-group's core values can coexist with TA in regard to out-groups; groups can insist on adherence to specific values within the group without expecting other groups to display the same values as well. In addition, should the out-group not display the same values that the in-group adheres to, the in-group does not necessarily have to perceive such incoherence as a threat because incoherence embraces differences (see Law 2004: 99). Finally, incompatible values, including in core areas, can coexist, provided that no actor exhibits a "militant missionary attitude toward them" (Deutsch et al. 1957: 124).

From the above, it follows that TA both as a concept and as a politics is itself ambiguous. Its application requires thinking about its limits in order to prevent its degeneration into indifference and complete arbitrariness. Constitutions, laws, charters and declarations establish limits within which

---

[6] Remember that in complex settings it is difficult to differentiate one policy area from others. Furthermore, all policy areas influence and communicate with one another in often surprising ways (see Chapter 2).

individuals and groups of people operate legitimately and beyond which they do not, defining what actions are permissible in a given context. Regarding ambiguity, too, they establish permissible interpretations from among all possible interpretations and meanings applicable to any given situation. TA and what it looks like precisely is, therefore, always dependent on context and culture; it cannot be fixed once and for all. As Holmes writes, "[c]ulture determines the 'style' with which we reduce complexity and ambiguity" (2015: unpaginated),[7] leading to differences between social groups in terms of their approach to ambiguity. As culture evolves, TA evolves, too: on a collective level, it shifts over time. TA varies across space and over time: the same social group possesses varying degrees of TA in different temporal settings, and different social groups display different degrees of TA at the same time.

Photoambiguity

Thus far, we have established that systems of human interaction are complex, that complex systems are ambiguous and that there are different ways to respond to ambiguity, among which we prefer responses based on TA rather than on disambiguation. We explained our preference in terms of the inherent complexity and messiness of the international system, which can always be perceived, interpreted, engaged with and responded to in multiple ways, the best or most appropriate of which cannot always easily be identified as many interpretations and responses seem equally permissible. None of the above, however, tells us how to achieve TA in a system that is often characterized by the opposite. In the remainder of the chapter, we want to sketch what we consider a particularly promising avenue toward TA in IR and peace and conflict studies: visuality. Regardless of several "pictorial" (Mitchell 1994: 11–34), "aesthetic" (Bleiker 2001) and "visual" (Callahan 2015; Pfonner and James 2020) turns in IR, the social sciences and humanities, images are still underexplored in terms of their TA-building capabilities. Just the opposite: they are often used to simplify complex situations and to visually illustrate what has already been established (or what authors want to establish) textually. We want to suggest that images' TA-building capabilities may help us to think and act better in a world saturated, not only with ambiguities

---

[7] It should be clear by now that we would prefer to say that culture determines the style with which we *approach* complexity and ambiguity.

but also with images, a world in which complexity and ambiguity appear visually. However, as John Berger explains, "[u]sually, in public the ambiguity of photographs is hidden by the use of words which explain, less or more truthfully, the pictured events" (Berger 2013: unpaginated). It is for this reason that exploration of the TA-building potentialities of images requires paying attention to the word–image relationship in photojournalism and elsewhere, following Fred Ritchin's advice that we have to read photographs, "not just the text surrounding them" (Ritchin 1999: 41). This is easier said than done, and we will investigate in Chapter 5 why it is so difficult to approach images *as* images.

Some images are designed such that they complexify habits of seeing by "illustrat[ing] the co-existence of contrary or simply different readings in the single image" (Mitchell 1994: 45). W. J. T. Mitchell (1994) refers to such images as "metapictures" (pp. 35–82) or "dialectical images" (pp. 45–57), such as the famous "Duck-Rabbit" or the equally classic "My Wife and My Mother-in-law," "emblem[s] of resistance to stable interpretation" (p. 50). Dialectical images—we prefer this term because an image's overall meaning is dialectically produced through "argument or dialogue" between different readings (p. 45)—are not "transparent representation[s] of something else" but rather "places where pictorial representation displays itself for inspection" (p. 48). What Mitchell calls the "ambiguity of their referentiality" invites the spectator "to return with fascination to the mysterious object whose identity seems so mutable and yet so absolutely singular and definite" (p. 48). Dialectical images, thus, are intentionally ambiguous, inviting spectators to reflect upon the different meanings they contain and the different readings they invite without prioritizing one reading or meaning over others.

We would not argue with any of this save for the implicit assumption that there are images that do *not* contain or invite different readings, that *only* dialectical pictures (or metapictures) are ambiguous and mysterious. They may be unique in the sense that their *explicit* purpose is to be "used to reflect on the nature of pictures" (Mitchell 1994: 57); as such, dialectical images are not only self-referential: they tell us a lot about the operating procedures and characteristics of other images as well. (Whether or not they are *used* to reflect on pictures' nature depends not on the image but on the observer.) However, not only a dialectical, purposefully ambiguous image but *every* image carries with it what David MacDougall calls "*excess* meaning" by which he refers to "many unintended sites of connotation," indeed "*too* many" such sites to control their meaning (MacDougall 1998: 68; first emphasis in original, second emphasis added). Images are non-coherent, embracing difference. Thus, every image resists stable interpretation. The camera, then, goes beyond that which the photographer subjectively intends to show even if she tries to completely anticipate what can be seen in the image (King 2003: 180). Even if she succeeds in completely anticipating what can be seen in the image—an idea that seems especially odd currently in an age of digitization where not only meanings but also images constantly evolve—she can never completely control the meaning(s) spectators assign to the image. This is so because such designation of meaning "has as much to do with the self of the observer as with the metapicture"— or, indeed, every picture—"itself" (Mitchell 1994: 48): what you see reflects who you are. Who you are can be dissociated neither from "specific discourses, disciplines, and regimes of knowledge" (Mitchell 1994: 48) nor from individual socializations and cultural memories that each observer brings with them to the encounter with an image. Consequently, "ways of picturing the world are different in different times and places" (Mitchell 1994: 43), and different observers will interpret the same image differently.

As we will suggest in Chapter 5, control of meaning is one of the functions of the word–image relationship in photojournalism as a specific regime of knowledge and knowledge production. As such, conventional photojournalism is an exercise in disambiguation and, therefore, mainly our negative reference point in our search for visuality's TA-building potentialities. However, disambiguation does not follow from an image's inherent characteristics but rather from designations of meaning assigned to the image and provided by means of captions or other accompanying texts. Captions tame an image's referential instability and reduce the multitude of meanings that each image carries with them to the one the photographer or the picture editor prefers. (It is up to the observer to accept this specific designation of meaning or not, but it is difficult to resist; after all, the photographer is supposed to know the exact conditions in which the photograph had been taken, and the caption is supposed to adequately reflect this knowledge.) As Susan Sontag puts it elegantly, captions are the photograph's "missing voice" (Sontag 1979: 108), intended to make sure that a photograph be read as intended by the photographer. However, she continues, even an entirely accurate caption is only one interpretation, *necessarily a limiting one*, of the photograph to which it is attached. And the caption-glove slips on and off so easily. It cannot prevent any argument or moral plea which a photograph (or set of photographs) is intended to support from being undermined by the plurality of meanings that every photograph carries. (Sontag 1979: 109; italics added)

While we are interested in such plurality of meanings as TA-building tools, photojournalists and commentators often are not. For example, photographer Ben Curtis, while acknowledging "the merits of being vague – providing more avenues of inference and this sort of thing," insists on adding as much and as accurate information as possible about his photographs before sending them to his editors because such information "makes the picture more powerful" (Curtis, as quoted in Morris 2014: 193).[8] When discussing James Nachtwey's photography, Susie Linfield strongly argues against photograph-only approaches to photojournalism, as such approaches ostensibly render difficult understanding and action, inviting instead "bewilderment and hopelessness" as well as "disgust and contempt" (Linfield 2010: 217). While we could gloss over the difference between our approach and the standard photojournalistic one by simply referring to different agendas necessitating different approaches to and understandings of images—the one focusing on TA-building, the other on accurate information and, thus, disambiguation—we suspect that it is indicative of more, to be explored in Chapter 5. Suffice it to say here that photojournalism visually increases the information we have about the world but, through accompanying text, also tends to fix the meaning of this information. It visually broadens our knowledge but then incorporates this knowledge by textual means into "dominant forms of discourse" (Shapiro 1988: 130), thus contributing to disambiguation and reproducing established forms of power and authority. Photojournalistic practice only rarely acknowledges that "photography is highly interpretive, ambiguous, culturally specific" (Ritchin 1999: 72), and it equally rarely capitalizes on these characteristics to help build TA. On the contrary, photojournalistic commentary and scholarship have tried to erase images' inherent ambiguity since the inception of photography precisely by trying to establish the definitive meaning of photographs, thus textually contributing to images' disambiguation. Consequently,

---

[8] Remember that we understand ambiguity in terms other than mere vagueness.

viewers have learned neither to read photographs *as* photographs nor to respect photography's inherent ambiguity, which, in photographic discourses, often appears as a liability rather than a merit.

If we want to understand an ambiguous world, then we have to appreciate and reinvigorate images' ambiguities and complexify viewing patterns. Thus, we are not interested in identifying *the* meaning of an image, nor are we interested in establishing a hierarchy of possible meanings derived from different degrees of credibility and plausibility. Instead, from the beginning of our encounter with an image, we respect ambiguities and ambivalences, gaps and omissions, the obvious and the obscure, the visible and the invisible, the central and the peripheral. Indeed, that an image's ambiguity is publicly hidden does not mean that it disappears from the image; rather, it awaits rediscovery by curious observers who are not afraid of hegemonic photographic discourses, who want to reclaim photography's ambiguity, and who wish to see more than they are supposed to see. Viewing, thus, becomes a political act: viewers might interrogate the politics of interpretation inherent in each single designation of meaning and invigorate images' "potential for political agency which depends on the possibility of a multitude of interpretations, ambiguities and differences" (Rubinstein and Sluis 2013: 154).

Conclusion

For many scholars, creative processes such as making or encountering visual art not only require the ability to cope with ambiguity inherent in various artistic expressions[9] but also offer the possibility to increase the capacity to endure ambiguous aspects of both art in particular and social situations in general. For instance, Miriam Ethel Bentwich and Peter Gilbey, in their study on the role of TA for junior physicians, suggest "that since the arts are a potential significant cultivator of imagination, they may be understood as vital for the enhancement of the tolerance for ambiguity" (2017: 7). They conclude "that visual art used in VTS [Visual Thinking Strategies; the authors] may contribute to developing medical students' tolerance of ambiguity, and that the latter is also related to empathy enhancement" (2017: 8). This is highly relevant for settings

---

[9] For example, Magdalena Szubielska et al. (2021) found that an individual's TA as well as her need for cognitive closure is relevant for the appreciation of ambiguous art.

characterized by violent conflict, too, as "[e]mpathy, after all, is a fundamentally creative act by which we connect previously unimagined lives to our own" (Holmes 2015: unpaginated). Following Proulx and Inzlicht, individuals possess capabilities for the "wholesale assembly of meaning frameworks in response to a given violation – in a sense, creating a new way to make our experiences feel familiar" (2012: 328). That means that if our meaning-making frameworks are challenged, for instance by ambiguities, creative processes—and we understand engaging with photojournalism as a creative process—can help us cope but also support us to construct new systems of meaning-making: "in the wake of uncertainty, we make something that makes sense to us" (Proulx and Inzlicht 2012: 329). In line with that, Franck Zenasni et al. found that TA might "contribute to the creative process because it empowers the intrinsically motivated exploration of novel, unusual or complex stimuli" (2008: 62). For this reason, it is not surprising that the link between creative processes such as making and consuming visual images and TA has attracted interest in other fields as well. Based on this research, it is a reasonable assumption that engaging with visual materials in an interactive and multisensory fashion involving open visual narratives will shape the audience's TA.

Up to this point, we have treated photojournalism as an aggregate term, which is another way of saying that we treated photojournalism as if there were only one approach and as if all photojournalists were basically doing the same thing. This, of course, is not the case. During and after the wars in the former Yugoslavia, Bosnia and Herzegovina served as a laboratory for the development of new photojournalistic approaches to war, genocide and overall violence, including mass civilian suffering. In the following chapter, therefore, we sketch selected photographies that emerged during that time and develop a typology of new photojournalistic approaches. It is this visual environment within which IR tries to make sense of what happened in Bosnia. It is this visual environment, too, within which—and beyond which—Fred Ritchin and Gilles Peress developed their project *Bosnia: Uncertain Paths to Peace*, which serves as the main visual data for our book (see Part III). It is this visual environment in relation to which we wish to discuss the visual potentialities for tolerance of ambiguity. We conclude the present chapter with the third of our Sarajevo photographs (Fig. 3.1) introduced in Chapter 2 in terms of photocomplexity.

Fig. 3.1 Sarajevo #3 (Photograph © Frank Möller)

References

Adler, Emanuel, and Michael Barnett, eds. 1998. *Security Communities*. Cambridge: Cambridge University Press.
Aggestam, Karin, Fabio Cristiano, and Lisa Strömbom. 2015. Towards Agonistic Peacebuilding? Exploring the Antagonism–Agonism Nexus in the Middle East Peace Process. *Third World Quarterly* 36 (9): 1736–1753.
Autesserre, Séverine. 2014. *Peaceland: Conflict Resolution and the Everyday Politics of International Intervention*. New York: Cambridge University Press.
Autesserre, Séverine. 2021. *The Frontlines of Peace: An Insider's Guide to Changing the World*. New York: Oxford University Press.
Bauer, Thomas. 2018. *Die Vereindeutigung der Welt: Über den Verlust an Mehrdeutigkeit und Vielfalt*. Ditzingen: Reclam.
Bentwich, Miriam Ethel, and Peter Gilbey. 2017. More Than Visual Literacy: Art and the Enhancement of Tolerance for Ambiguity and Empathy. *BMC Medical Education* 17 (1): 1–9.
Berger, John. 2013. *Understanding a Photograph*, ed. and introduced by Geoff Dyer. London: Penguin Classics.
Berger, Peter, and Thomas Luckmann. 1967. *The Social Construction of Reality: A Treatise in the Sociology of Knowledge*. London: Penguin.

Bleiker, Roland. 2001. The Aesthetic Turn in International Political Theory. *Millenium* 30 (3): 509–533.
Brigg, Morgan, and Roland Bleiker. 2011. Postcolonial Conflict Resolution. In *Mediating Across Difference: Oceanic and Asian Approaches to Conflict Resolution*, ed. Morgan Brigg and Roland Bleiker, 19–37. Honolulu: University of Hawai'i Press.
Bryan, Rebecca. 2016. Introduction: Everyday Coexistence in the Post-Ottoman Space. In *Post-Ottoman Coexistence. Sharing Space in the Shadow of Conflict*, ed. Rebecca Bryan, 1–38. New York and London: Berghahn Books.
Byrne, David, and Gillian Callaghan. 2023. *Complexity Theory and the Social Sciences: The State of the Art*. London and New York: Routledge.
Budner, Stanley. 1962. Intolerance of Ambiguity as a Personality Variable. *Journal of Personality* 30 (1): 29–50.
Callahan, William A. 2015. The Visual Turn in IR: Documentary Filmmaking as a Critical Method. *Millennium* 43: 891–910.
Caspersen, Dana. 2018. A Persistent Mobility of Perspective. In *Can Art Aid in Resolving Conflicts?*, ed. Noam Lemelshtrich-Latar, Jerry Wind, and Ornat Lev-er, 42–43. Amsterdam: Frame Publishers.
Chandler, David. 2017. *Peacebuilding: The Twenty Years' Crisis, 1997–2017*. Houndmills: Palgrave Macmillan.
Cilliers, Paul. 1998. *Complexity and Postmodernism: Understanding Complex Systems*. London and New York: Routledge.
Cobb, Sara. 2013. *Speaking of Violence: The Politics and Poetics of Narrative in Conflict Resolution*. New York: Oxford University Press.
Collins, Randall. 2008. *Violence: A Micro-sociological Theory*. Princeton: Princeton University Press.
Coser, Lewis. 1956. *The Functions of Social Conflict*. New York: The Free Press.
Couldry, Nick. 2000. *Inside Culture: Re-imagining the Method of Cultural Studies*. London: Sage.
Deutsch, Karl W., Sidney A. Burrell, Robert A. Khan, Maurice Lee, Jr., Martin Lichterman, Raymond E. Lindgren, Francis L. Loewenheim and Richard W. Van Wagenen. 1957. *Political Community and the North Atlantic Area: International Organization in the Light of Historical Experience*. Princeton: Princeton University Press.
Dingley, James. 2005. Constructive Ambiguity and the Peace Process in Northern Ireland. *Low Intensity Conflict & Law Enforcement* 13 (1): 1–23.
Dingli, Sophia, and Thomas N. Cooke. 2022. Political Silence, an Introduction. In *Political Silence: Meanings, Functions, and Ambiguity*, ed. Sophia Dingli and Thomas N. Cooke, 1–19. London and New York: Routledge.
Dube, Saurabh. 2022. Decolonial Dissonance. *IWM Post*, No. 130: 18.
Durrheim, Kevin, and Don Foster. 1997. Tolerance of Ambiguity as a Content Specific Construct. *Personality and Individual Differences* 22 (5): 741–750.

Empson, William. 1949. *Seven Types of Ambiguity*. London: Chatto and Windus.
Frenkel-Brunswick, Else. 1949. Intolerance of Ambiguity as an Emotional and Perceptual Personality Variable. *Journal of Personality* 18 (1): 108–143.
Furnham, Adrian, and Joseph Marks. 2013. Tolerance of Ambiguity: A Review of the Recent Literature. *Psychology* 04 (09): 717–728.
Furnham, Adrian, and Tracy Ribchester. 1995. Tolerance of Ambiguity: A Review of the Concept, Its Measurement and Applications. *Current Psychology* 14 (3): 179–199.
Gallo, Giorgio. 2012. Conflict Theory, Complexity and Systems Approach. *Systems Research and Behavioral Science* 30 (2): 156–175.
Geller, Gail. 2013. Tolerance for Ambiguity. *Academic Medicine* 88 (5): 581–584.
George, Jim, and David Campbell. 1990. Patterns of Dissent and the Celebration of Difference: Critical Social Theory and International Relations. *International Studies Quarterly* 34 (3): 269–293.
Golubović, Jelena. 2020. "To Me, You Are Not a Serb": Ethnicity, Ambiguity, and Anxiety in Post-war Sarajevo. *Ethnicities* 20 (3): 544–563.
Hancock, Jason, and Karen Mattick. 2020. Tolerance of Ambiguity and Psychological Well-Being in Medical Training: A Systematic Review. *Medical Education* 54 (2): 125–137.
Holmes, Jamie. 2015. *Nonsense: The Power of Not Knowing*. New York: Crown Publishers.
Juncos, Ana E. 2018. Resilience in Peacebuilding: Contesting Uncertainty, Ambiguity, and Complexity. *Contemporary Security Policy* 39 (4): 1–16.
Khanna, Parag. 2022. Ist eine Weltordnung möglich? *DIE ZEIT*, No. 33, (11 August): 47.
King, Barry. 2003. Über die Arbeit des Erinnerns. Die Suche nach dem perfekten Moment. In *Diskurse der Fotografie: Fotokritik am Ende des fotografischen Zeitalters*, ed. Herta Wolf, 173–214. Frankfurt: Suhrkamp.
Kruglanski, Arie W., and Donna M. Webster. 1996. Motivated Closing of the Mind: "Seizing" and "Freezing." *Psychological Review* 103 (2): 263–283.
Law, John. 2004. *After Method: Mess in Social Science Research*. London and New York: Routledge.
Linfield, Susie. 2010. *The Cruel Radiance: Photography and Political Violence*. Chicago and London: The University of Chicago Press.
MacDougall, David. 1998. *Transcultural Cinema*, ed. and introduction by Lucien Taylor. Princeton: Princeton University Press.
McLain, David L., Efstathios Kefallonitis, and Kimberly Armani. 2015. Ambiguity Tolerance in Organizations: Definitional Clarification and Perspectives on Future Research. *Frontiers in Psychology* 6: 344.
Mitchell, W.J.T. 1994. *Picture Theory: Essays on Verbal and Visual Representation*. Chicago and London: The University of Chicago Press.

Morris, Errol. 2014. *Believing Is Seeing (Observations on the Mysteries of Photography)*. London: Penguin.
Mouffe, Chantal. 2013. *Agonistics: Thinking the World Politically*. London, New York: Verso.
Müller-Christ, Georg, and Gudrun Weßling. 2007. Widerspruchsbewältigung, Ambivalenz- und Ambiguitätstoleranz: Eine modelhafte Verknüpfung. In *Nachhaltigkeit und Widersprüche*, ed. Georg Müller-Christ, Lars Arndt, and Ina Ehnert, 180–197. Münster: LIT Verlag.
Nagle, John. 2014. From the Politics of Antagonistic Recognition to Agonistic Peace Building: An Exploration of Symbols and Rituals in Divided Societies. *Peace & Change* 39 (4): 468–494.
Norton, Robert W. 1975. Measurement of Ambiguity Tolerance. *Journal of Personality Assessment* 39 (6): 607–619.
Pfonner, Michael R., and Patrick James. 2020. The Visual International Relations Project. *International Studies Review*. https://doi.org/10.1093/isr/viaa014.
Proulx, Travis, and Michael Inzlicht. 2012. The Five "A"s of Meaning Maintenance: Finding Meaning in the Theories of Sense-Making. *Psychological Inquiry* 23 (4): 317–335.
Rancière, Jacques. 2009. *The Emancipated Spectator*, trans. Gregory Elliott. London and New York: Verso.
Reis, Jack. 1997. *Ambiguitätstoleranz: Beiträge zur Entwicklung eines Persönlichkeitskonstruktes*. Heidelberg: Asanger.
Ritchin, Fred. 1999. *In Our Own Image*. New York: Aperture.
Rubinstein, Daniel, and Katrina Sluis. 2013. The Digital Image in Photographic Culture: Algorithmic Photography and the Crisis of Representation. In *The Photographic Image in Digital Culture*, ed. Martin Lister, 22–40. London and New York: Routledge.
Sacco, Joe. 2012. *Journalism*. London: Jonathan Cape.
Sennet, Adam. 2021. Ambiguity. In *The Stanford Encyclopedia of Philosophy*, ed. Edward Zalta, Fall 2021 ed. https://plato.stanford.edu/archives/fall2021/entries/ambiguity/.
Shapiro, Michael J. 1988. *The Politics of Representation: Writing Practices in Biography, Photography, and Policy Analysis*. Madison: The University of Wisconsin Press.
Shinko, Rosemary E. 2008. Agonistic Peace: A Postmodern Reading. *Millennium: Journal of International Studies* 36 (3): 473–491.
Short, Philip. 2014. *Mitterrand: A Study in Ambiguity*. London: Vintage.
Sontag, Susan. 1979. *On Photography*. London: Penguin.
Strömbom, Lisa. 2019. Exploring Analytical Avenues for Agonistic Peace. *Journal of International Relations and Development* 23 (4): 947–969.

Szubielska, Magdalena, Joanna Ganczarek, Karolina Pietras, and Anna Stolińska. 2021. The Impact of Ambiguity in the Image and Title on the Liking and Understanding of Contemporary Paintings. *Poetics* 87: 101537.

Widmaier, Wesley W., and Luke Glanville. 2015. The Benefits of Norm Ambiguity: Constructing the Responsibility to Protect Across Rwanda, Iraq and Libya. *Contemporary Politics* 21 (4): 367–383.

Willasey-Wilsey, Tom. 2022. US Policy on Taiwan and the Perils of Strategic Ambiguity. 23 September 2022. https://rusi.org/explore-our-research/publications/commentary/us-policy-taiwan-and-perils-strategic-ambiguity. Accessed 11 November 2022.

Winkler, Susanne. 2015. Exploring Ambiguity and the Ambiguity Model from a Transdisciplinary Perspective. In *Ambiguity: Language and Communication*, ed. Susanne Winkler. Berlin, Munich, and Boston: de Gruyter.

Zabotkina, Vera, Didier Bottineau, and Elena Boyarskaya. 2021. Cognitive Mechanisms of Ambiguity Resolution. In *Advances in Cognitive Research, Artificial Intelligence and Neuroinformatics Proceedings of the 9th International Conference on Cognitive Sciences, Intercognsci-2020, October 10–16, 2020, Moscow, Russia*, ed. Boris M. Velichkovsky, Pavel M. Balaban and Vadim L. Ushakov, 201–212. Cham: Springer.

Zenasni, Franck, Maud Besançon, and Todd Lubart. 2008. Creativity and Tolerance of Ambiguity: An Empirical Study. *The Journal of Creative Behavior* 42 (1): 61–73.

PART II

New Photographies and Visual Ambiguities

CHAPTER 4

The Crisis of Photojournalism and the Emergence of New Photographies

INTRODUCTION

In the previous chapters, we established that systems of human interaction are complex, that complex systems are ambiguous, and that there are different ways to respond to ambiguity. We explained our preference for responses based on tolerance of ambiguity (TA) rather than disambiguation with reference to the inherent complexity and messiness of the international system, which can always be perceived, interpreted, engaged with and responded to in multiple, equally permissible and, occasionally, mutually exclusive ways. Images can illustrate the plethora of permissible interpretations we regularly encounter in international relations but often they do not. Or more precisely, they *do*, but textual designations of meaning in photojournalism tend to contribute to disambiguation, thus undermining images' TA-building potentialities (as sketched in the previous chapter and further developed in Chapter 5). As we are interested in approaches to peace and conflict based on TA, we have to engage critically with photojournalism, explaining its conventional operating procedures and subsequently going beyond them (Part III). Our procedure should not be understood as a critique of photojournalism in general, as we regard photojournalism as necessary and indeed indispensable in a political and social environment dominated by visual images. Furthermore, we have tremendous respect for photojournalists who often

© The Author(s), under exclusive license to Springer Nature Switzerland AG 2023
R. Bellmer and F. Möller, *Peace, Complexity, Visuality*, Rethinking Peace and Conflict Studies,
https://doi.org/10.1007/978-3-031-38218-5_4

work in dangerous and occasionally life-threatening conditions to inform others, including us, of what is going on in the world. However, we believe that conventional photojournalism does not take advantage of all possibilities that photography offers (even within the confines of documentation), thus restricting spaces of possibility. Having treated photojournalism as an aggregate category in earlier chapters, we now want to disaggregate this category and introduce different photographies that emerged in response both to the specific challenges in Bosnia and Herzegovina in the 1990s and to what can be called the crisis of photojournalism.

A Blurring of Boundaries

There can be observed "a blurring of boundaries" (Patrick 2014: 238) mixing and connecting with one another different forms and genres of image production. Such blurring of boundaries can also be observed in the photography of individual photographers such as Paul Lowe, whose work in Bosnia, then and today, serves as a major inspiration for our study. As Val Williams explains, "Lowe's Bosnian photojournalism sits firmly in the tradition of modern photo documentary – speedy, topical and revealing" but also includes subjects that photojournalism tends to bypass—"calm and curious observation of texture, objects, landscapes, the crazy juxtapositions of conflict"—as well as panoramic photographs reminiscent of "the great cityscapes made in the nineteenth century" (Williams 2015: 3). Lowe's—and others'—photography thus challenged what Silvija Jestrovic calls

> the media's need to summarize complex conflicts by presenting the suffering of others in the clipped and clinically-informative language we have come to call news that is channeled into the comfort of our living rooms. In its translation of complex events onto two-dimensional screens and pages, many valuable layers are inevitably lost. (2013: 126)

Despite the blurring of genre boundaries and the frequent loss of "the multifaceted original" when translated into "two-dimensional" media narratives (Jestrovic 2013: 126), it is useful to treat—and respect—photojournalism as a separate genre of image production—a genre with its own histories, traditions, myths, conventions and rules of engagement, including ethical guidelines defining what photojournalists can do while going about their business and what is considered inappropriate. Understanding photojournalism's conventions is essential because photojournalism determines how we see the world.

Photojournalism's rules and guidelines determine not only photojournalism's operating procedures but also expectations among spectators. When exposed to an image that is said to be a photojournalistic one, spectators expect that the photographer adhered to a certain set of rules that art photographers or amateur photographers are neither expected nor required to respect. As photojournalist Ben Curtis explains: "If you're doing fine art photography, you can do what you want. But if your photos are intended to represent the truth, then it's a completely different situation" (quoted in Morris 2014: 194). A photograph's truth does not exclusively result from objectivity, neutrality and non-interference on the part of the photographer—in particular, photojournalists do not tamper with or arrange an image; they do not add anything to, and they do not remove anything from, the image (see Lange 1982: 46)—but also, as Curtis explicates, on truthful captions or, more precisely, on captions of which the photographer has reason to believe that they truthfully represent the scene depicted:

> As a photographer, when I write my captions, I'm very meticulous and methodical, and I go through and check them before I send them, and I have to establish to my own satisfaction that everything I've said in the caption is true, and that I can stand by it because I've witnessed it myself with my own eyes, or I've questioned the people in the field and I'm confident that I can stand by that information. (quoted in Morris 2014: 190)

However, Curtis's colleague Louie Palu alerts us to "the long-time practice of newspaper copy editors, who often replace the caption a photographer writes with quotes from the story the photograph accompanies, always over the photographer's objections" (Palu 2017: 59). Accordingly, Curtis concludes: "Everything that happens after my pictures hit the wire, it's not within my control" (quoted in Morris 2014: 193). However, regardless of authorship, captions offer possibilities for association and interpretation. Due to the surplus of meaning that all images carry with them, however, no image can be limited to the information provided in the caption (see Chapter 5), and what photographers think of as true because they have witnessed the situation depicted with their own eyes can always be challenged by other witnesses who have seen the same scene but interpret it differently.

As Palu explains, photojournalists follow "a code of ethics that, among other things, calls for independence and impartiality" although—like all human beings—journalists "may fall short of ethical aspirations" (Palu 2017: 59). Such a code of ethics demanding impartiality, while legitimizing the work of photojournalists in many circumstances and separating photojournalism from other photographic genres such as citizen photography (see Möller 2017a), becomes problematic in conditions where "one side [is] clearly the aggressor and the other the victim" (Lowe 2015: 5), as was arguably the case during the siege of Sarajevo (to which Lowe refers), the Spanish Civil War or (at the time of writing) the Russian aggression against Ukraine. In such cases, the photographer's impartiality appears problematic just as does "the objectivity of the camera" which, according to Sergey Tretyakov, "regards with indifference the just and the unjust" (as cited in Watney 1982: 166). Indeed, Robert Capa (who in many ways epitomizes photojournalism), Chim (David Seymour) and Gerda Taro are said to have "embraced the propagandistic uses of their [Spanish Civil War; the authors] photographs in support of the Republican cause" (Wallis 2010: 16). Furthermore, they are said to have understood that in order for photography to have purpose, "the photographer had to be engaged, had to have judged the political stakes in that story, and had to have taken sides" (Wallis 2010: 13). Here, photojournalistic ethics did not rule out taking political sides; rather, both conditioned each other, and this specific combination of photographic ethics and politics can be observed in the Bosnian case as well. Echoing the above position, the BBC's Martin Bell is said to have argued that

> journalists, while they have a duty to report as objectively and as honestly as possible, must consider the evidence. If that determines that one party is clearly the aggressor and the other the victim, then a neutral position is unacceptable. This he [Bell] termed the "journalism of attachment," in which identifying one side as morally wrong and therefore accountable for their crimes does not necessarily impinge on the professionalism of the journalist. (Morrison and Lowe 2021: 145)

However, not only did such reporting not result in the Western military intervention that many Western journalists demanded early in the conflict and hoped their reporting would contribute to; reporting from Sarajevo was also dismissed by many (politicians and journalists alike) as "biased reporting" (Morrison and Lowe 2021: 143), clearly favoring the position of the Bosnian government while claiming to sympathize merely with Bosnian citizens (Morrison and Lowe 2021: 143–147), thus ultimately weakening the influence journalists had on Western decision-making. Thus, photojournalism is more complex than the standard reference to neutrality, objectivity and impartiality would seem to imply. For example, it is one of photojournalism's rules that the photographer does not interfere in the situation depicted, but her very presence is already an interference to which people respond, as Radhika Chalasani confirms: "We're interfering with a situation by our very presence, and that automatically changes the dynamic."[1] Furthermore, journalists respond themselves to the conditions they depict and make judgments that cannot but influence their reporting.

Crisis of Photojournalism, Crisis of Confidence

With regard to the situation in Bosnia and Herzegovina in the 1990s, Lowe explains that "many of us in the media believed that if we told the story loudly enough … the world would take notice and intervention to stop the carnage would ensue" (Lowe 2015: 5). However, while photojournalists did tell the story loudly and produced many important and memorable images (often risking their lives while doing so),[2] the world, although taking notice, did not intervene for a long time (Donia 2009: 299). Thus, photojournalism is not always successful, if by successful we mean more than visually communicating information and raising awareness of the conditions depicted. Many photojournalists have a political agenda in the sense that they assume a direct connection between their photographs and politics: they expect others—the world, the international community, selected politicians, etc.—to respond to their images

---

[1] https://www.theguardian.com/media/2012/jul/28/gutted-photographers-who-didnt-help (accessed 4 January 2023). Journalists, Joe Sacco explains, "are not flies on the wall that are neither seen not heard." Their presence "is almost always felt" (2012: xi).

[2] last-despatches.balkaninsight.com reports that "[o]ver 150 journalists were killed during and after the 1990s wars in the Balkans – some of them foreigners who came to cover the conflicts, but most of them citizens of the warring republics" (accessed 3 January 2023). For the working conditions of journalists during the siege of Sarajevo, see Morrison and Lowe (2021).

by intervening in the conditions depicted with means that are politically more effective than those that photojournalists possess (see Möller 2013: 56–74). This attitude can be called pro-active documentation: strictly working within the parameters of documentation while simultaneously clearly taking political sides and advocating specific politics, e.g., military intervention. Should such intervention fail to materialize, disappointment is likely to follow, as testified by photographer Ron Haviv after the timely publication of photographs he had taken in Bijeljina documenting the execution of unarmed Muslim civilians by Serbian paramilitaries—some of the most famous photographs from the Bosnian war.[3] Haviv expected that "these pictures would provide a final push, so the world would stop this. But obviously nothing happened. It was really incredibly disappointing" (quoted in Lowe 2014: 218). Neither "advocacy journalism" nor "straightforward reporting," terms used by *Newsday* correspondent Roy Gutman (quoted in Morrison and Lowe 2021: 142)[4] to characterize the two different types of journalists working in Bosnia, made much impact on policy. That nothing happened undermined belief in photojournalism's political effectiveness and purpose and triggered what Kenneth Morrison and Paul Lowe call "something of a crisis of confidence" (2021: 143).

This belief, however, seems to have been based on a rather simplified understanding of the complex relationship among "perception, affection, comprehension and action" (Rancière 2009: 103) which is primarily a political, not a visual relationship. As Morrison and Lowe report, even within the media itself,

> despite the graphic nature of the visceral images emanating from Sarajevo, the equally powerful despatches in print media and the mounting numbers of civilian deaths, the story of the siege did not receive the same sustained media attention for the duration of the siege that it had during the summer of 1992 – the narrative of the Olympic city of Sarajevo being under siege while the Olympic games were taking place in Barcelona gave the story a particular resonance that was time-limited (Morrison and Lowe 2021: 141)

---

[3] For a selection of these and related images, see https://emuseum.mfah.org/objects/111774/ethnic-cleansing (accessed 18 March 2023).

[4] Note that, based on different perceptions and interpretations of a given situation, what qualifies as "straightforward reporting" for some may be perceived by others as "advocacy journalism" and vice versa.

and, therefore, unsustainable. More basically, news from the siege of Sarajevo stopped being news as the siege continued for years.[5]

Recognition of the fact that photojournalism cannot stop violence in Bosnia and Herzegovina (or in Rwanda or many other places, for that matter) does not, however, necessarily undermine the value of photojournalism. The world is not a social laboratory; we cannot replicate the wars in ex-Yugoslavia under laboratory conditions, exploring what the situation would have looked like had no photographer attempted to represent it or had photographers represented it differently. We have what we have and what we have is complex, defying simple answers. It is arguable, for example, that as much as or even more than reflecting photography's failure, frustration with photography's incapability of ending violence reflects exaggerated hopes pinned to photography since its inception. After all, how can photography be expected to achieve what politics cannot (or does not even want to) achieve? James Nachtwey, simultaneously one of the most famous and one of the most criticized photographers due to the graphic nature of many of his images and the absence of written contextualization characterizing many of his projects, puts it thus (quoted in Linfield 2010: 60): "The greatest statesmen, philosophers, humanitarians ... have not been able to put an end to war. Why place that demand on photography?"

Perhaps because, while critics emphasize photography's connection with war and violence (see Sontag 1979), historically, its supporters had linked it to such grand ideas as democracy, equality and human rights. As François Brunet explains, early proponents tried to increase photography's legitimacy vis-à-vis traditional forms of image making by calling it a "democratic art," an "art without art" and therefore "an art for all": "The cultural face of the political idea of equality, [photography] heralded a democratic art" (2019: xiii). In early French photographic discourses, for example, "democratic aspiration appeared as a major aspect of the idea of photography" (p. 7), linking (the idea of) photography closely with (the idea of) democracy, thus inviting interpretation of a failure of democracy in terms of a failure of photography. "In 2000," Brunet concludes, "the idea of photography was still linked with that of equality, and it is in this respect that a larger social consensus saw within it a legitimate expression of individuality" (p. 364). As noted in Chapter 3, complexity carries with

---

[5] Furthermore, "outside the periods of very heaving shelling and fighting, the city could be eerily still, with little to report" (Morrison and Lowe 2021: 119).

it a history of its emergence, and the history of photographic complexity includes strong connections between photographic representation and ideas such as democracy and equality. In addition, human rights can be singled out as an issue that was deeply influenced by visual representation—not only in the sense that photographs documented individual violations of human rights but also, as Sharon Sliwinski (2011) shows, in that the very idea of human rights emerged in part as a result of visual representations of atrocity. In avant-garde writings, photography appeared even as "an agent of human self-realization" (Kelsey and Stimson 2008: xviii). Perhaps, then, a possible answer to Nachtwey's above question would be that the demand to put an end to war was placed on photography by its proponents themselves by emphasizing its connection to democracy, equality, human rights and self-realization, all of which are ingredients of a broader understanding of peace.

At the time of the wars in ex-Yugoslavia, assumptions about the operating procedures of photojournalism had been exposed to critical investigation by, for example, Abigail Solomon-Godeau (1991), Susan Sontag (1979) Victor Burgin (1982) and Martha Rosler (2006, originally published 1981) in influential writings that continue if not to dominate than at least to influence photojournalistic discourses. Robin Kelsey and Blake Stimson (2008: xx) explain the pessimistic flavor of these critiques as follows:

> Most of the critiques of photography that emerged during the Vietnam War and its aftermath largely revived or elaborated those that the avant-garde had articulated as World War II approached, but now the critiques were sharper if not embittered, as no utopian alternative could be convincingly imagined, particularly after the student uprisings of 1968 seemed to produce only incremental change.

Critical investigation included double standards when, for example, beauty in photography appeared as a liability (very explicit in Sontag 1979, weaker in Sontag 2003) while it appeared as a merit in other forms of representation (such as literature): a beautifully written text describing human suffering appeared acceptable while a beautiful photograph of human suffering did not (see the discussion in Reinhardt, Edwards and

Duganne 2007).[6] As we summarized elsewhere, photographers, and especially photojournalists, were criticized for

> contributing to violence rather than merely documenting it; exploiting the subjects depicted, especially those in pain; making human suffering appear beautiful and, by doing so, aestheticizing and depoliticizing pain; and producing, as visiting photographers, ad hoc images without deeper knowledge of the structural, political and historical conditions on location. Claims to objectivity and neutrality were increasingly scrutinized from critical perspectives emphasizing the role photographers themselves played in the construction of what they were documenting, thus challenging the very idea of detached, objective documentation. (Bellmer and Möller 2022: 3; for the crisis of photojournalism, see also Prosser et al. 2012)

Often, it appeared that photographers were the cause of the conditions they depicted and that their depictions aggravated these conditions rather than merely documenting or even improving them. Such criticism was itself criticized as "approach[ing] photography … with suspicion, mistrust, anger, and fear" (Linfield 2010: 5). However, although occasionally exaggerated, it has no doubt contributed to the diversification of the theoretical perspectives on photography and to the evolution of the photojournalistic language in both theory and practice—not necessarily introducing but certainly strengthening self-reflection on the part of photographers, including reflection on the ethics of taking and publishing photographic images. As Palu puts it, photojournalists currently "consider the impact of their images"—including, we would like to add, their impact on the subjects depicted—"in a way that amateurs might not" (Palu 2017: 59) and that their professional predecessors did not, or did not always, do. Thus, if we understand a crisis as "an unstable or crucial time or state of affairs in which a decisive change is impending,"[7] then photojournalism seems to have emerged from its crisis perhaps not stronger than, but definitely different from, what it used to be before the crisis (and before digitization and citizen photography emerged as new

---

[6] One reason for this discrepancy may be that photographers "have to maintain a close, often uncomfortable, proximity to their subject(s)" (Morrison and Lowe 2021: 148) thus being painfully—and occasionally provocatively—visible when going about their business while writers can report from some distance and cultivate a more discrete attitude, taking mental notes or merely observing a scene.

[7] https://www.merriam-webster.com/dictionary/crisis (accessed 4 January 2023).

challenges). It derives its current strength to a large extent from the diversification of image making within the genre of photojournalism, including the introduction of art photography elements, the farewell to established credos emphasizing, for example, proximity to action, and the redefinition of what qualifies as an event in photojournalistic representation; in other words, diversification of what appears worthy of a photojournalistic image.

Indeed, Haviv, Lowe and many of their colleagues working in the Bosnian context or elsewhere translated their disappointment with the seeming political ineffectiveness of their images into a constructive search for new approaches to photojournalism that simultaneously also addressed many other ingredients of photography criticism. The typology presented in the next section is rough as the various approaches are characterized by both differences and similarities, politically as well as aesthetically.[8] We are interested primarily in identifying the basic lines of thought underlying these diverse photographies rather than in naming every photographer whose work could be associated with one or more of these categories. As always, some photographic work cannot be categorized compellingly, standing out as genre-defying and unique (see Part III).

NEW PHOTOGRAPHIES

In the Bosnian context, new forms of photojournalism emerged while conventional forms continued to exist.[9] In Sarajevo, for example, parked UN armoured vehicles would provide cover for civilians trying to cross intersections. Photographers, feeling "the need to document ... attacks on civilians ... were, quite literally, waiting to capture images

---

[8] We first presented this typology in our article 'Messiness in Photography, War, and Transitions to Peace: Revisiting *Bosnia: Uncertain Paths to Peace*' (Bellmer and Möller 2022). While the basic lines of thought inspiring this typology are identical, we refine it in what follows.

[9] Our use of the word "conventional" does not imply value judgment. We use the term to refer to those forms of photojournalism that stick closely to the tradition of war and conflict photography. Such photography is in itself neither inferior nor superior to its alternatives. For a collection of such images, see War Photo Limited: *The End of Yugoslavia*, at https://warphotoltd.com.

of someone being shot" by snipers (Morrison and Lowe 2021: 150)—images reflecting photojournalism's obsession with 'great' shots in proximity to 'action' (Capa,[10] Eddie Adams,[11] etc.) which, in the Bosnian war, were hard to obtain: the frontlines around the city did not change much during the siege, and journalists had to overcome numerous bureaucratic obstacles if they wished to visit them. Furthermore, while operating at the frontlines was synonymous with danger, it did not guarantee good pictures (Morrison and Lowe 2021: 121–123), thus inviting the search for 'great' pictures within the city's parameters. Here, periods of ceasefire and relative calm offered other photo opportunities than periods of shelling and fighting.

Local photojournalists documented the Bosnian war in general and the siege of Sarajevo in particular for local consumption, while their international colleagues flew in to inform an international audience. This is what photographers have done since the early days of photography. As early as 1855, for example, Roger Fenton photographed the Crimean War. Together with photographs produced during the American Civil War, his work serves as one of photography's early defining moments (see Oldfield 2019: 20–24). Largely due to technological limitations prevailing at the time, commercial considerations and his embeddedness with British troops, Fenton's images look strikingly different from today's photojournalistic work. "Fenton was, however, the first photographer to produce a substantial body of work documenting any conflict in any region, at a time when there was no expectation of what 'war photography' should be" (Gordon 2017: 43).

What war photography *should* be has been established subsequently in photographic discourses and practices (see Tucker and Michels with Zelt 2012; Oldfield 2019), moving from Fenton's "dignified and sanitized images of conflict" including "staged portraits of soldiers in full regalia" (Oldfield 2019: 20) to the 'great' shots in close proximity to action associated with such photographers as Capa, to the visual focus on civilian suffering in the work of, for example, Don McCullin and to the embedded photography of the wars of the late twentieth century. Ernst

---

[10] *Death of a loyalist militiaman, Cerro Muriano, Córdoba front, Spain (The Falling Soldier), September 5, 1936.*

[11] *South Vietnamese National Police Chief Brigadier General Nguyen Ngoc Loan executes a Viet Cong officer with a single pistol shot in the head in Saigon, February 1, 1968.*

Friedrich's 1924 book of images from military and medical archives—"photography as shock therapy" (Sontag 2003: 14)—showing bodies devastated from war and many other gruesome things depicts the consequences of war on people, animals, built environment and landscapes just as does Nachtwey's (equally unbearable) imagery of contemporary warfare, all of which show what human beings are capable of doing in times of war. Some of these images—not necessarily the most shocking ones—are discursively elevated to the status of "icon" (see Hariman and Lucaites 2007) and thus ingrained in collective pictorial memory. The world as it appears in photojournalism is indeed a world of war and violence. "Photojournalism came into its own in the early 1940s – wartime," writes Sontag (2003: 34), and this is yet another ingredient of the history current photography carries with it. It is also a reference point for the new photographies that emerged in the 1990s—a *negative* one in the sense that none of the new visual approaches seems to be particularly interested in 'action' or 'great shots,' conventionally defined; a *positive* one in that many approaches share with McCullin and others interest in civilian suffering, the continuation of violence after war, and the visualization of traumatic memories.

While new photographies could be developed in earnest only after the war, some photographers explored a new visual vocabulary already during the war. Lowe, for example, used a series of ceasefires to explore the architecture of Sarajevo and to document both destruction and defense:

> I lugged a large format panoramic camera and a heavy tripod with me, and explored the various ways in which the streets had been fragmented by artillery shells, mortars, rockets and bullets, and the extraordinary variety of defences that its citizens had improvised from concrete, shipping containers and vehicles to defend themselves from the fire. The panoramic format opened up the scene, transforming the usual media coverage of the intense moment into a more expansive view that showed the scale of the city and its texture. (Lowe 2015: 5)

According to Morrison, these images capture "the soul of a city and its people experiencing the worst of times" (2016: 137), and they do so largely without resorting to the visual conventions of war photography. They document a form of everyday peace, if by everyday peace we mean the continuation of everyday life (see Sheringham 2006) in times of violence: "eking out safe space in a conflict context and allowing a façade of normality to prevail" (Mac Ginty 2014: 555) in a situation that was anything but safe and normal. Such everyday peace is characterized by individual and collective microsteps indicating resistance, resilience and a profound will to survive, defying the logic of violence.[12] As Jestrovic notes, "Sarajevo was a place of tension and ambiguity rather than a mere embodiment of political violence" (2013: 158) as which it regularly appeared in photojournalistic representation. Surely, death was a part of everyday peace, "the new normality" (Abadžić 2022: 79). However, while often an expression of pure desperation, such microsteps may add up to something bigger: "the repetition of every day practices [may] carry within themselves the possibility to change their own course and through that the context within which they occur(ed)," as Thomas Telios et al. (2020: 7) suggest in a very different context. Their suggestion, we think, is nevertheless applicable to the context we are discussing as well and confirms, without romanticizing, the importance of such microsteps and their visual representation. Another example of the anticipation of new photographies that came to fruition only after the war is Chris Morris's forensic approach to photography, taking pictures of children in a morgue "like a forensic document" because no other photographic approach seemed feasible and appropriate in a situation characterized by "[p]ure horror" (quoted in Morrison and Lowe 2021: 152). What in Morris's work seems to have been a spontaneous reaction to a particular situation reflecting a lack of alternatives was after the war developed systematically as forensic photography.

Forensic Photography

The basic theme of forensic photography is justice after violence. If photography cannot stop violence, then it can try to contribute to post-violence justice because, in the absence of justice, violence continues. Photography can approach spaces and places as crime scenes (see

---

[12] For the cultural dimension of everyday peace thus understood, see Jestrovic (2013: 115–189), Morrison and Lowe (2021: 132–140) and Abadžić (2022: 84–86). As Jestrovic notes, "art was as important to Sarajevo's vitality as humanitarian aid but there was one major distinction: humanitarian aid of any kind necessitated help, that is, external intervention, while cultural production was inextricably linked to an internal process of resistance through which the city's identity was shaped and preserved" (2013: 123–124).

Gustafsson 2019), meticulously and systematically documenting and cataloging atrocities. Bones are "the most reliable witnesses to atrocity" (Danchev 2009: 41), and while it may be difficult on the basis of visual evidence alone to precisely identify the victim, images of bones show that victims do indeed exist. In a sense, then, forensic photographers "*reappear the disappeared* or they prevent the disappeared from disappearing completely" (Möller 2019: 159; italics in original) thus undermining a policy that aims not only at killing people but also at erasing them from history. Identifying them and giving them a proper burial is part of justice after violence.

Without denying the photographer's agency, forensic photography follows a positivist understanding of images as evidence and photographers as collectors of evidence—evidence that can subsequently be used in a court of justice. "Sometimes at the expense of human testimony, material objects such as bones found in mass graves have increasingly been used in court as evidence of the crimes under investigation" (Gade 2020: 368), thus revitalizing belief in photography's evidentiary potentialities (see Dufour 2015). The International Criminal Tribunal for Yugoslavia used photographs as evidence in a judicial sense, for example, images by Giles Penfound taken in 1993 in Ahmići during his work with British UNPROFOR troops based in Vitez (see Fairey and Kerr 2020: 157–158).[13] Commentary indeed frequently emphasizes the political rather than aesthetic values of forensic photography, although it is its aesthetic dimension that is said to "provide[ ] a public site for discussing the conditions of the possibility of politics" without succumbing to or reproducing the logics of politics (Gade 2020: 367).

In Bosnia, Gervasio Sánchez's work documents processes of victim identification that "can last for days, months or years" (2011: 144), thus requiring a photographer's long-term engagement. Sánchez also documents the annual reburial ceremonies at the Srebrenica-Potočari Memorial Center (2011: 168–179). Gilles Peress's forensic work *The Graves* (Stover and Peress 1998)—following a book created during the war and preceding another one produced in 1999 on Kosovo—focuses on the exhumation of mass graves. Peress, Susie Linfield (2010: 245) suggests, "brings us close … to the mass graves, whose obscenity is to

---

[13] Some of these rather graphic photographs can be seen at https://www.ahmici.sensecentar.org/#top. Penfound served as Chief Press Photographer for the British Army; see https://www.dodho.com/giles-penfound/ (both websites accessed 23 August 2021).

be found not just in the fact that these people were murdered but in the contempt with which their bodies were mutilated and dumped." The photographer himself explains the evolution of his work during that period as follows:

> [I have] started to take more still lifes, like a police photographer, collecting evidence as a witness. I've started to borrow a different strategy than that of the classic photojournalist. The work is much more factual and much less about good photography. I don't care that much anymore about 'good photography'. I'm gathering evidence for history, so that we remember. (quoted in Lowe 2014: 221)

Such photography can, of course, be "good photography" once we depart from the conventional understanding of good or great shots in the photojournalistic tradition: "a picture of an unexpected event seized in mid-action by an alert photographer" (Sontag 2003: 55). While Peress's forensic approach is said to move "emphasis from the general to the specific" (Lowe 2014: 221), it may be more fruitful to think about the relationship between the specific and the general in Peress's work in dialectical terms or as a copresence: the one opens up the possibility for understanding the other (and vice versa), only seemingly simplifying complex issues while simultaneously complexifying the seemingly simple by "playing with the audience's expectations of how such genre images operate" (Lowe 2014: 220). "The viewer," Linfield concludes, "must work to complete the photograph by digging into what it suggests and endowing it with deeper insights" (2010: 238). Relying on the viewer to complete the photograph, paradoxically, complicates photography's role as evidence, as different viewers are likely to draw different conclusions from what they (believe to) see.

For Ziyah Gafić, photography resembles memory work, identity work and forensics. In *Quest for Identity*, Gafić documents the personal effects of victims of the Srebrenica genocide, collected from bodies after exhumation from mass graves (Gafić 2015). It is as much the substance of the photography as its organization and presentation that touches viewers, reminding them of the indiscriminateness with which people were killed: "the images are all shot in the same, simple, frontal style, set on the stainless steel mortuary table at the identification centre in Tuzla" (Lowe 2014: 227). According to the photographer, these images are an inventory of genocide, "a visual archive that survivors could easily browse [...]

In all their simplicity," Gafić continues to explain, "these items are the last resort of identity, the last permanent reminder that these people ever existed."[14] The items depicted are extraordinary in their ordinariness, inviting viewers to identify with and emotionally respond to them (see Lowe 2014: 227). Read together with *Heartland* (Gafić 2016), Gafić's tableaux offers a compelling, albeit pessimistic, visual narrative of post-war Bosnia and Herzegovina which is anything but post-conflict. In *Heartland*, Ozren Kebo notes, the photographs "do not offer us a future, nor do they debate with the past, and it is in his [Gafić's] photographs that we learn, in the most painful way, what a bitter present has settled between the two" (2016: 84–86). Aftermath photographs do not offer us a future either, but they do debate with the past.

Aftermath Photography

Aftermath photography is a direct response to photojournalists' habit of leaving a conflict zone immediately once physical violence is, or seems to be, over. Photojournalism, thus, tells *"only half the story,"* as the founder and director of The Aftermath Project, Sara Terry, puts it (Terry and van der Heyden 2018: 3; italics in original). While it is not possible to neatly separate one half from the other—war from post-war or even conflict from post-conflict—photojournalism's focus on representations of physical violence is a radical simplification in need of correction. Aftermath photography offers such a correction by acknowledging—and visualizing—a given conflict's continuation in what seems to be post-conflict conditions, thus visually interrogating the *post* in post-conflict (Baker and Mavlian 2014). Does *post* indicate the end of the conflict or merely its transformation into something less tangible and less visible, something—perhaps—less photographable? Frequently focusing on the visualization of traumatic memories of both combatants and civilians—"the psychological trauma of war" (Chouliaraki 2018: 71)—and the destruction inflicted upon landscapes and built environment, aftermath photography favors slow photography and "elegiac and mournful modes" of representation, replacing "the notion of the photograph as an act of interruption, displacement, interrogation, rearticulation" with that of photography

---

[14] Ziyah Gafić, *Quest for Identity*, at https://www.lensculture.com/articles/ziyah-gafic-quest-for-identity (accessed 12 August 2021).

"as a site of 'glacial' contemplation" (Roberts 2014: 110), thus critically engaging with Capa's famous demand that a photographer must be as close to action as possible. While adhering to photojournalism's self-understanding in terms of documentation and evidence, aftermath photography acknowledges the existence of ambiguities and interpretive openness. Aesthetically, it is closer to fine art photography than to photojournalism. Quite paradoxically, however, it often infringes upon its own ambiguities through textual explanations of what can be seen in a given image (Lisle 2011).

In Bosnia, Sara Terry's *Aftermath: Bosnia's Long Road to Peace* is among the first books about Bosnia's recovery, the "Herculean task of returning to homes haunted by tragedy and lingering hostilities" (2005: 10). It is a book about "learning to live again" (p. 10), about grief and joy, hope and hopelessness among those who had survived the war but were now facing the challenge of "surviv[ing] the peace," as the university student Edib Palalic, quoted in the book (p. 15), puts it. Regarding the temporalities of the aftermath, Steve Horn's book *Pictures without Borders* is particularly interesting, as it combines photographs taken a long time before the war (1970–1971) with photographs taken some years after the war, thus visually encapsulating the war without showing it directly. However, according to the photographer, "the deepest significance" of his return journey in 2003 "was in bringing pictures back to Bosnia, not taking new ones away" (Horn 2005: 8)—a very important mission given that the war was an attack not only on people but also on their histories and memories and many survivors lost everything including photographs with which to remember the past.

Simon Norfolk's aftermath photographs are examples of what Alex Danchev calls "meditations on the ethics of response and responsibility" (2009: 42) on the part of both the photographer and the viewer—ethics that do not evaporate with the end of the war. Research-based and produced with considerable temporal distance, Norfolk's work "project[s] a moment in the apparent present backwards into the past" (Lowe 2014: 223). It challenges simplified notions of temporal linearity and time's progressiveness, thus complexifying the notion of past and rendering difficult the notion of closure. In terms that are typical of aftermath photography, Lowe discovers a "multiplicity of meaning" and disorientation in Norfolk's work. For him, beauty serves as a tool to involve viewers and to "advance his [Norfolk's] moral message better" (2014: 224–225; see also Möller 2013: 36–38). However, while using beauty, Norfolk also reveals a degree of skepticism of it by providing captions to explain the circumstances his photographs are meant to reference. As

Debbie Lisle observes, "reveal[ing] his [Norfolk's] authorial intention when creating a particular picture ... encourages a singular and unidirectional interpretive journey to the preferred meaning" of the image (2011: 885), thus undermining the photograph's narrative openness and, with it, one of the strengths of aftermath photography. Thus, different aftermath photographers (and commentators), while jointly criticizing the conventions of photojournalism, pursue different visual agendas. In the Bosnian context, there can be observed a certain emphasis on aftermath representations of trauma and the legacies of the past. This emphasis is both legitimate and understandable, but it might create memory bubbles defining rather narrow spaces of possibility within which current and future politics unfold and from which it is difficult to escape. Aftermath photography tends to get arrested in the original event that it photographically prolongs; only rarely does it ask: "when does it [the aftermath] start exactly? When does it end? Does it end? ... What comes after the aftermath? ... If peace follows the aftermath, when exactly does the aftermath become peace?" (Möller 2017b: 317).[15] Offering visual paths "from the aftermath to peace" (Möller 2017b) is not always part of aftermath photography and photographic discourses revolving around it (see, however, Terry and van der Heyden 2018).

Post-conflict Photography

Terry notes that "what happens in the aftermath of war is as newsworthy, if not more so, than the destruction and horror of war ... I became convinced that we need post-conflict images to remind us of our humanity" (2005: 10). Rather than looking back, exploring the continuation of the past in the present as aftermath photography does, post-conflict photography—or peace photography—looks forward. It acknowledges, and tries to visualize, the constructive potentialities inherent in social conflict. Without ignoring the legacies of the past, it is future-oriented, aspiring to proactively visualize or anticipate peace (Allan 2011; Ritchin 2013: 122–141; Möller 2019). Rather than limiting peace

---

[15] In the exhibition *Conflict · Time · Photography* at Tate Modern (20 November 2014– 15 March 2015) the answer to the question "When does the aftermath end?" seems to have been: "never," as photographs taken one hundred years after a violent event were still regarded as aftermath photographs (see Baker and Mavlian 2014).

to "an ephemeral space between wars" (Knight 2020: 9), such photography understands peace as a photographic subject in its own right which can be strengthened by representing it.

One important aspect of post-conflict photography is its interest in activism, aid and advocacy (see Allan 2011; Sliwinski 2011; Walsh 2019, section three); another is its focus on everyday activities in post-conflict societies indicating a certain degree of civic normality (see Horn 2005: 63–65). This is important in contexts such as Bosnia where peace, conventionally understood, appears paralyzed (see Bennett 2016) or even under threat. Haviv, in conversation with Lauren Walsh (2019; Chapter 6), reflects upon his frequent return journeys to the Balkans and identifies them as "a project focusing on peace." He asks:

> What does the aftermath of war look like, even decades later? What are the visual narratives of peacetime? It's important not just to focus on the conflicts, but to raise awareness about post-conflict society and to examine when and how peace plays out and where, in cases, it fails.

The strict binary separating "the conflicts" from the "post-conflict society" is a simplification, but Haviv's interest in "visual narratives of peacetime" hints at a photographic agenda different from traditional photojournalism and aftermath photography. His focus on the potential "use [of] memory to move past the loss and create one nation for all Bosnians" (Haviv 2020: 211) is extremely important in a society apparently characterized by the opposite. We will have more to say on this genre of photographic image production in Part III.

Participatory Photography

Participatory photography aims at community building through photographic projects in which citizens participate as "agents of their own image" (Möller 2012: 66) rather than being objects of the photography of others or being visually ignored altogether. Often ascribed a democratizing role, participation in such projects is regarded as equally important as the final product, as it helps increase communication and social cohesion among the participants. Participatory photography targets the in-group—the participants—in terms of community building but also out-groups: it potentially shapes the in-group's image in the eyes of others, thus counteracting visual stigmatization (Möller 2013: 116). Participatory photography "is repeatedly framed as 'giving voice' to individuals [who] are commonly unheard or even silenced by powerful forces," thus enabling participants to determine how "they want to be seen by others rather than being represented by others in terms other than their own, e.g., as victims" (Bellmer and Möller 2022: 5).

Tiffany Fairey and Rachel Kerr (2020) have explored participatory projects in Bosnia, some of which are based on photography, to emphasize certain best practices while also acknowledging limitations and restrictions. They highlight two projects involving the History Museum of Bosnia and Herzegovina and the Post-Conflict Research Centre (PCRC), a Sarajevo-based NGO. Both projects included participatory elements such as workshops based on visual arts in the case of the Museum or "creative multimedia and photo-features on relevant regional and civil society issues" (Fairey and Kerr 2020: 152) on an online multimedia platform implemented by the PCRC. The authors conclude:

> Both of these initiatives were found to have engendered a form of participatory creative practice that created a multiplier impact enabling different sectors of Bosnian society – youth and artists – to play an active role in carving out new spaces for deliberation about the past, present and future, which we argue is a critical element of transitional justice and reconciliation. (Fairey and Kerr 2020: 156)

For Fairey and Kerr, these participatory visual initiatives both established a space for Bosnian youth to "engage public audiences and build their legitimacy as civil society actors on their own terms" through creative means and "made visible locally driven narratives" (2020: 159–160). The projects thus enable participants to express their stories but also provide opportunities to include them in public discourse: giving voice to individuals and making those voices heard *in their own context* rather than in contexts provided and conditioned by visiting photographers or artists (see Jestrovic 2013). However, Fairey challenges the notion of 'giving voice' to people as "naïve and overly simplistic" (2018: 112). Rather, participatory photography "projects are sites for negotiating rather 'giving' voice," understanding "photographic 'voice' as a negotiated, uncertain and emergent practice" (pp. 111–112). As a result, "there is no authentic voice that emerges out of participatory photography projects but rather a range of stories and perspectives that are considered and edited according to a particular strategic aim embedded within a particular set of power relations" (p. 121). Instead of searching for an "authentic voice," then, such an approach to post-conflict photography points toward the "great potency of photography," namely, its "plurality and its open-ended capacity for re-invention and re-appropriation" (p. 121).

Conclusion

The purpose of this chapter was to disaggregate photojournalism and to show that many photographies currently coexist and communicate with one another. Indeed, the conventional distinction between photojournalism and fine art photography is a radical and misleading simplification. Some of the new photographies are deeply entrenched in the traditions, conventions and myths of photojournalism, while others cultivate distance to this tradition or to parts of it. The more radical approaches allow ambiguities to operate on observers in an uncontrolled and uncontrollable way—in a way, that is to say, that is anathema to conventional photojournalism—thus extending both the limits of photojournalism and spaces of possibility. Sometimes, tradition and innovation coexist. For example, some aftermath photography visually generates ambiguities, thus inviting "viewers to create alternative, surprising, and potentially oppositional interpretations" (Lisle 2011: 885) but simultaneously renders such oppositional interpretations difficult by providing captions explaining the photographer's intentions: words tame images. Paradoxically, such photography lets the genie out of the bottle and at the same time tries to put it back into the bottle. Here, the power of the photojournalistic tradition seems to outweigh the power of innovation and imagination, thus catering to the conventional belief that captions are needed to fix an image's meaning.

In the following chapter, we will discuss the tolerance of ambiguity-enhancing potentialities inherent in visual images. We resume the lines of thought introduced in Chapter 2 (photocomplexity) and Chapter 3 (photoambiguity) and identify the plurality of meanings that images carry with them, their ambiguity and interpretive openness as merits rather than liabilities if we want to create a space for thinking differently about complexity, difference of perspective, and, ultimately, the political and social Other. To this end, we connect critical debates surrounding images' ambiguity with discussions on the concept of tolerance of ambiguity. We conclude the present chapter with the fourth of our Sarajevo photographs (Fig. 4.1) introduced in Chapter 2 in terms of photocomplexity.

Fig. 4.1 Sarajevo #4 (Photograph © Frank Möller)

References

Abadžić, Amra. 2022. *Sarajevo: The Longest Siege*. Sarajevo: Scena MESS.
Allan, Stuart. 2011. Documenting War, Visualizing Peace: Towards Peace Photography. In *Expanding Peace Journalism: Comparative and Critical Approaches*, ed. Ibraham Seaga Shaw, Jake Lynch and Robert A. Hackett, 147–167. Sydney: University of Sidney Press.
Baker, Simon, and Shoair Mavlian, eds. 2014. *Conflict Time Photography*. London: Tate Publishing.
Bellmer, Rasmus and Frank Möller. 2022. Messiness in Photography, War, and Transitions to Peace: Revisiting 'Bosnia: Uncertain Paths to Peace'. *Media, War, and Conflict* 16 (2). https://doi.org/10.1177/17506352211072463.
Bennett, Christopher. 2016. *Bosnia's Paralysed Peace*. London: Hurst & Company.
Brunet, François. 2019. *The Birth of the Idea of Photography*. Toronto: RIC Books.
Burgin, Victor, ed. 1982. *Thinking Photography*. Houndmills and London: Macmillan.
Chouliaraki, Lilie. 2018. The Humanity of War: Iconic Photojournalism of the Battlefield, 1914–2012. In *Visual Security Studies: Sights and Spectacles of Insecurity and War*, ed. Juha A. Vuori and Rune Saugmann Andersen, 71–90. London and New York: Routledge.
Danchev, Alex. 2009. *On Art and War and Terror*. Edinburgh: Edinburgh University Press.
Donia, Robert J. 2009. *Sarajevo: A Biography*. London: Hurst & Company.
Dufour, Diane (ed.). 2015. *Images of Conviction: The Construction of Visual Evidence*. Paris: LE BAL.
Fairey, Tiffany. 2018. Whose Photo? Whose Voice? Who Listens? 'Giving', Silencing and Listening to Voice in Participatory Visual Projects. *Visual Studies* 33 (2): 111–126.
Fairey, Tiffany, and Rachel Kerr. 2020. What Works? Creative Approaches to Transitional Justice in Bosnia and Herzegovina. *International Journal of Transitional Justice* 14 (1): 142–164.
Gade, Solveig. 2020. Forensic (Im)probabilities: Entering Schrödinger's Box with Rahib Mroué and Hito Steyerl. In *(W)archives: Archival Imaginaries, War, and Contemporary Art*, ed. Daniela Agostinho, Solveig Gade, Nanna Bonde Thylstrup and Kristin Veel, 365–385. Berlin: Sternberg Press.
Gafić, Ziyah. 2015. *Quest for Identity*. Millbrook: de.Mo Design.
Gafić, Ziyah. 2016. *Heartland*. Sarajevo: Connectum.
Gordon, Sophie. 2017. *Shadows of War: Roger Fenton's Photographs of the Crimea, 1855*. London: Royal Collection Trust.
Gustafsson, Hendrik. 2019. *Crime Scenery in Postwar Film and Photography*. Houndmills: Palgrave Macmillan.

Hariman, Robert, and John Louis Lucaites. 2007. *No Caption Needed: Iconic Photographs, Public Culture, and Liberal Democracy*. Chicago and London: The University of Chicago Press.

Haviv, Ron. 2020. Bosnia and Herzegovina Now. In *Imagine: Reflections on Peace*, ed. Constance Hale and Fiona Turner, 211–227. Paris: Hemeria.

Horn, Steve. 2005. *Pictures without Borders: Bosnia Revisited*. Stockport: Dewi Lewis in association with the Bosnian Institute.

Jestrovic, Silvija. 2013. *Performance, Space, Utopia: Cities of War, Cities of Exile*. Houndmills: Palgrave Macmillan.

Kebo, Ozren. 2016. Looking into a Radical Wasteland. In *Heartland*, ed. Ziyah Gafić, 84–93. Sarajevo: Connectum.

Kelsey, Robin and Blake Stimson. 2008. Introduction: Photography's Double Index (A Short History in Three Points). In *The Meaning of Photography*, ed. Robin Kelsey and Blake Stimson, vii–xxxi. Williamstown and New Haven and London: Sterling and Francine Clark Art Institute and Yale University Press.

Knight, Gary. 2020. Preface: Out of War. In *Imagine: Reflections on Peace*, ed. Constance Hale and Fiona Turner, 7–11. Paris: Hemeria.

Lange, Dorothea. 1982. *Photographs of a Lifetime. With an Essay by Robert Coles. Afterword by Therese Heyman*. New York: Aperture.

Linfield, Susie. 2010. *The Cruel Radiance: Photography and Political Violence*. Chicago and London: The University of Chicago Press.

Lisle, Debbie. 2011. The Surprising Detritus of Leisure: Encountering the Late Photography of War. *Environment and Planning D: Society and Space* 29: 873–890.

Lowe, Paul. 2014. The Forensic Turn: Bearing Witness and the 'Thingness' of the Photograph. In *The Violence of the Image: Photography and International Conflict*, ed. Liam Kennedy and Caitlin Patrick, 211–234. London and New York: I.B. Tauris.

Lowe, Paul. 2015. *Ožiljak (Scar). Field Study* 21.

Mac Ginty, Roger. 2014. Everyday Peace: Bottom-up and Local Agency in Conflict-Affected Societies. *Security Dialogue* 45 (6): 548–564.

Möller, Frank. 2012. Celebration and Concern: Digitization, Camera Phones and the Citizen-Photographer. In *Images in Mobile Communication: New Content, New Uses, New Perspectives*, ed. Corinne Martin and Thilo von Pape, 57–78. Wiesbaden: VS Research.

Möller, Frank. 2013. *Visual Peace: Images, Spectatorship, and the Politics of Violence*. Houndmills: Palgrave Macmillan.

Möller, Frank. 2017a. Witnessing Violence through Photography. *Global Discourse: An Interdisciplinary Journal of Current Affairs and Contemporary Thought* 7 (2–3): 264–281.

Möller, Frank. 2017b. From Aftermath to Peace: Reflections on a Photography of Peace. *Global Society: Journal of Interdisciplinary International Relations* 31 (3): 315–335.

Möller, Frank. 2019. *Peace Photography*. Houndmills: Palgrave Macmillan.

Morris, Errol. 2014. *Believing Is Seeing (Observations on the Mysteries of Photography)*. London: Penguin.

Morrison, Kenneth. 2016. *Sarajevo's Holiday Inn on the Frontline of Politics and War*. Houndmills: Palgrave Macmillan.

Morrison, Kenneth, and Paul Lowe. 2021. *Reporting the Siege of Sarajevo*. London: Bloomsbury Academic.

Oldfield, Pippa. 2019. *Photography and War*. London: Reaktion Books.

Palu, Louie. 2017. Image Control in the Age of Terror. In *Art as a Political Witness*, ed. Kia Lindroos and Frank Möller, 57–64. Opladen, Berlin, Toronto: Barbara Budrich Publishers.

Patrick, Caitlin. 2014. Ruins and Traces: *Exhibiting Conflict in Guy Tillim's Leopold and Mobutu*. In *The Violence of the Image: Photography and International Conflict*, ed. Liam Kennedy and Caitlin Patrick, 235–255. London and New York: I.B. Tauris.

Prosser, Jay, Geoffrey Batchen, Mick Gidley, and Nancy K. Miller, eds. 2012. *Picturing Atrocity: Photography in Crisis*. London: Reaktion Books.

Rancière, Jacques. 2009. *The Emancipated Spectator*, trans. Gregory Elliott. London and New York: Verso.

Reinhardt, Mark, Holly Edwards and Erina Duganne (eds.). 2007. *Beautiful Suffering: Photography and the Traffic in Pain*. Williamstown and Chicago: Williams College Museum of Art and The University of Chicago Press.

Ritchin, Fred. 2013. *Bending the Frame: Photojournalism, Documentary, and the Citizen*. New York: Aperture.

Roberts, John. 2014. *Photography and Its Violations*. New York: Columbia University Press.

Rosler, Martha. 2006. *3 Works*. Halifax: The Press of the Nova Scotia College of Art and Design.

Sacco, Joe. 2012. *Journalism*. London: Jonathan Cape.

Sánchez, Gervasio. 2011. *desaparecidos—Disappeared*. Barcelona: Blume.

Sheringham, Michael. 2006. *Everyday Life: Theories and Practices from Surrealism to the Present*. Oxford: Oxford University Press.

Sliwinski, Sharon. 2011. *Human Rights in Camera. Foreword by Lunn Hunt*. Chicago and London: The University of Chicago Press.

Solomon-Godeau, Abigail. 1991. *Photography at the Dock: Essays on Photographic History, Institutions, and Practices. Foreword by Linda Nochlin*. Minneapolis: University of Minnesota Press.

Sontag, Susan. 1979. *On Photography*. London: Penguin.

Sontag, Susan. 2003. *Regarding the Pain of Others*. New York: Farrar, Straus & Giroux.

Stover, Eric and Gilles Peress. 1998. *The Graves: Srebrenica and Vukovar*. Zurich: Scalo.

Telios, Thomas, Dieter Thomä, and Ulrich Schmid. 2020. Preface. In *The Russian Revolution as Ideal and Practice: Failures, Legacies, and the Future of Revolution*, ed. Thomas Telios, Dieter Thomä, and Ulrich Schmid, 1–16. Houndmills: Palgrave Macmillan.

Terry, Sara. 2005. *Aftermath: Bosnia's Long Road to Peace*. New York: Channel Photographics.

Terry, Sara and Teun van der Heijden. 2018. *War Is Only Half the Story: Ten Years of The Aftermath Project*. Stockport: Dewi Lewis.

Tucker, Anne Wilkes and Will Michels with Natalie Zelt. 2012. *War/Photography: Images of Armed Conflict and Its Aftermath*. Houston: The Museum of Fine Arts.

Wallis, Brian. 2010. Recovering the Mexican Suitcase. In *The Mexican Suitcase: The Rediscovered Spanish Civil War Negatives of Capa, Chim, and Taro, Vol. 1: The History*, ed. Cynthia Young, 13–17. New York: International Center of Photography/Göttingen: Steidl.

Walsh, Lauren. 2019. *Conversations on Conflict Photography*. London and New York: Bloomsbury.

Watney, Simon. 1982. Making Strange: The Shattered Mirror. In *Thinking Photography*, ed. Victor Burgin, 154–176. Houndmills and London: Macmillan.

Williams, Val. 2015. What Happened Here: A Photographer in Sarajevo 1992–1996. *Field Study* 21: 2–3.

CHAPTER 5

Visual Ambiguities: Controlling the Meaning of Images in a Digital and Interactive World

INTRODUCTION

In earlier chapters, we established that systems of human interaction are complex, that complex systems are ambiguous and that there are different ways to respond to ambiguity. We prefer responses based on tolerance of ambiguity (TA) because they reflect the complexity and messiness of the international system, including peace and conflict dynamics, better than responses based on disambiguation. Images can illustrate this messiness and, by so doing, enlarge spaces of possibility. However, textual explanations (especially in photojournalism) often limit these spaces. Photojournalism, thus, is an exercise in disambiguation. As we are interested in approaches to peace and conflict based on TA, we have sketched in the preceding chapter selected new photographies that emerged in response to the situation in Bosnia and Herzegovina in the 1990s and the crisis of photojournalism and that emancipated photography, even documentary photography, from the conventions of photojournalism. Some of the new photographies follow poststructuralist thinking and embrace ambiguities (aftermath photography, e.g.), while others, reflecting positivist thinking in one way or another, do not (forensic photography, e.g.).

© The Author(s), under exclusive license to Springer Nature Switzerland AG 2023
R. Bellmer and F. Möller, *Peace, Complexity, Visuality*, Rethinking Peace and Conflict Studies,
https://doi.org/10.1007/978-3-031-38218-5_5

In Chapter 2, we introduced the term *photocomplexity* not only because complexity includes visual experience but also because the visual experience is, in itself, complex. Furthermore, the relationship between an image and that which it depicts is complex just as is the relationship between words and images, addressed differently in different genres of image production. It is a corollary of visual complexity that different people interpret the same image differently. Very often, they have good reasons for so doing although they are not always aware of them—reasons reflecting their visual socialization and viewing experience as well as their embeddedness in specific political, social and cultural configurations. Some readers respond primarily to an image's visual ingredients, others to its textual elements and others, again, to both without necessarily being capable of distinguishing the one from the other. Every image is a composite of different ingredients, and how these ingredients relate to one another and operate on observers is never easy to say. Complexity theory helps us identify different layers of visual/textual complexity and serves as a frame of reference and a way of thinking about images. Furthermore, it helps us understand that visual culture is linked to the real world in the sense that meanings assigned to an image and meaning-making processes have real consequences in this world if the resulting meaning is shared by a significant number of people. To think about the relationship between images and the real in this way is more fruitful than trying to explicate the real-ness of visual representation, as is often done in discourses revolving around notions of truth and truthfulness.[1]

In Chapter 3, we used the term *photoambiguity* to refer to images' inherent ambiguities and to the surplus of meaning that all images carry with them. We suspect that these characteristics may help us to think and act better in a world saturated with both ambiguities and images, a world in which complexity and ambiguity appear visually and politics are visualized on the basis of what can be seen. Thus, we have to reverse processes of disambiguation that can frequently be observed in photojournalism and political image interpretation. Luckily, such disambiguation does not reflect an image's inherent characteristics; instead, it proceeds by ignoring these characteristics. It is a logical consequence that if we want to utilize images to build TA, we have to rediscover their plurality of meanings,

---

[1] Such discourses are not identical with discourses on the *politics* of truth which can be explored critically in visual approaches in the vein of "investigative aesthetics" (see Fuller and Weizman 2021).

defend images from one-dimensional designations of meaning and reinvigorate their ambiguities, thus inevitably complexifying viewing patterns and challenging control of meaning, which seems to be at the core of many image interpretations. What we mean by control of meaning and how it can be challenged will be explored in this chapter.

As the sociology of knowledge has shown, "knowledge must always be knowledge from a certain position" (Berger and Luckmann 1966: 22), not only (quite inevitably) reflecting but also supporting and strengthening—or at least aiming to support and strengthen—this position. Knowledge production derived from images is no exception, including "processes in the course of which that which is socially constructed is believed to be"—and, in a sense, *becomes*—"objectively true" (Möller 2019: 84). Ideology, Raymond Williams notes, becomes hegemony if the "expression of the interests of a ruling class" is accepted "as 'normal reality' or 'commonsense' by those in practice subordinated to it" (1976: 145). Hegemony—the conflation of the interests of the ruling class and normal reality—works as much through visual as through other forms of representation. It is a reasonable assumption that, in a world "hypersaturated with images" (Sontag 2003: 105), hegemony works more through visual than through other forms of representation.

Whether or not critics "like photographs, or the act of looking at them" (Linfield 2010: 5)—which, according to Susie Linfield (2010: 5), they do not—is politically irrelevant if we follow Jacques Rancière's assessment that images, rather than with critical intent, are often "employed in the official system of information" (2009: 95). Analyzing the operation of visual images within such a system is a political and a critical act, if by 'critical' we mean more than "the mere recognition of established opinion or the extrapolation from established versions of facticity" (Shapiro 2015: 10). After all, this system of information and its representatives decide what we, as spectators, see: not only do they select the images that we see (in contrast to the huge number of images that we are not exposed to) but they also regularly tell us and explain what we see, thus determining spaces of possibility derived from, and legitimized with reference to, the visual. This system of information works by "selecting the speaking and reasoning beings who are capable of 'deciphering' the flow of information about anonymous multitudes" (Rancière 2009: 96), thus reducing the act of looking to passive and unreflective as well as uncritical and unpolitical consumption. Against such consumption we need, among other things, time to analyze images; we need the courage to call into question the ostensible expertise of image interpreters who often claim to be, while hardly ever in fact being, neutral observers (occasionally with little democratic accountability); we have to distinguish what an image is *said* and "*supposed* to generate" from what it is "*capable* of generating" (Möller 2019: 85; italics in original); we have to increase our own space of interpretation by not blindly following what others say we see; and we have to be aware and critical of what Ekkehard Krippendorff (2000: 91) calls *Herrschaftswissen*—knowledge in the service of power and domination which can be produced by many means including visual ones. In short, we have to radicalize visual analysis. Whether or not we like photographs does not really matter. It helps, however, because spending time with something you like is easier and more rewarding than spending time with something you do not like.

Control of Meaning

Visuality poses conundrums that are hard to solve. A selection:

> There is "tension … between the little a photograph reveals and all that it promises to reveal but cannot" (Hirsch 1997: 119).

> We cannot address images on their own terms because "'language' (in some form) usually enters the experience of viewing photography or of viewing anything else" (Mitchell 1994: 282). The use of the word "usually," however, implies that this is not always the case: viewing may be possible without recourse to language.

> Although a "verbal representation cannot represent … its object in the same way a visual representation can" (Mitchell 1994: 152), we regularly translate images into words, thus inevitably missing some ingredients of the object we want to describe.

> For photographers, at least fine art photographers, "[w]ords are proof that the vision they had is not, in the opinion of some at least, fully there in the picture" (Adams 1994: 33). Words thus testify to the failure of the photographer *as* a photographer, the photograph *as* a photograph. Or, in the words of actor Christoph Waltz: "If it

[the actor's part; the authors] requires explanation, you have to ask yourself a few questions."[2]

There is "a sense of unease and even danger" as regards the visual because it is "too open to misinterpretation" while at the same time being "too seductive" (MacDougall 1998: 68).

"As photographs bring more into view, they also reinforce the invisibility of some things by overtly focusing on others" (Smith 2013: 14). Visibility and invisibility are not opposites but condition each other.

We use images to remember. "But photographs of people I know and love are actually a poison to memory, because they remain strong while my memories weaken" (Elkins 2011: 114–115). In the absence of photographs, however, our memories weaken as well so don't blame the photographs.

"The problem is not that people remember through photographs, but that they remember only the photographs" (Sontag 2003: 89). For people who have nothing else by which to remember the people they knew and loved, however, photographs are not a problem but a blessing.

"A picture is what it is … It wouldn't make any sense to explain them. Kind of diminishes them … I mean, they're right there, whatever they are" (William Eggleston).[3]

Rather than solving these (and other) conundrums inherent in visual representation, we want to engage them in order to explore the question of how visual images can contribute to TA. This is, in itself, an exercise in TA: we do not insist on one specific way of understanding and approaching the operation of images but accept and welcome the coexistence of different permissible approaches. We regard conversations among them as important and fruitful if we want to take advantage of all the possibilities images offer (e.g., to increase TA in a political context).

[2] https://www.theguardian.com/film/2023/apr/27/christoph-waltz-my-only-regret-is-that-i-didnt-attack-nigel-farage-enough (accessed 27 April 2023).

[3] https://www.theguardian.com/artanddesign/2004/jul/25/photography1 (accessed 13 January 2023).

Likewise, we wish to capitalize on narrative openness and the plurality of meanings that images carry with them to instigate conversation not only about images but also about peace and conflict dynamics and power constellations in the international system as they appear visually. To this end, we have to endure that there are many things we either do not know or cannot say with one hundred percent certainty; the visual cannot give us assurance. Photographic genres such as aftermath photography (as discussed in the preceding chapter) capitalize on such a lack of assurance to nudge viewers into critical reflection on both their own habits of seeing and the relationship between these habits and others' habits of seeing.

For example, we might be able to describe how a given image affects us, but we have no way of knowing how it affects you; simply assuming that it affects you in the same way it affects us would not only be arrogant but also pure conjecture, ignoring that how a person interprets an image cannot be separated from the self of that person (see Chapter 3). Pretending to speak in the name of 'spectators,' 'the audience' or 'people' without offering evidence that a significant group of people indeed shares our interpretation would mean conflating textual analysis and social analysis (see Couldry 2000: 76–77). Regarding images, even judgment informed by the history and theory of visual culture and image production (documented in abundance; see, e.g., Wells 2003; Kelsey and Stimson 2008; Kromm and Benforado Bakewell 2010; Emerling 2012) may lead to different and equally compelling analyses. This makes generalization so difficult and the search for it—for example, for a generally applicable definition of the relationship between words and images—almost pointless. To be sure, such a search is business as usual in the social sciences because the alternative—living in a kind of definitional limbo, exposed to tension between different points of view without being capable of resolving it—is not only unusual but also hard to endure. It is a part of photoambiguity.

The Eggleston quote above illustrates this well and serves as a good starting point for discussion. Eggleston argues that written or verbal explanations diminish images (see Möller 2013: 31–32): they take something away from them rather than adding something, as is regularly argued in the literature. This is a perfectly legitimate position, but as we will see below, it is not the only legitimate position. In the article from which the above quote was taken, Eggleston also says:

> I've never noticed that it helps to talk about them [individual photographs; the authors], or answer specific questions about them, much less volunteer

information in words ... People always want to know when something was taken, where it was taken, and, God knows, why it was taken. It gets really ridiculous.

Like Robert Adams in the above quotation, Eggleston suggests assigning value to the image and appreciating it as image. "Editorial photography," on the other hand, treats images often as mere "illustration of preexisting ideas" (Ritchin 1999: 26), as a supplement to text, and photo editors are said to represent "a medium which is almost everywhere considered secondary to the text" (Ritchin 1999: 99). Such an understanding—images merely illustrating text—would diminish images, treat them as accessory to text and establish a hierarchy in which text, while benefiting from images, would appear superior to them. This position, too, is legitimate; it reflects what W. J. T. Mitchell calls "an ancient tradition ... which argues that language is the essential human attribute: 'man' is the 'speaking animal.'" In this tradition, the image appears as "the medium of the subhuman, the savage, the 'dumb' animal, the child, the woman, the masses" (1994: 24). And while we hope that currently no one would strictly adhere to this tradition—it can, however, still occasionally be encountered in disparaging comments on comics and graphic novels—we also suspect that suspicion about images does linger on in many visual and verbal discourses. Furthermore, constructing words versus images is part of an equally powerful tradition that sees the world in binaries—exercises in disambiguation.

Many commentators and image producers would refrain from constructing the word–image relationship in such dichotomous and hierarchical terms and instead argue that images accompany words (see Palu 2017: 59). This could indicate many things. In a rather refined approach, Peter Gilgen, for example, addresses the word–image relationship in what he calls picture magazines in terms of "an intellectual stereoscopic effect: the image gains in profile through the verbal information conveyed in the caption; from the accompanying image this information gains persuasive power" (2003: 56). While the effect is mutually supportive—Gilgen also uses the term "integration" to describe the operation of photograph and caption—the caption nevertheless strengthens the image's profile, while images merely accompany the caption's information. According to photographer Ben Curtis (in Morris 2014: 193), information conveyed in the caption "makes the picture more powerful," and Linfield (2010:

217–218) seems to be of the same opinion when criticizing photographer James Nachtwey for presenting photographs without captions. This position would then seem to be the opposite of diminishment, in terms of which Eggleston discusses the impact of words on images (see above). Rather than diminishing them, words strengthen images and make them more powerful.

The term "accompanying" might also merely indicate that words and images are somehow in association with each other, that the one cannot be thought of without the other but that the precise nature of this association is hard to establish. This is one possible understanding of "accompanying" (while "He will be *accompanying* her on the piano" leaves little doubt as to who is seen as the more important person).[4] In such a case, empirical analysis would have to clarify the precise appearance of such an association in specific cases and among specific audiences. Without necessarily implying that one is subordinate to the other, thus assuming a hierarchical relationship, there may still be a difference in terms of initiative or agency: if B (e.g., an image or a piano player) is said to accompany A (e.g., a newspaper article or a vocalist), then B can be expected to exhibit less agency than A, which is another way of saying that A conditions B stronger than the other way round (while B also influences A, only weaker).

Not every use of the term "accompanying," then, would demote images; some can be read vaguely as "being in association with" each other; others may indicate a mutually supportive relationship. However, no matter how we address the word–image relationship, images find it difficult to escape words. Even if we approach or contextualize images visually, such an approach presupposes the use of language: it is through language that we think about how to address images visually. Thus, a neat separation of images from words is as impossible as is a categorical definition of the word–image relationship. Images and words are somehow always in association with each other, and this is as close as we can get to an understanding of this relationship without unduly simplifying it. Indeed, from our complexity point of view, more important than trying to establish the 'correct' relationship between words and images, generalizable over time and across cases, is acknowledgment of its inherent vagueness or, in a better term, its ambiguity (referring to the coexistence

---

[4] See https://www.merriam-webster.com/dictionary/accompany (accessed 14 January 2023).

of many permissible understandings rather than mere underspecificity). We sketched some of these understandings above; many more could be added. Vagueness or ambiguity can help us open the door to the possibility of using images for the purpose of enhancing TA rather than serving disambiguation which inevitably happens when we try to fix the meaning of an image or categorically define the connection between images and words or images and anything else.

The above discussion may reveal merely different approaches to the word–image relationship in different genres of image production, all of which are permissible in the context in which they appear. However, we suspect that it is also indicative of something else, namely, a position that, while trying to erase images' inherent ambiguities, is in itself ambiguous. Western commentators' worries about images' ambiguities and the plurality of meanings they carry with them coexist with fascination bordering upon obsession with images—but only on the condition that it is possible to stabilize the "instability of meaning" (Rubinstein 2010: 199) that visual images possess.[5] Such stabilization, however, is impossible because "[w]hatever its [a photograph's; the authors] 'obvious' meaning ... there is too much *excess* meaning and, as distinct from written description, too many unintended sites of connotation" (MacDougall 1998: 68; italics in original). In another manifestation of photoambiguity, then, the photograph is both "too seductive" and "too engaging, for it draws the viewer into an interpretive relationship that bypasses professional mediation" (MacDougall 1998: 68) thus undermining the traditional role of professional mediators—the "speaking and reasoning beings who are capable of 'deciphering' the flow of information" (Rancière 2009: 96) referred to above—and assigning to the viewer a high degree of codetermination, even co-authorship. Skepticism of images, therefore, joins hands with skepticism of viewers and their capability, when confronted with many possible interpretations of an image, of reading the image as intended by the image-maker and as connoted by the conditions shown in it.

However, even captions won't really help. As Susan Sontag notes, "the plurality of meanings that every photograph carries" will ultimately undermine the argument presented in the caption (1979: 109)

---

[5] Note that we use the terms "plurality of meanings," "surplus of meaning," "excess meaning" and "instability of meaning" interchangeably although they might mean slightly different things in the source texts.

and destabilize the meaning that the text tried to establish. Photographic meaning constructed through texts is always only temporary, waiting for its replacement; it is mandatory only until another meaning gains the discursive upper hand. This can even be said about archival images, seemingly fixed and unmovable but waiting for the rediscovery of hidden and marginalized meanings outside the archive (see Roberts 2014: 114–115). According to Sontag (2003: 29), "one day captions will be needed, of course" to prevent "misreadings" and "misrememberings" of photographs that were initially presented without captions because viewers, at the time of publishing, could be assumed to know anyway what they were looking at.[6] Captions, however, will always have to compete with the power of the image, which cannot be reduced to the textually prescribed meaning. Indeed, in light of images' plurality of meanings, the very idea of *mis*reading images appears problematic, as there is no objective standard with which to establish an image's 'correct' meaning.

And then there are those authors who claim that images do not have any meaning at all that could be fixed by means of language. In the words of the filmmaker and photographer Wim Wenders: In contrast to words,

> there is no accord whatsoever on what images mean. They don't 'mean', to begin with! They 'imply', 'suggest', 'hint' or whatever ... You can right away start a new conflict when you want to 'define' what images really mean. (in Wenders and Zournazi 2013: 38)

Attempting to tame an image's plurality of meanings by textual means or insisting on the existence of meaning despite its absence amount to reducing the image to what can be said about it, addressing it in terms other than its own and, ultimately, erasing from the image that which constitutes it as an image. Such an attempt is bound to failure: captions may invite a certain interpretation of an image, but they cannot erase all the other meanings and connotations that the image carries with it, some of which can be articulated by means of words while others cannot (see Chapter 12). These meanings are still there in the image, waiting for

---

[6] Sontag refers to the exhibition *Here Is New York*, staged in Manhattan immediately after the attacks on the World Trade Center on 11 September 2001, and assumes that visitors "had, if anything, a surfeit of understanding of what they were looking at" (2003: 29). The book documenting the exhibition, published in 2002, while revealing the photographers, does not include captions, thus inviting readers to construct their own narratives—either based on individual photographs or by combining images (see George and Peress 2002).

rediscovery and articulation. Acknowledging both that "pictures alone cannot make for us the discriminations that we might like to make" (Hirsch 1997: 71) and that captions only *appear* to remedy the problem amounts to a loss of control—of the image, its meaning and its operation in society. This is not good news for those who wish to "purposefully misuse[]" photographs' alleged objectivity and "perceived credibility ... to manipulate the public ... for political and commercial goals" (Ritchin 2009: 19), but it is not good news for those who wish to use photographs for democratic or emancipatory purposes, either. Regardless of the goal you want to achieve (commercial, political or otherwise), you can always be challenged on visual grounds; the meaning you assign to an image can always be identified as only one meaning among many permissible others.

However, how can you lose control of meaning if you did not possess it in the first place? How can you lose something, the possession of which has always been an illusion? And would such a loss necessarily be a problem for those who wish to use images for political purposes? After all, images' "potential for political agency ... depends on the possibility of a multitude of interpretations, ambiguities and differences" (Rubinstein and Sluis 2013: 154). Following this line of thought, to "start a new conflict" (Wenders) when trying to define what an image means would not be problematic, either, unless conflict is reduced to its destructive potentialities thus ignoring its potentially constructive contribution to the improvement of relations within and among social groups, as elaborated in the sociological and anthropological conflict literature (see Coser 1956; Fry 2007). If we want to understand a complex world, then we have to appreciate and reinvigorate images' ambiguities and complexify viewing patterns. We have to engage critically with Western societies' penchant for disambiguation—their proclivity for such seemingly world-ordering but ultimately inadequate binaries as we versus them, good versus evil, rights versus wrong, words versus images and so on—to order the world in such a way that it (bene)fits Western interests and prescribe this order to others. This practice reflects Western epistemology where reality is, and has to appear, consistent; realities are "more serious [than dreams and art; the authors]. They demand singularity"—in contrast to "non-coherent multiplicities"—"and singularity demands experts, a single point of view. Non-coherent realities disappear into art, or the realm of the personal" (Law 2004: 98). The resulting practice of disambiguation undermines images' capability of illustrating available spaces of possibility and by doing so helping viewers cope with an ambiguous world.[7]

If we want to use visual images to increase TA, then we are neither interested in identifying *the* meaning of an image nor in establishing a hierarchy of possible meanings derived from different degrees of plausibility reflecting the social position of the person who tries to establish such a hierarchy. Likewise, we are not trying to fix the word–image relationship. Instead, from the beginning of our encounter with an image, we respect ambiguities and ambivalences, gaps and omissions, the obvious and the less obvious, the general and the peripheral, the visible and the invisible, and the actual and the potential. This, we would like to show in what follows, is exactly what digitization invites—and expects—us to do.

Digitization and Interaction

We can summarize digitization's most important dimensions in our context as follows: digitization increases ambiguity, invites interaction and exacerbates control of meaning. It does so among other things by "creating discrete and malleable records of the visible that can and will be linked, transmitted, recontextualized, and fabricated" (Ritchin 2009: 141). While digitization affects all forms of image-making, not all image-makers appreciate it equally. For example, forensic photographers, bearing witness to atrocities, can be expected to be much more skeptical about digitization than aftermath photographers interested in visual ambiguities or peace photographers aiming at visualizing a plurality of paths to peace. Digitization adds potential to actual images and multiplies the actual image, thus undermining visual images' function as stable reference points in visual-discursive constructions of reality and rendering difficult identification of an image's author. As we noted in Chapter 2, if you mention *The Falling Soldier*, visually educated people of a certain generation will recognize this image and remember (i.e., recall from their pictorial memory) what it looks like. Meanings assigned to this image changed over time, reflecting, for example, questions pertaining to its authenticity and the photographer's responsibility for what can be seen in the picture

---

[7] We do not want to imply that *only* Western societies apply strategies of disambiguation. However, presenting our argument firmly within Western discursive constructions, we do not wish to make uninformed and unreferenced claims about non-Western politics and societies.

(see Whelan 2007; Susperregui 2016). The image, however, remained the same. Audience interaction was limited to discussing meaning and responsibility rather than altering visual contents (save for artistic appropriations). If you mention Roger Fenton or Robert Capa, Nick Ut, Eddie Adams, Don McCullin or Susan Meiselas, to name but a few of the most famous war and conflict photographers, then many people with an interest in the history of photojournalism will immediately reactivate one or more images stored in their pictorial memory. Or take the following description of another iconic image from the history of photojournalism:

> The little girl is naked, running right toward you, looking right at you, crying out. The burns themselves are not visible, and it is her pain – more precisely, her communicating the pain she feels – that is the central feature of the picture. Pain is the primary fact of her experience, just as she is the central figure in the composition.

Robert Hariman and John Louis Lucaites (2010: 175) are no doubt describing Nick Ut's *Accidental Napalm*, one of the most often reproduced photographic representations of the Vietnam War. They show that this photograph is not only one of the most famous pictures documenting the horrors of war—not only the horrors of this specific war but also the horrors of war in general—but also one of the most copied pictures, adapted to the political and commercial contexts within which it appeared. The original, however, remained the same, immediately recognizable, no matter how many artists tampered with it and in how many different contexts it was shown (Hariman and Lucaites 2010: 171–207). Thus, meanings assigned to this photograph changed; over time, "the image has accrued layers of (mis)interpretation" (Oldfield 2019: 36). The photograph itself, however, did not change.[8] It remains a stable visual reference point determining spaces of possibility. Like every photographic icon, it "make[s] some beliefs and actions more intelligible, probable, and appealing, and others less so" (Hariman and Lucaites 2010: 8).

It has often been noted in the context of photography and memory that photographs serve as stable visual reference points.

---

[8] With regard to this particular image, the terms "the original" and "the photograph itself" are problematic as we will show in Chapter 11 when discussing this photograph.

> The more often I look at a photograph of someone I loved who is no longer alive, the more my own faltering memory tries to accommodate itself to the unchanging image (which remains insistently itself, obstinately particular and stubbornly slightly different than what I had recalled),

James Elkins (2011: 115) writes. This process of accommodation continues

> until my memory is nothing but a tattered shadow clinging to the photograph, pretending to be the very face in the photograph, which it never was, clinging and growing weaker, until it disappears entirely. (p. 115)

Photographs replace—and become—memories. The original memories disappear or at least weaken anyway, but photographs arguably accelerate this process by offering stable visual reference points to which memory can adapt. According to Susan Sontag (2003: 89), "remembering through photographs eclipses other forms of understanding, and remembering" but, as we noted above, for people who have nothing else by which to remember the people they loved and whose original memories are fading—like most memories do—photographs are a blessing, not a problem. Photographer Steve Horn writes about this experience in the context of his return journey to Bosnia (2005: 8):

> I was also driven by my instinct to share the earlier pictures with people who had been cut off from their past. I had photographed a group of children playing high up on a hill in the historic Bosnian town of Jajce. On my return I found two of those children, now adults with families of their own. The photographs became their only childhood pictures. I began to see that the deepest significance of the trip was in bringing pictures back to Bosnia, not taking new ones away.

Or elsewhere: "Together we witnessed the power of photographs to connect, in a place where so many reminders of the past had been destroyed" (Horn 2005: 107). Similar to Horn, photographer Gilles Peress observes that for most families returning to Sarajevo at the end of the siege, "the only traces of the past were images. Images were everywhere, littering the floor inside homes, in the street, family images to be caressed, political images to be torn, private and public memories of times now gone."[9]

Now imagine a situation characterized by the absence of stable visual reference points—a situation where memories are fading until they disappear altogether and images are changing; a situation where images are not only changing but are also *meant* to change; and a situation in which images are not only meant to change (while the original remains the same, unaltered) but where there is no longer an original that could serve as a stable visual reference point both for our memories and for all the image alterations and appropriations built upon the original image. In other words, imagine digitization. Martin Lister (2013: 8) explains that

> it is in the nature of digital networked images to exist in a number of states that are potential rather than actual in a fixed and physical kind of way. Such images are fugitive and transient, they come and they go, they may endure for only short periods of time and in different places, maybe many places simultaneously.

"Digital media," Fred Ritchin (2009: 17) adds, "translate everything into data, waiting for an author or an audience (or a machine) to reconstitute it." He continues by saying that "the digital photograph can be conceived of as a meta-image, a map of squares, each capable of being individually modified and, on the screen, able to serve as a pathway elsewhere" (p. 141). This notion of images as meta-images cannot easily be reconciled with the traditional understanding of images as stable reference points. Indeed, the changes inflicted upon visual representation through digitization are substantial:

> Rather than being fixed and given, digital images are both elusive and ephemeral – they exist in different states simultaneously and successively. Single, identifiable creators morph into networks of actors, including anonymous ones. Neither networks nor actors can be easily or completely controlled, even by powerful agents such as states or international tech companies. Seemingly finite processes of image-production resulting in a "final" image (that, after completion, is available for analysis) are transformed into infinite processes where users engage with existing visual material. (Möller et al. 2021: 3)

---

[9] https://archive.nytimes.com/www.nytimes.com/specials/bosnia/suburbs/grbavica/transition/grbavica_first_day.html (see also Part III).

Thus, "we are not dealing with mere variations in image making that could be addressed by mere variations in theory" (Möller and Bellmer 2023: 7) à la digitizing Benjamin, Barthes, Sontag and so on. We are not dealing with mere variations in the extent to which images and their meanings can be controlled, either. In the digital age, the very idea of control of meaning—fixing *the* meaning of an image—is anachronistic and attempts at regaining such control are bound to failure. In addition, digital images are always in the process of becoming; they are always emerging, constantly changing. Questions pertaining to authorship—individual image-makers, networks or machines—are increasingly difficult to answer. Furthermore, digital images always exist, at least potentially, in more than one state; they not only wait for but actively invite engagement (often, their very purpose is engagement), and their capability of serving as stable reference points in a complex, ambiguous and constantly changing world decreases.

Reflecting these changes, Ritchin concluded a number of years ago that the "introduction of digital photography, noted for its nearly effortless malleability, provides a propitious moment to ask whether this [photography's; the authors] evidentiary role can and should be retained, or even expanded" (2009: 19). Some responses to this question should not surprise us. Demands for disambiguation are never far away, equating digital images' malleability with, and mistaking it for, mere propaganda or misinformation rather than understanding it as an integral component of digitization regardless of the image-maker's intentions. Such demands follow the conventional conviction that 'we inform' while 'others misinform.'[10] Such recourse to yet another binary—information ('we') versus misinformation ('they')—tries to superimpose some order on what seems to be increasingly confusing and out of order, aiming to reestablish discursive and, consequently, political high ground.[11] It is politically understandable and has real consequences, but it is also sadly predictable and incredibly unimaginative.

One key to understanding the social functions of digitization is interaction. Among the more promising approaches to digitization in our

---

[10] Of course, we are not saying that digital images are not manipulated for political purposes. The history of photography is a history of photo manipulation and digital photography is no exception. However, digital photography cannot be limited to manipulation and misinformation without totally missing what it is about.

[11] Remember our insistence, in chapter three, on *permissible* interpretations. We acknowledge the possibility of, and the need to resist, deliberate misinformation. Therefore, we ask for interpretive frames within which tolerance of ambiguity can be performed *legitimately*.

context, then, are those that understand that interaction helps us to take advantage of all possibilities that ambiguity offers. Such approaches respect that all images are ambiguous, carrying with them a plurality of meanings—no matter how they have been produced, regardless of the social and cultural configurations in which they operate, and irrespective of the genre to which they are assigned. Appreciating images' ambiguities in art photography (TA) while rejecting them in photojournalism (disambiguation), for example, not only restricts the possibilities of photojournalism, which we will explore in Part III but also assigns to photojournalism a task that no image can achieve, namely, showing things *as they really are*. The image "is not a mere reproduction of what is out there in front of the photographer or the filmmaker," Rancière explains and continues by saying that the image "is always an alteration that occurs in a chain of images which alter it in turn" (2009: 93–94). Approaches to digitization revolving around interaction also understand that digitization invites us to engage with ambiguities actively and constructively (TA) instead of reverting to disambiguation. Digitization, thus, expects audience interaction with digitally produced images (or with analog images digitally transformed into data). It not only invites and enables interaction—which had been possible prior to digitization as well, albeit on a smaller scale (see Bennett 2012: 54); it comes to fruition *only* if audiences do engage with it in fact.

Instead of "situat[ing] knowledge in the object" and expecting audiences merely to identify "what the creator intended," pausing in front of the artwork in awe of the artist's genius, as traditional art worlds are said to have operated (Sutherland and Acord 2007: 127), digitization enables and expects audiences to become creators themselves, adding layers of meaning to an existing artwork by changing its visual contents. Identifying the intended meaning of an object may still be a part of the encounter with the image, but it is accompanied by adding new meanings and new contents reflecting the experience and socialization of the observer. Since digitization transforms everything into data, adding content, thus developing the original object further in light of the interactor's skills, interest and experience, is easier than ever before (and raises numerous legal and copyright issues that we cannot address here). In the process, the original object may even disappear altogether. What the creator of the original wanted to say and show joins hands with what the user wants to show and say. It may be challenged and altered or confirmed and strengthened. In any case, the intentions of the creator of the original communicate implicitly or explicitly with the intentions of the interactor. Combined, both create a new work that cannot be anticipated; its component parts cannot be neatly dissected and subsequently reassembled, either. It cannot be grasped in terms of change of meaning: the artwork itself changes. The new work serves, again, merely as a starting point for further alterations and more changes in a potentially infinite process. This process renders obsolete the notion of *the* meaning of *the* image, the idea that such meaning can be controlled, and also the separation of artists from spectators.

None of the above has anything to do with the notion of qualitative improvement, which is why we referred above to the *social* functions of digitization. As long as we stick to the established—yet always emerging—conventions of what qualifies as a good painting or a great photograph, you cannot improve a Rembrandt painting by taking a photograph of it and then altering the photograph digitally; you cannot improve a Cartier-Bresson or Salgado photograph, either. And while you may be able to improve the quality of a digitally or AI-produced image, the issue here is primarily one of transforming viewing into an essentially political act of interrogating the politics of image-making, dissemination and interpretation. Accepting the existence of ambiguities and explicitly leveraging them—creating new ambiguities by adding or removing visual contents—will produce new spaces of possibility within which we can think about ambiguity, difference of perspective and, ultimately, politics and society.

All of the above undermines the notion of images as stable reference points, the meaning of which can be fixed, and invites interpretation of images as starting points for image creation, image alteration and political communication. The role of artists thus understood is "to construct aesthetic systems of mediation, affording experience" (Sutherland and Acord 2007: 135). Such an "exercise in political democracy" (Sutherland and Acord 2007: 135) can be observed in artistic and aesthetic image-making in all sorts of participatory and performance art, although occasionally audiences, rather than becoming democratic co-artists, function merely as the artist's accessory or vicarious agents (see Bishop 2012). It is, of course, a big step from open artistic narratives in participatory art capitalizing on the technical possibilities of digitization to image-making in the context of photojournalism with its strong, albeit partially mythical, connection to facts and truth. Before exploring this context in Part III, we will briefly and schematically sketch different modes of interaction with which audiences become involved in the production processes of images subdivided, following Audrey Bennett (2012), into passive and active modes of interaction.

Everything—passive as well as active interaction—"starts with the sense of sight" (Bennett 2012: 54). Without the sense of sight, there is no interaction. (Theoretically, however, interaction could, e.g., also start with the sense of touch or smell when the interactor touches or smells a painting or a photograph and by doing so interacts non-visually with it and that which it depicts—forms of interaction hardly to be recommended in museum contexts and totally pointless when the encounter with the image takes place on the computer screen.)[12] The one-way passive mode of interaction begins and ends with the sense of sight: it "is unisensory in that it relies only on the sense of sight for interpretation to occur" (p. 54). In the two-way passive mode of interaction, the user interprets an image through her sense of sight but also mobilizes "additional sensory interaction" (p. 55) to intensify the experience of the image and activate the information contained in it. In such a case, the image includes "the option to use other senses to experience it" (p. 55), but it is the user's decision whether or not she will use this option. For example, she can, but does not necessarily have to, call a telephone number or scan a code included in the image to receive more information. The passive mode of interaction becomes active once the unisensory visual experience is replaced by a multisensory one.

Thus, in the one-way active mode of interaction, the user, after having started the interaction with her sense of sight, "use[s] other senses, like her sense of touch, to interpret the image and complete the communication transaction" (p. 62). Zooming in or out by means of a computer mouse is one option. In the two-way active mode of interaction, the communication transaction goes beyond viewing and includes changing: "the user looks at the image to begin the process of interaction; however, she uses one or more of her other senses to modify the content and form and complete the process of interpretation" (p. 63). We have described this process already above in terms of changing visual contents by adding something to an image or removing something from it; a simple procedure in the digital environment but one that is anathema in photojournalism (see Chapter 11). In the three-way active mode of interaction, finally, the communication transaction goes beyond viewing

---

[12] The experience of touching a print of an analog photograph and feeling the aging process of the material reflects the aging process of memories thus counteracting Elkins's observation, quoted above, that memories weaken while photographs remain the same.

and modifying and includes sharing the modified image with others—a process that Bennett considers optional (p. 65) but that, we think, is essential because it distinguishes a two-way from a three-way mode of interaction. In addition, it adequately reflects one of the features of digitization, i.e., its open-endedness referred to above in terms of a potentially infinite process of image alteration involving many viewers on social media.

Interaction, as Bennett understands it, refers to "an image that engages the user in a visual, physical or other sensory 'give and/or take' exchange of information; a dialogue, so to speak" (p. 54). One might ask: can images be thought of *without* interaction, and can (should) interaction be limited to the exchange of *information*? After all, even the most passive spectators nevertheless use their sense of sight to engage in the act of looking and might be affected emotionally even without obtaining any information from the encounter with the image. While "images have always been interactive" (p. 54), digitization offers new possibilities for interaction, especially regarding the two-way and three-way modes of active interaction (see, e.g., Möller et al. 2021). To conclude this chapter, then, we would like to move from image and interaction theory to brief reflections on readers' engagement and interaction with the photographs included in this book.

Conclusion

In Chapter 2, we introduced the term photocomplexity to indicate that viewing is a complex experience and complexity is a part of visuality. In Chapter 3, we suggested that photoambiguity can help us develop tolerance of ambiguity and make us think and act better in a world saturated with both ambiguities and images, a world in which complexity and ambiguity appear visually. In the present chapter, we argued that this is true especially in the era of digitization where images not only constantly change and evolve but are *meant* to change and evolve. While losing the capability of serving as stable visual reference points, digital images show the fluidity and malleability as well as the evolution and unpredictability of social relations, including peace and conflict dynamics. In a complex world, neither social relations nor digital images can be controlled entirely because numerous permissible developments and interpretations always coexist. We sketched some forms of passive and active interaction through which users contribute to the evolution of the digital image and morph into what, elsewhere, we call image-actors, i.e., users who "firmly locate images in digital culture's visual framework, conditioned by active interaction" (Möller et al. 2021: 2). In our earlier academic work, we followed the interactive logic of seeing—changing—sharing when we introduced "appropriation" as a method for the study of international relations. Appropriation has a long history in visual culture, but in our context it simply refers to the "reuse of existing visual material – either in its entirety or in part – without substantially altering the immanent characteristics of the appropriated visual material" (Möller et al. 2021: 6; italics omitted). The images presented in the present book also invite interaction—passive interaction, i.e., interpretation by means of the sense of sight to construct narratives that are, or are not, in association with the text presented in the book, but also active interaction through modification and alteration of the images including digital modification on the computer screen, physical modification if you possess and wish to destroy a hard copy of the book and mental modification without infringing upon the materiality of the image. Obviously, the images included in a hard copy can easily be transformed into data by digitally photographing them.

It should be clear by now that the photographs included in this book at the end of each chapter (Sarajevo #1–Sarajevo #12) are not meant to illustrate the text or anything else. Nor are they meant to operate according to some intellectual stereoscopic effect (see above) or another effect combining with each other words and images. They can, but need not be, linked to the text. They can be regarded individually or in search of a narrative emerging from the combination of two or more images. Since they are presented in this book and the book consists mainly of words organized in a certain manner, readers may assume—or construct—some connection between words and images, including connections we are neither aware of nor interested in. However, being in association with each other may merely mean that this book co-presents words and images, nothing more.

The Bosnian context is a possible, but certainly not the only, context in which the images can be positioned. Those images that are presented at the end of each chapter rather than embedded within them may also work quite independently, inviting narratives that have nothing to do with the chapters' written narratives. We would certainly hope that readers pay attention to both text and images, but we cannot anticipate actual reading patterns. We can anticipate neither the meanings readers might assign to the photographs nor the effects the images may have on readers. Which may actually be a good thing because, following Rancière, images can establish "a new landscape of the possible" only "on condition that their meaning or effect is not anticipated" (2009: 103). We are interested in such landscapes and refer to them throughout the book as spaces of possibility that TA might help enlarge. In accordance with Rancière, then, we would like to suggest that images expand spaces of possibility "if they are not anticipated by their meaning and do not anticipate their effects" (Rancière 2009: 105).

Thus, we are not suggesting a certain reading or a certain narrative of the images by, for example, providing detailed captions explaining when they were taken, where they were taken exactly, why they were taken and what can be seen in them. All photographs were taken in Sarajevo, and all photographs were taken a long time after the siege, 2018–2022. We do not compare the situation then with the situation today. And while we announced in Chapter 2 clarification later in the book of the relationship between the written and the visual, we now understand that such clarification would imply disambiguation and thus undermine the purpose of the book. We conclude this chapter with the fifth of our Sarajevo photographs (Fig. 5.1).

Fig. 5.1 Sarajevo #5 (Photograph © Frank Möller)

REFERENCES

Adams, Robert. 1994. *Why People Photograph: Selected Essays and Reviews*. New York: Aperture.
Bennett, Audrey. 2012. *Engendering Interaction with Images*. Bristol: Intellect.
Berger, Peter, and Thomas Luckmann. 1966. *The Social Construction of Reality: A Treatise in the Sociology of Knowledge*. London: Penguin.
Bishop, Claire. 2012. *Artificial Hells: Participatory Art and the Politics of Spectatorship*. London and New York: Verso.
Coser, Lewis. 1956. *The Functions of Social Conflict*. New York: The Free Press.
Couldry, Nick. 2000. *Inside Culture: Re-imagining the Method of Cultural Studies*. London, Thousand Oaks and New Delhi: Sage Publications.
Elkins, James. 2011. *What Photography Is*. New York and London: Routledge.
Emerling, Jae. 2012. *Photography: History and Theory*. London and New York: Routledge.
Fry, Douglas P. 2007. *Beyond War: The Human Potential for Peace*. Oxford: Oxford University Press.
Fuller, Matthew, and Eyal Weizman. 2021. *Investigative Aesthetics: Conflicts and Commons in the Politics of Truth*. London and New York: Verso.
George, Alice Rose and Gilles Peress (eds.). 2002. *Here Is New York*. Zurich, Berlin and New York: Scalo.
Gilgen, Peter. 2003. History after Film. In *Mapping Benjamin: The Work of Art in the Digital Age*, ed. Hans Ulrich Gumbrecht und Michael Marrinan, 53–62. Stanford: Stanford University Press.
Hariman, Robert, and John Louis Lucaites. 2010. *No Caption Needed: Iconic Photographs, Public Culture, and Liberal Democracy*. Chicago and London: The University of Chicago Press.
Hirsch, Marianne. 1997. *Family Frames: Photography, Narrative, and Post-memory*. Cambridge and London: Harvard University Press.
Horn, Steve. 2005. *Pictures without Borders: Bosnia Revisited*. Stockport: Dewi Lewis Publishing in association with The Bosnian Institute.
Kelsey, Robin and Blake Stimson (eds.). 2008. *The Meaning of Photography*. Williamstown and New Haven and London: Sterling and Francine Clark Art Institute and Yale University Press.
Krippendorff, Ekkehard. 2000. *Kritik der Außenpolitik*. Frankfurt: Suhrkamp.
Kromm, Jane and Susan Benforado Bakewell (eds.). 2010. *A History of Visual Culture: Western Civilization from the 18th to the 20th Century*. Oxford and New York: Berg.
Law, John. 2004. *After Method: Mess in Social Science Research*. London and New York: Routledge.
Linfield, Susie. 2010. *The Cruel Radiance: Photography and Political Violence*. Chicago and London: The University of Chicago Press.

Lister, Martin. 2013. Introduction. In *The Photographic Image in Digital Culture*, 2nd ed., ed. Martin Lister, 1–21. London and New York: Routledge.

MacDougall, David. 1998. *Transcultural Cinema*. Edited and with an introduction by Lucien Taylor. Princeton: Princeton University Press.

Mitchell, W.J.T. 1994. *Picture Theory: Essays on Verbal and Visual Representation*. Chicago and London: The University of Chicago Press.

Möller, Frank. 2013. *Visual Peace: Images, Spectatorship, and the Politics of Violence*. Houndmills: Palgrave Macmillan.

Möller, Frank. 2019. *Peace Photography*. Houndmills: Palgrave Macmillan.

Möller, Frank, and Rasmus Bellmer. 2023. Interactive Peace Imagery: Integrating Visual Research and Peace Education. *Journal of Peace Education*. https://doi.org/10.1080/17400201.2023.2171374.

Möller, Frank, Rasmus Bellmer and Rune Saugmann. 2021. Visual Appropriation: A Self-Reflexive Qualitative Method for Visual Analysis of the International. *International Political Sociology* 16 (1). https://doi.org/10.1093/ips/olab029.

Morris, Errol. 2014. *Believing Is Seeing (Observations on the Mysteries of Photography)*. London: Penguin.

Oldfield, Pippa. 2019. *Photography and War*. London: Reaktion Books.

Palu, Louie. 2017. Image Control in the Age of Terror. In *Art as a Political Witness*, ed. Kia Lindroos and Frank Möller, 57–64. Opladen, Berlin, Toronto: Barbara Budrich Publishers.

Rancière, Jacques. 2009. *The Emancipated Spectator*, trans. Gregory Elliott. London and New York: Verso.

Ritchin, Fred. 1999. *In Our Own Image*. New York: Aperture.

Ritchin, Fred. 2009. *After Photography*. New York: W.W. Norton & Company.

Roberts, John. 2014. *Photography and Its Violations*. New York: Columbia University Press.

Rubinstein, Daniel. 2010. Tag, Tagging. *Philosophy of Photography* 1 (2): 197–200.

Rubinstein, Daniel, and Katrina Sluis. 2013. Concerning the Undecidability of the Digital Image. *Photographies* 6 (1): 151–158.

Shapiro, Michael J. 2015. *War Crimes, Atrocity, and Justice*. Cambridge and Malden: Polity.

Smith, Shawn Michelle. 2013. *At the Edge of Sight: Photography and the Unseen*. Durham and London: Duke University Press.

Sontag, Susan. 1979. *On Photography*. London: Penguin.

Sontag, Susan. 2003. *Regarding the Pain of Others*. New York: Farrar, Straus & Giroux.

Susperregui, José Manuel. 2016. The Location of Robert Capa's *Falling Soldier*. *Communication & Society* 29 (2): 17–43.

Sutherland, Ian and Sophia Krzys Acord. 2007. Thinking with Art: From Situated Knowledge to Experiential Knowing. *Journal of Visual Art Practice* 6(2): 125–140.
Wells, Liz, ed. 2003. *The Photography Reader*. London and New York: Routledge.
Wenders, Wim and Mary Zournazi. 2013. *Inventing Peace: A Dialogue on Perception*. London and New York: I.B. Tauris.
Whelan, Richard. 2007. *This Is War! Robert Capa at Work*. New York: International Center of Photography/Göttingen: Steidl.
Williams, Raymond. 1976. *Keywords: A Vocabulary of Culture and Society*. London: Fontana.

PART III

Bosnia: Uncertain Paths to Peace

CHAPTER 6

Introducing *Bosnia: Uncertain Paths to Peace*

INTRODUCTION

In Chapter 2, we introduced the term photocomplexity to indicate that viewing is a complex experience and complexity is a part of visuality. Even a seemingly simple picture can be understood in many different ways, communicating different things to different observers. Complexity theory as a way of thinking helps us to identify different layers of complexity inherent in photographs. In Chapter 3, we suggested that images, understood as carriers of multiple meanings, can help us to develop tolerance of ambiguity and make us think and act better in a world saturated with both ambiguities and images, a world in which complexity and ambiguity appear visually. We used the term photoambiguity to grasp that every image is ambiguous, always carrying with it a plurality of meanings that cannot be limited to one meaning, mandatory for all observers. We argued that if we want to understand an ambiguous world, then we have to appreciate images' plurality of meanings, welcome their ambiguities and complexify viewing patterns. In Chapter 4, we suggested that this is not what photojournalism normally does and introduced different photographies that emerged in the 1990s in response to the crisis that photojournalism faced at the time. In Chapter 5, we argued that in the current era of digitization, images not only constantly change and evolve but are *meant* to change and evolve. Thus, not only meanings assigned

© The Author(s), under exclusive license to Springer Nature Switzerland AG 2023
R. Bellmer and F. Möller, *Peace, Complexity, Visuality*, Rethinking Peace and Conflict Studies, https://doi.org/10.1007/978-3-031-38218-5_6

to an image change but also the image, losing its capability of serving as a stable visual reference point. This is inherent to digitization, regardless of the intentions of individual image-makers. Control of meaning declines. In an ever-changing and hardly controllable visual environment, tolerance of ambiguity is more important than ever before to challenge hegemonic acts of disambiguation.[1]

In violent conflicts, the complexity of social reality is commonly reduced. Take, for example, "the ethnic hatreds storyline" (Andreas 2008: 11) with which many commentators addressed and tried to make sense of the wars in the former Yugoslavia, thereby "mask[ing] far more complex and ambiguous realities on the ground" (Andreas 2008: 11).[2] Narratives and stories surrounding a conflict become simplified when incorporated into strategic considerations, but simplification also promises assurance and predictability in an environment characterized by the opposite. Conflict fosters coherence of the in-group at the expense of its relationship to out-groups (see Coser 1956). Trained in critical international relations and peace and conflict studies, however, we are skeptical of such binaries. In-group and out-group are aggregate categories in need of differentiation if we want to understand the complexities of social conflicts. Indeed, we have learned that dividing the world into binaries is one of the basic problems of Western rationality. This is one of the reasons why we think about the operation of visual images in peace and conflict dynamics in terms of their relation to the complexity of social life. Does an image tell us anything new? Does it display a perspective that is commonly underrepresented in (visual) discourse? Do we gain a better understanding of a conflict, an understanding that reflects its complex dynamics? Does the image increase the visibility of such dynamics? Does it challenge the tendency to simplification underlying much published photojournalistic work, its proclivity for disambiguation? Does it help us to understand that in complex situations, there is never just one cause and there is never just one path to conflict resolution or transformation? Does it prevent

---

[1] Reflecting upon the controversy revolving around *documenta fifteen* in Kassel 2022, for example, the sociologist Natan Sznaider recently emphasized the need for tolerance of ambiguity to confront a reality in which there exist not only dichotomies in terms of either-or but also equivalency in terms of as-well-as. See www.zeit.de/hamburg/2023-02/documenta-antisemitismus-skandal-hbfk-symposium (accessed 2 February 2023).

[2] For early accounts of the disintegration of Yugoslavia, see Glenny (1996) and Silber and Little (1997).

us from constructing, while trying to answer such questions, new binaries such as tolerance of ambiguity versus disambiguation or simplification versus complexification?

Regarding the siege of Sarajevo, photojournalists tried to visualize that "one side was clearly the aggressor and the other the victim" (Lowe 2015: 5). Among the aggressors and among the victims, however, different subject positions can be identified, coexisting but also changing over time and exhibiting different degrees of relevance to the conflict. Peter Andreas (2008: 12), for example, argues that there were those who were victims of the external siege imposed on the city by the Bosnian Serb army while simultaneously benefitting from "a less visible internal siege (made possible by the external siege conditions)" including theft, looting and profiteering. In his most recent novel, located in Sarajevo during the early stages of the siege, Dževad Karahasan writes about the radical division of Sarajevo's society into those who "gobble up, steal, rescue, and appropriate" and those who would not even pick up a cigarette that wasn't theirs; on the one hand, those who understood the confusing conditions prevailing in the city as an opportunity to gather and grab everything that was not nailed down and those who, on the other hand, understood these conditions as a duty and opportunity to show restraint and to renunciate everything that did not rightfully belong to them. Why, Karahasan wonders, weren't there any people who positioned themselves between these two groups (2023: 84–85, 110; our translation of the German translation)? However, also within these two groups, different people experienced the siege differently. Analysis, thus, must pay

> attention to discrepancies between the formal scripts and the more informal behavior behind the scenes, the multiple roles that actors can simultaneously play, and the relationship between the visible, audience-directed official "face work" on the front stage and the less visible, unofficial action backstage. (Andreas 2008: 3–4)

Human beings are always parts of social groups and define themselves and their actions largely as members of groups, including tensions resulting from memberships in different groups. In the city, different social groups could be separated from one another—most basically those who benefitted from the siege from those who did not and those who stayed in the city from those who left it. The citizens of Sarajevo—who identified themselves as *Sarajlije*, "cosmopolitan citizens of a modern, open world" (see

Markowitz 2010: 47)—could be differentiated both from the refugees who came to the city from rural Bosnia, "mostly peasants, who've fled from rape and massacre and their burning villages" (Sacco 2004: 73), and from foreign journalists and military personnel. People with connections to companies or associations that helped them survive the siege and gain access to seemingly scarce goods—'seemingly' because for those with connections, everything was available "while the vast majority of the residents of the city survived on meagre rations of UN humanitarian aid" (Morrison and Lowe 2021: 113)[3]—could be distinguished from those without such connections (Karahasan 2023: 178).

At the same time, one of Karahasan's characters, Senada, is said to exhibit tenderness and discomfort, anxiety and gratitude, grief and irritating joy (2023: 118) thus necessitating tolerance of ambiguity—the ability to recognize and deal with the coexistence of positive and negative characteristics in the same subject or object—on the part of her friends and acquaintances. Things were complex indeed. How could it have been otherwise? "I didn't believe there was much ambiguity there," Christiane Amanpour of CNN remembers, "and I was always clear about how I reported the story." But the story of the "Bosnian Serb Army behav[ing] disgracefully" and "violat[ing] international norms and humanitarian law by targeting civilians and journalists and … plac[ing] an entire city under siege" (quoted in Morrison and Lowe 2021: 146) was only one story among many others. Andreas differentiates "the front-stage cameras in Sarajevo" covering the siege of the city comprehensively from lack of journalistic attention to the war elsewhere in the country (2008: 38)[4] but also within Sarajevo; different aspects of life under siege were covered differently with a lot of journalistic attention devoted to life and death at the barricades (see Chapter 4).

In the present chapter, we will introduce a photojournalistic project that emerged in the 1990s, Fred Ritchin and Gilles Peress's *Bosnia: Uncertain Paths to Peace*, a project that is in part still (as of spring 2023) available on the Internet.[5] This interactive online project combined text,

---

[3] Andreas notes, however, that "on its own, humanitarian aid was far from sufficient to sustain the city's population" (2008: 13).

[4] "With Sarajevo occupying center stage, much of the rest of Bosnia was treated as a sideshow" (Andreas 2008: 38) and journalistic reporting became a part of the siege dynamics (pp. 71–79). See also Morrison and Lowe (2021: 89–117).

[5] See https://archive.nytimes.com/www.nytimes.com/specials/bosnia/index.html.

audio snippets and images in an original manner and without establishing a hierarchical relationship among them. The project's high degree of interactivity invited a plurality of simultaneously existing narratives that are neither prescribed by the project's creators, hierarchically ordered, nor assessed in light of their truth value. As such, it deviates substantially from conventional journalistic reporting. It also challenged the authorial voice of its creators while allowing for an unusual degree of audience participation and co-authorship thus appealing to tolerance of ambiguity rather than to disambiguation.

We follow quite closely the narrative of one of the project's creators, Fred Ritchin, and discuss it in light of what we wrote in Chapter 3 about ambiguity and in Chapter 4 about photojournalism. We will review the project's basic lines of thought—its photophilosophy—in this chapter and proceed with a description of the website's structure and our own navigation in the next chapter, zooming in on the grid structure and interactivity in the following chapters. Obviously, as a project launched in 1996, *Bosnia: Uncertain Paths to Peace* could not utilize the possibilities that digitization (as described in the previous chapter) currently offers. In a sense, then, we take one step back to the early stages of interactivity and digitization. This step, however, helps us avoid getting lost in the quicksand of technological developments, which are hard to follow as technology is constantly evolving. It also helps us understand the basic lines of thought underlying the project, especially their connection to photocomplexity and photoambiguity.

THE PHOTOPHILOSOPHY OF *BOSNIA: UNCERTAIN PATHS TO PEACE*

Launched in 1996 by *The New York Times on the Web*, *Bosnia: Uncertain Paths to Peace* co-presented photographs taken in two different locations in the Bosnian capital city, Sarajevo, at the end of the siege, audio messages, written narratives and background material to communicate to the users a sense of place and its complexity at this particular point in time and to outline peace perspectives following the state of exception that had dominated Sarajevo between 1992 and 1995 (see Karahasan 2014, 2023; Andreas 2008; Demick 2012; Abadžić 2022). The project aimed to realize some of Ritchin's ideas regarding the future of journalistic reporting post-print media, relying on the visual approaches Peress had developed in earlier projects so as to make photojournalism more relevant. This could be done by both engaging the conventions of photojournalism and taking advantage of all possibilities that digitization promised to offer. As an early example of peace photography (Ritchin 2013: 122–141; Möller 2019), the project did not aim to visualize the violence, widely defined, that continued to shape everyday life in the city even after the end of the siege (Holbrooke 1999: 350, 363)[6] but, rather, to contribute to peace proactively. Photojournalistically speaking, thus, it was not interested in a 'good' story or in 'great' images and, as such, challenged the genre's established conventions. Tellingly, IFOR's[7] "easy, untroubled entry" into Bosnia in December 1995 did not attract much media attention although "*this* was the real story; and it was important" (Holbrooke 1999: 324; italics in original). It is easy to imagine the media frenzy if IFOR had faced major resistance.[8]

According to Ritchin, "newspapers and magazines publish a continuous stream of generally interchangeable images of violence's apex, milking it for its realism without an exploration of its unfolding or underlying causes" (1999: 27). They rely on both "the photograph's perceived authority" (Ritchin 1999: 26)—its realism—and the photographer's perceived authority as witness with a camera. After all, the photographer was there, on location, when something happened that she documented without interfering in it. This is a part of the myth of photojournalism— presence on location, non-partisanship, non-interference, proximity to action (see Möller 2017 and Chapter 4)—but it is a very powerful myth, carefully cultivated by professional photojournalists, critics and commentators and challenged only by a few.

---

[6] For example, Morrison and Lowe report that one person was killed and nineteen were injured in January 1996 when a projectile hit a tram in Sarajevo. Formally, the siege was lifted at the end of February 1996 although gas and electricity had begun to reach the city in October 1995 (Morrison and Lowe 2021: xxvi–xxvii).

[7] Deployed in December 1995, IFOR (Implementation Force) was NATO-led and tasked with implementing military aspects of the Dayton Peace Agreement. It was replaced by SFOR (Stabilization Force) a year later. See https://www.nato.int/cps/en/natohq/topics_52122.htm (accessed 25 March 2023).

[8] "Unable to show any tension or conflict between the arriving American forces and the local population, television exaggerated the dangers facing the troops, and covered the arrival in a sort of retro-Vietnam style that misled the American public as to the dangers the troops faced," Holbrooke (1999: 324) reports.

In photojournalism, "the visual vocabulary has particularly stagnated" because national contests and international competitions cater to established conventions and "expected clichés ... Rather than discuss and value differences as providing new ideas for an expanding set of approaches, even in a weakened field a conformity reigns that constricts possibility" (Ritchin 2013: 51). In order to challenge such conformity, Ritchin discusses photography in terms of its "capability ... to engage itself otherwise, less obviously, in subtle ambiguity, in soaring metaphor, in questioning the nature of reality rather than delineating conventional responses" (1999: 126) and appreciates Peress's 1980 work in Iran as "engaging the reader in an open-ended, non-authoritative dialectic" (1999: 101). "Authoring the Image" (Ritchin 1999: 98–115) implies acknowledging the viewer as co-author because, regardless of its dependence on "contextualization by text and layout," photography is also always "highly interpretive, ambiguous, culturally specific" (Ritchin 1999: 72). As Susan Sontag had already noted twenty years earlier, textual designations of meaning "cannot prevent any argument or moral plea which a photograph (or a set of photographs) is intended to support from being undermined by the plurality of meanings that every photograph carries" (1979: 109).

How can this be translated into a photojournalistic project without undermining both the photographer's authority and (photo)journalism's association with truth—its schizophrenic mission of showing the truth[9] while at the same time acknowledging that this is not possible? Ritchin and Peress's project—*Bosnia: Uncertain Paths to Peace*, shown on the Internet for three months in summer 1996 following the end of the siege—suggests that the photographer's authority can be strengthened precisely by acknowledging its limits. One of the project's conditions of possibility was the signing of the Dayton Accords in December 1995 (see Holbrooke 1999: 231–312), after which photographic (and other) possibilities emerged in the city that had been impossible, or much harder to realize, earlier. Another precondition for the project was interest on the part of the *New York Times* to expand the limits of print journalism: to experiment with and "take advantage of the new strategies made possible by the Web – nonlinear narratives, discussion groups, contextualizing information, panoramic imaging, the photographer's reflective voice"

---

[9] See, for example, the 2017 *New York Times* campaign: **Truth**. The alternative is a lie.

(Ritchin 2009: 102). A third precondition was the cooperation between Ritchin—an experienced picture editor—and Peress—an internationally acclaimed photographer who in earlier projects, including in Bosnia, had already gone beyond the conventional forms of photojournalistic representation (see Chapter 4). According to Ritchin, Peress understood "his role" in the project "as not only that of a photographer but an author in the largest sense of the world [*sic*]" (2013: 102). In a time-consuming process, he provided the photographs not as raw material to be assembled by others but edited and organized the images and their appearance on the website himself. In addition, he provided commentary (including audio commentary) to contextualize the images and reflect upon his position as a photographer which, elsewhere, he defines "as a witness."[10]

Susie Linfield (2010) provides insights into the evolution of Peress's photographic work, which are important in our context as well. Peress, according to Linfield, "became a photographer because he no longer *believed* in language" (p. 234; italics in original)—in particular in language which was concerned *only* with language, not with reality; and while according to Linfield, he does not seem to think that there is a direct connection between photography and change, he believes that if you want to change the world you have to look at it rather than hiding behind the poststructuralist insistence on the world's non-representability (p. 236).[11] Indeed, for Peress, Linfield suggests, "photography is a way to think about the world. His photographs seem to be arguments with and about what he is seeing rather than documentations of it" (p. 234):

> Peress's pictures are often hard to decipher, but they are never about the absence of reality. His subject is more complex: the difficulty of finding, conveying, and, most of all, making meaning *from* reality. And because that is a hard, indeed often impossible, thing to do, Peress's photographs are about failure: not as an individual shortcoming that can be fixed but as an inescapable aspect of the human condition that can only be endured. (p. 234; italics in original)

---

[10] http://artsmia.org/get-the-picture/print/peress.shtml (accessed 6 February 2023).

[11] Regarding Peress's 1995 Rwanda photographs, Piotr Cieplak argues that the framing of these images "hints at the inevitable partiality of representation, and, at the same time, its stubborn possibility" (2017: 65).

Making meaning from images that try to make meaning from reality but often fail to do so is as difficult a task as enduring the inevitable shortcomings of the human condition. Linfield (p. 235) suggests that Peress "rejects the conventional wisdom that remembering history prevents its repetition" but he nevertheless documents what human beings are capable of doing in times of war and violent conflict. However, in his more recent work, he does so rather indirectly by photographing bones and graves rather than actual acts of violence when they are perpetrated—as a "witness," "a detective" and "a philosopher" (p. 235) engaging in and developing a personal version of the aesthetics of forensic, aftermath and trauma photography (see Chapter 4) including its tendency to assign a lot of work to the viewer who "must work to complete the photograph by digging into what it suggests and endowing it with deeper insights" (p. 238).

In his 1994 book, *Farewell to Bosnia*, Peress, in Linfield's interpretation, is "showing us a society as it is torn apart" thus "mak[ing] visible, or at least imaginable, the bonds of human connection – the communities of citizens – that existed before the slaughter" (p. 242). In a similar vein, Anne Wilkes Tucker writes about a photograph showing the evacuation of Jews from Sarajevo in 1993 that "Peress's image of hands touching through a bus window conveys the wrenching separation felt by those leaving on the bus and the family members left behind in a city besieged by shelling and snipers as well as suffering from shortages of food and clean water" (Wilkes Tucker and Michels with Zelt 2012: 456). Do these visualizations imply that such bonds may be recreated after the slaughter, that reunification is possible, or is all lost? With regard to peacebuilding, John Paul Lederach uses the term "the moral imagination" to designate "the capacity to imagine and generate constructive responses and initiatives that, while rooted in the day-to-day challenges of violence, transcend and ultimately break the grips of those destructive patterns and cycles" (2005: 29) but, perhaps, some patterns—and some images—are too violent, too destructive and too traumatic to allow for such an imagination. Negative peace photography visualizes the need for peace by showing its absence, but sometimes the absence of peace is all there is to see, overwhelming imagination and limiting what can be thought of as possible.

After the publication of *Farewell to Bosnia*, it took one more year until the Dayton Accords ended the war (Fig. 6.1).[12] And because it took such a long time for Western powers to get involved in the conflict decisively, the subject of Peress's photographs, Linfield suggests, "is 'us' – what we did and failed to do – as well as 'them'" (p. 243). However, 'they' certainly did not need a photographer to show them what it is like and what it feels like to be "abandoned by the world" (p. 243)[13] so the main subject of this photography appears to be 'us' rather than 'them' and one of its main objectives is to shame 'us'—western audiences and politicians,[14] international organizations and the international community—into action in response to the conditions depicted.[15] This is perfectly in accordance with one of photojournalism's traditions, namely, intervening in a conflict photographically to make others intervene with more efficient means to end the conflict. Peress does not "spare us" subjects we would rather not see, and Linfield asks: "why should he?" (p. 244; see also Cieplak 2017: 62–73). However, an equally important question is: should photographers perhaps dispense with showing the suffering of others altogether and thus prevent the victims from being exposed to the view of distant spectators who, by looking, prolong the suffering (see Bal 2007; Reinhardt 2007)? Such thoughts may have triggered Peress's move toward forensic photography, as explored in Chapter 4, when he returned to Bosnia in 1996.

A forensic approach to photography required a new photographic practice using "'crime scene'-like close-up images of the still lives of the aftermath of atrocities" (Lowe 2014: 219). As photographer Gary Knight (one of the proponents of such photography) explains, he is no longer interested "in creating beautiful photographs and more interested

---

[12] The Dayton Peace Agreement "was a means to end a war, not the basis of a permanent solution to the Bosnian Question" (Bennett 2016: 9; see also Holbrooke 1999: 133 and 170).

[13] Avishai Margalit differentiates what it *is* like from what it *feels* like in *The Ethics of Memory* (2004).

[14] Peress is "mostly known in the widely defined Western world" where his images circulate (Cieplak 2017: 61). Cieplak notes with regard to Peress's photographs from Rwanda that "even if the images were widely accessible in the country, it isn't at all clear whether people would want to see them" (p. 61). The same can be said about his photographs from Bosnia.

[15] However, it was certainly not due to a lack of photographic representation that Western governments postponed decisive action until August 1995.

6 INTRODUCING *BOSNIA: UNCERTAIN PATHS TO PEACE* 145

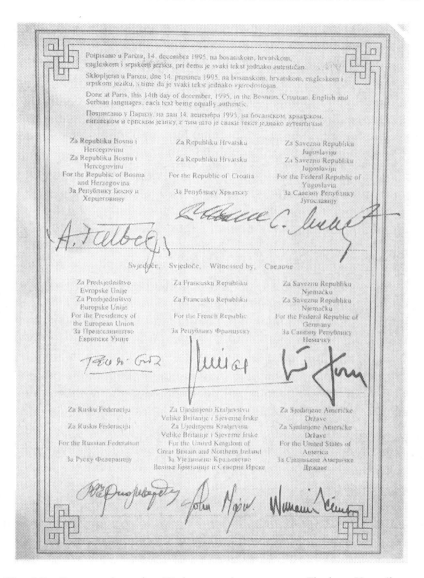

Fig. 6.1 Dayton Accords (Dokumentationszentrum Flucht, Vertreibung, Versöhnung, Berlin)

in using photography as a means to an end" (quoted in Lowe 2014: 220). Using photography as a means to an end is not a new photojournalistic strategy: photojournalists have used photography to raise awareness, create solidarity and call for intervention and so on. However, the end has changed and is now a legalistic one: producing detailed, visual evidence that, while still addressing a mass audience, "can carry legal force" (Lowe 2014: 221) or, in Peress's words (quoted in Lowe 2014: 221), producing photographs "that are plausible evidence but also plausibly meaningful to the public in the abstract or to the judicial system."

The current media landscape is defined by the Internet and this "opens up all sorts of possibilities for photographers and viewers" (Linfield 2010: 256). As Peress explained in a November 2008 conversation with Linfield (p. 257):

> We are entering into an age in which visual language is defined by a dialogue between photographers and audiences.
>
> This means not just the democratic posting of images but the democratic *interpretation* of images. (italics in original)
>
> There is no longer a voice of authority, with univocal images created from above ... We need deep humility, humbleness, in relation to our formulation of reality now.

The call for humility and humbleness reflects insights into both the limitations of photography and the complexity of the world, only parts of which can be partially represented, revealing something while simultaneously obscuring other things. However, humility and humbleness do not rule out ambition. From the beginning of their joint project *Bosnia: Uncertain Paths to Peace*, then, Ritchin and Peress

> tried to be ambitious. Rather than publish the conventional photographs of war, sensationalizing victimization and emphasizing the grotesquerie of violence, we preferred photographs that would strive to understand the problematic and possibility of peace. We were attempting to ask how people who viciously killed one another for years might live together, and provided forums for readers to discuss strategies for resolution. (Ritchin 2009: 105)

The photographer—as the one who was not only familiar with the contents and contexts of his photography but also with what he had left out of the frame—"had to articulate the multiple meanings of each image as a way of deciding upon accompanying texts and images, and to strategize possible linkages to photographs and media on the other screens that would make up the site," Ritchin elaborates (2009: 102) after explaining that his own experience in print media was insufficient for a multimedia, online project. He explains how his own sense of being an editor evolved:

> In this need to interrogate every image for possible meanings there was a sharper sense of my own distance, as editor, from the events and people being depicted and, concurrently, a heightened desire to understand them. I wanted to know the people that were photographed as individuals rather than as symbols; furthermore, with all the nonlinear, multimedia possibilities of the Web, generic imagery of a suffering mother or wounded combatant would not propel the narrative. In fact, such simplistic imagery would squelch it. (pp. 102–103)

Peress had photographed on conventional film but, reflecting digital culture's penchant for turning everything into data, digitized his photographs by scanning them thus enabling digital storytelling and facilitating audience interaction. Dealing with an audience as yet largely unaccustomed to such storytelling, crucial questions concerned user involvement: How would a user approach such data? "Why would a reader want to become involved in such a new form of reading"—which was time-consuming, involving a high degree of co-authorship—and when would a reader's interest be lost? (p. 104) Perhaps the best approach would be sending the reader on an adventure tour through the website and, by implication, through the city—to some extent surprising and unpredictable—just like a journalist arriving in Sarajevo without knowledge of what to expect, "where to go, what specific story to explore" (p. 104) but without the risks and dangers the visitors to the city were facing. Just like a journalist, the website's users could prepare themselves for this trip by studying background material presented on the website—a map, glossary and bibliography, a copy of the Dayton Accords and links to other websites providing further information—or they could jump back and forth on the website, moving from images to background information or vice versa; or they could follow Peress's narrative in words and images—except that they could *not* because "[e]ach click of the cursor would put a reader on another screen with new perspectives and unknown possibilities" (p. 104).

The grid structure of some pages invited users to construct their own story line by jumping from an image to any other image in the grid without being able to anticipate where in the story one would land or whether there existed a story in the first place (see Chapter 8). In contrast to a book or a chronologically organized website or a website organized according to subjects where one image would logically follow the preceding one and anticipate the following one, *Bosnia: Uncertain Paths to Peace* "offered no way of quickly flipping forward to assess the path" (Ritchin 2013: 123). The user's path through the website was as unclear and unpredictable as was Bosnia's path to peace, with surprising and unexpected challenges looming behind every corner and on every page, and it only seemed to be facilitated by a relatively simple navigation device (see Chapter 7). Lost on the website, users could always leave it and join one of the discussion groups to share their experience with others, again just like journalists regularly shared their individual experience with others in the lobby of Sarajevo's Holiday Inn hotel (see Morrison 2016).

One of the things missing from most conventional photojournalistic representation is the photographer's voice. In fine art photography, this voice is deliberately missing; its inclusion in the visual artwork would indicate the failure of the artwork, showing that the artist's vision "is not … fully there in the picture" (Adams 1994: 33). In journalism, the caption functions as the photograph's "missing voice" (Sontag 1979: 108), but it is not always written by the photographer herself. In *Bosnia: Uncertain Paths to Peace*, the team decided to include the photographer's voice in the project by pairing his images "with his own written text and recorded voice to add other points of view. His emotional reactions and philosophical questions would help to contextualize and extend the imagery beyond what the typical identifying captions could accomplish" (Ritchin 2009: 105). In one audio commentary, Peress articulates the "wish to be corrected by people who lived there" and refers to the Internet as "one of the places where my misconceptions will be corrected"[16] thus acknowledging the limits of his own knowledge. Peress, thus, "was given center stage" (Ritchin 2009: 106) but, in a sense, the user was given center stage,

---

[16] www.nytimes.com/specials/bosnia/gallery/peress.3.au (accessed 2 February 2023). See also the next chapter.

too, navigating, while communicating and interacting with the photographer, the subject and the website, her own way through the material thus constructing her own narratives. Or, chronologically speaking: "While the photographer initially had center stage on this project – it was up to him to articulate the pertinent links among the many possible images – the reader was then responsible for their reassembly" (Ritchin 2013: 123).

The acceptance or non-acceptance of designations of meaning depends on the social and professional position from which such designations are made. Peress's position was strong due to his presence on location and his reputation as a photographer. There is little doubt that *The New York Times* also enjoyed a high degree of respectability and authority at the time as one of the world's leading newspapers on which *Bosnia: Uncertain Paths to Peace* relied to some extent (in addition to the *Times*'s financial power and organizational prowess). However, while benefitting from the authority of the outlet, the project also undermined it both by engaging its users in "a relatively open and unresolved fashion" (Ritchin 2009: 106) and by inviting users to correct the positions shown and articulated on the website—an invitation that is normally absent from journalistic reporting.

In addition to Peress's (explicit) and Ritchin's (implicit) positions, the website also featured, in the forums,[17] assessments by rather well-known scholars, media personalities and politicians, thus establishing yet another discursive frame within which the website's contents could be read. Such frames are important; they try to regulate engagement with the website and its ambiguities in such a manner that it takes place within (what the creators regard as) permissible spaces of interpretation. However, "the discussion groups were quickly dominated by some of the most racist and vitriolic comments ever to appear in the *New York Times*" (Ritchin 2009: 107). Many of the forums "were dominated largely by pro-Serbian commentators abroad who felt their cause was being vilified by the conventional media" (p. 108) and, apparently, also by unconventional projects such as *Bosnia: Uncertain Paths to Peace*. The plurality of meanings and interpretive openness the project offered did not always result in envisioning paths to peace, as its creators had hoped.

---

[17] The project included fourteen forums: Introduction; Healing and Reconciliation; Will Bosnia Survive Dayton?; Religion and War; U.S. Interests, U.S. Achievements; International Justice; War Crimes; Nationality and Nationalism; Will History Teach us Nothing?; Bosnia's Cultural Heritage; Genocide: How Should We Respond?; The Irony of Media Coverage; Truisms; Comment on the Site.

In retrospect, such a hope may seem to have been naïve, but it reflected widespread belief in the democratizing potentialities of the Internet—giving voice to people formerly excluded from public discourse—that prevailed at the time. However, "the same leaders who had started the war were still trying to silence those who called for multiethnic cooperation" (Holbrooke 1999: 362). Such attempts could have been prevented from entering the discussion groups of *Bosnia: Uncertain Paths to Peace* only through editorial intervention.[18] Such intervention, however, would have undermined the project's basic lines of thought. And the hostility articulated in the discussion groups to the idea of peaceful, multiethnic coexistence was indicative of the long way Bosnia still had to travel to peace. Revealing such hostility was an important, if unintended, result of the project: "a reader could learn more from them than from any news report as to how extensive, irrational, and personal the contested claims could be" (Ritchin 2009: 108).

Visual Controversies

Implicitly and inadvertently confirming that which a project sets out to criticize is always a danger inherent in critical projects, regardless of whether these projects are political, academic, journalistic or artistic. To some extent, every approach confirms the categories it wishes to criticize simply by using them as negative reference points: not every user will agree that they are *negative* reference points. Every project relying on images may strengthen, through reproduction, the power even of those images it wishes to criticize; every project has only limited power over the meanings readers will discover. Furthermore, every project has to make numerous choices as to the question of what issues it wishes to cover—and how it wishes to cover them—in contrast to those that remain at the margins or uncovered altogether.

While referring to *Bosnia*'s paths to peace in its title, the project has very little to say on Bosnia and a lot to say about Sarajevo. The focus on the capital was as understandable as it was problematic in light of the project's title, implicitly equating the situation in Sarajevo with the situation elsewhere in the country. During the siege, "the agony of Sarajevo

---

[18] The former *New York Times* foreign editor Bernard Gwertzman is said to have issued "entreaties for civility" (Ritchin 2009: 108).

became the embodiment of the Bosnian war's savagery and senselessness," the historian Robert Donia writes (2006: 287). If anything, the situations in rural areas and cities such as Mostar were even worse than the conditions in the capital (see Andreas 2008: 4), which explains why only a few journalists dared to leave Sarajevo during the war. While the conditions there were well covered, the brutality of the war elsewhere in the country was not: maximum visibility in Sarajevo joined hands with minimum visibility elsewhere (see Andreas 2008: 38–39). However, the reasons for the focus on Sarajevo were compelling. Given its status as host city of the 1984 Winter Olympics and its international reputation in terms of cosmopolitanism and multiculturalism, Sarajevo attracted international attention during the siege, including visits by politicians such as then French president François Mitterrand and then UN Secretary General Boutros Boutros-Ghali (Andreas 2008: 7) and intellectuals such as Susan Sontag (Jestrovic 2013: 115–128; Moser 2019: chapters 34–36). The city "could be expected to attract more audience interest than a smaller city or rural area would have generated" (Bellmer and Möller 2022b: 12). After all, "urban areas are typically the hubs and nodes that link internal conflicts to the external world" (Andreas 2008: 5). Furthermore, for journalists, Sarajevo was relatively safe—at least when compared with other parts of the country—and, due to the airlift, the city was relatively easily accessible, providing the necessary transport connections and basic infrastructure for long-term media coverage (Morrison and Lowe 2021).

Importantly, *Bosnia: Uncertain Paths to Peace* covered two distinct areas of the city—*Sarajevo* and *The Suburbs*—thus directing attention to the multilayeredness of life in the city, its contradictions and ambiguities. Like every project, *Bosnia: Uncertain Paths to Peace*

> entered and visually documented the conflict at a specific point thus, although including a chronology that users could study, paying little *photographic* attention to the conflict's pre-violence history without which understanding of the current conditions was bound to be limited and biased. (Bellmer and Möller 2022b: 13; italics added)

The project succeeded in offering an alternative to conventional (photo)journalistic reporting, but it also visually reproduced photojournalism's disregard of the "unfolding or underlying causes" of violence (Ritchin 1999: 27), noted above. The time of the project was nevertheless well chosen because the signing of the Dayton Accords on 14 December 1995 made the search for paths to peace both compelling and necessary.

Bosnia: Uncertain Paths to Peace applies both disambiguation and tolerance of ambiguity. This is, in itself, already an exercise in TA building since it acknowledges the existence of more than one approach to the visual material presented in the project:

> The multiple meanings of the photographs were often not at all apparent. Ultimately, ... it was possible either to collapse each photograph's potential meanings into one that could be called a defining caption, or to sustain the ambiguities in the presentation so as to provoke new thinking, not only about each image but also about the larger conflict in Bosnia. (Ritchin 2009: 103)

Thus, both disambiguation and TA building are possible. Since it is neither feasible to identify *all* potential meanings that a photograph carries nor to collapse them into *one* defining caption thus exerting control of meaning, even the first option will have to acknowledge that some meanings will inevitably escape both the photographer and the editor, to be identified by users who, by so doing, construct their own narratives and position the image in association with them. This possibility does not guarantee the emergence of new thinking, however, since users may see only what they believe anyway (following Errol Morris's dictum that Believing Is Seeing; Morris 2014) thus utilizing the variety of possible interpretations of the image merely to confirm their own point of view that already existed prior to the viewing experience. A project such as *Bosnia: Uncertain Paths to Peace* can only *offer* plurality of meanings and interpretive openness; it is for the users to decide whether they want to accept this offer or reject it, in which case no new thinking would emerge.

Provoking new thinking and discussing strategies for conflict resolution was at odds, we think, with some of the contents included in the project, in particular "a 360-degree panoramic showing a Serbian cemetery filled with empty holes where bodies once were – the caskets were being dug up by relatives afraid that the dead might soon be desecrated by vengeful enemies" (Ritchin 2009: 106). While the periscope-style view offered a view on the cemetery that conventional photographic representation could not offer, we feel that "recreat[ing] some of the eerily disconnected feeling of what it was to stand in the middle of that cemetery, where many of the relatives, fueled by alcohol, were unburying family members" (p. 106) is an unpromising path to peace, bound to failure and likely to tear open old wounds. At the same time, offering a view on the cemetery from different perspectives may have functioned as an invitation to regard—or imagine—other images from different perspectives as well, thus supporting the notion that every subject can legitimately be regarded from different angles—both literally and metaphorically. The photographer's selection of a point of view is never unpolitical because it determines what can be seen in an image and how it appears.

Peress's wish to be corrected by readers and on the Internet is at odds with conventional photojournalistic conventions. After all, he was on location and could, therefore, claim with some degree of legitimacy knowledge of what can be seen in his photographs. No matter how unusual his position is in light of these conventions, it is also at odds with the lines of thought that we wish to present throughout the book. Rather than understanding readers' response to the images as "correction," we would prefer an attitude that accepts different narratives as equally valuable, non-hierarchically standing side-by-side and inviting conversation (see Bellmer and Möller 2022a), reflecting different individual experiences without assigning priority to any of these experiences or ontological superiority to the 'correcting,' rather than the 'corrected,' voice. Peress, as a visitor, may have missed some of the meanings that the people who lived in the city immediately recognized. However, the photographer may also have identified meanings that the city's inhabitants took for granted and therefore disregarded.

The word 'correction' implies that there is a correct—the one and only legitimate—point of view, to which all other possible points of view have to be adapted, a position we critically engage with in this book. Thus, we agree with Peress that the people who lived in Sarajevo during the siege and who, in contrast to most journalists, could not leave the city easily if at all, will, in all likelihood, assign meanings to (at least some of) the images that differ from the meanings Peress notes in his written and verbal commentary. However, we wish to see these different meanings as coexisting rather than in need of correction and wonder what meaning(s) people who did *not* live in Sarajevo during the siege might assign to the images.

Conclusion

In this chapter, we presented an introduction into the basic lines of thought inspiring *Bosnia: Uncertain Paths to Peace*, its photophilosophy. We argued that this photojournalistic project deviates in many important ways from photojournalistic conventions, especially by assigning an unusually high degree of co-authorship to the users and by presenting a narrative that is anything but linear. We suggested that this project strengthened the photographer's authority precisely by acknowledging the limits of his—and, by implication, everyone's—knowledge and by presenting the photojournalistic truth as the sum of many narratives, not all of which are mutually supportive and all of which are contingent, changeable over time and across space. While inviting viewers to correct his positions accords with the plurality of narratives the project wishes to establish, it does not reflect our interest—informed by complexity theory and tolerance of ambiguity—in establishing narrative plurality non-hierarchically, including narratives that are difficult to tolerate. Thus, rather than correcting one position by another, we would prefer coexistence of different, equally valuable narratives, voices and forces. And, in a sense, this is what *Bosnia: Uncertain Paths to Peace* achieves: no matter how many corrections users submitted to the discussion groups and no matter how substantial these corrections were, Peress's original voice is still present on the website. It has not disappeared; it does not seem to have been updated in light of users' corrections, either. Rather, it continues to present one frame of interpretation—one space of possibility—within which, or in contrast to which, experienced users and newcomers can approach the website. In the following chapter, we will sketch different navigational paths on which users, such as us, can experience the website and connect to that which it depicts: post-siege Sarajevo in two distinct locations within the city—the center and the suburbs. We conclude the present chapter with the sixth of our Sarajevo photographs (Fig. 6.2) introduced in Chapter 2 in terms of photocomplexity.

Fig. 6.2 Sarajevo #6 (Photograph © Frank Möller)

References

Abadžić, Amra. 2022. *Sarajevo: The Longest Siege*. Sarajevo: Scena MESS.
Adams, Robert. 1994. *Why People Photograph. Selected Essays and Reviews*. New York: Aperture.
Andreas, Peter. 2008. *Blue Helmets and Black Markets: The Business of Survival in the Siege of Sarajevo*. Ithaca and London: Cornell University Press.
Bal, Mieke. 2007. The Pain of Images. In *Beautiful Suffering: Photography and the Traffic in Pain*, ed. Mark Reinhardt, Holly Edwards, and Erina Duganne, 93–115. Williams College Museum of Art: Chicago University of Chicago Press/Williamstown.
Bellmer, Rasmus, and Frank Möller. 2022a. Active Looking: Images in Peace Mediation. *Peacebuilding* 11 (2). https://doi.org/10.1080/21647259.2022.2152971.
Bellmer, Rasmus, and Frank Möller. 2022b. Messiness in Photography, War, and Transitions to Peace: Revisiting 'Bosnia: Uncertain Paths to Peace'. *Media, War, and Conflict* 16 (2). https://doi.org/10.1177/17506352211072463.
Bennett, Christopher. 2016. *Bosnia's Paralyzed Peace*. London: Hurst & Company.

Cieplak, Piotr. 2017. *Death, Image, Memory: The Genocide in Rwanda and its Aftermath in Photography and Documentary Film*. Houndmills: Palgrave Macmillan.
Coser, Lewis A. 1956. *The Functions of Social Conflict*. New York: The Free Press.
Demick, Barbara. 2012. *Besieged: Life Under Fire on a Sarajevo Street*. London: Granta.
Donia, Robert. 2006. *Sarajevo: A Biography*. London: Hurst and Company.
Glenny, Misha. 1996. *The Fall of Yugoslavia: The Third Balkan War*. London: Penguin.
Holbrooke, Richard. 1999. *To End a War*. New York: The Modern Library.
Jestrovic, Silvija. 2013. *Performance, Space, Utopia: Cities of War, Cities of Exile*. Houndmills: Palgrave Macmillan.
Karahasan, Dževad. 2014. *Sara und Serafina*, trans. Barbara Antkowiak. Frankfurt: Suhrkamp.
Karahasan, Dževad. 2023. *Einübung ins Schweben*, trans. Katharina Wolf-Grießhaber. Frankfurt: Suhrkamp.
Lederach, John Paul. 2005. *The Moral Imagination: The Art and Soul of Building Peace*. Oxford: Oxford University Press.
Linfield, Susie. 2010. *The Cruel Radiance: Photography and Political Violence*. Chicago and London: The University of Chicago Press.
Lowe, Paul. 2014. *The Forensic Turn: Bearing Witness and the 'Thingness' of the Photograph*. In *The Violence of the Image: Photography and International Conflict*, ed. Liam Kennedy and Caitlin Patrick, 211–234. London and New York: I.B. Tauris.
Lowe, Paul. 2015. *Ožiljak (Scar)*. Field Study 21.
Margalit, Avishai. 2004. *The Ethics of Memory*. Cambridge: Harvard University Press.
Markowitz, Fran. 2010. *Sarajevo: A Bosnian Kaleidoscope*. Urbana, Chicago, and Springfield: University of Illinois Press.
Möller, Frank. 2017. Witnessing Violence Through Photography. *Global Discourse: An Interdisciplinary Journal of Current Affairs and Contemporary Thought* 7 (2–3): 264–281.
Möller, Frank. 2019. *Peace Photography*. Houndmills: Palgrave Macmillan.
Morris, Errol. 2014. *Believing Is Seeing (Observations on the Mysteries of Photography)*. London: Penguin.
Morrison, Kenneth. 2016. *Sarajevo's Holiday Inn on the Frontline of Politics and War*. Houndmills: Palgrave Macmillan.
Morrison, Kenneth, and Paul Lowe. 2021. *Reporting the Siege of Sarajevo*. London: Bloomsbury Academic.
Moser, Benjamin. 2019. *Sontag: Her Life and Work*. New York: HarperCollins.

Reinhardt, Mark. 2007. Picturing Violence: Aesthetics and the Anxiety of Critique. In *Beautiful Suffering: Photography and the Traffic in Pain*, ed. Mark Reinhardt, Holly Edwards, and Erina Duganne, 13–36. Williams College Museum of Art: Chicago University of Chicago Press/Williamstown.
Ritchin, Fred. 1999. *In Our Own Image*. New York: Aperture.
Ritchin, Fred. 2009. *After Photography*. New York: W.W. Norton.
Ritchin, Fred. 2013. *Bending the Frame: Photojournalism, Documentary, and the Citizen*. New York: Aperture.
Sacco, Joe. 2004. *The Fixer: A Story from Sarajevo*. London: Jonathan Cape.
Silber, Laura, and Allan Little. 1997. *Yugoslavia: Death of a Nation*. London: Penguin.
Sontag, Susan. 1979. *On Photography*. London: Penguin.
Wilkes Tucker, Anne, and Will Michels with Natalie Zelt. 2012. *War/Photography: Images of Armed Conflict and Its Aftermath*. Houston: The Museum of Fine Arts.

CHAPTER 7

Navigating *Bosnia: Uncertain Paths to Peace*

INTRODUCTION

Bosnia: Uncertain Paths to Peace[1] is what users make of it, which is another way of saying that users may approach the website as intended by its creators, the picture editor Fred Ritchin and the photographer Gilles Peress, or not. The creators offer commentary, explanations, written and spoken reflections, instructions and recommendations, but how users approach the website in fact is mostly outside their control. Images always draw viewers "into an interpretive relationship that bypasses professional mediation" (MacDougall 1998: 68) thus inviting a plurality of narratives to emerge from the images—narratives that can neither be anticipated nor controlled completely. This explains skepticism about images even on the part of many of those who frequently use them. Professional mediators such as journalists use captions to undermine images' uncontrollability, thus restoring their (the mediators') authority and increasing the probability that images will be read as intended. However, as Jacques Rancière argues, images—and especially images of art—can expand the limits of

---

[1] Fred Ritchin, Gilles Peress, and *The New York Times on the Web, Bosnia: Uncertain Paths to Peace* (1996), at https://archive.nytimes.com/www.nytimes.com/specials/bosnia/index.html.

© The Author(s), under exclusive license to Springer Nature Switzerland AG 2023
R. Bellmer and F. Möller, *Peace, Complexity, Visuality*, Rethinking Peace and Conflict Studies, https://doi.org/10.1007/978-3-031-38218-5_7

the possible only "on condition that their meaning or effect is not anticipated" (2009: 103), which is why *Bosnia: Uncertain Paths to Peace* is so important.

In *Bosnia: Uncertain Paths to Peace*, lack of control is intended just as is the emergence of unanticipated narratives. Interactivity is utilized to transcend print media's "limitations of storytelling" (Ritchin 2009: 105). It enables the construction of multiple narratives within a visual and discursive frame suggested both by the visual and textual information included in the project, especially in the forums, and by the larger social, political and cultural configurations within which the project operates (e.g., Western culture, whatever that means precisely).

Bosnia: Uncertain Paths to Peace includes a huge variety of possible stories—some intended by the creators, others emerging from individual navigations—of which users can select one or several. Users decide *for what purpose* they visit the website: they may, for example, deliberately want to search for multiple narratives thus expanding the limits of their personal experience and knowledge, or they may want to reflect upon the narratives they bring with them to their encounter with the website and interrogate these narratives in light of the alternatives the project offers. They may want to explore their own reading and viewing habits, or they may want to think about the project's subjects—Bosnia and peace—in a new way. Alternatively, they might just want to learn something about an issue on which they do not yet have an opinion and therefore look for an authoritative interpretation of the events in Bosnia to be provided by an experienced journalist. They may visit the website to explore its technical possibilities without being particularly interested in Bosnia, or they may want to explore the situation in Bosnia without being particularly interested in the website's technical organization. Finally, they may want to look for confirmation of preexisting ideas thus ignoring the possibility of exploring alternatives. Such readers are not interested in "a new landscape of the possible" (Rancière 2009: 103) but in strengthening the existing one. These readers will also find on this website what they are looking for.

The website's creators do not take the users by the hand. Instead of guiding them through the project, they want to engage "the reader in an open-ended, non-authoritative dialectic" (Ritchin 1999: 101), as Gilles Peress is said to have done in his earlier work in Iran. As a result, they do not infringe on dialectic openness by prescribing viewing and navigation patterns. Indeed, some ideas to nudge viewers into particular viewing patterns had to be abandoned (Ritchin 2009: 107), largely for technical reasons but also because such a practice would have undermined the project's basic ideas. The result is a project whose meaning cannot be controlled and whose narratives can neither be anticipated completely nor reduced to one binding story, mandatory for all users. It necessarily co-presents different stories. It offers neither assurance nor the guiding hand of a mediator. It expects users to be curious and active, participating—as co-authors—in the construction of (some of) the multiple storylines that can be identified or constructed. Thus, *Bosnia: Uncertain Paths to Peace* does not offer anything a reader might expect from a newspaper project. While some readers may regard the resulting ambiguity as an adequate expression of the complexity of the situation in Bosnia at the time, other readers may reject the very idea that there is more than one way of making sense of the situation or even find it insulting. Such readers may navigate the website aiming at disambiguation. Finally, viewers may be confused by the way the website is organized, but such confusion "seemed slight compared to what had actually been going on in Bosnia" (Ritchin 2013: 124).

As we explore in this book the tolerance of ambiguity-enhancing potentialities of visual culture, we are interested in the ways the project "take[s] advantage of the new strategies made possible by the Web"— new, that is, in 1996: "nonlinear narratives, discussion groups, contextualizing information, panoramic imaging, the photographer's reflective voice" (Ritchin 2009: 102). Most of these ingredients contribute to acknowledgment of the plurality of meanings that images and projects utilizing them always carry with them rather than to the reduction of such plurality to one binding, mandatory meaning. To borrow words used by the sociologist Natan Sznaider,[2] we are interested in the as-well-as inherent in visual culture rather than approaching it in terms of either-or, which is so typical of Western ways of making sense of the world. Images co-present "centered and peripheral details in the same frame" (MacDougall 1998: 69); they show and allude to the general *and* the particular, the intended *and* the unintended, the visible *and* the invisible. As Nick Couldry (2000: 4) reminds us:

---

[2] See Chapter 6, footnote 1.

We should always reject short cuts in cultural description, not because we want complexity for its own sake, but because this is the only way to think culture in a non-dominative way, to recognize it as a space of multiple voices and forces. ... We need the tools to think about, and research, cultural complexity in a manageable way.

Does *Bosnia: Uncertain Paths to Peace* offer such tools?

Entering *Bosnia: Uncertain Paths to Peace*

The project's opening screen seems manageable enough.[3] Users do not have many choices. Indeed, wherever they click, they will be directed to a page introducing the project. This page ('About the Project') contains information about the project and its context in very basic terms. Neither the opening screen nor the following page has anything to say about the photograph that opens the essay[4] and that also appears on the project page, albeit rather small in the upper, right-hand corner. This is what the users learn about the project:

> For four years, Bosnia and Herzegovina was torn by the bloodiest and most ruthless European conflict since World War II. Its capital, Sarajevo, was the focus of an epic siege. Its territory was riven into ethnic enclaves, and accounts of mass killing and rape shook the world's conscience.
>
> With the signing of the Dayton accords last December, Bosnia is emerging from that torment. Now it faces the challenge of reconstruction and reconciliation, of carrying out free elections and of bringing accused war criminals to justice.

---

[3] We would have liked to reproduce some of the project's pages or at least include screenshots of selected pages, or parts of selected pages, such as the opening page or the project page. However, the publisher insists on permissions when third-party material is used (including screenshots from a website that is almost thirty years old and freely accessible on the Internet). Such permissions would have been obtainable from the *New York Times* (or the agency representing the *Times*) but very expensive for a non-commercial book such as ours. Furthermore, even with permission from the *Times*, we would still need permission from every individual who can be seen and identified in the images—a hopeless endeavor. The only thing we can do is ask our readers to visit the website when reading our analysis.

[4] The use of the word 'essay' in this context may be irritating as it normally references a written piece of work, but we are merely following the terminology used on the website and in Ritchin's explanatory texts.

"**Bosnia: Uncertain Paths to Peace**" is both a photographic chronicle and a worldwide discussion of this crucial passage in Bosnia's struggle.

An <u>interactive photo essay</u> by the French photojournalist <u>Gilles Peress</u>, with the photographer's narrative, documents the last weeks of the siege of Sarajevo in February and March, including the exodus of Serbs from the suburbs from which the siege had been mounted.

A collection of <u>forums for discussion</u>, led by scholars, diplomats, artists, humanitarian leaders and other experts, will be active for one month, starting June 10, and open to contributions from the entire Internet community. Connections have been established in Sarajevo, at the war crimes tribunal in The Hague and at the United Nations to encourage participation by those closest to the Bosnian conflict and its resolution.

And <u>resources for context</u> are available, including chronologies, maps, links to other Internet sites, a glossary and who's who, a reading list and recent coverage of the Bosnian events from The New York Times.

We welcome your feedback about this project.[5]

Clicking on 'interactive photo essay' will lead users to a page containing navigation devices and two photographs (henceforth, Project Page), one of which we have already seen on the opening screen but we still do not know what it shows; clicking on 'Gilles Peress' will open a page with information about the photographer; clicking on 'forums for discussion' will open a page that offers access to twelve such forums[6] plus four additional buttons (INDEX | CONTEXT | FORUMS | PHOTO ESSAY) of which the last one leads the user to the Project Page, the first one to a complete index offering a wealth of information about the organization of the website including multimedia links to audio and video, and the second one to the same page that the user would also have accessed had she clicked on 'resources for context' on the page 'About the Project.' This context page presents links to references and resources regarding the status of Bosnia after the Dayton Accords including maps and chronologies and links to *New York Times* articles and *National Public Radio* broadcasts. Furthermore, the page 'About the Project' contains at the bottom three links: 'Continue to the Photo Essay' (which again leads the

---

[5] https://archive.nytimes.com/www.nytimes.com/specials/bosnia/intro.html.

[6] See Chapter 6, footnote 17. 'Introduction' and 'Comment on the Site' cannot be accessed directly on this path but through the INDEX button on the bottom of this page.

user to the Project Page); 'About the Navigation' (which leads the user to a page with detailed yet incomplete[7] descriptions of how to navigate the website); and 'A Complete Guide to the Site,' the index which elsewhere on the website can be accessed by clicking on INDEX. 'About the Navigation' presents at the bottom seven buttons—the same buttons that also appear below the photographs on the page 'Continue to the Photo Essay' and these are the basic navigational devices for the whole website:

INDEX | GRID   CONTEXT | FORUMS   PREVIOUS | MORE | NEXT

We already know what INDEX, CONTEXT and FORUMS indicate. While we do not yet know what GRID means, we can expect PREVIOUS and NEXT to indicate a linear journey through the website, while MORE can be assumed to offer additional information (although it cannot be clicked on here, only on selected pages later in the essay; clicking first on MORE, when available, and then on TO MAIN will bring the user to the same page she would also have accessed by clicking directly on NEXT, thus rejoining the narrative). We can easily check the meaning of GRID by clicking on it: we open a page containing 35 small images, organized like a grid (7 images × 5 images). We are told that if we click on any of these images, we "will join the narrative at that point."[8] In addition to the already familiar buttons INDEX | GRID and CONTEXT | FORUMS, the page also contains a button TO SARAJEVO GRID, which makes us assume that the grid we see before our eyes is not the only one. We still do not know the subject(s) of the grid that we are seeing right now and have to move the cursor over the images to learn from the URL that appears on the bottom of the page that all these pictures were taken in the suburbs, albeit in different ones: Vogošća, Ilidža and Grbavica. We remember that the page 'Navigating the Photo Essay' included information about the suburbs and can consult that page if we want to know more. If we click on the button TO SARAJEVO GRID, we will open a page that is organized similarly to the suburbs grid but contains fewer

---

[7] The project's creators "decided, without telling the reader, that clicking on a photo would link to the same screen as if MORE had been selected; the idea was that choosing a photo indicated sufficient interest so that the reader should be shown more than the linear narrative would provide" (Ritchin 2009: 104).

[8] https://archive.nytimes.com/www.nytimes.com/specials/bosnia/grid/suburbs_grid.html.

images, only fifteen (organized grid-like 5 images × 3 images). The GRID button on this page is only decorative; no further page opens if we click on it. In contrast to the SUBURBS GRID, the background throughout the SARAJEVO GRID appears in white, giving the grid a less sinister atmosphere.

At this early stage, we already have different options. For example, we can spend a lot of time on the CONTEXT page, preparing ourselves thoroughly for our visual journey. Such preparation would certainly take more than the four hours it took one user to go through the site, according to Ritchin (2009: 107). We can study the 'Navigation page' to make our journey more predictable. We can simply always click on the NEXT button thus following the path prescribed by the creators. Or we can jump head over heels into our journey by engaging, without preparation, with the images presented in the GRIDS. These "uncaptioned photographs ... were meant to encourage a more intuitive, visual reading" (Ritchin 2009: 105), but such a reading is inhibited by the very small size of the images. However, more than any other ingredient of the website, the grids epitomize nonlinearity and interpretive openness, which are at the core of the whole project (and we will have more to say on them in Chapter 8). Simply "join[ing] the narrative" by clicking on one of the grid images seems difficult, however, as users would have no clue what narrative it is that they would be joining.

Or we can spend a lot of time with the image that opens the whole project. At this point, the website does not tell us anything about the image and its subjects. We would not know that, as Ritchin explains elsewhere, this photograph "was, in fact, a rephotographed snapshot of a Muslim family in which the face of each family member had been erased by a drill bit; the disfigured snapshot was all that was left when this family returned home after four years of conflict" (Ritchin 2009: 105–106). We would not know, either, that we will re-encounter this image later on our journey through the suburbs, namely, on the page titled 'conclusion'—provided that we reach that particular page on our individual journey. On that page, we learn that

> Amela Fako, a 24-year-old Muslim woman, found this photograph of her family when she returned to her home in Ilidza after the war. That was about all she found. Bosnian Serbs had cleaned out almost everything in her home but left this image, defaced by a drill bit, "a primitive message,

part of the other war, one not done with guns," she said. "It was the war of fear, the war on the mind. They wanted to make it difficult for us to come home."[9]

And because we would know none of the above, we could start our own process of interpretation, combining what we (believe to) see with what (we think) it might mean or what, in Wim Wenders's words, it might "'imply,' 'suggest,' 'hint' or whatever" (Wenders and Zournazi 2013: 38). Essentially, we would start our own interpretation *not* to be *corrected* later when we find additional information on the website or elsewhere but to understand the multilayeredness of every image, images' irreducibility to one meaning and the multiplicity of stories that each image tells.

First Navigation

We could continue describing the website's organization, but such a description would result in a rather tedious reading experience. Instead, we wish to introduce four different navigational approaches to the website. We claim neither that one approach is superior to the others nor that no other approaches could be chosen. Different users will choose different approaches, and the same user will use different navigational paths when visiting the site several times, exploring the possibilities it offers for users to co-construct meaning and to become involved in storytelling. Ordering these four approaches hierarchically in terms of analytical superiority would undermine our interest in a non-dominative way of approaching the website.

It is arguable that, although deviating from standard photojournalistic conventions, *Bosnia: Uncertain Paths to Peace*—just like conventional photojournalism—aims to capitalize on a specific relationship between words and images, described earlier in Chapter 5 of the book in terms suggested by Peter Gilgen (2003: 56), namely, as "an intellectual stereoscopic effect" connecting words and images with one another in a mutually supportive way without superimposing the meaning assigned to words on that assigned to images or vice versa. (This effect is also meant

---

[9] https://archive.nytimes.com/www.nytimes.com/specials/bosnia/suburbs/grbavica/transition.html. For the family's story, see also Loyd (2020: 206–207) and Ron Haviv's photograph of this particular photograph in Hale and Turner (2020: 194).

to be critical in a very Benjaminian way.)[10] On the introduction page to the suburbs, for example, we see blocks of text alternating with images: four blocks of text separated from one another by two photographs at a time. The text is written by Gilles Peress and dated "*Bosnia, Feb 19*" (1996). At the bottom of the page, we find the by now familiar standard navigation device—INDEX | GRID, CONTEXT | FORUMS and PREVIOUS | MORE | NEXT. MORE is disabled; clicking on NEXT brings us to the suburb of Vogošća, a destination we would also reach by clicking on any of the images. To learn where this suburb is exactly located in Sarajevo's urban structure, we could click on INDEX, then on 'Maps' and finally on 'Sarajevo and suburbs' and see that Vogošća is located north-west of Sarajevo quite some distance from the city's central part.[11] Peress's narrative provides a sense of the atmosphere of the scenes depicted in the images but is much more personal than is normally the case in photojournalistic captions:

> As I am walking through this destroyed landscape, through the remains of a war now gone, I am overwhelmed by the silence, the absence of explosions. I can hear the birds singing. The ending of war is almost more depressing than war itself because once you don't have to run for your life, the evidence of waste is fully there to contemplate as slowly as you want, inch by inch, bullet hole by bullet hole.

Photograph 1   Photograph 2

> The sense of hangover of the day after the party, after the house was trashed, after the family was destroyed, the children dispersed, colors every one of my feelings. There is a bitter taste. People in Sarajevo and in the Serbian suburbs are sullen; there is none of the joy that one would expect from the coming of peace.

---

[10] Gilgen explains that "the heteronomous element of the caption safeguards against a possible revival of auratic effects in the photographic image. ... And while captions serve to bridge this spatio-temporal gap [i.e., the distance between the spectator and the depicted scene; the authors] by actualizing the historicity of the image, they simultaneously mark it as irreducible" (2003: 56).

[11] https://archive.nytimes.com/www.nytimes.com/specials/bosnia/context/sarajevo. GIF.html.

| Photograph 3 | Photograph 4 |

I am listening to the BBC World Service when a sudden announcement on the 6 o'clock news explodes like a shell in the middle of a sunny day: the Serbs have to leave Sarajevo's suburbs within three days. We, and I suspect they, all thought that the deadline was a month later: the 19th of March.

| Photograph 5 | Photograph 6 |

I quickly check the information; the deadline has been moved for some of the suburbs so that the evacuations would be staggered. The Serbian neighborhoods will go over to the Bosnian authority one after the other at intervals of six or seven days. The first one to go -- in three days, as announced on the radio -- is Vogosca.[12]

Reading this page as Gilgen's intellectual stereoscopic effect suggests is one way of reading it. The images are not explained individually but provide a visual sense of place that strengthens, and is strengthened by, Peress's written narrative. Co-presented on the same page, it is a reasonable assumption that words and images are indeed meant to be read together, although nothing prevents the user from reading only the text, jumping from one block to the next without paying attention to the images. Alternatively, she could also pay attention only to the images or to one image and build a narrative upon her visual experience regardless of the textual information included in Peress's narrative. The vision that the photographer had may indeed be fully there in the picture; users could, therefore, concentrate on the images and start to construct a narrative derived from their visual impression, unaffected by the text. As the images' relationship to the surrounding text blocks is far from obvious, tensions may result from reading them in parallel or stereoscopically. These images do not simply illustrate the text. They do something else, but what they do exactly is hard to say.

[12] https://archive.nytimes.com/www.nytimes.com/specials/bosnia/suburbs/suburbs_intro2.html.

If you start your journey in Sarajevo, you will find the same navigational devices at the bottom of the page. Four images and four blocks of text are organized diagonally from the upper left-hand corner to the lower right-hand corner of the page (text blocks and photographs 1–3) and then counterbalanced by the fourth image–text pair, providing the page with an artistic sense normally absent from photojournalism. One photograph appears left to the first block of text, a second one left to the second text block, a third one left to the third text block and the fourth image right to the fourth block of text. Clicking on each of the (very small) images will bring you to the same page you would also open by clicking on NEXT (Sarajevo chapter opener). This procedure is by now familiar to us. When compared to the introduction to the suburbs, Peress's text is much shorter, like a poem, distinctly un-photojournalistic, describing his arrival in the city and establishing the mood and the atmosphere dominating the whole narrative.[13]

---

[13] https://archive.nytimes.com/www.nytimes.com/specials/bosnia/sarajevo/sarajevo_intro.html.

Photograph 1	Flying above the land frozen and virgined by the snows, I start to see the scars,					
		Photograph 2	the trenches, rows of homes, suburbs of a better life, wrecked by house-to-house combat,			
				Photograph 3	by front lines through living rooms, gardens turned into mine fields. From this vantage point,	
					embracing the totality of destruction, silenced by the winter air, we drift upon the city: Sarajevo.[a]	Photograph 4

Due to the very small size of the images, what they depict is hard to decipher. Clicking on them will not, as would be the case currently, enlarge the image but lead you to the next page, thus offering no assurance whatsoever what these images show. It would not help approach Sarajevo through the Sarajevo grid, either, as this particular page is not included in it.

Second Navigation

We have described our own initial navigation experience in the spring of 2021 elsewhere (Bellmer and Möller 2022: 7–9). Without repeating what we have already written above about the website's basic organization, we want to reproduce our navigational experience here without suggesting that this is the only or the best way of approaching the website. It is simply one path among many others, and its selection is as arbitrary as it seemed to be logical at the time. We wish to clarify also from the beginning that "our personal experience with the website and its effects on us certainly differ from those the original users had back in the 1990s" (p. 7)—the digital environment is a completely different one just as is the political environment. Furthermore, looking is always a personal experience reflecting who you are, what you bring with you to the visual encounter and what you are interested in. We do not wish to speculate how the original users experienced the website,[14] and we do not know who the original users were. We do speculate, however, that people in Sarajevo and the suburbs, in the spring of 1996, had many other things to do than engaging with an online project exploring a situation they were utterly familiar with anyway: local people did not need the website to show them how it felt like to have been exposed to the siege for almost four years. And we know from Ritchin's report that plans to set up a computer terminal in the university of Sarajevo "encountered problems," as a result of which it "was slow to go online" (Ritchin 2009: 107). In addition, the possibilities that the early Web offered were quite limited when compared to today's standards. Not surprisingly, then, many forums "were dominated largely by pro-Serbian commentators *abroad*" (Ritchin 2009: 108; italics added). This domination shows how difficult

---

[14] Some clues can be found in the forums. However, only a very small number of comments is still available, all of which praising the project. See https://archive.nytimes.com/www.nytimes.com/specials/bosnia/forums/bosnia_comments.html.

it is to give voice to people directly affected by violence. We remember our navigation experience as follows (Bellmer and Möller 2022: 8–9):

> Used to highly self-explanatory user interfaces, we are tempted to go directly into the essay without bothering to familiarize ourselves with the navigation. We consider ourselves experienced and knowledgeable users of digital interfaces. How could such a simple design possibly confuse us? [...] Without having read the navigation instructions, a feeling of being overwhelmed emerges. What do we have to click to experience the 'whole' story in the 'correct' order? How do we avoid missing a part? Can we click PREVIOUS and choose a different image to see the other photographs, to read other written texts? (p. 8)

In the previous chapter, we quoted the photographer's wish to be corrected by users and criticized this wish from a complexity point of view. In our first encounter with Peress's voice, we found what he had to say both fascinating and irritating. It was fascinating because it introduced us both into his personal way of trying to make sense of the world and into a world that was completely alien to us—life under siege conditions, for example, or the world of the sniper—thus revealing many facets of life (and death) in the city we were not familiar with. At the same time, his self-reflective and self-effacing voice was irritating, as it

> undermine[d] our belief in and our reliance on the photographer's authority. After all, he was on location, in contrast to us. Shouldn't he be able to give us an authoritative reading of what happened and what his photographs were meant to express? Is this not what we expect photographs and photographers in a journalistic context to give us? What is the use of photography if it requires corrections of a given photographer's misconceptions? (p. 8)

Furthermore, we wondered,

> how are the 'people who lived there' supposed to 'correct' the photographer's conception? How are users who did not live there supposed to navigate the plurality of views bound to result from such correction? Will such correction not result in viewers' confusion? And does it make sense in the first place to expect anyone to be capable of providing a 'correct' conception if by *correct* we mean a conception that is relevant beyond first-person assumptions, no matter how convincing and justified such assumptions might be in light of personal experience? We realize that,

although we are only at the beginning of the project, we are already drawn into its dynamics. (pp. 8–9)

And what do the photographer's reflections mean for us visiting the website more than 25 years after its construction? Indeed,

> Peress's voice sucks us into his story and his understanding of his own role as a photographer, visiting a location without being of/from this location, a guest, a stranger, uninvited. Furthermore, his reflections, acknowledging his own limitations, make us think about the role assigned to us, as users who did not live 'there' during the siege. We understand that this project will not give us the assurance we expected it to give us when we started our navigation. (p. 8)

And we also begin to understand *our* misconceptions. This website is not meant to give us assurance. There are only fragments of stories to explore that do not necessarily culminate in a 'whole' story, and there is no correct order in which to read and make sense of the pages. However, while we begin to understand our misconceptions, we are still caught in the logics and standard procedures of photojournalism that are not easy to abandon, as our next navigation shows.

Third Navigation

We return to the website a few days later, choosing a different path to navigate it. Even though the website seems highly simplistic, almost embarrassingly so, it still confuses us. For example, if we click on an image to see a larger version of it, we are directed to a different page, showing more images and text. We return to the original image and click NEXT only to find ourselves on the same page that we had already entered by clicking on the photograph.[15] After clicking on a couple of images in the Sarajevo storyline, we end up on a page displaying five photographs accompanied by a text saying:

> One of the deep regrets for many of the Serbs fleeing the suburbs to more distant destinations was that they would no longer be able to take the tram into Sarajevo and wander into a coffee shop.[16]

---

[15] See footnote 7 above.
[16] https://archive.nytimes.com/www.nytimes.com/specials/bosnia/sarajevo/sa5.html.

We wonder if the people depicted had nothing else to regret than the somewhat longer distance to a coffee shop. What do we have to do to experience the 'complete' story, the 'real' story of the siege of Sarajevo? Embarrassed, once again, we hesitate, but this time we are embarrassed with ourselves and our patronizing attitude, not with the website. Indeed, the impossibility of visiting a coffee shop is an important part of the complete story. Going about your daily routines is an essential ingredient of everyday peace or everyday resistance, "eking out safe space in a conflict context and allowing a façade of normality to prevail" (Mac Ginty 2014: 555) thus maintaining and insisting on "a residue of the ethical or perhaps merely aesthetic standards from an earlier life" (Emcke 2016: 27; our translation). Showing that *that* is no longer possible is an important element of the website, communicating to its users the day-to-day dimension of violent conflict, which tells us as much about the lived reality in the city as the standard photojournalistic focus on the terror at the barricades. However, after some additional clicks, we see those images that we expect to see; after all, this is said to be a photojournalistic project: finally, a dead body, destroyed cars. Once again, however, we are wrong, as the caption reveals:

> Walking through Sarajevo while the suburbs were burning and people in flight, I came upon people shooting a feature film about the four-year siege that had just ended. This man is not dead, for once, but an actor.[17]

We wonder what kind of story we would have constructed if we had not read the caption—probably a story about the ongoing violence and the hopelessness of the overall situation in the city after the end of the siege. It seems that we are still prisoners of the expectations we brought with us to the viewing experience, shaping what we expected to see and determining how we interpreted what we saw. After all, *Bosnia: Uncertain Paths to Peace* does not operate in a political or visual vacuum. It operates within a visual environment that, as regards Sarajevo immediately after the siege, was dominated by images of war, genocide, destruction and traumatic memories—an environment within which *Bosnia: Uncertain Paths*

---

[17] https://archive.nytimes.com/www.nytimes.com/specials/bosnia/sarajevo/sa7.html (see also Ritchin 2009: 103: "only four days after the shelling had stopped," a feature film about the siege of Sarajevo was being produced on location—another facet of the grotesquerie of the overall scenario).

to Peace too was being experienced. Even today, laudable institutions such as the *Galerija 11/07/95* in Sarajevo,[18] dedicated to the memory of the Srebrenica genocide, visually document and, in a sense, reconstruct the conflict: "such projects run the risk of repeating the trauma of the past or even perpetuating rifts between communities," Pippa Oldfield notes with regard to this particular gallery, but "they may also provide a 'safe' space to reflect upon life-altering violence and honor those who are gone" (2019: 168). What they do not offer is a visual path from the aftermath of violence to peace (see Möller 2017). Thus, the visual encounter with Sarajevo and its galleries and museums today is still dominated by the history of violence, genocide and siege.

Perhaps, then, the reason for our confusion is to be found not in the images but in our preconceptions, in which case we would be among the main addressees of the project. This is indeed good photography: it helps us acknowledge the preexisting conceptions, visual and otherwise, that we brought with us to the viewing experience, revealing dimensions of the conflict we were not aware of and thus producing new knowledge. As such, it is not only good photography but also critical photography based on "conceptual innovation" that makes users "*think* about atrocities" (Shapiro 2015: 10; italics in original) committed in Sarajevo and elsewhere. At the barricades *and* in the coffee house, every error and every miscalculation could mean death—every correct step and every correct assessment could mean survival.

Fourth Navigation

In addition to images and written texts, nine audio files are embedded into selected subpages presenting the photographer's voice. Thus, users can read Peress's narrative but also listen to his personal reflections on his experiences during his visit to Bosnia. The introduction of audio files with the photographer's voice is one of the most innovative and unusual elements of a project that is full of innovations such as slide shows, videos, hyperlinks, unconventionally presented sequences of images, philosophical and poetic narratives, nonlinear storytelling and so on. Photography is often said to be silent, and the caption is said to be the photograph's "missing voice" (Sontag 1979: 108); in *Bosnia: Uncertain Paths to Peace*,

---

[18] See www.galerija110795.ba.

however, the photograph's—or the photographer's—voice is not missing but very present. Thus, we have to engage with it without reducing the photographs to what the photographer has to say about them. His voice is one voice among many. Furthermore, often he does not have to say much about the photographs but, rather, about the environment within which he took them. Thus, interpreting the images within this environment is still the user's task. From our notes:

peress.4.au[19]

The camera itself is an author because the camera speaks with its distinctive voice. And you (who) look at the picture – a reader clicks to more, clicks to next or clicks to context or index or goes back to previous or whatever – in how you look and you made mind associations (?) about an image is also an author. So there is not one author to an image.

peress.3.au[20]

I really wish to be corrected by people who lived there. And I hope that the Web is one of the places where my misconceptions will be corrected – both in terms of ideas and images and captions and so on. [I see it as a] democratic space, a space of dialogue.
→ one view – the photographer's – can and perhaps should be replaced by another, more correct view – the view of the person who lived there – rather than accepting a plurality of views.

peress.2.au[21]

… it is not about escaping the bullets; it's the eye that is able to aim and decide to kill or not to kill. So you enter into a world that's [yeah] almost like a theatrical sense of screens, a reality that's calculated to the millimeter where the sniper can see you from here to there and not beyond there. It's almost like a [pool?] table where every angle is calculated. It's both a physical world with physical and real consequences; but at the same time it's a virtual world that's in your mind where you have to compute always the angles of things. And that's what sniper's world is about: it's a terrifying

---

[19] https://www.nytimes.com/specials/bosnia/gallery/peress.4.au.

[20] https://www.nytimes.com/specials/bosnia/gallery/peress.3.au.

[21] https://www.nytimes.com/specials/bosnia/gallery/peress.2.au.

world, and at the same time it's a fascinating world where every error can mean death.

Looking at our notes almost two years after we made them, not all of them are entirely clear to us. Our handwritten notes are hard to decipher and the paper has not aged well. We could check the transcription by relistening to the material, but such a procedure would undermine the authenticity of the notes. What is clear, however, is our interest—then and now—in how the photographer ponders his subject position *as* photographer, inviting users to correct him and identifying the Internet as a democratic place where such a correction could take place. Such identification reflects the widespread optimism and enthusiasm that prevailed at the early stages of the Internet regarding its democratizing potentialities, which have long since been replaced by a much more sober and skeptical attitude. However, Peress's basic idea is still fascinating—the idea of a photographer, a photojournalist, merely offering visual raw material for users' interpretation rather than imposing on the users a specific way of making sense of the images. His captions aren't captions in a photojournalistic sense—"neutral, informative: a date, a place, names" (Sontag 2003: 45). Self-reflective and poetic, they do not offer "directives" or "signposts" that Walter Benjamin recommended against "freischwebende Kontemplation" ("free-floating contemplation") on the part of viewers (Benjamin 1963: 21). Instead, Peress encourages "the free play of the spectator's faculties" (Gilgen 2003: 56), which can then be translated into active interaction (see Chapter 5). However, the basic problem remains: if you are interested in a plurality of open-ended narratives, then there is no way to control the emergence of narratives without undermining the project's basic lines of thought. Ritchin reports that they

> had wanted to automatically keep track of a reader's movement so that some mixing of pathways through the essay could take place based upon previous choices. For example, a reader who continually chose photos depicting Serbs might be given more photos representing Serbs or maybe would be required to look at more images that showed Muslims. (2009: 107)

Such editorial interference into users' choices was not only impossible at the time due to technical restrictions; it would also have undermined the notion of users as co-authors on an equal footing with the project's creators, responsible for the construction of their own narratives, regardless of the narratives suggested by the project's creators or its structure. Some narratives will inevitably emerge with which other users will not identify at all, requiring tolerance of ambiguity even though it may be difficult to tolerate some of the emerging narratives. If you understand, recognize and appreciate culture "as a space of multiple voices and forces" (Nick Couldry, quoted above), then you also have to recognize those voices and forces that you do not appreciate. Recognizing those voices does not mean agreeing with them, but the decision to agree with them or to disagree requires knowledge of them and their coming into being. You can disagree but nevertheless understand how they emerged; and even if you do not agree, they will have real consequences and these consequences can, to some extent, be anticipated once you understand the narratives underlying them. This is at the core of tolerance of ambiguity as we see it (within certain limits—limits to be specified in accordance with the requirements of every individual situation). *Bosnia: Uncertain Paths to Peace* helps understand how, simply by navigating the website on individual, idiosyncratic paths, different voices emerge, accompanied by the photographer's images and his voice but ultimately rather independent of them.

Indeed, this multi-sensory element, which must have been very unusual to users at the time, offers highly diverse perspectives. Ritchin assigns importance to the photographer's "emotional reactions and philosophical questions" that go far beyond traditional, factual captions in photojournalism (2009: 105). However, if not even the photographer knows exactly what happened on location and what his photography shows, then how are we—users navigating the website from our save places, temporally and spatially, our homes or offices, users who did not experience the war in Bosnia and the siege of Sarajevo first-hand, users who did not personally experience any war or any siege—supposed to make sense of it? This website, we realize, will not allow us to be passive and neutral observers of a straightforward narrative or consumers of pre-formulated ideas and assessments that we can either accept or reject.

Conclusion

In this chapter, we have sketched four different navigational approaches to *Bosnia: Uncertain Paths to Peace*. Much can be criticized from the point of view of conventional photojournalism; much can be praised from a complexity point of view. Our navigational sketches do not present a complete picture. Every user will choose her individual path just as we use different paths each time we revisit the website, diversifying our experience. We have learned to appreciate what we initially found confusing. We have also learned to appreciate the residue of confusion we still encounter when we visit the website. There is no 'complete' story to discover by choosing the 'right' path, only fragments of stories. Assembling several such fragments on several successive visits will not lead to a complete story, either, just to a larger fragment. We may miss parts of the narrative, but the people of Sarajevo will, in all likelihood, also have missed parts of the story of the siege when it took place while simultaneously experiencing many things that no website can communicate to the uninitiated.

We understood that what we expect to see depends very much on the experience we bring with us to the encounter with a project and that it is not easy to change one's habits of seeing, especially in an image context that is still very much dominated by the conventions and standard procedures of photojournalism. We learned to appreciate the photographer's modesty and insights into the limitations of his own knowledge, even though he was on location—in contrast to us. Inevitably, a certain degree of skepticism emerged about other photographers, other journalists and other photojournalists but also about academics who pretend to know the whole story. Complexity theory tells us—and *Bosnia: Uncertain Paths to Peace* shows us—that we will never know the whole story, that the whole story, while being composed of a multitude of individual stories, is always more than the sum of its sub-stories. In the following two chapters we proceed by taking a closer look at two ingredients of the website—the grid structure and the invitation to inter-activity—to further explore its potentialities for nonlinear storytelling, narrative plurality and the emergence of tolerance of ambiguity. We conclude the present chapter with the seventh of our Sarajevo photographs (Fig. 7.1) introduced in Chapter 2 in terms of photocomplexity.

Fig. 7.1 Sarajevo #7 (Photograph © Frank Möller)

References

Bellmer, Rasmus, and Frank Möller. 2022. Messiness in Photography, War, and Transitions to Peace: Revisiting 'Bosnia: Uncertain Paths to Peace. *Media, War, and Conflict* 16 (2). https://doi.org/10.1177/17506352211072463.

Benjamin, Walter. 1963. Das Kunstwerk im Zeitalter seiner technischen Reproduzierbarkeit. In *Das Kunstwerk im Zeitalter seiner technischen Reproduzierbarkeit. Drei Studien zur Kunstsoziologie*, 7–44. Walter Benjamin. Frankfurt: Suhrkamp.

Couldry, Nick. 2000. *Inside Culture: Re-imagining the Method of Cultural Studies*. London, Thousand Oaks, and New Delhi: Sage.

Emcke, Carolin. 2016. *Von den Kriegen. Briefe and Freunde*. Frankfurt: Fischer.

Gilgen, Peter. 2003. History after Film. In *Mapping Benjamin: The Work of Art in the Digital Age*, ed. Hans Ulrich Gumbrecht and Michael Marrinan, 53–62. Stanford: Stanford University Press.

Hale, Constance, and Fiona Turner, eds. 2020. *Imagine: Reflections on Peace*. Paris: Hemeria.

Loyd, Anthony. 2020. God Won't Have Forgotten. In *Imagine: Reflections on Peace*, ed. Constance Hale and Fiona Turner, 196–209. Paris: Hemeria.

MacDougall, David. 1998. *Transcultural Cinema*, ed. and with an introduction Lucien Taylor. Princeton: Princeton University Press.

Mac Ginty, Roger. 2014. Everyday Peace: Bottom-Up and Local Agency in Conflict Affected Societies. *Security Dialogue* 45 (6): 548–564.

Möller, Frank. 2017. From Aftermath to Peace: Reflections on a Photography of Peace. *Global Society: Journal of Interdisciplinary International Relations* 31 (3): 315–335.

Oldfield, Pippa. 2019. *Photography and War*. London: Reaktion Books.

Rancière, Jacques (2009) *The Emancipated Spectator*, trans. Gregory Elliott. London and Brooklyn: Verso.

Ritchin, Fred. 1999. *In Our Own Image*. New York: Aperture.

Ritchin, Fred. 2009. *After Photography*. New York: W.W. Norton.

Ritchin, Fred. 2013. *Bending the Frame: Photojournalism, Documentary, and the Citizen*. New York: Aperture.

Shapiro, Michael J. 2015. *War Crimes, Atrocity, and Justice*. Cambridge and Malden: Polity Press.

Sontag, Susan. 1979. *On Photography*. London: Penguin.

Sontag, Susan. 2003. *Regarding the Pain of Others*. New York: Farrar, Straus & Giroux.

Wenders, Wim, and Mary Zournazi. 2013. *Inventing Peace: A Dialogue of Perception*. London and New York: I.B. Tauris.

CHAPTER 8

The Grids: Architectural Space and Panel-to-Panel Transitions

Introduction

In Chapter 6, we introduced *Bosnia: Uncertain Paths to Peace*, an interactive, online project designed by the picture editor Fred Ritchin and the photographer Gilles Peress in association with the *New York Times on the Web* in the spring of 1996.[1] The project was meant to illustrate and illuminate the living conditions in two selected areas of the Bosnian capital city of Sarajevo at the end of the siege that had paralyzed the city since 1992: the city center and the suburbs. In contrast to conventional photojournalistic projects, Ritchin and Peress's work aimed to visualize "the tentative making of peace" (Ritchin 2009: 102)—"the problematic and possibility of peace" (p. 105)—outlining paths to peace in a city that had been dominated for almost four years by the opposite. Explicitly inviting users to respond to Peress's photo essay, the project acknowledged the existence of a plurality of narratives with which either to make sense of the situation from an individual perspective or to acknowledge that the situation did not make sense, conventionally understood. Ritchin and Peress did not even try to establish an authoritative narrative derived from the photographer's experience in the city. The project expanded the limits of print journalism and developed new ways of journalistic storytelling,

[1] https://archive.nytimes.com/www.nytimes.com/specials/bosnia/index.html.

© The Author(s), under exclusive license to Springer Nature Switzerland AG 2023
R. Bellmer and F. Möller, *Peace, Complexity, Visuality*, Rethinking Peace and Conflict Studies,
https://doi.org/10.1007/978-3-031-38218-5_8

relying on the possibilities the Internet offered in terms of establishing nonlinear narratives and inviting a plurality of stories to be constructed on the basis of the material presented on the website. It enabled a multisensory experience on the part of viewers by combining images with written and recorded texts and asked for active interaction.

In Chapter 7, we described selected navigational paths through the website that helped us understand not only how the website is organized but also to what extent our own perceptions and impressions depend on the preconceptions we bring with us to our navigation. We criticized the photographer's hope that his misconceptions will be corrected by users engaging with the contents of the website as misleading from a complexity point of view. Our own preconceptions were certainly revealed by our navigation through the website and its deliberate gaps and obstacles, dead ends and redundancies, surprises and challenges, which helped expose the fallacies in our beliefs. We argued that *Bosnia: Uncertain Paths to Peace* indeed presents good and critical photography because, based on conceptual innovation, it goes beyond recycling photojournalistic conventions and makes viewers think about what they see. The project also provides new knowledge by directing viewers' attention to the everyday experience of life after the siege and the continuation of the past in the present without, however, getting stuck in the past as aftermath photography tends to do. The term 'uncertain' in the project's title can still be applied to Bosnia today, more than 25 years after the project, but the word 'peace' is equally important because it shapes what users think of as possible when they visit the website and reflect on Bosnia's future. The longer peace prevails, the less it will be visualized, and this is a problem because for peace to prevail; it has to be seen as functioning for the benefit of the citizens. "While peace – once established – may not seem for photographers to be an *event* worthy of photographic attention, peace is never established ...; it is always emerging and always under threat ... and, therefore, always in need of photographic representation" (Bellmer et al. forthcoming; italics in original).

In this chapter and in the following chapter, we will focus on selected ingredients of *Bosnia: Uncertain Paths to Peace*—the grid structure and inter-activity—to explore the project's potentialities for nonlinear storytelling, narrative plurality and the emergence of tolerance of ambiguity. Rather than interrogating the website in light of the reality in the city (whatever that may have been), our critique is largely work-immanent.

MESSINESS, ANXIETY AND APPREHENSION

The term 'the siege of Sarajevo' is an aggregate term in need of differentiation. Using the term generically will hide more than it reveals about life in the city between April 1992 when the shelling started and the end of February 1996 when the siege formally came to an end. Indeed, "the Sarajevo siege provides a powerful illustration of the merits of disaggregating conflict and analytically embracing its messiness" (Andreas 2008: 165).[2] Merely separating a conflict into its constituent parts and reassembling these parts after analysis will, from a complexity perspective, not result in understanding the conflict in its entirety. While such a procedure tends to disregard the evolution of complex and changing dynamics operating among the different parts, it is nevertheless an important and necessary step toward understanding. This is an ambiguous result of thinking in terms of complexity: disaggregation leads to incomplete results but is nevertheless indispensable for analysis. Analysis equals disaggregation.

Arguably, disaggregation reflects the experience of most citizens at the time, as their experience was also incomplete. The Ritchin–Peress project exemplifies how such disaggregation can be accomplished by visual means. It does so, most basically, by separating the city of Sarajevo from its suburbs and visually assigning different conditions and different dynamics to these areas. Dividing the city into two entities is also a simplification, of course. Within these two areas, different dynamics prevailed, some of which the project covers while others remain obscure. However, it is analytically superior to treating Sarajevo as a unitary actor or even as a unitary non-actor passively exposed to the violence inflicted on it. *Bosnia: Uncertain Paths to Peace* addresses the problem of "two-dimensional translations" by rendering visible the "multifaceted" and "chaotic original" (Jestrovic 2013: 126), and while the project does not succeed completely, it shows the complexity of subject positions and inhibits assurance through narrative closure.[3] After all, there "can never be a final and

---

[2] In a microstudy, Barbara Demick (2012) has described the living conditions during the siege and afterward of the people of one Sarajevo street—Logavina. This is maximum disaggregation.

[3] See also Jelena Golubović's (2020) insightful account which renders ethnic ambiguity in post-conflict Bosnia visible through disaggregation thus complexifying preconceived notions of inter-ethnic relations.

definitive interpretation of any image because in each new situation, in each new encounter with an audience or viewers, the image will acquire new interpretations and meanings" (Rubinstein and Sluis 2013: 36).

Regarding the story of the siege of Sarajevo—and, for that matter, regarding *any* story—there are as many narratives as there are people telling them:

> Each person carries with them an individual history of reflection which cannot be reduced to shared cultural patterns. Partly pure accident, and partly structured, this history is the trace of that person's perceiving, absorbing, interacting, reflecting, retelling, reflecting again, and so on, a sequence endured by that person alone. This very particular 'structure' is what we mean by 'experience'. (Couldry 2000: 51)

We need to add two qualifications: first, in the process of retelling a story, the story changes. Primo Levi wrote in the context of the Holocaust that memory, "expressed in the form of a story, tends to become fixed in a stereotype, in a form tested by experience, crystallized, perfected, adorned" (1989: 24), replacing memory. Such a stereotype can simplify or complexify the original narrative, but experience can also be composed of both simplification and complexification, as some parts of the story may become simpler while other parts of the story may become more complex in the process of retelling (see Chapter 12). The capability of replacing—and becoming—memory has also been observed with regard to photographs and visual storytelling (see Chapter 5). Second, there are even more stories because individuals, as members of social groups, narrate their individual stories differently in different contexts, in part adapted to how they want to be seen by others, in part tailored to what they believe their respective audience expects them to say and wants to hear. Human beings are social beings, always responding to or anticipating the presence of others, identifying partially with others. And while we may refer to other people as negative reference points to help us define who we are by establishing who we are not, we still have something in common with them, as images show inevitably and redundantly (see MacDougall 1998: 246–247). This is one of their functions in peacebuilding, albeit an underappreciated one: it is *too* obvious to make a fuss about it. Remember, for example, the photograph—actually a photograph of a photograph—that opens *Bosnia: Uncertain Paths to Peace* discussed in the preceding chapter: although the faces of the people depicted have been erased there can be no doubt that what we see are human beings with whom we—and the people who defaced the photograph, too—have something in common. It may even be speculated that these people felt the need to destroy parts of the photograph's surface exactly *because* they knew that they had something in common with the people depicted. However, this photograph still conveys what David MacDougall calls "features of human appearance and sociality" (1998: 247). A despicable act meant to call into question the humanity of the people depicted did, in fact, confirm it. We would not expect the people depicted to share this position, but we think that it is arguable.

Ritchin and Peress present individual visual stories and emphasize the anxieties and vicissitudes of everyday life. In an image with accompanying text, for example, Peress describes an encounter between the Serb Zoran and some Bosniak men: "Suddenly it's all hugs and kisses – they happened to know Zoran, and some were old friends." Challenging preconceived notions of Serb–Bosniak antagonism, Peress continues by reporting: "He then turned around and pointed at Zoran, jokingly saying, 'It's him! He threw the shell at me! It's his fault!' Zoran, then taking on a childlike voice and joining his hands as if in supplication, said, 'So sorry.'" By presenting photographs of such encounters, Peress and Ritchin acknowledge that each person—including the photographer—possesses a multitude of subject positions, including and perhaps especially during a violent conflict, adapted to the circumstances.[4] The illustration of a multitude of complex subject positions, difficult to disentangle, reminds us of the need for decision-making—including decisions as to what we see—with "a large degree of caution (and humility) while at the same time demanding that we think through the possible ramifications" (Hughes 2012: 116) of which there are many.

The complexity lens does not argue that we will be able to fully understand a system by looking at the individual parts. However, it helps us develop positions and interpretations in a less totalizing way; it teaches us humility (Coleman 2006: 340) and modesty (Cilliers 2010: 8). "[C]omplexity," according to Antoine Bousquet and Robert Geyer (2011: 1), "embodies an inherently humble approach that is conscious of

---

[4] For the story, see https://archive.nytimes.com/www.nytimes.com/specials/bosnia/suburbs/vogosca/zoran_returns/vogosca_zoran_returns.html and https://archive.nytimes.com/www.nytimes.com/specials/bosnia/suburbs/more/vogosca_zoran_returns.more.html (accessed 1 October 2021).

the limitations to predictability and control which are built into the very fabric of the world and our positions as observers and actors within it." As Paul Cilliers (2010: 4) argues, while "[w]e cannot reduce rich, nonlinear difference to simple descriptions, ... we need descriptions nonetheless." *Bosnia: Uncertain Paths to Peace* offers descriptions and disaggregates the whole into smaller, individual pieces thus making visible the messiness and complexity of the subject at hand and forcing us to accept the limitations of our knowledge.

Navigating the Grids

Grids are networks:

> Grid:
> [...]
> 2b: a network of uniformly spaced horizontal and perpendicular lines (for locating points on a map)
> *also*: something resembling such a network
> [...][5]

We live in networked societies. Network also appears to be a key term when describing Sarajevo's urban structure during the siege. As Mirjana Ristic has put it: "The violence and terror transformed Sarajevo's urban space into a network of danger zones in which anyone at any time was a moving target" (2018: 17). During the siege, Sarajevo was "composed of a network of dangerous and forbidden zones," "a network of danger zones that were exposed to snipers' positions," "a network of dangerous and forbidden zones in which any mundane, everyday activity became potentially lethal" (pp. 51, 55 and 59, respectively). Human relations are organized in networks, and networks increasingly replace individual actors. Networks are spaces where people interact with one another; grids are spaces in which images communicate with one another. An image acquires meaning from the ever-changing "network of relations around it" (Rubinstein and Sluis 2013: 36). Network, thus, appears to be a key term in digital societies: "The network does not have opening hours, weekends, past or future. It is always in the present and it is everywhere

---

[5] *Merriam-Webster.com Dictionary*, Merriam-Webster, https://www.merriam-webster.com/dictionary/grid (accessed 16 February 2023).

at the same time" (Rubinstein and Sluis 2013: 31). In *Bosnia: Uncertain Paths to Peace*, two networks or grids—one composed of images from the suburbs and the other from images of the center of Sarajevo[6]—invite inter-activity on the part of users. These grids take center stage with regard to the project's nonlinearity, inviting a plurality of narratives to emerge from the user's encounter. These grids

> would allow the reader to decisively *reject any linearity* by clicking on an image to leap to any other part of the reportage. The *uncaptioned* photographs that made up the grid were meant to encourage a more *intuitive*, visual reading. (Ritchin 2009: 105; italics added)

In what follows, we would like to engage with the italicized elements in the above quotation, starting with the lack of captions that, as elaborated in earlier chapters, is indeed a major deviation from standard forms of representation in photojournalism, inviting navigation without mediation, guidance and editorial paternalism. A photograph, MacDougall argues, "draws the viewer into an interpretive relationship that bypasses professional mediation" (1998: 68). For this reason, photojournalism often uses captions to offer professional mediation and to ensure that the photograph is read as intended, thus inhibiting individual interpretive acts on the part of individual viewers. Captions have other functions as well. They are meant to counteract a feeling of helplessness when confronted with an image, the meaning of which cannot be deciphered immediately. In the case of these grids, however, professional mediation by the photographer or the editor is deliberately avoided, thus leaving the user in limbo. These images are what viewers make of them; how they approach the grid is entirely up to them. The way the grids are organized may suggest certain navigational approaches rather than others, but no one prevents the user from ignoring such suggestions and doing something completely different. Presenting images without captions is also a deviation from the other pages of the project which, as described in the previous chapter, mostly co-present text and images. The grids, thus, require a different navigational approach (see Fig. 8.1).

---

[6] The Sarajevo grid includes photographs that were not taken in the city center (the hills surrounding it, for example). Likewise, the sniper's view is not normally associated with the city center but rather with the surrounding hills or high-rise buildings in the suburbs from which the city center was targeted.

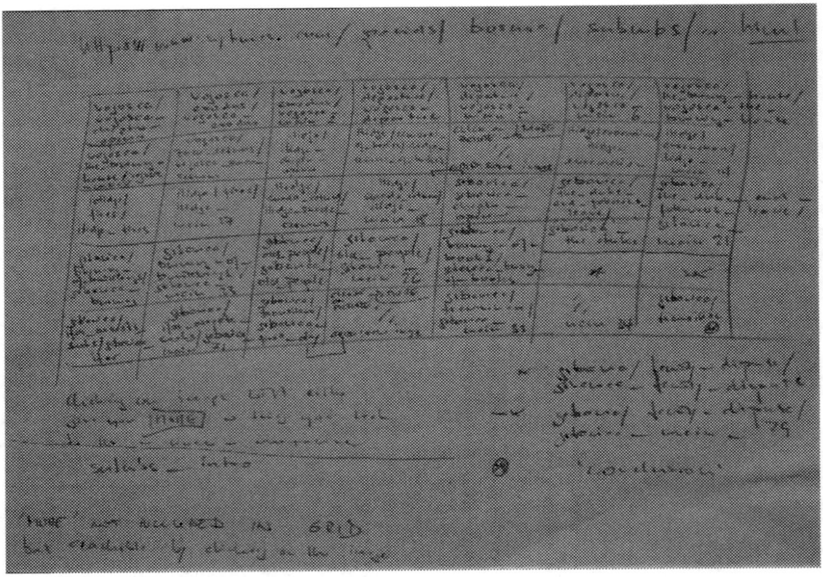

190   R. BELLMER AND F. MÖLLER

Fig. 8.1 Trying to make sense of the suburbs grid, notes, February 2023

If you click on GRID on the photo essay's opening page, you will be directed to the suburbs grid but that this network of images (seven images by five images) is indeed the suburbs grid is not immediately clear unless you check the URL on your computer screen. It specifies that you are visiting a *New York Times* special on Bosnia and that the grid is related to the suburbs.[7] Apart from that, nothing tells you that you are seeing images taken in the suburbs (although a button TO SARAJEVO GRID at the bottom of the page suggests at least that you are not exposed here to images from Sarajevo). The website invites users to "join the narrative" by clicking "on any of the images." *Joining* the narrative would be difficult, however, as users would have no clue as to what narrative it is that they are supposed to be joining by clicking on an image; it is like starting to read a book in chapter four without even knowing the book's title. If users click on an image, they will open a page that displays

[7] https://archive.nytimes.com/www.nytimes.com/specials/bosnia/grid/suburbs_grid.html.

only a photograph or a number of photographs, a text–image combination or a text–image combination with an additional link to an audio file. Embedded in the text, there are occasional links to other pages, including the glossary. Some pages offer the possibility of clicking on MORE; some images, too, will lead you to MORE if you click on them but others will merely lead to the next page—the page that you would also have opened by clicking on NEXT. At least one photographic motive appears twice, shot from slightly different angles, thus inviting different stories or variations of the same story.[8] The final image revisits the scene we are already familiar with from the project page showing people with their faces erased. From there, you will be directed to the Sarajevo grid, the background of which appears in white, thus inviting a viewing experience that is different from the one the SUBURBS GRID with its black background offers.

If you move the cursor across the photographs assembled on the grid page, the URL of each image appears in the bottom-left corner on the screen, revealing that, instead of rejecting any linearity, the grid images are organized with some degree of logic and, indeed, linearity, namely, according to suburbs—first Vogošća, followed by Ilidža and Grbavica[9]— provided that, as many Western users will probably be inclined to do, you start in the top-left corner and then move from left to right and from the top to the bottom. Furthermore, if you start your navigation in the top-left-corner and proceed in the same manner (from left to right and from the top to the bottom of the grid until you reach the final image in the bottom-right corner) then you will follow the same narrative that you would also have followed by always clicking on NEXT—the main narrative suggested by the project's creators. Following this path would be the least imaginative way of approaching the grid, although it would make sense from a narrative point of view, conventionally understood. For example, following this path, Zoran's return would follow Zoran's departure rather than the other way around. For Western users, accustomed to Western reading patterns, this would be an almost natural path through

---

[8] https://archive.nytimes.com/www.nytimes.com/specials/bosnia/suburbs/grbavica/grbavica_chapter_opener.html and https://archive.nytimes.com/www.nytimes.com/specials/bosnia/suburbs/grbavica/ifor_arrests_serbs/grbavica_ifor.html.

[9] We follow Ritchin and Peress by designating Grbavica a suburb although it is located quite centrally in the city, just a short distance from the political center yet located on the southern bank of the Miljacka river.

the grid—a path, however, that would not allow the user to take advantage of all the possibilities these networked images offer. The resulting "conversation among photographer, subject, and reader" (Ritchin 2009: 106) would be quite limited and conventional.

Instead, the user could indeed click on *any* image *except* the one in the left-hand top corner, try to join the narrative, or develop her own narrative derived from the contents of this particular page—image(s), text and/or audio. She could intuitively or arbitrarily select several images successively and, again, construct her own narrative derived from the pages' contents and the way she connects the chosen pages with one another, as if picking up a book and reading the chapters in an arbitrary order. The emerging story will most likely be an original story, authored by the user. Alternatively, she could open one of the pages where only images appear and construct a narrative on the basis of these images or disregard the textual information that accompanies other images on other pages. Thus, the grid indeed invites the user to be creative, to reject any implicit linearity, and to approach the network intuitively inspired, perhaps, by Roland Barthes's *punctum*—"that accident which pricks me" (2000: 27) ("when it happens to be there)" (p. 42). As a property of any individual user—"it is mine and only mine" (Elkins 2011: 38)—the *punctum* cannot be generalized. As we noted in the preceding chapter, such a navigation might be *both* arbitrary, i.e., incomprehensible to other users who follow their own paths, *and* completely logical from the individual user's point of view. It would not make any sense to *explain* individual navigations, which is why we, while exploring the possibilities the grids offer, keep our own navigations to ourselves (save for our initial encounters as sketched in the preceding chapter). Our navigations are hard to reconstruct anyway. At the same time, we invite readers to explore the grids on their own, thus becoming co-authors of *Bosnia: Uncertain Paths to Peace*.

Rather than joining the narrative, users can also radically construct their own narratives by what we consider the most imaginative approach to *Bosnia: Uncertain Paths to Peace*, namely, by *not* clicking on the images at all and treating them in their own terms, i.e., as images (but remember what we wrote about the text–image relationship in Chapter 5). Users may select one or two (or more) images and look at them individually or in terms of panel-to-panel sequences, just as they would approach sequential art such as comics or graphic novels, or they might disregard the sequentiality of the images altogether. Just imagine the vast number of possible panel combinations that the suburbs grid offers. Thirty-five individual images and unaccountable panel-to-panel sequences, combining with one another two images, three images, four images and so on including images that are not situated next to each other in the grid. Connecting the third image from the left in the first row with the second image from the left in the fourth row and the third image from the right in the fifth row, to give just one, totally arbitrary example, would result in a visual narrative that is completely different from the story that would emerge by connecting with one another three other images or, indeed, the same three images in a different order. Stories will emerge that noone has anticipated and that no-one can anticipate because each user will construct them by combining the images with her individual experience. Some of these stories will traverse several suburbs. On the screen, the images appear rather small, but it is possible to recognize something (even though different users will recognize different things, pricked by different *punctums*). By means of screenshots, the images can also be reproduced and subsequently enlarged. The choice of the images can be informed by the images' URL if, for example, a user wants to combine a photograph from Vogošća with one from Ilidža and one from Grbavica or ignored if no such deliberate combination is intended. Re-photographed images can be used as a starting point for active interaction as described in Chapter 5 in terms of seeing, changing and sharing. Once again, new images and new stories will emerge. The grid offers no limits to users' imagination. The same procedures can also be applied to the Sarajevo grid (see Table 8.2), the URLs of which are less revelatory than those of the suburbs grid (Table 8.1) thus infringing even less on the user's imagination.

Above, we wrote that both the grids' structure and Western reading patterns (e.g., the habit of reading text from left to right) suggest certain navigational approaches and panel combinations rather than others. Because all images in the grids are situated next to others, it is a logical assumption that they are somehow in association with one another. Just as we preferred the term "being in association with one another" when we talked about the relationship between words and images in earlier chapters, we prefer this term here too when reflecting upon the relationship between and among the grids' individual images because the precise nature of this relationship is hard to establish. More importantly, in light of complexity theory and tolerance of ambiguity, it is not even useful to try to establish this relationship once and for all because each such establishment would reduce complexity rather than acknowledging

Table 8.1 Suburbs grid, Uniform Resource Locators (URLs)

vogosca/ vogosca_ chapter_ opener	vogosca/ exodus/ vogosca_ exodus	vogosca/ exodus/ vogosca_ main2	vogosca/ departure/ vogosca_ departure	vogosca/ departure/ vogosca_ main5	vogosca/ departure/ vogosca_ main6	vogosca/ the_ burning_ house/ vogosca_ the _ burning_ house
vogosca/ the_ burning _ house/ vogosca_ main8	vogosca/ Zoran_ returns/ vogosca_ zoran_ returns	ilidja/ ilidja_ chapter_ opener	ilidja/ removal_ of_bodies/ ilidja_ removal_ of_bodies	ilidja/ removal_ of_bodies/ ilidja_ removal_ of_bodies	ilidja/ evacuation/ ilidja_ evacuation	ilidja/ evacuation/ ilidja_ main14
ilidja/ fires/ ilidja_fires	ilidja/ fires/ ilidja_ main17	ilidja/ suada_ returns/ ilidja_ suada_ returns	ilidja/ suada_ returns/ main18	grbavica/ grbavica_ chapter_ opener	grbavica/ the_ duke_ and _ followers_ leave/ grbavica_ the_duke	grbavica/ the_ duke_ and _ followers_ leave/ grbavica_ main21
grbavica/ burning_ of_ buildings/ grbavica_ burning	grbavica/ burning_ of_ buildings/ grbavica_ main23	grbavica/ old_ people/ grbavica_ old_people	grbavica/ old_ people/ grbavica_ main26	grbavica/ burning_ of_books/ grbavica_ burning_ of_books	grbavica/ family_ dispute/ grbavica_ family_ dispute	grbavica/ family_ dispute/ grbavica_ main29
grbavica/ ifor_ arrests _ serbs/ grbavica_ ifor	grbavica/ ifor_ arrests _ serbs/ grbavica_ main31	grbavica/ transition/ grbavica_ first_day	grbavica/ transition/ grbavica_ first_day	grbavica/ transition/ grbavica_ main33	grbavica/ transition/ grbavica_ main34	grbavica/ transition

Source https://www.nytimes.com/specials/bosnia/suburbs/...html

it (and the conditions it references). Instead, we wish to sketch different ways of approaching the grids in terms of as-well-as rather than either-or. Our sketch is not exhaustive, and users may choose different approaches, reflecting their individual experience and interests.

Table 8.2 Sarajevo grid, Uniform Resource Locators (URLs) plus key words from the Index page

sarajevo_ chapter_opener	sa2	sa3	sa4	sa5
Crossroads*	Scenes*			Tram*
sa6	sa7	sa8	sa9	sa9a
Night*	Film*		Library*	1993 victims*
sa10	sa11	sa12	sa13	sa14
Montage*	Sniper's world*			Conclusion*

*Terms used on the page 'Index to the Site' to reference direct links to these particular pages. sa3 and sa4 (containing additional 'Scenes'), sa8 (containing more on the 'Film'), and sa12 and sa13 (containing more about the 'Sniper's world') cannot be directly accessed from the 'Index' page. The 'Index' page includes only 21 links to the suburbs although the suburb grid contains 35 images
Source https://www.nytimes.com/specials/bosnia/sarajevo/...html

APPROACHING THE GRID STRUCTURE IN TERMS OF INDIVIDUAL IMAGES

The images are in association with one another, but they are also separated from one another by a small margin that, just like the pages' overall background, appears in black (suburbs grid) and white (Sarajevo grid). This margin—the space between individual images—is a part of the grids' overall structure. Michel Foucault wrote about "the small space running above the words and below the drawings" in illustrated books as the space where there "are established all the relations of designation, nomination, description, classification" (1982: 28). In *Bosnia: Uncertain Paths to Peace*, there is such a space between the bottom row of images and the invitation to join the narrative by clicking on any of the images, but there is also space between the individual images. While we would not want to exaggerate the meaning of this space, we also think that it is there for a reason. It helps differentiate one image from its neighbors, but it also offers a space for contemplation, slowing down the navigation, making the user rest and reflect on whether to return to the preceding image, to move on to the next image or to do something entirely different.

Although organized in a grid, each image—supported by the space that separates it from its neighbors—claims individuality and asks the viewer to respect its individuality rather than seeing it only as a part of a succession of images. Individual images can be reduced neither to what connects them with others nor to what separates them from others. They are defined by both. While the grid expects the user to treat images both individually and collectively, however, the grid in its entirety cannot be completely understood by merely describing or analyzing its individual parts and reassembling these parts after description or analysis. The grid can thus be understood in terms suggested by complexity theory; its inherent ambiguities resulting from the countless possibilities of interpreting and combining its individual parts must be acknowledged. Tensions resulting from different interpretations and combinations must be endured, which is another way of saying that there is no such thing as a coherent whole. Alternatively, if we understand the whole as the sum of all possible interpretations and combinations of the images included in the grid, then we have to acknowledge that we will never be capable of understanding it in its entirety, no matter how hard we try. Such an understanding, acknowledging not only the incompleteness of our knowledge at any point but also the impossibility to fully comprehend the situation, would be similar to an approach to Bosnia and Sarajevo at the time in terms of "sheer randomness" (Donia 2009: 320, referring to "death in the city") and "senselessness" (Holbrooke 1999: 154), indicating that the prevailing situation could not be grasped in its entirety if at all.

The Ritchin–Peress project is not the first visual project that arranges images in grids or networks. In art photography, for example, the work of Bernd and Hilla Becher is an important example of individual photographs organized in grids, inviting viewers both to consider them individually and to ponder connectivity. As Jae Emerling (2012) explains, the Bechers' photographs of water towers and other industrial structures are "typological studies of industrial forms done in a documentary photographic style in which several individual images are presented together in the form of grid-tableaus" (p. 149). The images are arranged "into various numbers (three, six) so that each image is an independent unit and yet entirely dependent on the set as a whole" (p. 149). Although the Bechers' images are completely different from the photographs presented in *Bosnia: Uncertain Paths to Peace*[10] and belong to a different

---

[10] The artists use "black-and-white film, standardized format and ratio of figure to ground, uniform, full-frontal view, flat lighting conditions or the approximation of such conditions in the processing of the print, lack of human presence, uniformity in print quality, sizing, framing, and presentation" (Emerling 2012: 149).

photographic genre—art photography rather than photojournalism—they evoke the same question that the grids in *Bosnia: Uncertain Paths to Peace* evoke: "The question arises as to whether in arranging pictures in grids of different numbers, which negates the isolation and autonomy of an individual image, is there movement (or narrativity) from image to image? How are the images connected? Is it a network, a series, a set, a sequence – an archive?" (pp. 149–150). After discussing and dismissing several art historical interpretations, Emerling suggests that the grid structure presents photographs that initially appear identical; only upon closer inspection (facilitated by the viewer-friendly size of the photographs), the viewer will recognize that they are *not* identical and begin "the aesthetic and epistemic labor of discerning differences" (p. 153). Thus, the grid structure and the similarity of the images included in it trick viewers into engagement with individual photographs, the individuality of which, however, can only be appreciated in the context, i.e., in comparison with other images included in the grid.

In the Ritchin–Peress grids, the photographs do not appear identical. Although their small size makes it difficult to see what they display exactly, it is immediately obvious that these images are thirty-five (Suburbs) or fifteen (Sarajevo) *different* images.[11] Although they are small, they are large enough for viewers to have an idea of what they might show; although they are large enough to suggest an interpretation, they are too small to give viewers assurance. Which is another way of saying that the grid structure reconstructs the situation in Sarajevo and the suburbs during and immediately after the siege, "the actual chaos in Bosnia" compared to which "[a]ny confusion" the website's users may have felt then and may feel now "seemed minimal" (Ritchin 2009: 105)—except that we would prefer to talk about the complexity and ambiguities of the situation in Sarajevo which the grids communicate to users. However, the grid structure itself is ambiguous in the sense that it offers the user a huge variety of equally possible and equally permissible navigations and interpretations to be explored (as suggested above) in terms of as-well-as rather than either-or.

One key to understanding the operations of the grids is by following the distinction between representations of landscape and representations of architecture, as suggested by Ernst van Alphen (2005: 71–95). Both

---

[11] Only the photographs referenced in note 8 above appear similar but even these images do not appear identical.

are "means by which the space of representation is explored, challenged, and exposed" (p. 73), but they operate differently on observers: the space of architecture operates by "setting up obstacles that make the viewer more and more eager to look behind them." The space of landscape, in contrast, "is predicated on a relationship of attraction, or seduction" (p. 72); it "engages vision by seducing you or inviting you" (p. 92). Grids are architectural spaces *par excellence,* and such spaces have a specific way of operating on viewers:

> Architectural space engages vision by raising obstacles. And obstacles encourage the desire to conquer them, to do something when it is forbidden, to try something when it is impossible, to intrude on a space that is not yours and has to be respected as secret or someone else's. (pp. 91–92)

Not all of these descriptions seem adequate when applied to *Bosnia: Uncertain Paths to Peace*—for example, visiting the images is not forbidden; users are explicitly invited to visit them (though we do not know what the subjects depicted think about such a visit). Thinking about the grid structure in terms of architectural space as a means with which to engage vision is nevertheless useful because it was not clear that (or why) a reader would "want to become involved" in such a new form of reading as the one required in *Bosnia: Uncertain Paths to Peace* (Ritchin 2009: 104). Thinking about the grids as architectural space helps us specify the ways in which the grids make users want to become involved: grids raise obstacles and users want to conquer them. They can conquer them only by engaging with them. Such engagement, however, includes intrusion on a space that is not theirs, thus complexifying the relationship between users and the subjects depicted, especially if the subjects depicted appear to be people in pain.[12] The result of such engagement cannot be anticipated. The desire to conquer obstacles is one thing, but succeeding in conquering obstacles is a different thing entirely; and what does "conquer" mean in the context of representation anyway? If users begin "the aesthetic and epistemic labor" of elaborating on difference— which is what, according to Emerling (quoted above), they are supposed

---

[12] The literature on what has been called "Beautiful Suffering" is substantial. See, for example, Sontag (2003), Reinhardt et al. (2007), Rancière (2009), Grønstad and Gustafsson (2012), and Möller (2013: 36–55).

to do when confronted with grid structures—then they will expect some kind of reward for their work, but what kind of reward could the grid possibly offer?

Grids show us the limitations of our view (Alphen 2005: 90). Comprehension of such limitations helps us understand the limits of comprehension we are regularly facing both when visiting (trying to conquer) grids and when engaging with that which the grids reference, in this case, the complexities and ambiguities of the situation in Bosnia at specific locations at a specific time. Grids, thus, teach us modesty and humility and, as such, perform an important function in the context of this book in addition to visualizing the limits of comprehension and complexifying users' subject positions. Encountering grids by focusing on sequentiality and movement from image to image, i.e., reading images not as isolated images but, rather, in connection with the preceding one(s) and the following one(s), is a different navigational approach. It does not simplify our task.

Approaching the Grid Structure as Sequential Art

Exploring the images assembled in the grids in terms of sequentiality basically means denying the individuality of the images and understanding them as elements in a progression of images. This is the normal operating procedure of comics and graphic novels as sequential art.[13] Sequential art relies on the expectations readers bring with them to the reading experience, among which the idea that the artwork tells a coherent story figures prominently. Individual panels can be studied or admired for their creator's ingenuity, but in the context of sequential art, they make sense only if seen as a part of the whole story (save for experimental comics such as Art Spiegelman's early work). Due to technical reasons, the distance between individual panels in comics and graphic novels is relatively large; it is the reader's task to bridge this distance by assembling fragments into a whole. Thus, in contrast to what we said above about *Bosnia: Uncertain Paths to Peace* (which, obviously, is not a comic), comics (except experimental ones) and graphic novels present complete narratives suggested by the artist but ultimately constructed by the reader by connecting individual panels with one another in such a way that a coherent narrative emerges—coherent, that is, in the eyes of the individual

---

[13] In the Bosnian context, Joe Sacco's work (2000, 2004, 2005) is outstanding.

reader (see McCloud 1994). From this, it follows that if you understand the grids presented in *Bosnia: Uncertain Paths to Peace* as sequential art, the reading experience will be completely different from the experience of approaching the Ritchin–Peress project as described above, i.e., with a focus on individual images. This is neither a question of right or wrong nor one of either-or. Moreover, while *Bosnia: Uncertain Paths to Peace* is meant to be read as a work of journalism, not as a comic or graphic novel, nothing prevents the reader from approaching the project, especially the grids, as sequential art, thus capitalizing on the operating procedures of sequential art to diversify reading experience, construct new narratives and assume the subject position of co-author. With such a subject position, (co-)responsibility for the story emerges, and such responsibility involves the reader/co-author in the story more strongly than would otherwise be the case.

Sequential art cannot be thought of without "closure" which designates the "phenomenon of observing the parts but perceiving the whole" (McCloud 1994: 63).[14] As Scott McCloud explains, comics is "a medium where the audience is a willing and conscious collaborator and closure is the agent of change, time and motion" (p. 65). Above, we have already encountered the place where closure takes place: it is the space between panels—the "gutter"—where "human imagination takes two separate images and transforms them into a single idea" (p. 66). Essentially, in comics readers connect with one another two (or more) *neighboring* images; they do not usually assemble, say, the first, the fourth, and the seventh panel on a page into a narrative (one of the procedures we suggested above with regard to the grid structure in *Bosnia: Uncertain Paths to Peace* to diversify the reading experience) but *all* images appearing on a page, starting (when socialized in Western reading patterns) in the top-left corner and proceeding to the bottom-right corner. It is a habit, or experience, on the part of readers on which comic artists rely when presenting their story.

Above, we approached the margin between images as the place where individual images are *separated* from one another, thus enabling the viewer to approach them individually as visual starting points for the construction of individual stories; now, we are going to suggest the opposite, i.e., approaching the gutter as the place that *connects* individual

---

[14] Quotations from McCloud's work appear in normal writing without italicization, capitalization and other peculiarities typical of comics.

images with one another, thus enabling the viewer to construct a story based on panel-to-panel sequences. Both approaches are possible and permissible, but the story you will construct depends very much on the approach you choose. While the chosen approach depends, in turn, very much on the expectations users bring with them to their encounter with the image, nothing prevents them from changing their expectations and, thus, their reading patterns in the course of such an encounter.

If users decide to approach *Bosnia: Uncertain Paths to Peace* in terms suggested by sequential art, then (once again) they have different options. As McCloud (pp. 70–72) elaborates, panel-to-panel transitions appear in different categories:

– moment-to-moment,
– action-to-action,
– subject-to-subject,
– scene-to-scene,
– aspect-to-aspect or
– non-sequitur

all of which require reader involvement, although to different degrees. Even with regard to the most abstract panel-to-panel transition—non-sequitur—where panels appear "to be totally unrelated to each other … a relationship of some sort will inevitably develop. … By creating a sequence with two or more images, we are endowing them with a single overriding identity, and forcing the viewer to consider them as a whole" even if they do "not make 'sense' in any traditional way" (p. 73). From this, it follows that even if the distance between individual images assembled in the grids in *Bosnia: Uncertain Paths to Peace* seems quite large and even if the relationship between them is far from obvious, readers will construct "a relationship of some sort" between them, provided that they approach the Ritchin–Peress project in terms suggested by sequential art. Furthermore, even images based on what seems to be a non-sequitur panel-to-panel transition are not entirely unrelated to each other: all of them appear in the same project, coexisting in space and time. Thus, there is an overall frame within which readers will approach these images; the frame is Bosnia at the end of the siege.

If, on the one hand, readers "choose to see stories as connected series of events," then they will look primarily for panel-to-panel transitions in terms of action-to-action, subject-to-subject and scene-to-scene, which "show things happening in concise, efficient ways" (p. 76). On the other hand, if they choose to see stories as existing of random and unconnected points in space and time, then they will look for, and ultimately appreciate, non-sequitur panel-to-panel transitions, acknowledging the absence of any sense, traditionally defined. And if they see stories as consisting of connected series of events that are occasionally interrupted by unpredictable, random incidents then they will look for non-sequiturs embedded in more conventional forms of panel-to-panel transitions. Arguably, this is the most promising way of approaching *Bosnia: Uncertain Paths to Peace* as sequential art, but it is not the only one. Whatever approach readers choose, it will reflect the operating procedures of sequential art but also, and equally importantly, the personal experience and the expectations readers bring with them to the reading experience. And if readers approach *Bosnia: Uncertain Paths to Peace* as sequential art, they will stop being readers in a traditional sense and instead become the photographer's "silent accomplice" (p. 68). The photographer may imply, suggest or hint at something by presenting selected images in a certain sequence, but ultimately the reader, by connecting individual images with one another and "endowing them with a single overriding identity" (McCloud, as quoted above), becomes not only a participant in "a conversation among photographer, subject, and reader" (Ritchin 2009: 106) but also an author of a story that is the individual property of this reader/author and this reader/author alone. With authorship comes responsibility, and this is where approaching *Bosnia: Uncertain Paths to Peace* in terms of sequential art becomes uncomfortable. However, paraphrasing Ritchin, we might say that any uncomfortable feeling that may result for the reader from co-authoring the story seems minimal compared to the actual lack of comfort in Bosnia at the time.

Conclusion

Characteristically enthusiastically, McCloud proclaims that "the potential of comics is limitless and exciting" (McCloud 1994: 3). Approached in terms suggested by sequential art, then, the potential of *Bosnia: Uncertain Paths to Peace* is equally limitless and equally exciting. Observing some of sequential art's reading conventions, readers may follow the linearity suggested in the grid structure, thus confirming rather than rejecting (Ritchin 2009: 105) linearity. More adventurous readers may ignore such conventions and construct their own linearity by selecting the images in the grids randomly, connecting them with one another in an idiosyncratic and unique manner and assigning meaning to non-sequitur panel-to-panel transitions. Alternatively, as elaborated in earlier parts of this chapter, they could approach the images assembled in the grid structure individually, constructing narratives based on selected, individual images rather than sequences of images.

Concluding this chapter, we want to suggest three ways in which the grid structure of *Bosnia: Uncertain Paths to Peace* could have been altered, and the images included in the grid could have been presented, such that it would have allowed the user "to decisively reject any linearity" (Ritchin 2009: 105). The original grid structure already intended to reject linearity but realized such rejection only half-heartedly. First, if the user—informed by typical Western reading patterns—starts her navigation in the upper-left corner and then proceeds from left to right and from the top to the bottom until she reaches the final image in the bottom-right corner, then she will follow the same path that she would also have explored by always clicking on NEXT. In other words, she will follow the main navigational path through the website, the implicit master narrative suggested by Ritchin and Peress. Ordering the images assembled in the grid differently would have guaranteed a different navigational path even if the reader had followed a typical Western reading style. Second, obscuring the URL in the suburbs grid that appears on the screen when moving the cursor across the images would have exacerbated users' orientation. The images may be "uncaptioned" (Ritchin 2009: 105), but the URL is the images' silent voice. In the suburbs grid, scrutinizing only those images taken in one of the three suburbs represented in the grid is possible by out-selecting images from the other suburbs, as indicated in the URLs (see Table 8.1). Anonymized or less specific URLs would have increased both users' confusion and the project's nonlinearity.

Third, one major omission in the project is a grid combining Sarajevo and the suburbs. *Bosnia: Uncertain Paths to Peace* "facilitates open narratives within the two-story lines but renders it difficult to transcend them" (Bellmer and Möller 2022: 12). While it is possible to move from one main grid page to the other, once you entered the suburbs narrative (or the Sarajevo narrative, for that matter), you cannot easily join the other narrative; instead, you have to go back to the GRID or the INDEX first. Furthermore, the different background colors chosen for the two grids—suburbs: black; Sarajevo: white—give the impression of separate, closed narratives. Finally, there is no single grid showing all fifty images that appear in the suburbs grid *and* in the Sarajevo grid:

> Such a grid, presenting all photographs in random order, would have added to the intended confusion the inter-actor experiences anyway when navigating the website; simultaneously, it would have worked against an understanding of the city – and, by implication, of Bosnia – as clearly divided between two communities thus ignoring inter-ethnic communication that prevailed before and, to some extent, also during the siege. (Bellmer and Möller 2022: 12)

A combined grid with images arranged randomly and URLs obscured would have been a radical embodiment of the project's basic lines of thought, its interest in narrative plurality, nonlinearity and non-dominative ways of making sense of the project's contents.

During the siege, for many residents living outside the city center, it was impossible "to take the tram into Sarajevo and wander into a coffee shop."[15] Today, the citizens of Sarajevo once again insist on, demonstrate and performatively emphasize the city's unity through a variety of everyday routines, including the *šetanje*—the evening stroll. Many inhabitants of the suburbs, rather than performing it in their local neighborhood, "come by bus, tram, or car to walk in the city center to assert their inclusion among the Sarajlije [the citizens of Sarajevo]" (Markowitz 2010: 35) and to insist on, and participate in, common life. We conclude this chapter with the eighth of our Sarajevo photographs (Fig. 8.2) introduced in Chapter 2 in terms of photocomplexity.

---

[15] https://archive.nytimes.com/www.nytimes.com/specials/bosnia/sarajevo/sa5.html (see also Chapter 7).

Fig. 8.2 Sarajevo #8 (Photograph © Frank Möller)

References

Andreas, Peter. 2008. *Blue Helmets and Black Markets: The Business of Survival in the Siege of Sarajevo*. Ithaca and London: Cornell University Press.
Barthes, Roland. 2000. *Camera Lucida: Reflections of Photography*, trans. Richard Howard. London: Vintage.
Bellmer, Rasmus, and Frank Möller. 2022. Messiness in Photography, War, and Transitions to Peace: Revisiting 'Bosnia: Uncertain Paths to Peace.' *Media, War, and Conflict* 16: 2. https://doi.org/10.1177/17506352211072463.
Bellmer, Rasmus, Tiffany Fairey, and Frank Möller. Forthcoming. Peace Photography, Visual Peacebuilding and Participatory Peace Photography. In *The Routledge Handbook of Conflict and Peacebuilding Communication*, ed. Stefanie Pukallus and Stacey Connaughton. New York: Routledge.
Bousquet, Antoine, and Robert Geyer. 2011. Introduction: Complexity and the International Arena. *Cambridge Review of International Affairs* 24 (1): 1–3.
Cilliers, Paul. 2010. Difference, Identity and Complexity. In *Complexity, Difference and Identity, an Ethical Perspective*, ed. Paul Cilliers and Rika Preiser, 3–18. Dordrecht, Heidelberg, London, New York: Springer.

Coleman, Peter T. 2006. Conflict, Complexity, and Change: A Meta-Framework for Addressing Protracted, Intractable Conflicts—III. *Peace and Conflict: Journal of Peace Psychology* 12 (4): 325–348.

Couldry, Nick. 2000. *Inside Culture: Re-imagining the Method of Cultural Studies*. London, Thousand Oaks, New Delhi: Sage.

Demick, Barbara. 2012. *Besieged: Life Under Fire on a Sarajevo Street*. London: Granta.

Donia, Robert J. 2009. *Sarajevo: A Biography*. London: Hurst & Company.

Elkins, James. 2011. *What Photography Is*. New York and London: Routledge.

Emerling, Jae. 2012. *Photography: History and Theory*. London and New York: Routledge.

Foucault, Michel. 1982. *This Is Not a Pipe*. With Illustrations and Letters by René Magritte, trans. and ed. James Harkness. Berkeley, Los Angeles, London: University of California Press.

Golubović, Jelena. 2020. "To Me, You Are Not a Serb": Ethnicity, Ambiguity, and Anxiety in Post-war Sarajevo. *Ethnicities* 20 (3): 544–563.

Grønstad, Asbjørn, and Henrik Gustafsson, eds. 2012. *Ethics and Images of Pain*. New York: Routledge.

Holbrooke, Richard. 1999. *To End a War*. New York: The Modern Library.

Hughes, Bryn. 2012. Peace Operations and the Political: A Pacific Reminder of What Really Matters. *Journal of International Peacekeeping* 16 (1–2): 99–118.

Jestrovic, Silvija. 2013. *Performance, Space, Utopia: Cities of War, Cities of Exile*. Houndmills: Palgrave Macmillan.

Levi, Primo. 1989. *The Drowned and the Saved*, trans. Raymond Rosenthal. New York: Vintage.

MacDougall, David. 1998. *Transcultural Cinema*, ed. and with an intro. Lucien Taylor. Princeton: Princeton University Press.

Markowitz, Fran. 2010. *Sarajevo: A Bosnian Kaleidoscope*. Urbana, Chicago and Springfield: University of Illinois Press.

McCloud, Scott. 1994. *Understanding Comics: The Invisible Art*. New York: HarperCollins.

Möller, Frank. 2013. *Visual Peace: Images, Spectatorship, and the Politics of Violence*. Houndmills: Palgrave Macmillan.

Rancière, Jacques. 2009. *The Emancipated Spectator*, trans. Gregory Elliott. London: Verso.

Reinhardt, Mark, Holly Edwards, and Erina Duganne, eds. 2007. *Beautiful Suffering: Photography and the Traffic in Pain*. Williamstown: Williams College Museum of Art/Chicago: University of Chicago Press.

Ristic, Mirjana. 2018. *Architecture, Urban Space and War: The Destruction and Reconstruction of Sarajevo*. Houndmills: Palgrave Macmillan.

Ritchin, Fred. 2009. *After Photography*. New York: W. W. Norton & Company.

Rubinstein, Daniel, and Katrina Sluis. 2013. The Digital Image in Photographic Culture: Algorithmic Photography and the Crisis of Representation. In *The Photographic Image in Digital Culture*, 2nd ed., ed. Martin Lister, 22–40. London: Routledge.

Sacco, Joe. 2000. *Safe Area Goražde: The War in Eastern Bosnia 1992–95*. Seattle: Fantagraphics Books.

Sacco, Joe. 2004. *The Fixer: A Story from Sarajevo*. London: Jonathan Cape.

Sacco, Joe. 2005. *War's End: Profiles from Bosnia 1995–96*. Montreal: Drawn & Quarterly.

Sontag, Susan. 2003. *Regarding the Pain of Others*. New York: Farrar, Straus and Giroux.

van Alphen, Ernst. 2005. *Art in Mind: How Contemporary Images Shape Thought*. Chicago and London: The University of Chicago Press.

CHAPTER 9

Interactivity and the Author-Audience Relationship

Introduction: Bosnia, 1993–1996

In 1993, the photographer Gilles Peress traveled to Bosnia to document the raging war and human suffering in the former Yugoslavia. *Farewell to Bosnia*, published the following year, cumulates the photographs he took during six months on location. They were dedicated to "bear[ing] testimony to the brutality and devastation of the 1990s Balkan conflict."[1] Peress's photography corresponds with the conventional and for photojournalism foundational linkage between documenting photographically, raising awareness for a sociopolitical problem and stimulating a political response to this problem. The "belief in a straight line between perception, affection, comprehension and action" (Rancière 2009: 103) was, however, disappointed in Bosnia (and elsewhere) although many photographers, journalists and photojournalists, rather than hiding behind journalistic neutrality, took sides, clearly distinguishing aggressors from victims and communicating this distinction to their audiences (see Morrison and Lowe 2021; see also Chapter 4). In Bosnia, Peress and his fellow photographers were forced to realize that a strong and comprehensive political response was not forthcoming until the end of 1995.

---

[1] https://www.magnumphotos.com/newsroom/conflict/gilles-peress-farewell-to-bosnia/, accessed 31 August 2021.

© The Author(s), under exclusive license to Springer Nature Switzerland AG 2023
R. Bellmer and F. Möller, *Peace, Complexity, Visuality*, Rethinking Peace and Conflict Studies,
https://doi.org/10.1007/978-3-031-38218-5_9

Although atrocities and violence were globally broadcast throughout the siege and memorable images were published all around the world, it was only in response to the *Markale* market hall massacre of 28 August 1995 that Western governments decided to act (see Ristic 2018: 63–65). The media's failure to trigger an earlier "intervention to stop the carnage" (Lowe 2015: 5) made Peress, and many others, rethink their approach to photography and conflict (see Chapters 4 and 6). As he explains in conversation with Paul Lowe, his interest changed from "good photography" to "gathering evidence for history, so that we remember" (Lowe 2014: 221). We argued in earlier chapters that gathering evidence for history can—and in Peress's case, does—result in good photography.

In spring 1996, Peress returned to Bosnia and, together with the picture editor Fred Ritchin, developed *Bosnia: Uncertain Paths to Peace*.[2] This time, the context was completely different: the Dayton agreement[3] had been signed in Paris on 14 December 1995, that is, shortly before his visit. It was meant to end the bloodshed and pave the way to a more peaceful future for the people living in Bosnia. People who had survived the war were now facing the formidable challenge of "surviv[ing] the peace," as the Sarajevo university student Edib Palalic told photographer Sara Terry (2005: 15) when she came to Bosnia a couple of years later, convinced that "what happens in the aftermath of war is as newsworthy, if not more so, than the destruction and horror of war" (Terry 2005: 10). As Richard Holbrooke, one of the designers of the Dayton Accords, remembers, "all sides carried deep scars and many still sought revenge instead of reconciliation. Most troubling, the same leaders who had started the war were still trying to silence those who called for multiethnic cooperation" (1999: 362).

The Dayton agreement's focus was primarily on ending the war (see Holbrooke 1999); it was not meant as a sustainable and permanent solution to the problems that Bosnian society was facing (see Bennett 2016: 9). It is thus unfair to criticize the agreement and its designers in retrospect for the agreement's failure to establish a permanent solution. At the time, the Dayton Accords were seen as the precondition for, and as a decisive step toward, peace and reconciliation between the different social groups involved in the conflict. Hope and optimism were certainly

---

[2] https://archive.nytimes.com/www.nytimes.com/specials/bosnia/index.html.
[3] https://www.osce.org/files/f/documents/e/0/126173.pdf.

damaged when violence and expulsion continued after the signing of the agreement (Holbrooke 1999: 335–359). Formerly Serb-dominated areas in Sarajevo, such as Grbavica, where Peress took some of his pictures, were integrated into the Federation of Bosnia-Herzegovina in early 1996 (Ristic 2018: 132). Peress captures this integration/expulsion in words and images in the suburb of Vogošća.[4] Some people were forced to leave their neighborhoods while others were prevented from returning to theirs, as *Bosnia: Uncertain Paths to Peace* shows in the suburbs part. However, the idea of peace-to-come was planted. The Dayton agreement—as incomplete and problematic as it may be—continues to be the main formal arrangement within which the peace process unfolds (Bennett 2016) despite its many flaws, including the "institutionaliz[ation of] many of the national divisions that had dominated society since 1990" (Donia 2006: 335) and "extraordinarily intrusive levels of external intervention as part of the peacebuilding process" (Mac Ginty 2006: 57), which undermine "the crucial modern political articulation of all spatiotemporal relations"—"the principle of state sovereignty" (Walker 1993: 6). Sarajevo was "territorially divided along the siege line" and "the violent war was transformed into a 'cold war' through the post-siege transformation of Sarajevo's architecture and urban space" (Ristic 2018: 132).

Pessimism, optimism and weariness coexisted. For example, Bosnian president Alija Izetbegović referred to the agreement in terms of an "unjust peace" (quoted in Bennett 2016: 79), although his government's position is said to have "paid dividends on all the most sensitive issues" (Bennett 2016: 78). For photojournalists such as Peress, the new question was how to document, accompany and support this troublesome peace process photographically, adding a *proactive* element to photography's traditional documentary function. Images of heads of states signing an agreement—a standard way of visually depicting peace—neither seemed to do justice to the developments on the ground nor adequately reflected the degree of frustration and skepticism among many people. Such rather formal images tried to communicate optimism; Holbrooke, for example, notes the usefulness of even the most ritualistic photograph "as a sign of momentum toward peace" (1999: 139). However, violence continued,

---

[4] See the part of the suburb narrative dedicated to Vogošća, starting in the introduction: https://archive.nytimes.com/www.nytimes.com/specials/bosnia/suburbs/suburbs_intro2.html.

albeit on a much lesser scale, and "the wartime mindset" (Bennett 2016: 82) prevailed. However, at the same time, cooperative interactions between individuals and social groups took place. Such actions could be photographed to visualize the fragile peace and anticipate sustainable forms of dealing with conflict without recourse to violence, thus adding an *anticipatory* dimension to photography's documentary role. "Peace," as Peress notes, "is an extraordinary concept, one in which we imagine that things go back to the way they were. But they don't."[5] Showing that multiethnic cooperation is possible even in conditions that are not conducive to cooperation is, therefore, an important element of a photography of and for peace.

What concerns us in this chapter is *interactivity* (especially the photographer–audience interaction) as a crucial element of both *Bosnia: Uncertain Paths to Peace* and current digital media practice. Peress understood the Internet as "a democratic space, a space of dialogue" where his "misconceptions will be corrected both in terms of ideas and images and captions and so on"—corrected, that is, "by people who lived there."[6] In earlier chapters, we criticized the photographer's wish to be corrected from a complexity point of view, arguing that rather than replacing one conception with another, the aim should be to acknowledge the coexistence of different conceptions, reflecting both different individual and collective experiences and the messiness of the overall situation that cannot be grasped by a single conception, a single narrative, however "correct" it may be. We also noted that Peress, as a visitor, may have seen things that local people took for granted and, thus, disregarded. Peress's wish is noteworthy all the same because it reveals a new understanding of the audience and the photographer as co-authors. The Peress–Ritchin project is a highly relevant precursor of current-day interactive media and documentary formats. Despite, or perhaps because of, the project's relative simplicity (reflecting technological limitations prevailing at the time), *Bosnia: Uncertain Paths to Peace* is a good vehicle to explore changes in photojournalism. We suggest that projects such as Peress and Ritchin's change the role of creators, photographers, outlets and audiences. This change implies not only evolution and shifts in terms of responsibility assigned to all those actors but also offers new possibilities to

---

[5] https://archive.nytimes.com/www.nytimes.com/specials/bosnia/sarajevo/sa9a.html.

[6] https://www.nytimes.com/specials/bosnia/gallery/peress.3.au.

report on peace and conflict dynamics, the messiness of which is increasingly recognized in both the literature (Andreas 2008; Mac Ginty 2014) and photographic practice. Recording this messiness adequately requires multi-author perspectives and visual-narrative plurality. In this chapter, we will go beyond what we have already said in earlier chapters both by understanding *Bosnia: Uncertain Paths to Peace* as an early embodiment of interactive documentaries and by discussing its operating procedures in light of such documentaries.

In what follows, we will briefly discuss the relationship between the Peress–Ritchin project and the media environment at the time. We will then relate the project to today's digital and interactive media environment, identifying it as a precursor of current interactive documentary formats based on one-way, two-way and/or three-way interaction. In the next step, we will show that even such a rather simple interactive project (simple, that is, in comparison with current interactive formats) enables narrative openness and nonlinear storytelling, explored here in terms of authorship, responsibility on the part of the interactors and visual disaggregation of the conflict. We conclude that despite the project's many merits, Ritchin and Peress's hope to be corrected by the website's users clashes with some of the website's features and the overall digital environment which make such correction difficult.

BOSNIA: UNCERTAIN PATHS TO PEACE AND THE MEDIA ENVIRONMENT AT THE TIME

The experiences during the Balkan wars led many photographers to invent new approaches to report on war and peace, thus reformulating their discipline's function and practice. Concepts such as aftermath photography, forensic photography, participatory photography and visual post-conflict narratives, to name but a few new approaches, emerged at the time in Bosnia but also in other contexts, diversifying visual approaches to violent conflict by acknowledging both that "war is only half the story" (Terry 2005: 10) and that the aftermath is equally newsworthy (see Chapter 4). While citizen photography and social media had not yet started to challenge professional photography's monopoly on the visual reporting of war and violent conflict, photojournalism had for some time been "at the dock" (Solomon-Godeau 1991). With *Bosnia: Uncertain Paths to Peace*, Peress and Ritchin addressed several aspects that also inspired other practitioners to take new routes, responding to such established criticisms as photojournalism's ad hoc character, its voyeuristic and predatory tendencies, its focus on war, violence and destruction, its tendency to reduce human beings to victims devoid of own agency, its self-congratulatory mood celebrating photographers working in dangerous conditions in search of "great" shots without deeper interest in the causes underlying the conditions depicted and so on. The emerging new photographies also understood that the reenactment of violence in traumatic memories and its continuation in discriminatory actions in ostensibly peaceful times needed to be visualized in order to achieve a fuller picture of war and its consequences. By aiming to show forward-looking perspectives toward peace, Ritchin and Peress assumed a proactive photographic position, acknowledged that there was more than one path to peace and suggested that photography could contribute to peace. In the context of this chapter, the most important aspect of the Peress–Ritchin project lies in its interactive design as an online project enabling audience participation. However, the project not only *enabled* such participation; its success was also to some extent *dependent* on active audience participation.

Bosnia: Uncertain Paths to Peace was on display online for the duration of three months during the summer of 1996. Instead of restricting itself to the limitations of print publications, it was intended "to take advantage of the new strategies made possible by the Web – nonlinear narratives, discussion groups, contextualizing information, panoramic imaging, the photographer's reflective voice" (Ritchin 2009: 102). For Peress and Ritchin, interaction of and with the audience was crucial. In "a conversation among photographer, subject, and reader" (p. 106), "the author/photographer is," as Darcy DiNucci wrote, "simply the most prominent participant" (quoted in Ritchin 2009: 108). Prominence, however, does not imply superior knowledge derived, for example, from the photographer's presence on location or his experience in conflict situations. Peress himself explicitly calls into question the aptness of his observations in words and images and, as we noted above, asks to be corrected by local people. As already quoted, for Peress—reflecting the spirit of optimism regarding the democratizing potentialities of the Internet prevalent at the time—the place for such correction is the Internet: a "democratic space, a space of dialogue." What does such democratization imply regarding the authority of the photographer, the limits of photographic knowledge production, the responsibility of the audience and the general process of experiencing peace and conflict through photography? Does it reflect what Ritchin calls "an open-ended, non-authoritative dialectic" (1999: 101) or is it better understood in terms of passing the buck, i.e., allocating responsibility to the audience for assigning meaning to a situation characterized, in Holbrooke's (1999) words, by "senselessness" (p. 154) as well as "absurdity" and "stupidity" (p. 232)?

For Peress and Ritchin, the Internet was bound to change the logic and functioning of both images and news reporting. Rather than continuing to operate within the confines of the print media, journalists were asked to translate the new digital possibilities into "better journalism" (Ritchin 2009: 101). However, at the time, they were still facing severe obstacles. While today, one of digitization's most outstanding features is its capability of making images and other information public in real time, *Bosnia: Uncertain Paths to Peace* needed two months of editing and site building to make the project, "made with film" and subsequently digitized, operational—a process that, according to Ritchin, "was equivalent to making three books or one feature film" (2009: 102). Gaining time, thus, was not the crucial issue. While digital storage capabilities seem infinite today, up- and download speed and server capacities at the time were still quite limited. Thus, increasing the amount of data wasn't the issue either.[7]

In the preceding chapter, we explained the merits of the website in terms of *nonlinearity*; in this chapter, we would like to emphasize *interactivity* as a crucial feature distinguishing *Bosnia: Uncertain Paths to Peace* as it appeared on the Internet from the project if it had appeared in book format. Indeed, Ritchin and Peress used the web's opportunities to establish an interactive environment where photographers and users, inspired by the material, could start a conversation with each other. This interactive environment enabled such an exchange mainly in two specific ways. First, Peress and Ritchin included the possibility for the audience to engage both with the project and with one another in fourteen discussion groups in a digital forum, enabling "readers to discuss strategies for resolution" (Ritchin 2009: 105). The forums were introduced by such famous personalities as then US Ambassador to the United Nations and later US Secretary of State Madeleine Albright. While this might have increased

---

[7] In terms of quantity, the written and visual material published on the website could easily have been presented in book format; the audio files could have been transcribed into written text—although *reading* the transcriptions might have affected the user differently from *listening* to the photographer's voice, undermining the project's multisensory dimension.

the forums' topicality, it also implied a problematic conflation of journalistic and political agendas, suggesting an overall interpretive frame within which the whole project appeared—a frame that was as much political as it was journalistic.

Second, the reader was assigned a major role in assembling a storyline, a narrative. In the preceding chapter, we have shown how such an assemblage could unfold in the grids. Unlike a printed newspaper or a conventional photo-essay published online, *Bosnia: Uncertain Paths to Peace* required the visitor to take the initiative and to actively explore the website. As Ritchin explains, "there was no way of quickly flipping forward [or scrolling down; the authors] to assess and select a path" (2009: 104). Instead, it is the user's task to navigate through the website, assembling a story by choosing on which link, button or image to click: "Each click of the cursor would put a reader on another screen with new perspectives and unknown possibilities" (p. 104). Even when following the website's main narrative by always clicking on NEXT, the reader still had to conquer obstacles posed by the distance between individual pages. Consequently, every user might choose a different path through the narrative, allowing for strongly varying viewing experiences. Users, when *re*-visiting the website, were also likely to choose a path other than the one they had opted for earlier thus diversifying their individual experience with the website and the conditions it reflects as well. For example, while their initial experience may have been dominated by the images, when revisiting the website users may have been attracted by the photographer's voice as it appears in the nine audio files integrated into selected subpages. This multi-sensory element, which must have been very unusual to users at the time, offers highly diverse perspectives on the topics addressed in the audio files and invites users to compare the impressions derived from the images with impressions derived from Peress's commentary.

The website, however, not only invites users to compare with one another the impact of different media but also invites them to amend Peress's perspectives in light of their own, thus transforming users into coauthors. The fact that Peress reflects on his own position and his (limited) knowledge makes us, too, reflect about what it means that we can engage with his images from war-torn Sarajevo right now, from our save places—temporally and spatially—our homes, as users who did not experience the war in Bosnia and the siege of Sarajevo first-hand and who have no clue what it feels like to be exposed to armed aggression. Interactive documentaries, Paolo Favero notes, "have the potentiality to connect social actors in different locations with each other turning, through the shared used [*sic*] of digital images, scattered individuals into a community" (2014: 171). This website, we realize, will not allow us to be passive and neutral observers of a straight-forward narrative that we can either accept or reject; rather, we are a part of a virtual community of co-authors, the exact manifestation of which depends to some extent on the degree of interaction we chose.

INTERACTIVITY AND INTERACTIVE DOCUMENTATION

Today, "media participation can be seen as the defining characteristic of the internet in terms of its hyperlinked, interactive and networked infrastructure and digital culture" (Deuze 2007: 245). Digitization equals interaction: digital images are expected to be experienced, modified and shared (see Bennett 2012). Moreover, *all* "[d]igital media translate everything into data, waiting for an author or an audience (or a machine) to reconstitute it" (Ritchin 2009: 17).[8] Digital image production, thus, is not adequately understood by looking for a 'final' image that, after completion, is simply *there* for pleasure or analysis; rather, digital image production is an infinite process in the course of which elusive and ephemeral images come into being. These images "exist in a number of states that are potential rather than actual" (Lister 2013: 8).

When *Bosnia: Uncertain Paths to Peace* was developed and published, digitization was just in the starting position. The project's design would be very different in the current-day's techno-media environment. It is not difficult to imagine how it would look today, consisting of a more variegated mixture of moving and still images, accompanied by audible and written texts, allowing the user a degree of interactivity with the project that would go far beyond the options the original design provided. It is also conceivable that current editors would nudge users into certain paths, invisibly guiding them through the website, as Ritchin and Peress contemplated. Owing to technological restrictions, such plans had to be abandoned (Ritchin 2009: 107); they would have undermined the open character of the project anyway.

---

[8] As noted above, *Bosnia: Uncertain Paths to Peace* was made with film and subsequently scanned and digitized.

Recent digital reporting formats such as interactive documentaries,[9] then, increasingly connect multimedia and interaction. For Kate Nash, such documentaries anticipate the future of the documentary format: "non-linear, multi-media, interactive, hybrid, cross-platform, convergent, virtual, or something else as yet un-thought" (2012: 197). This future is strikingly similar to the one Peress and Ritchin envisioned in 1996. In this digital media environment, the differentiation between distinct media blurs (Favero 2014: 169); in conversations, practitioners tend to "use the terms film, video, images, [and] data interchangeably" (Favero 2014: 171). Therefore, it appears difficult to maintain a distinct separation between photojournalism and other visual documentation, such as documentary filmmaking; such practices converge.[10] This convergence directly affects the conventions and professional self-conceptions that both photojournalism and documentary film established and aim to sustain. Both fields of documentary reporting testify to a so-called profilmic reality, i.e., the reality that exists beyond and before the camera (Favero 2014: 167), thus independent of it. Both formats "aim[] to convey a fairly unfiltered, unmediated and near-experience vision of the actual" (Favero 2013: 261).

On the one hand, photojournalism (ideal-typically) insists on "resemblance between image and reality-as-seen" (Saugmann et al. 2020: 7), often referred to as objective reporting or even as truth even though many photojournalists acknowledge that their images always imply an ideological perspective and are based on their personal moral convictions.[11] Documentary filmmakers, on the other hand, appear to have

---

[9] Those formats are commonly called "collab-docs, trans-media docs, cross-media docs, database docs and hypertext docs" (Aston and Gaudenzi 2012: 134) or "i-doc, webdoc, web documentary and interactive documentary, the latter being the most popular" (Vázquez-Herrero and López-Garcia 2019: 248). Aston and Gaudenzi suggest that "any project that starts with an intention to document the 'real' and that uses digital interactive technology to realize this intention can be considered an interactive documentary" (2012: 125–126).

[10] The introduction of the Digital Story Telling Award by the World Press Photo Foundation in 2011 speaks to this development. In 2019, the headline award *Interactive of the Year* was established. See for instance: https://witness.worldpressphoto.org/10-years-of-digital-storytelling-e71a5107a8ea, accessed on 18 May 2021.

[11] For example, Ron Haviv (in Walsh [2019, unpaginated]) prefers the term "a fair representation" rather than an objective one and acknowledges that "[p]hotography by its nature is subjective. I'm choosing the frame. I'm choosing the moment. I do it while I'm taking the picture, and then I'm doing it again with the edit."

different priorities; they "make claims" more actively and openly, "propose perspectives and evoke feelings in support of a particular view of the world" (Nash 2012: 196). Documentaries, Bill Nichols suggests, "are the product of a persuasive, or at least poetic, intent to have an audience see and act differently" (2001: 587). This is particularly so due to the importance and ostensible necessity of including a narrative of some sort, which "imbues time with historical meaning" and "allows documentary to endow occurrences with the significance of historical events" (Nichols 2001: 589).

If the current digital media environment makes separation between photojournalism and other visual documentation increasingly difficult, such a "blurring of boundaries" (Patrick 2014: 238) impacts the conventions and myths surrounding a profession. Moreover, the borders between professional and citizen journalism (Allan 2013) and those "between the journalistic field and the interactive non-fiction world are blurring, also due to technological shifts" (Vázquez-Herrero and López-Garcia 2019: 245) and recent media practices. However, Nash (2012: 198) argues that despite this blurring of boundaries between these visual formats, "it is not improbable to think that audiences will conceptualize their experience of the webdoc on the basis of their familiarity with traditional documentary," thus for the time being seeing and experiencing the webdoc as a variation of traditional documentary rather than a profound departure from it. This was also the case for us when we addressed *Bosnia: Uncertain Paths to Peace* rather conventionally (see Chapter 7): we expected a sophisticated interactive format to function like a conventional photo-essayistic format and thus initially missed the point completely. Furthermore, according to Favero, "iDocs seem to foreground the relationality, participation, multisensoriality, and materiality that today are being addressed as key characteristics of images in the contemporary world" (2018: 23); "new, creative, non-linear forms of engagement and interaction between viewers, authors and the material itself, [open] up the terrain for a new politics of viewing and meaning-making" (2013: 260).

From the above, it follows that *Bosnia: Uncertain Paths to Peace* qualifies as an early-stage interactive documentary, combining various digital media and allowing a certain degree of interaction between story and viewer. Ritchin and Peress certainly wanted to persuade the website's users to see Bosnia and Bosnians differently—not only as victims and perpetrators of violence but also as ordinary people doing, in different subject positions, ordinary things in extraordinarily difficult circumstances. Their agenda was a proactive one, i.e., outlining and visually anticipating paths to peace, rather than a merely documentary one. They infringed upon their own authority as journalist/photographer by acknowledging their own limitations and actively invited users to contribute to the website by submitting comments and participating in the discussion groups.

INTERACTIVITY AND NARRATIVE OPENNESS
Changing Roles, Changing Responsibility

When compared with today's standards, *Bosnia: Uncertain Paths to Peace*'s level of interactivity was rather limited. It is a huge step indeed to, for instance, the first interactive non-children's movie on Netflix which reportedly offered more than a trillion different narratives[12] enabled by tremendously enhanced digital processing and server capacities. Limited as it may have been, *Bosnia: Uncertain Paths to Peace* did, however, present many more navigation possibilities than individual users were likely to explore. As shown in the preceding chapter, viewers could combine the individual images assembled in the grids in a huge variety of panel-to-panel sequences thus changing from passive users following a pre-given narrative to interactors constructing new and original storylines.

Following Audrey Bennett's conceptualization, such construction would reflect a "one-way, active mode of interaction, in which the user looks at the image to begin the process of interpretation and use[s] other senses, like her sense of touch, to interpret the image and complete the communication transaction" (2012: 62). Using other senses is indeed inevitable when engaging with *Bosnia: Uncertain Paths to Peace*: clicking on buttons or images to continue the communication transaction, moving the cursor across the images in the grids or listening to the audio files all require senses other than looking. Two- and three-way modes of active interaction require changing, modifying, removing or adding individual images (see Bennett 2012: 62–65), an option that *Bosnia: Uncertain Paths to Peace* did not offer. Thus, while a more ambitious interaction with *images* was difficult, interaction with *texts* and *comments* was not only possible but also explicitly encouraged.

---

[12] https://www.cnet.com/news/interactive-black-mirror-bandersnatch-is-here-to-add-to-A-twisted-2018/, accessed 15 April 2021.

A three-way mode would also require the user to share changed and added images with other users, thus "redirecting distribution of the image to others (e.g., through social networking venues)" (Bennett 2012: 65). Interactivity, in its third active mode, extends the general goal of documentary reporting and becomes a delivery mechanism that changes the relationship between the viewer and the material, thus radically re-shaping the goal and possibilities of documentary projects. Digital culture consists of both actual and potential elements, and potential ingredients can be actualized by adding them to the already existing material and sharing the altered material with others, thus changing the overall project. In *Bosnia: Uncertain Paths to Peace*, such re-shaping was limited to text and comments; it took place in the discussion forums where users shared comments with others in ways not always appreciated by Ritchin and Peress (Ritchin 2009: 107–108; see also below). Thus, while the possibilities for active interaction with images that *Bosnia: Uncertain Paths to Peace* offered were very limited, the idea of altering the relationship between author and viewer was firmly planted in the project, thus anticipating today's interactive documentaries. Designed today, *Bosnia: Uncertain Paths to Peace* would probably include the option of uploading users' images. It might even include the invitation to appropriate the images published on the website in order to diversify perspectives (for appropriation, see Möller et al. 2022): if the photographer felt the need to be corrected by local people, then his photographs would seem to have been the most appropriate place for such a correction.

However, even in its simpler, one-way incarnation, interactivity is commonly associated with narrative openness or nonlinear storytelling. Enabling the viewer to actively decide on the steps she wishes to take allows a multitude of storylines to develop. Consequently, "a user may seldom be able to recreate the exact same viewing sequence again" (Favero 2013: 264).[13] Thus, not only different viewers but also individual viewers follow different viewing sequences. Narrative openness and the resulting "multiple informational pathways [...] challenge[] the concept of narrative coherence that has been so central to film and television documentary" (Nash 2012: 199), but they do so *only* if narrative coherence is seen to result exclusively from the original author's design. If we accept

---

[13] Every viewing experience is different from previous ones, reflecting personal background, time and location thus rendering difficult comparison between viewing experiences by one or even several individuals.

that each and every viewer will construct their own storylines and look for (and find!) narrative coherence within them, then interactive documentaries, rather than abandoning the idea of narrative coherence, will end up with a plurality of narratively coherent stories—coherent, that is, from the point of view of the individual viewer who put the story together.

The "lack of authorial voice" in interactive projects offers a space in which the project's designer does not impose one perspective on the audience (Aston and Gaudenzi 2012: 133). Interactivity resulting in narrative openness might for this reason "offer more scope for in-depth engagement with a set of complex ideas through the presentation of multiple entry points and simultaneous storylines" (Aston and Gaudenzi 2012: 133). Thus, rather than lamenting the lack of the authorial voice and narrative coherence we welcome, from a complexity perspective, the emergence of a plurality of authors and voices reflecting upon the same source material and adding new material to explore diverse connections between this material and the reality it (cl)aims to represent. For Ritchin, this is exactly why he had proposed an interactive and nonlinear project to the *New York Times on the Web* in the first place: "nonlinearity can be a more supple approach in the exploration of lives and situations that are themselves multifaceted" (2009: 110). Ritchin compares nonlinear storytelling with a conversation in the "oral tradition" (2009: 108). With every image, especially in the grids, Peress offers talking points, and the interactor can take up from wherever she wants and follow her personal interests. Thus, for Ritchin, the hyperlinks he and Peress provided allow "a more zigzag approach" (2009: 108) instead of blindly following the authorial voice of the creator by automatically moving from one NEXT button to the next.

In summary, "interactivity is a key element of the webdoc's structure and, therefore, meaning" (Nash 2012: 203). Here, the audience "is positioned within the artefact itself, demanding him, or her, to play an active role in the negotiation of the 'reality' being conveyed" (Aston and Gaudenzi 2012: 126). Thus, the involvement of the viewer gains central importance in the meaning-making process. Moreover, by engaging the viewer and allowing different and equally valuable, uncensored narratives on the same platform, *Bosnia: Uncertain Paths to Peace* questioned the authority of the presumably all-knowing author. However, this very questioning increased the credibility and authority of the overall project as a mirror of society: by co-presenting different narratives (including mutually exclusive ones) in a non-hierarchical manner, the project testified to the complexities of the social conditions it aimed to reveal. Audiences were not presented with the authoritative voice of the expert journalist and the all-seeing eyes of the photographer; they navigated their own individual paths through the project, including paths that differed from those envisioned by the project's creators. By doing so, audiences created their own narratives in an individual, idiosyncratic manner for which they were ultimately themselves responsible. Thus, audiences "begin to bear some of the responsibility of collaborator and 'coauthor'" (Ritchin 2009: 110).

Interactivity and Authorship

Interactivity transforms the relationship of the viewer and the creator: the viewer, by altering or adding material or assembling material in new ways, becomes a creator, and the creator becomes a viewer of the altered material. Despite its rudimentary character, *Bosnia: Uncertain Paths to Peace* treats the audience not only as "receptors of messages created by engaged imagemakers and curators. Rather, they are, through their very capacity to be, to communicate, and to function as conveyers of information, the very co-producers of these works" (Favero 2018: 36). Audiences—or what Jay Rosen calls "people formerly known as the audience"[14]—have morphed into interactors: people who engage actively with media content. The digital interactor is no mere variation of the historical figure formerly referred to as spectator, emancipated (see Rancière 2009) or not, but a substantial departure from it. At the same time, we should not exaggerate these changes: the encounter with images has always been an interactive one (Bennett 2012: 54), and genres such as graphic novels have long since understood readers as co-authors (see McCloud 1994: 68). However, there is no doubt that digitization offers completely new possibilities for active interaction, the radical realization of older ideas and the radicalization of new ideas.

Transforming viewers into interactors has significant consequences for the authorship of a story, especially regarding photojournalism with its emphasis on truthful representation. By becoming reality's co-producer, the interactor takes part in its visual construction, rather than being merely on the receiving end, getting shown the creator's way of perceiving truth. As Judith Aston and Sandra Gaudenzi (2012: 128) suggest, "the

---

[14] Rosen uses this term in the documentary Bellingcat: Truth in a Post-Truth World, directed by Hans Pool and produced by Cinephil Philippa Kowarsky (submarine in co-production with VPRO, 2019), 7′14″.

'moment of truth' is now also placed into the actions and decisions of the user/participant." This "destabilization of the author-audience paradigm" (Rubinstein and Sluis 2013: 32) also shifts the responsibility involved in acts of representation. Although the ethical responsibility of the viewer has been acknowledged in the literature, the main ethical burden has traditionally been placed on the photographer. In times of the digital image, especially when used in interactive documentary formats, the photographer, or rather the initiator of an encounter with an image, "cannot guarantee the function of an image" (McQuire 2013: 226), that is, its meaning and its operation in society. Instead, the viewer as interactor actively participates in the construction of reality and visual meaning-making and, therefore, also obtains the obligation to reflect on the ethical consequences of this process, "confound[ing] the old dichotomy of active and passive looking" (Bate 2013: 84) that characterized the conventional relationship between photographer and audience.

At the same time, this also changes the role of actors such as Peress and Ritchin, who we consider to be curators[15] rather than only editors, authors or producers of images, providing a space for active interaction between them, the materials and the interactors. This development, consequently, shapes visual documentary reporting, which strongly relies on the authority of the disciplines, the image-makers and the outlets publishing the visual material. Interactivity seemingly poses a contradiction to the paradigm of narrative authority and the truth-value claimed to be inherent in documentary filmmaking and photojournalism. This is an issue that Ritchin (2009: 106) acknowledges for his project: "And rather than produce the site primarily relying on the authority of the *New York Times*, by acknowledging and encouraging a conversation among photographer, subject, and reader we could be seen as undermining it."

Ritchin and Peress deliberately expanded the limits of photojournalistic representation and explored the possibilities that digitization offered to engage with exactly these limits. They aimed to improve traditional photojournalistic practice but also to critically engage with it and its

---

[15] A curator is "a person who organizes and arranges a showing of art or other objects of interest." https://dictionary.cambridge.org/dictionary/english/curator, accessed 4 May 2021.

underlying conventions in a way that, paradoxically, strengthened its narratives and increased its power by undermining some of the established and taken-for-granted principles (and myths) on which photojournalism's legitimacy was based, thus resuscitating photojournalism in a time of crisis. "Good journalism" (Ritchin), then, is journalism composed of many voices engaging in a critical conversation with one another.

Approaching War, Conflict and Peace Interactively

As we have shown above, *Bosnia: Uncertain Paths to Peace* does not merely *invite* the visitor of the website to become active herself; she is *compelled to become active* to engage with the project. Without interaction, the project would not make much sense; without interaction, the user could not proceed beyond the project's opening page. Already here, decisions are required just as are senses other than looking to continue the communication process. The interactor inevitably needs to make decisions about where to start and how to proceed; she has to assemble the pieces either to construct a seemingly coherent narrative or, ultimately, to acknowledge the absence of coherence—from the project and perhaps also from the reality it aimed to depict. From a complexity point of view, this would not be the worst result of an encounter with the project, as it demands modesty by showing the limits of what we can possibly know—about the conditions in the city and the suburbs at the end of the siege, about the overall situation in Bosnia, about the implementability of the Dayton Accords, about the prospects of reconciliation, about peace perspectives and so on. "Non-coherence," John Law suggests, "may be what keeps the system held together" (2004: 99). Interactors encounter parts of the events and can hardly avoid facing diverse perspectives. Some of these perspectives may even seem to be contradictory and mutually exclusive; others may challenge the interactors' preexisting ideas in uncomfortable ways. Instead of deciding beforehand on a highly limited set of possible meanings of each photograph by integrating it into a strict (written) narrative, *Bosnia: Uncertain Paths to Peace* decidedly aimed "to sustain the ambiguities in the presentation so as to provoke new thinking, not only about each image but also about the larger conflict in Bosnia" (Ritchin 2009: 103). The narratives' nonlinear design could, then, more adequately represent the complexity and multilayeredness of the lives and situations depicted (Ritchin 2009: 110). Indeed, "the Sarajevo siege provides a powerful illustration of the merits of disaggregating conflict and analytically embracing its messiness" (Andreas 2008: 165), and *Bosnia: Uncertain Paths to Peace* is a good example of how such disaggregation can be done visually.

While refraining from establishing a binding narrative, Ritchin and Peress aimed at the creation of specific *feelings* on the part of the interactors—apprehension, anxiety and confusion—and utilized the website's design to achieve this. When we approached the website with the aim of experiencing it 'completely,' it took us several hours to reach the 'end' of the two narrative sections. Even then, we could not be totally confident that we had actually explored the entire story including all detours embedded in it; we could not even be fully sure, either, that there was a full story that could be explored in the first place. We had not even started interacting with all additional links and resources available on the website, including the genealogy of the conflict. As such, we were still lacking orientation, very much like "the journalist who arrives at the Sarajevo airport not knowing where to go, what specific story to explore" (Ritchin 2009: 104). The emergence of anxiety and confusion on the interactors' part was indeed intended (p. 105). Being transformed into interactors actively engaging with the project, we are denied assurance about what we see and what we are told. We surely appreciate that we can easily leave Bosnia at any point. This escape route was unavailable to most residents of Sarajevo during the siege for a variety of reasons, including the Bosnian government's unwillingness to let people go because they were needed "both for the defense of the city and to maintain high levels of international attention and sympathy" (Andreas 2008: 63). People suffered, among other things, for the production of images of suffering people appealing to international solidarity—one way in which journalists became implicated in the siege dynamics and politics.

However, following Nash (2012: 200), we need to ask once again, "what is the relationship between user contributions and the voice of the webdoc?" The website was relatively simple, and the degree of interactivity was relatively limited. As noted above, while users assemble the storyline, thus constructing visual reality, they can barely contribute to the body of *visual* material. The collection of material is fixed and defined by Peress and Ritchin. Users' contribution, therefore, is limited to written comments in the discussion forums. The curators asked for "feedback about this project"[16] but they do not seem to have adapted the website regularly in light of comments and feedback. Such feedback could have included readers' photographs, but such photographs are not reproduced on the website. Thus, the visual dimension of interaction is very limited indeed. Furthermore, at the time, online participation was not possible for everyone,[17] probably even less so to individuals fleeing violence or trying to make ends meet in difficult and unpredictable circumstances. Their chances to perform a correcting role would have been slim even if they had been interested in assuming such a role. (Today, due to technological advances and massively increased access to mobile internet, active interaction can involve an individual's first-hand reports from conflict areas, as citizen photography shows.) Finally, while the project invites interaction between the photographer and the users, it does not explicitly invite interaction between the photographer and the subjects depicted (at least not in the openly accessible material where the people depicted seem bereft of the possibility to correct the stories or at least to co-write them). It is Peress's narrative we read and see, and not the narrative of the people who appear in his photographs. Thus, while the audience appears to be a co-producer of the project, the people depicted in the photographs do not.

With regard to the forums and the democratic space they seemed to offer, interaction proved very difficult as well—not because no one interacted but, rather, because the 'wrong' people interacted: the forums were "quickly dominated by some of the most racist and vitriolic comments ever to appear in the *New York Times*," Ritchin (2009: 107) reports, attracting commentary that presented a rather one-sided view on the events (p. 108). Certain opinions called for violence and aimed to delegitimize other points of view, thus undermining both the forums' democratic potentialities and the project's peace potentialities. Rather than showing tolerance of ambiguity, then, these voices preferred disambiguation. As we noted in earlier chapters, this can hardly be avoided when

---

[16] https://archive.nytimes.com/www.nytimes.com/specials/bosnia/intro.html.

[17] Ritchin reports that an Internet center "planned for Sarajevo University encountered problems and was slow to go online" (2009: 107).

narrative plurality is invited. Censorship would have been an option—publishing only selected comments—but such intervention would have undermined the project's basic lines of thought. If you invite comments, then the comments you receive will include intolerable and offensive comments. (As current attempts to regulate online content on social media clearly show, there is no easy solution to this problem—especially when you look at it from the perspective of tolerance of ambiguity: it is easy to be tolerant of positions that only slightly deviate from your own; it is a different question entirely to be tolerant of positions with which you fundamentally disagree. However, tolerance of ambiguity is not primarily about agreement or disagreement but, rather, about recognition and acknowledgment.) If you allow only comments that are positioned within a project's parameters, redundancy and an uncritical congratulatory mood loom. Moreover, the discussion groups did have an important function, namely, showing how long Bosnia's path to peace would be: being "racist and vitriolic," these "rampantly hostile" contributions were also "painfully revelatory" (Ritchin 2009: 107–108).

Conclusion

Digitization has changed how image-makers and viewers interact with each other. Their relationship is going to evolve further, shifting authority and responsibility, a process that *Bosnia: Uncertain Paths to Peace* anticipated and actively sought. Rather than passing the buck to the audience and expecting audience members to identify *the* meaning of the material presented on the website, the Ritchin–Peress project—through its interactive and messy design—succeeds in communicating to the audience the messiness of both the Bosnian conflict and the fragile peace of 1996. It can be seen as a precursor to current forms of interactive documentaries, giving the audience a degree of co-authorship and, thus, responsibility that goes far beyond the function that photojournalism conventionally assigns to spectators. Rather than trying to capture complex, ambiguous and contradictory stories in the ostensibly authoritative voice of the photographer/journalist, it allows for the emergence of a plurality of authors and voices co-constructing the story in its complexity and shifting roles, authorities and responsibilities.

However, questions abound: Is Sarajevo at the end of the siege the most suitable place for the exploration of narrative plurality? How open can (and perhaps should) a journalistic (or artistic, or any other) narrative be without completely hiding the curator's voice (and her politics)? As Ritchin (2009: 109–110) asks: "How can the author maintain a voice or a vision when the reader is filling in so many of the gaps, adding materials, making connections that the author may never have envisioned or even known about?" The short answer to this question would be that the author cannot maintain her own voice; rather, the author's voice becomes a part of a concert including dissonances, tensions and occasional resolutions. As we have shown in this chapter, this does not necessarily have to be a bad thing as long as one is interested in narrative plurality. However, are there limits to openness, frames within which openness is to be encouraged while beyond which it is not? Are all narratives and perspectives equally valid and equally acceptable? For current-day visual reporting, the question remains: How can interactivity—which in the digital era needs to be thought of as inevitable—be utilized to create more comprehensive and complex reporting as well as experience on the side of the interactors without falling into the trap of disambiguation, hate speech, dehumanization and other attempts at Otherizing? Finally, if a curator opts for an interactive format in which narratives can unfold freely and openly, we should not forget the role of decisions made before and during such a project. As Nash (2012: 207) notes, how users will interact with a documentary "will be strongly influenced by the way in which information is structured and presented to the user via the interface." Freedom of choice on the users' part is often only an illusion. We conclude this chapter with the ninth of our Sarajevo photographs (Fig. 9.1) introduced in Chapter 2 in terms of photocomplexity.

Fig. 9.1 Sarajevo #9 (Photograph © Frank Möller)

References

Allan, Stuart. 2013. Blurring Boundaries: Professional and Citizen Journalism in a Digital Age. In *The Photographic Image in Digital Culture*, 2nd ed., ed. Martin Lister, 183–200. London and New York: Routledge.

Andreas, Peter. 2008. *Blue Helmets and Black Markets: The Business of Survival in the Siege of Sarajevo*. Ithaca and London: Cornell University Press.

Aston, Judith, and Sandra Gaudenzi. 2012. Interactive Documentary: Setting the Field. *Studies in Documentary Film* 6 (2): 125–139.

Bate, David. 2013. The Digital Condition of Photography: Cameras, Computers and Display. In *The Photographic Image in Digital Culture*, 2nd ed., ed. Martin Lister, 77–94. London and New York: Routledge.

Bennett, Audrey G. 2012. *Engendering Interaction with Images*. Bristol and Chicago: Intellect.

Bennett, Christopher. 2016. *Bosnia's Paralysed Peace*. London: Hurst & Company.

Deuze, Mark. 2007. Convergence Culture in the Creative Industries. *International Journal of Cultural Studies* 10 (2): 243–263.

Donia, Robert J. 2006. *Sarajevo: A Biography*. London: Hurst & Company.

Favero, Paolo. 2013. Getting Our Hands Dirty (Again): Interactive Documentaries and the Meaning of Images in the Digital Age. *Journal of Material Culture* 18 (3): 259–277.

Favero, Paolo. 2014. Learning to Look Beyond the Frame: Reflections on the Changing Meaning of Images in the Age of Digital Media Practices. *Visual Studies* 29 (2): 166–179.

Favero, Paolo S.H. 2018. *The Present Image: Visible Stories in a Digital Habitat*. Houndmills: Palgrave Macmillan.

Holbrooke, Richard. 1999. *To End a War*. New York: The Modern Library.

Law, John. 2004. *After Method: Mess in Social Science Research*. London and New York: Routledge.

Lister, Martin. 2013. Introduction. In *The Photographic Image in Digital Culture*, 2nd ed., ed. Martin Lister, 1–21. London and New York: Routledge.

Lowe, Paul. 2014. The Forensic Turn: Bearing Witness and the 'Thingness' of the Photography. In *The Violence of the Image: Photography and International Conflict*, ed. Liam Kennedy and Caitlin Patrick, 211–234. London and New York: I.B. Tauris.

Lowe, Paul. 2015. *Oziljak (Scar)*. Field Study #21.

Mac Ginty, Roger. 2006. *No War, No Peace: The Rejuvenation of Stalled Peace Processes and Peace Accords*. Houndmills: Palgrave Macmillan.

Mac Ginty, Roger. 2014. Everyday Peace: Bottom-Up and Local Agency in Conflict Affected Societies. *Security Dialogue* 45 (6): 548–564.

McCloud, Scott. 1994. *Understanding Comics: The Invisible Art*. New York: HarperCollins.

McQuire, Scott. 2013. Photography's Afterlife: Documentary Images and the Operational Archive. *Journal of Material Culture* 18 (3): 223–241.

Möller, Frank, Rasmus Bellmer, and Rune Saugmann. 2022. Visual Appropriation: A Self-reflexive Qualitative Method for Visual Analysis of the International. *International Political Sociology* 16: 1. https://doi.org/10.1093/ips/olab029.

Morrison, Kenneth, and Paul Lowe. 2021. *Reporting the Siege of Sarajevo*. London: Bloomsbury Academic.

Nash, Kate. 2012. Modes of Interactivity: Analysing the Webdoc. *Media, Culture & Society* 34 (2): 195–210.

Nichols, Bill. 2001. Documentary Film and the Modernist Avant-Garde. *Critical Inquiry* 27 (4): 580–610.

Patrick, Caitlin. 2014. Ruins and Traces: Exhibiting Conflict in Guy Tillim's *Leopold and Mobutu*. In *The Violence of the Image: Photography and International Conflict*, ed. Liam Kennedy and Caitlin Patrick, 235–255. London and New York: I.B. Tauris.

Rancière, Jacques. 2009. *The Emancipated Spectator*, trans. Gregory Elliott. London and Brooklyn: Verso.

Ristic, Mirjana. 2018. *Architecture, Urban Space and War: The Destruction and Reconstruction of Sarajevo.* Houndmills: Palgrave Macmillan.

Ritchin, Fred. 1999. *In Our Own Image.* New York: Aperture.

Ritchin, Fred. 2009. *After Photography.* New York: W.W. Norton & Company.

Rubinstein, Daniel, and Katrina Sluis. 2013. The Digital Image in Photographic Culture: Algorithmic Photography and the Crisis of Representation. In *The Photographic Image in Digital Culture*, 2nd ed., ed. Martin Lister, 22–40. London and New York: Routledge.

Saugmann, Rune, Frank Möller, and Rasmus Bellmer. 2020. Seeing like a Surveillance Agency? Sensor Realism as Aesthetic Critique of Visual Data Governance. *Information, Communication & Society* 23 (14). https://doi.org/10.1080/1369118X.2020.1770315.

Solomon-Godeau, Alison. 1991. *Photography at the Dock: Essays on Photographic History, Institutions, and Practices.* Minneapolis: University of Minnesota Press.

Terry, Sara. 2005. *Aftermath: Bosnia's Long Road to Peace.* New York: Channel Photographics.

Vázquez-Herrero, Jorge, and Xosé López-García. 2019. When Media Allow the User to Interact, Play and Share: Recent Perspectives on Interactive Documentary. *New Review of Hypermedia and Multimedia* 25 (4): 1–23.

Walker, R.B.J. 1993. *Inside/Outside: International Relations as Political Theory.* Cambridge: Cambridge University Press.

Walsh, Lauren. 2019. *Conversations on Conflict Photography.* London: Bloomsbury Visual Arts.

PART IV

Leveraging Ambiguity for Peace

CHAPTER 10

Embracing Difference: Learning from Bosnia?

Introduction

In the previous parts of the book, we have argued for regarding complexity and ambiguity not as a danger for or a threat to peaceful development but as a resource to be capitalized on to improve the quality of social relationships and come closer to peaceful cohabitation based on a more adequate understanding of socially constructed reality than procedures derived from disambiguation and the reduction of complexity are capable of generating. Moreover, we have elaborated that both images, as ambiguous and non-coherent forms of representation that always carry with them a plurality of meanings, and engagements with images might act as tools to enhance our ability to accept and constructively deal with complexity and ambiguity. Our argument was one in support of tolerance of ambiguity because such tolerance reflects the complexity, messiness, uncertainty and unpredictability of the social world better than disambiguation with its tendency to see and construct the world in polarizing and mutually exclusive dichotomy. In Part III, we have exemplified our approach by discussing the photojournalistic online project *Bosnia: Uncertain Paths to Peace*, which actively engages (and makes users engage) with the complexity of its subject—Bosnia and Sarajevo—in the immediate post-siege period. The project's design enables narrative openness and interactivity; the stories it tells result from both the information assembled on the website and the particular ways in which individual users navigate the website. The project deviates in a constructive manner from standard photojournalistic procedures. While such procedures aim to clearly establish *the*—one and only—story based on a knowledgeable journalist's work on location, *Bosnia: Uncertain Paths to Peace* self-critically interrogates the limits of journalistic knowledge production. It acknowledges the plurality of stories that can be derived from the material presented on the website and avoids hierarchical ordering of these stories in terms of, for example, truthfulness thus recognizing that journalistic knowledge—and, by implication, any form of knowledge—is always limited.

In Part IV, we want to move to some extent away from *Bosnia: Uncertain Paths to Peace* and, similar to the book's first two parts, present our argument in more generic terms, applicable to our case study but also beyond it. Reflecting the name of this part of the book, we wish to leverage ambiguity for peace. To this end, we will take a closer look at two additional aspects of the visual construction of reality. First, we want to discuss a specific and largely disregarded image component with which to increase the complexity of an engagement with visual images that we deem a promising venue for thinking differently about images and the stories they (supposedly) tell. This procedure arguably enables us to arrive at a different and more nuanced understanding of an image's subject(s), thus diversifying viewers' experience, challenging their habits of viewing and directing their attention to the politics of representation inherent in every visual image and every designation of meaning. We want to engage with what James Elkins (2011: 116–117) calls the *surround*—non-iconic, peripheral and unwanted image components—as a place for the emergence of narrative plurality (Chapter 11). Second, we will introduce the concept of *active looking* as a visual-discursive practice that includes images as a mode of expression and contribution to meaning-making capitalizing on specific characteristics of images, specified in Chapter 12, with the aim of (re)complexifying (conflict) narratives. Both chapters serve as venues for the visual complexification of narratives in the narrative tradition of peacebuilding and help us embrace difference rather than searching for identity and (absolute) sameness, which are often said to be preconditions for peaceful conflict resolution. Before turning toward the *surround* and *active looking* as places where complexity and ambiguity can be explored and appreciated, in this chapter, we will sketch why we consider embracing difference a relevant resource for peace, first against the backdrop of the Bosnian and the Sarajevan context and then in regard to more general and (photo-)philosophical reflections. We are well aware that conceptualizations of *difference* (or *différance* in French discourse) are among the most complex, contested and sophisticated politico-philosophical writings in the social sciences and humanities. Our aim here surely is not to review this literature but, rather, to look for inspiration based on the assumption that how we address difference affects our approach to ambiguity, predetermining whether we look at a specific area in search of tolerance of ambiguity or disambiguation. We thus assume that tolerance of ambiguity varies across different areas rather than being a person's individual personality trait (see Chapter 3).

Learning from Bosnia?

To suggest learning from Bosnia is a provocation. After all, Bosnia is regularly supposed to learn from and adapt to standards set by the European Union and, in fact, required to do so if it wishes to enter the EU at some point, abandoning its policymakers' notorious indolence and developing skills in rational policymaking that the EU allegedly possesses while Bosnia ostensibly does not. Such a position is a caricature of both the EU and Bosnia. "The norm of territorial and cultural alignment, with its nexus between sovereignty and identity, is," as David Campbell argued in the aftermath of the Balkan Wars of the 1990s, "central to international relations' construction of the world as comprising sovereign states in an anarchic realm" (1998: 165). This norm was also central to Western policymakers' position on the dissolution of Yugoslavia, fervently supported by nationalist politicians in most of the country's constituent parts, while those politicians who did not support it did not manage to counteract it decisively (see Glenny 1996: 148–149). What worked reasonably well in Slovenia and less so in Croatia proved to be a disaster in Bosnia; and while the reasons for this disaster are manifold and, indeed, complex, it also reflects an incomprehension on the part of Western policymakers of Bosnia's specific institutional and identity-political arrangements and the history from which these arrangements stemmed. Concepts such as sovereignty insisting on territorial and cultural alignment are social constructions, and problems emerge if policymakers forget that these are social constructions, treating as natural and mandatory what are contingent and always emergent political and discursive arrangements and imposing them on entities that are neither prepared for nor easily capable of absorbing them. Western policymakers were conceptionally unable to integrate Bosnia adequately into their frames of mind, conditioned by sovereignty—which is another way of saying that they lacked political imagination—while Bosnian social reality (constructed and otherwise) could not be adapted to these frames of mind and their political manifestations without recourse to violence. In Campbell's words:

> In the case of Bosnia, abhorrence of aggression has proved insufficient as a basis to bring about an effective response because restoration of sovereignty, revisiting the status quo ante, could not be the goal. Since the dissolution of Yugoslavia in 1991, there has been no going back. The absence of such conventional grounds — combined with the seeming inability of humanitarian concerns to muster the requisite support to deal with the political dynamics of the conflict rather than just its symptoms — means alternative rationales for action have been required. A deterritorialization of responsibility is needed.
>
> The fatal predicament for Bosnia has been the absence of such alternative grounds in the discourse of the international community. (1998: 166)

Perspectives on identity and difference exemplify Campbell's point. Embracing difference need not signify a lack of identity or a weakly developed sense of identity. Dževad Karahasan explains that the traditional openness of the Bosnian culture for a different view, a different perspective, did not stem from a missing identity or a weak identificatory consciousness but, rather, from a willingness to assign relevance and soundness or solidity to other perspectives (1993: 84). This willingness has emerged, with ups and downs, over centuries, reflecting, among other things, Bosnia's geographical position, patterns of migration, population changes and external political influence as well as cultural and religious diversity. Acknowledging the existence of the identity of the other was the condition of possibility for confirming one's own identity (p. 93). Without acknowledging difference, then, the formulation of one's own identity would not have been possible. Thus, one's own and others' identities are entangled, mutually constitutive and dependent; the one cannot be thought of without the other: by discovering the other, I discover myself, as Karahasan (p. 18) puts it. Importantly, however, others' identities were not perceived as a *negative* reference point or even as a threat against which one had to defend oneself; rather, engagement with others' identities enriched one's own identity. The recognition of difference was a part of the plurality of life for those who wanted to live together and rejoice at that which separated one person from another (p. 80). In Sarajevo, difference was celebrated and, paradoxically, simultaneously neutralized in the Old Town (Baščaršija; see Fig. 10.1) by embracing commonalities. Visiting coffee houses, for example, transcended difference, while the co-presence of people representing different social groups made such visits more interesting; hence, the deep regret that many people felt during the siege when such visits were no longer possible (see Chapter 7). Sameness, on the other hand, was cultivated in the individual neighborhoods (mahalas) and private houses and gardens with their peculiar arrangements of insides and outsides and their unique technical, functional and semantic positionings toward the city (pp. 20–23).

Bosnian culture, thus, was based on tolerance of ambiguity—so much so that just before the war started, many people in Sarajevo emphatically ruled out the possibility of the city becoming "the next Lebanon, or worse" (Jestrovic 2013: 110). Sarajevo was considered "too mixed, its close-knit and ethnically diverse community … would never be divided across ethnic lines" (Jestrovic 2013: 110–111). The Bosnian war and the siege of Sarajevo followed different ideas—ideas based on modes

Fig. 10.1 Baščaršija (Photograph © Frank Möller)

of absolutizing what was merely relative, naturalizing what was socially constructed and strictly, without exception, separating what used to be closely connected. The siege aimed to annihilate both the *social practices* of a multiethnic city and the *idea* of multiculturalism. In tandem with the post-siege reconstruction of the city and the establishment of two urban entities—(Bosniak-dominated) Sarajevo and (Serb-dominated) East Sarajevo largely reproducing the siege lines—it seems to have been fairly successful. As Mirjana Ristic explains:

> Many of the ruined public buildings and spaces linked to all ethnic groups together and/or the shared Bosnian-Herzegovinian state remained derelict for years after the war while the post-war construction of new religious and cultural buildings related to either ethnicity boomed in both cities. Also, both cities have engaged in the construction of various commemorative forms that largely shape two parallel ethnic histories and versions of the war. Although there are a number of projects coming mostly through non-governmental initiatives that question or challenge the ethnic division, Sarajevo and East Sarajevo function largely as arenas for new forms of ethnic struggle. …
>
> The city was transformed into two relatively mono-ethnic cities in which architecture, urban space, heritage and memories of war work to mark ethnic boundaries, inscribe particular ethnic identities in place and exclude Others. (2018: 18)

"With the signing of the Dayton Peace Accords and the constitution that derived from them," Fran Markowitz adds, "wartime goals of dividing the citizenry according to ethnicity became accomplished facts, which silenced the commonalities that had united the region's inhabitants" (2010: 145). Today's Bosnian commonalties comprise, according to Markowitz, only "Bosnian stew, Bosnian coffee" (see Fig. 10.2), "Bosnian houses, and the Bosnian way – some might add the Bosnian language." Paradoxically or ambiguously and, as such, typical of Bosnian politics and society, both the Bosnian way and the Bosnian language "may be refuted, even as [they are] enacted" (p. 162).

The Bosnian way—Bosanski način—may be perceived as, mistaken for and reduced to a standstill, indolence, tentative discursive meandering without decision-making. However, to decide *not* to make a decision in a given situation—to postpone the decision for some time or at least until after the next coffee—*is* a decision and it may be the best possible decision in that particular situation, expecting from (non-)decision-makers to

Fig. 10.2 Bosnian coffee (Photograph © Frank Möller)

accept, for the time being, the coexistence of different positions thus requiring tolerance of ambiguity. Importantly, then, the Bosnian way "expresses an aesthetic that not only celebrates live and let live but also borrows from, incorporates, criticizes, and appreciates possibly contradictory elements that somehow fit together in a fluid, incongruous pattern that expresses the lived-in cultural understandings of its practitioners" in a mental and geopolitical positioning toward Europe in which both Bosnia and the Bosnians "are not one or the other, but both and in-between" (Markowitz 2010: 162)—as-well-as rather than either-or. The use of the word 'somehow' in the above quotation is important, as it implies that it is not possible to explain completely how this arrangement, including contradictory and almost schizophrenic elements, works. As the city's biographer, Robert Donia, notes, "Sarajevans have almost unanimously rejected communism as an ideology, yet they hold fond memories of life before the war, a time when communists ruled the city. Most of them reject national exclusivity in principle, yet they have repeatedly opted to put nationalist political leaders in office" (2009: 351–352). Even during the siege, the newspaper *Oslobodjenje* continued, against all odds, telling a multiethnic story thus serving as "a symbol of the Bosnian-Herzegovinian ethnic mixture and resistance to nationalism" (Ristic 2018: 83). Serbian journalists kept working for the newspaper and "sharply condemned the violence" of the Bosnian Serb Army. "This Serbian voice was particularly significant because Bosnian Serb politicians could not represent it as Bosniak propaganda" (Ristic 2018: 82).[1]

The post-war situation in Bosnia, too, is shaped by the tension between a tendency to deal with complexity by reducing it and the obvious existence of various identities and personal experiences that defy simple categories. Take, for example, a story told by the scholar Jelena Golubović about a conversation between a Serb woman and a Muslim man in Sarajevo soon after the end of the siege. "She told him she felt nervous about being a Serb in the post-war city. He turned to her and said, 'Oh, but to me, you are not a Serb. To me, you are... Bosnian Orthodox!'" For the woman, this remark struck her self-identification, also in relation to other social groups in the city and the country. As she told Golubović: "Why should I now be Bosnian Orthodox? The Muslims are all Bosniaks now. They're building a nation for themselves, but they want to tear mine down? [...] I didn't want to be Bosnian Orthodox; I didn't want a new name. I just wanted to keep being a Serb like I was before the war, and I wanted that to not be a problem." In Golubović's analysis, this encounter speaks to an overall trend in the country: "Before the war, ethnicity was one identity marker among numerous others, and there was meaningful space for citizens to hold multiple, hybrid, or ambiguous ethnic identities. But the logic of war and of the post-war state has polarized people into discrete ethnic groups and solidified the boundaries between them" (all quotes from Golubović 2020: 2).

Perhaps, then, one way of addressing Bosnian ambiguities is in terms of a patchwork, an edifice and historically and culturally conditioned system of beliefs and social practices "composed of miscellaneous or incongruous parts."[2] To borrow a term used by Bernadette Buckley in a different context, these parts are "(con)fused" (2009: 836), and this mixture of fusion and confusion, this non-coherence, has to be captured visually and analytically. Complexity theory can help because it warns us that

---

[1] It is noteworthy that the newspaper continued operating throughout the siege and "never missed a day of publication." Its multiethnic team of journalists operated from "the building's underground atomic shelter" and risked their lives when entering and exiting the building in the heavily attacked Nedžarići neighborhood at the western end of the Socialist town (Ristic 2018: 82–83).

[2] "Patchwork." *Merriam-Webster.com Dictionary*, Merriam-Webster, https://www.merriam-webster.com/dictionary/patchwork (accessed 21 March 2023).

entities cannot be completely understood by disaggregating them into component parts, analyzing these parts separately from one another and reassembling them subsequent to analysis. Such disaggregation is a necessary but not a sufficient path to knowledge, and whatever path we chose, the resulting knowledge will be incomplete. The aim of visualization and analysis, then, is not to reduce the complex (con)fusion of Bosnian social reality but to represent it more adequately, as we argued in Part III when analyzing *Bosnia: Uncertain Paths to Peace*. Such analysis includes acknowledgment that different people have different understandings of what qualifies as an adequate representation. Such differences are part of the (con)fusion of everyday life.

Another part of the (con)fusion of Bosnian social reality is, according to Lana Bastašić, that "[t]here's no finish line in Bosnia, all roads seem to be equally languid and pointless; they lead you in circles even when it looks like you're making progress" (2021: 87). The absence of a finish line should not irritate us, however, as crossing such a line—achieving peace in a Galtungian sense of positive peace—is as utopian and impossible as is reaching closure in complex systems. What matters is the trajectory: from war/siege to the aftermath and from the aftermath toward peace, which, however, is unattainable. Equally important is the absence of regression to physical violence, and in this regard, post-war Bosnia and post-siege Sarajevo seem to have been reasonably successful despite a plethora of political, economic, demographic and social problems and rhetorical attacks on the Dayton Accords and the country's territorial integrity (see Rhotert and Rolofs 2020).

However, a return to the multiethnicity of the pre-war city (both as an idea and as a social practice) seems as unlikely in the foreseeable future as a return to, or further development of, the Bosnian way as described above—not least due to the memories of violence and the trauma of the war which, according to Miljenko Jergović, solidified into a "foundational myth," an "identity-establishing"—and, therefore, stable and self-perpetuating—"narrative which characterizes the inhabitants of the city until today" (2015: 105; our translation from the German translation). This is one of the reasons for what John Roberts calls "a melancholic closure of the event-as-aftermath" (2014: 112), which can be observed in Bosnian memorial practices, looking back at the siege rather than moving on. And while we try to encourage thinking about and visualizing the path from the aftermath to peace (Möller 2019: 105–158), we also have to develop tolerance toward those perspectives that insist on the continuing relevance of the aftermath. Thus, we have to learn to be tolerant of perspectives we do not share and accept them as permissible, as they reflect individual experiences that are different from ours. (Perhaps we would share these perspectives if we had the same experience.) We cannot call the legitimacy of such perspectives into question, but we can try to understand that different experiences make different people consider different things permissible and legitimate, as the remainder of this section, derived from our fieldnotes and written from a first-person perspective, illustrates.[3]

> Reflecting on the visualization of peace, one situation plays vividly in front of my eyes that I encountered on a summer day at the Baščaršija square in Sarajevo, Bosnia and Herzegovina. At the center of the square, you can find Sebilj, a wooden fountain from the Ottoman era (see Fig. 10.3). Regarding this fountain, it is said that travelers who drink from its water will one day return to Sarajevo. Amidst the crowded square, filled with tourists and locals, I saw a little boy, maybe three or four years old, standing on the step of the fountain. What stroke me was seeing this little boy holding and playing with a toy rifle. He happily aimed at random passers-by, imitating shooting sounds. The boy attracted a lot of people's attention, most of whom were laughingly pointing at him, being entertained, some even actively engaging with him, acting as if they were hit by a bullet, pretending to fall to the ground, fatally wounded by the boy's rifle.
>
> For me, this was a deeply confusing encounter, firmly ingrained in my pictorial memory. For a visitor coming to Sarajevo, the legacy of the violent war in the region is omnipresent. Many buildings still reveal broken facades and display bullet holes (see Fig. 1.3). Many main tourist attractions are linked to the Yugoslavian war or the siege of Sarajevo more specifically. Dark tourism indeed. Seeing people simulating war with that child felt strongly cynical in that context.
>
> Growing up and being educated in Germany, a country that I perceive as having a reserved attitude toward publicly displayed militarism, my first impression was that this situation at Baščaršija Square reflected the political and social conflicts that prevail in the country. (The social scientist in me was also immediately thinking about such concepts as militarized masculinities and the normalization of war in the everyday.) It reminded me of

---

[3] For the complete text, see "Ways of Showing Peace (II): Visualizing Contested Peace" at https://www.imageandpeace.com/2021/05/03/ways-of-showing-peace-ii-visualizing-contested-peace/.

Fig. 10.3 Sebilj (Photograph © Frank Möller)

conversations with young and liberal people in Sarajevo, people 'like me,' who announced that they would take up arms and fight if, for instance, the Republic Srpska, one of the two entities of the country and dominated by Serbs, would declare independence or unification with Serbia. They explained that this, to them, would mean that the Serbs would have won the war in the end. This would mean to them that the genocide in Srebrenica would have succeeded after all. "The peace that follows many contemporary conflicts is often un-satisfactory and marked by a continuation of inter-ethnic tensions, lack of order and eruption of violence. The lack of sustainable peace arrangements is illuminated in the body of literature, which conceptualises peace as temporary and contested in terms of fragile, precarious, unstable, or turbulent peace" (Aggestam and Björkdahl 2009: 24). Therefore, my encounter at Sebilj, from my point of view, would not qualify as an image of peace.

At the same time, in the situation I described above, people were laughing. To me, laughter seemed out of place.[4] They, however, appeared

---

[4] For laughter out of place as a coping strategy in adverse conditions, see Goldstein (2003).

to adore the little boy and his toy. After all, playing war is different from waging war. The boy's performance didn't seem to be anything extraordinary and possibly harmful to other people I observed. Couldn't the laughter, the joyful encounter with the boy be a positive sign that the trauma of the violent conflict in the country is not that dominating for local people anymore? That a toy-weapon is less a reminder of danger than an inter-generational tool linking a young child with the adult passers-by? Could laughter not be a sign of agency, a strategy to cope with intricate pasts and presents and equally intricate memories, very difficult to assess and understand for outsiders inclined to make premature moral judgments derived from their own experience?

For me, when dealing with the question of the visualization of peace, this image in my mind serves as a reminder – a reminder of my positionality toward the question of peace (and conflict), toward other people's experiences of peace (and conflict), a reminder of the complex relationship between the horrors of the past, present contestations of peace, and the hope for peaceful relations in the future. This encounter in Sarajevo became a strong point of reference for me.

EMBRACING DIFFERENCE, TRANSFORMING CONFLICT

Can we transform conflict by embracing difference, by understanding the ways in which difference enriches our lives, by acknowledging that difference, although constitutive of who we (think we) are, does not necessarily have to be regarded as a *negative* reference point? Embracing difference implies recognizing conflict, which, in its most basic understanding, signifies merely (more or less) serious disagreement or (factual or constructed) perceived incompatibility. Conflict, often reduced to violent conflict, can be found at the core of many approaches in international relations. For advocates of the agonistic peace approach, for example, conflict (as in different and even opposing positions, interpretations and perspectives) is the pre-condition for the existence of "the political" (Mouffe 2013: 2). It cannot be avoided, as this multitude of positions, resulting from the foundational construction of an I/we and the respective you/they, is central to our societies (Shinko 2008: 478). Following this understanding of conflict, the foundational "we/they opposition" (Mouffe 2013: 9) requires institutions, mechanisms and ways of thinking/acting that prevent antagonistic and violent forms of dealing with difference from taking over (Nagle 2014: 471; Strömbom 2019: 949). Chantal Mouffe, therefore, argues that "many us/them relations are merely a question of recognizing difference" (Mouffe 2013: 5). Difference, once recognized, and conflict resulting from difference can serve as negative or positive points of reference. Embracing difference constructively, then, implies looking for those ingredients of conflict that help improve social relations by, for example, replacing the rigid we/they opposition with relational thinking, understanding us as less them and them as less us, thus acknowledging that whatever separates us from them, there is something we ultimately have in common—something that could serve as a social bond to improve the relationship. This 'something' can be visualized. Improving social relations does not necessarily require conflict resolution; acknowledging conflict and recognizing it as a social bond may be a more fruitful approach aiming at creating a space where the conflictual contest between different positions can take place in an agonistic form without recourse to antagonism.

The "moral imagination"—the step from what is to what does not yet exist but what might exist at some point, the step from what is to what may be imagined and thought of as possible—"rises," according to John Paul Lederach, "with the capacity to imagine ourselves in relationship" (2005: 29), and such imagination requires the recognition of difference. Conflict, unless it displays unlimited violence, is a social relation, and "once relations have been established through conflict, other types of relations are likely to follow" (Coser 1956: 122). The moral imagination also rises with "the willingness to embrace complexity without reliance on dualistic polarity, the belief in the creative act, and acceptance of the inherent risk required to break violence and to venture on unknown paths that build constructive change" (Lederach 2005: 29). As we have argued throughout the book, visual images can help embrace complexity and deal constructively with conflict resulting from complexity. In contrast to Lederach, however, our approach is not primarily interested in "simplicity as a source of energy" (2005: 33)[5] but rather in complexifying narratives to better represent the social reality these narratives are meant to address. Replacing the we/they opposition with more relational thinking is one such complexification.

Thus, as we have noted earlier, from our point of view, it need not be a problem that "a new conflict" can emerge "when you want to 'define'

---

[5] Lederach understands complexity as "*the* great challenge of peacebuilding" and suggests "locat[ing] a core set of patterns and dynamics that generate the complexity" rather than targeting complexity directly (2005: 33; italics in original).

what images really mean," as Wim Wenders warns (Wenders and Zournazi 2013: 38), as long as all parties to the emerging conflict agree to deal with it constructively, i.e., in search of commonalities and conflict transformative potentialities and without recourse to violence. We can talk about images without 'defining' what they mean—we can (try to) describe what they mean to us without necessarily expecting others to share our description—and surely without trying to establish what they "really" mean, i.e., without assigning to our interpretation ontological superiority. As we have emphasized in this book, images mean different things to different people, and it is through dialog about these differences that individuals and groups of people learn to understand and to partially identify with one another. This is another way of saying that images help us understand *both* that no one can be reduced to what they have in common with others *and* that no one can be reduced to what distinguishes them from others (Möller 2007: 254). We have something in common even with the Other (with a capital O) with whom agreement seems, or is said to be, impossible. Thus, while there is always something that separates an individual from other individuals, there is also always something they have in common—not least the "commonalities of being human" that images show "explicitly and redundantly" (MacDougall 1998: 246). Even if some such commonalities cannot be seen in an image, the viewer will nevertheless visualize them through closure in one of the two senses of the word used in this book, for example, in Chapter 8: seeing only parts but visualizing the whole. *In extremis*, the commonalities of being human can be visualized even in images devoid of people, as "most images without faces or people are actually full of people: they are places where people can find themselves in imagination" (Elkins 2011: 50).

Returning to the Bosnian way: "Perhaps at its fullest, the Bosnian way means living with contradictions, refusing to accept in its entirety any one path or creed. It means bending the rules while accepting the game and keeping an eye open to critique and modify everything" (Markowitz 2010: 161). Learning from the Bosnian way, then? To be sure, the prewar Bosnian way is to some extent a social construction, a narrative reflecting interests and identities; referring to the Bosnian way today involves some degree of nostalgia and retrospective myth building. Its relationship with Bosnian reality is and has always been complicated. Terms such as multiculturalism derived from Western discourse should be applied to Bosnian social reality with some degree of caution. However, while as Campbell notes, the term was often used "as a means of mobilizing support in 'the West'" without necessarily being grounded in Bosnian discourse, its absence "does not mean that the contingent and hybrid senses of identity ... are alien to Bosnia." On the contrary, ethnographic work has demonstrated "their centrality to the identity marked as Bosnian/Muslim" (1998: 211). However, according to Donia (2009), "[c]ommon life and tolerance were most at risk in times of political instability" (p. 355), "excesses and instances of revenge" did occur (p. 356) and "at no time" have such values as "the city's common life, openness, response to cultural influences, and receptivity to outsiders ... completely triumphed" (p. 356). According to one protagonist in Joe Sacco's *The Fixer*, due to the influx of refugees from rural areas during the siege, "THERE IS NO MORE 'SPIRIT OF SARAJEVO' ABOUT WHICH EUROPEANS ARE ALWAYS TALKING" (2004: 74). Currently, the Bosnian way is just as absent from large portions of Bosnian sociopolitical reality as it is absent from the social and political realities of those countries (including western European ones) that often, and occasionally quite patronizingly, interfere in Bosnia-Herzegovina. The country is exposed to "extraordinarily intrusive levels of external intervention as part of the peacebuilding process" (Mac Ginty 2006: 57), intervention understood not in terms of mutual learning but, rather, as one-sided adaptation. Yet as an *idea*, the Bosnian way, expanding what we think of as possible, is still intriguing, especially in the context of this book and its interest in tolerance of ambiguity.

Societal polarization seems to have increased in recent years in Bosnia (see Rhotert and Rolofs 2020) and elsewhere, while communication between different sociopolitical groups has decreased. Social groups cultivate their own cultures, amplified through social media reflecting strict and uncompromising differentiation between social groups where others appear as a threat or a deviation rather than as an inspiration. Or they appear in "parody form" only, which happens when we fail to "see 'others' as having something in common with us – something that requires recognition" (Couldry 2000: 120). Difference is often used to increase the in-group's coherence at the expense of both divergent opinions within the in-group, thus stifling internal dissent, and dialogue with out-groups thus making communication impossible. The techniques are always the same. They have been identified in the literature on the social construction of reality—i.e., the conflation of that which is socially constructed with that which is objectively true—in terms of, for example, therapy and nihilation as mechanisms of social control (see Berger and Luckmann 1967: 130–134). Captions in photojournalism also have a control function, regardless of what other purposes they serve. Owing to communication failures and other component parts of the operating procedures of social media as well as to the general decline of the critical function of the media, they are probably more effective currently than they used to be.

To prevent increasing polarization from eroding social cohesion and trust, we need to appreciate difference as a building block of, rather than an obstacle to, communities. This is one of the main statements of this book. The Bosnian way as described by Markowitz in the above quotation outlines a possible approach to difference: accepting contradictions rather than trying to resolve (all of) them; rejecting as unacceptable the idea that there is only one permissible way of doing things; being open-minded toward criticisms and adjustments; and exhibiting flexibility with regard to individual rules and narratives while simultaneously acknowledging as binding the overall societal frame within which these rules and narratives operate. The Bosnian way thus understood is quite sophisticated, as it requires working "*with* difference and not by *reducing* difference" thus offering "a common space of intellectual and political commitment" that Nick Couldry demands for cultural studies (2000: 21–22; italics in original). Such a space might also adequately represent the increasingly complex and ambiguous social environments in and beyond Bosnia. In the context of this book, all of the above has to be reflected upon in light of the question of how it may help increase tolerance of ambiguity.

Conclusion

In Chapters 2, 3 and 5, we outlined our approach to complexity and ambiguity and explained both why, in a complex and ambiguous world, we prefer tolerance of ambiguity rather than disambiguation and how images can contribute to an increase in such tolerance. The disappearance of visual images as stable reference points and the emergence of a plurality of visual narratives connected with and derived from any image—inevitable features of digitization—will strengthen existing ambiguities and create new ones. These ambiguities cannot, and should not, be tamed by mandatory verbal or written designations of meaning if we are interested in the production of new spaces of possibility within which we can think about complexity, ambiguity, difference and, ultimately, politics and society. As Daniel Rubinstein and Katrina Sluis note, "technologies of representation ... can be harnessed toward a view of life that embraces change, uncertainty, spontaneous becoming and difference" (Rubinstein and Sluis 2013: 24). In the following two chapters, we develop two more ways of approaching visual material with which to strengthen such a view of life. We conclude the present chapter with the tenth of our Sarajevo photographs (Fig. 10.4) introduced in Chapter 2 in terms of photocomplexity.

Fig. 10.4 Sarajevo #10 (Photograph © Frank Möller)

References

Aggestam, Karin, and Annika Björkdahl. 2009. Introduction: War and Peace in Transition. In *War and Peace in Transition: Changing Roles of External Actors*, ed. Karin Aggestam and Annika Björkdahl, 15–31. Lund: Nordic Academic Press.
Bastašić, Lana. 2021. *Catch the Rabbit*. London: Picador.
Berger, Peter, and Thomas Luckmann. 1967. *The Social Construction of Reality: A Treatise in the Sociology of Knowledge*. London: Penguin.

Buckley, Bernadette. 2009. The Workshop of Filthy Creation: Or Do Not Be Alarmed, This Is Only a Test. *Review of International Studies* 35 (4): 835–857.
Campbell, David. 1998. *National Deconstruction: Violence, Identity, and Justice in Bosnia.* Minneapolis and London: University of Minnesota Press.
Coser, Lewis. 1956. *The Functions of Social Conflict.* New York: The Free Press.
Couldry, Nick. 2000. *Inside Culture: Re-imagining the Method of Cultural Studies.* London: Sage.
Donia, Robert J. 2009. *Sarajevo: A Biography.* London: Hurst & Company.
Elkins, James. 2011. *What Photography Is.* New York and London: Routledge.
Glenny, Misha. 1996. *The Fall of Yugoslavia: The Third Balkan War.* London: Penguin.
Goldstein, Donna M. 2003. *Laughter Out of Place: Race, Class, Violence, and Sexuality in a Rio Shantytown.* Berkeley, Los Angeles, and London: University of California Press.
Golubović, Jelena. 2020. "To Me, You Are Not a Serb": Ethnicity, Ambiguity, and Anxiety in Post-war Sarajevo. *Ethnicities* 20 (3): 544–563.
Jergović, Miljenko. 2015. *Vater*, trans. Brigitte Döbert. Frankfurt: Schöffling & Co.
Jestrovic, Silvija. 2013. *Performance, Space, Utopia: Cities of War, Cities of Exile.* Houndmills: Palgrave Macmillan.
Karahasan, Dževad. 1993. *Tagebuch der Aussiedlung*, trans. Klaus Detlef Olof. Klagenfurt: Wieser Verlag.
Lederach, John Paul. 2005. *The Moral Imagination: The Art and Soul of Building Peace.* Oxford: Oxford University Press.
MacDougall, David. 1998. *Transcultural Cinema*, ed. and with an introduction by Lucien Taylor. Princeton: Princeton University Press.
Mac Ginty, Roger. 2006. *No War, No Peace: The Rejuvenation of Stalled Peace Processes and Peace Accords.* Houndmills: Palgrave Macmillan.
Markowitz, Fran. 2010. *Sarajevo: A Bosnian Kaleidoscope.* Urbana, Chicago, and Springfield: University of Illinois Press.
Möller, Frank. 2007. *Thinking Peaceful Change: Baltic Security Policy and Security Community Building.* Syracuse: Syracuse University Press.
Möller, Frank. 2019. *Peace Photography.* Houndmills: Palgrave Macmillan.
Mouffe, Chantal. 2013. *Agonistics: Thinking the World Politically.* London and New York: Verso.
Nagle, John. 2014. From the Politics of Antagonistic Recognition to Agonistic Peace Building: An Exploration of Symbols and Rituals in Divided Societies. *Peace & Change* 39 (4): 468–494.
Rhotert, Alexander, and Oliver Rolofs. 2020. 25 Jahre nach Dayton: Hält der Frieden in Bosnien und Herzegowina? *Südosteuropa Mitteilungen* 6: 25–38.

Ristic, Mirjana. 2018. *Architecture, Urban Space and War: The Destruction and Reconstruction of Sarajevo*. Houndmills: Palgrave Macmillan.

Roberts, John. 2014. *Photography and Its Violations*. New York: Columbia University Press.

Rubinstein, Daniel, and Katrina Sluis. 2013. The Digital Image in Photographic Culture: Algorithmic Photography and the Crisis of Representation. In *The Photographic Image in Digital Culture*, 2nd ed., ed. Martin Lister, 22–40. London and New York: Routledge.

Sacco, Joe. 2004. *The Fixer: A Story from Sarajevo*. London: Jonathan Cape.

Shinko, Rosemary E. 2008. Agonistic Peace: A Postmodern Reading. *Millennium: Journal of International Studies* 36 (3): 473–491.

Strömbom, Lisa. 2019. Exploring Analytical Avenues for Agonistic Peace. *Journal of International Relations and Development* 23 (4): 947–969.

Wenders, Wim, and Mary Zournazi. 2013. *Inventing Peace: A Dialogue on Perception*. London and New York: I.B. Tauris.

CHAPTER 11

Exploring the Surround, Appreciating Complexity

INTRODUCTION

This chapter explores the *surround*—non-iconic, peripheral and unwanted image components (Elkins 2011: 116–117)—as place for the emergence of narrative plurality in *Bosnia: Uncertain Paths to Peace* and elsewhere. In this chapter—and in the following one—we create some distance between our argument and the Ritchin–Peress project. What we have to say is relevant to this project but also to other encounters with images. Similar to Fred Ritchin and Gilles Peress, we do not wish to guide our readers but rely on their own initiative and curiosity when exploring the project's surround. Indeed, regarding the surround may lead you *anywhere*, and anywhere is an extremely interesting place from a complexity point of view, indicating unpredictability of visual encounters: In the surround, the limits of what is permissible can be moved in such a way that meanings emerge which "exceed [an image's] simple superfluous illustration" as provided by the dominant media (Rancière 2009: 96). In addition to "the necessity of reading photographs, not just the text surrounding them" (Ritchin 1999: 41), the surround—the visual components surrounding an image's main figure—must be read as well, not just the central figure. Spectators have to develop their own agency with regard to meaning-making rather than blindly following designations of meaning made by others, and they have to look for meaning in both obvious and less

© The Author(s), under exclusive license to Springer Nature Switzerland AG 2023
R. Bellmer and F. Möller, *Peace, Complexity, Visuality*, Rethinking Peace and Conflict Studies,
https://doi.org/10.1007/978-3-031-38218-5_11

obvious parts of the image. This chapter, then, aims to capitalize on images' often unacknowledged and "unintended sites of connotation" (MacDougall 1998: 68) to identify places where alternative narratives may emerge so as to achieve a better, i.e., more complete and diverse, understanding of *Bosnia: Uncertain Paths to Peace*.

The surround tells us a lot, provided that we pay attention to it rather than disregarding it as insignificant and focusing attention on what appears in the center of an image. What it tells us cannot be anticipated; it tells different viewers different things. As such, exploring the surround will diversify the viewing experience and enable narratives to emerge that would otherwise remain hidden. The surround defies incorporation into established ways of seeing and patterns of interpretation. Similar to the operating procedures of the grids discussed in Chapter 8, what narrative(s) emerge(s) depends on the viewer. Whatever narrative emerges, it will be a property of the viewer, and it will be different from the narrative that emerges from regarding only central image components.

We present our arguments in two parts. In the first part, subdivided into two sections, we explore the surround—marginalized in photographic discourses or dismissed as irrelevant—theoretically and conceptually. We emphasize the *archived* character of the Ritchin–Peress project and argue that archived images wait for rediscovery by viewers interested in thorough visual investigation liberated from the "the urgency"—or tyranny—"of the present tense" (Phelan 2012: 53). Such investigation may focus on an image's main figure, its surround or the relationship between the main figure and the surround. Whatever focus the viewer chooses, imagination is required—the more so as the images in the Ritchin–Peress project appear rather small. What appears in the surround, thus, is hard to decipher. This, however, is not an insurmountable obstacle. Viewers, by interacting with the image, can choose to appropriate and enlarge those image ingredients they are most interested in, and these ingredients may be found in the surround.

Photographers do not normally appear in photojournalistic images; the photographer is "a person never shown in the frame" (Butler 2010: 81). In the second part, therefore, we explore how the encounter with an image changes when a photographer appears in it. In our case, the photographer appears in the surround. This appearance connects the chapter's second part with its first part and enables us, once again, to appreciate Peress's presence in *Bosnia: Uncertain Paths to Peace*—not in the images but as author of the narrative and provider of audio comments where he self-critically discusses his own subject position as a photographer. Such discussion is not a clever act on the part of the photographer to pass the buck to the viewer who is given the task to make sense of the images; rather, it is an important vehicle to nudge the viewer into engagement, to make her interrogate what photojournalism often takes for granted (e.g., the presence of the photographer) and to change her subject position from (passive) spectator (a myth anyway) to co-author. Emancipating the viewer from the authoritative voice of the photographer, the emerging narratives, rather than being hierarchically ordered or mutually exclusive, are seen as coexisting. Put together, they approximate a complete understanding of *Bosnia: Uncertain Paths of Peace*, which, however, is unattainable.

Analysis of the surround may reveal meanings that analysis of the image's main figure missed: it may confirm but also challenge, complement or even correct earlier interpretations of the image's meaning derived from analysis of its main figure.[1] Essentially, center–surround dynamics occur and are indicative of patterns of visibility and invisibility operating *within* the image. This is different from patterns of in|visibility mirroring "representability," i.e., inclusion in or exclusion from the frame (Butler 2010: 73).[2] Even *within* the frame of representation, there is a hierarchy of things observed and things ignored. Visibility and invisibility do not simply follow patterns of inclusion and exclusion linked to an inside and an outside, respectively: the outside may be inside. Indeed, while images may show "what is hidden by what is being said in print" (Hariman and Lucaites 2003: 41), what is being said and written about images may also hide parts of what is being shown in the picture, singling out certain aspects while ignoring others. As Jennifer Mason and Katherine Davies explain, "because photographs manifestly contain visible images of people and their physical characteristics, people sometimes say *less* than they might otherwise do about those things, because there seems to be no real imperative to explain them" (2009: 594–595; italics in original). David MacDougall (1998: 246–247) adds that verbal and written

---

[1] Different viewers may identify different main figures and surrounds. Neither 'main figure' nor 'surround' is an objective criterion.

[2] For Judith Butler, representability is linked to "state permission," i.e., "the state seeks to establish control over it, if always with only partial success." Furthermore, "[p]rior to the events and actions represented within the frame, there is an active if unmarked delimitation of the field itself" conditioning what can be included in an image (p. 73).

descriptions of images tend to focus on "a few notable details" because the general "features of human appearance" are *too* obvious to be specifically mentioned; mentioning them would seem to be redundant as they can be seen in the image anyway.

Interpretive-aesthetic and hermeneutical approaches to image analysis increase the invisibility of some image components by emphasizing other components; they always reflect a choice differentiating what seems to be important in a given context from allegedly irrelevant image ingredients—irrelevant to the photographer's mission, the image's overall message, aesthetic gratification, political mobilization and so on. Photographs, as Shawn Michelle Smith notes, "reinforce the invisibility of some things by overtly focusing on others" (2013: 14), but discourse does pretty much the same thing: photography crops reality and discourse crops photographs—the one by visual, the other by verbal and written means. It is, therefore, necessary to pay attention to what is visible in the image but excluded from discourse to achieve a better understanding of what an image shows and how it operates in the context of *Bosnia: Uncertain Paths to Peace* (or, for that matter, in any context). In what follows, then, we will discuss the surround from two different angles, first by analyzing its potentialities quite generically and, second, by focusing on one specific disappearance from visual representation, namely, that of image-makers.

Revisiting Images, Reordering Events

We wish to suggest both revisiting photographs—or other forms of visual culture possessing a surround—and focusing analytical attention not on the image's main figure but on the surround. Scholars revisit images all the time, for example, to connect images with other images to establish a photographic genre such as war photography (see Tucker et al. 2012) or in search of changes over time in their relation to society or, alternatively, the lack of changes indicating some degree of stability of the meanings assigned to the image (see Hariman and Lucaites 2007). By revisiting images, researchers can engage with established and stable meanings sedimented in society rather than with ad hoc and tentative meanings still competing with others. As Alex Danchev and Debbie Lisle explain, "returning to earlier work" may help identify "its continued significance, often overlooked" (2009: 775), but it may also make us see the picture in a new light, identifying what earlier reflections missed. Some of the meanings images always carry with them exist potentially rather than actually—similar to digital images, which "exist in a number of states that are potential rather than actual in a fixed and physical kind of way" (Lister 2013: 8)—and can be vitalized discursively. Returning to an image tells us something *new* about the image, and *what* it tells us is indicative of politics and society within which both we and the image operate. This is so even if revisiting images confirms and thus strengthens earlier interpretations, as is often the case when photographic icons are the objects of reflection because iconicity requires a certain degree of discursive stability (Hariman and Lucaites 2007; Boudana et al. 2017).

Photographic icons are immediately recognizable, known beyond the sphere of photography specialists, often quoted and reproduced (including in contexts that have little or nothing to do with the original context) and "*understood to be representations of historically significant events*" (Hariman and Lucaites 2007: 27; italics in original).[3] Iconicity, however, equals partial invisibility *despite* representation. On the one hand, iconic status freezes a given image's meaning for some time: as we argued in earlier chapters, everyone with some knowledge on the history of photojournalism will connect, for example, *The Falling Soldier* with specific assumptions, imagine those image elements that condition its iconic status, and understand what this image represented politically, historically and culturally. On the other hand, those image elements that were discursively assigned secondary importance to the image's status or ignored altogether as irrelevant remain out of focus, assigned to oblivion. An image's meaning is a consequence of discursive designations repeatedly articulated from positions of authority and shared among a significant number of people so that it becomes sedimented in culture, largely unquestioned, conditioning group coherence and legitimizing all sorts of politics. Meaning becomes ideology once all traces of its constructedness are erased (Sutherland and Acord 2007: 127).

Re-appearing such erased traces is an important ingredient of critical work. Discursively constructed meaning might change over time, reflecting the always evolving political, social and cultural configurations within which such construction unfolds. Even if seemingly fixed at a given point in time and stabilized over time by verbal and written accounts,

---

[3] Here, an event's historical significance precedes visual representation while visual representation can also be said to endow an event with historical significance. Either way, once discursively established, iconic images "*activate strong emotional identification or response, and are reproduced across a range of media, genres, or topics*" (p. 27; italics in original).

meaning is permanently in the process of becoming. Some meanings assigned to images are more stable than others and several meanings may coexist. In principle, however, the meaning(s) of every image can change. Such change reflects politics and society; often, it tells us more about politics and society than it does about the image. Changes in meaning may be motivated by what can be seen in the surround. Analyses of the surround, however, are neither automatically nor necessarily critical, if by critical we mean practices that go beyond "the mere recognition of established opinion or the extrapolation from established versions of facticity" (Shapiro 2015: 10).[4]

As a method aimed at knowledge production derived from a plurality of narratives, revisiting an image does not require an immediate cause; it can be done at any time. The absence of an immediate cause liberates (re-)interpretation from the (perceived) need to respond to this cause. Revisiting an image is also an exercise in reflexivity that interrogates processes of knowledge production: an image's meaning is not simply *there* in the image, awaiting discovery by an objective observer. Rather, what the observer identifies as an image's meaning(s) reflects her own subject positions and political and visual socialization, analysis of which has to be a part of the procedure: what we see reflects who we are. Revisiting images is certainly an exercise in "slow looking" (Bal 2007: 113–115; Shapiro 2008)—"a chronicle of precise looking" (Stepanova 2020: 354; our translation). Surround analysis requires curiosity, unwillingness to be blinded by what only seems to be obvious (Morris 2014) and skepticism about binding and inflexible designations of meaning. It does not require, however, specific methods of visual analysis. Visual appropriation, for example, may transform peripheral image ingredients into central ones, thus increasing their visibility and facilitating analysis (see Möller et al. 2021). Photography may also be reclaimed from the archive where things have been collected and meanings have been produced through what John Roberts (2014) calls "accumulation (the result of prior judgment, editorial decisions, and so on)" (p. 114). Such reclamation "always

---

[4] Systematically analyzing that which is not obvious to a casual observer including peripheral details and assembling these details into a coherent narrative is what forensic photography does. Such photography also produces new knowledge and assumes critical functions (see Fuller and Weizman 2021). However, it is often based on a rather positivist understanding of images in terms of "evidence as indisputable facts" (Gade 2020: 380) while social-constructivist, interpretive analysis of the surround is not.

promises a practice of counterproduction, of counterarchiving, of interruption and reordering of the event" (p. 114). Archives as "structures of meaning in process" (p. 114) are image repositories waiting for rediscovery, reconstruction and reinterpretation. *Bosnia: Uncertain Paths to Peace* is an archived project waiting for such rediscovery, reconstruction and reinterpretation. Its photography, certainly representing a historically significant event, is not often included in accounts of photojournalistic icons, but this omission tells us next to nothing about the quality of the photographs (see Chapter 4). Photographic reconstruction can, in principle, be endless; it can be done at any time; and it can aim at reordering established meaning by either focusing on the main figure or, as in what follows, on the surround. When focusing on the surround, analysis can concentrate either on the relationship between the main figure and the surround or on the surround as an independent object of analysis.

IMAGES AND THE SURROUND

Similar to the distinction between an image's main figure and the surround, MacDougall separates centered from peripheral details coexisting in images. Peripheral details "are open to interpretation, as mere fragments or as mistaken signifiers, and they are also potential distractions from the author's purpose" (1998: 69). Critical analysis, however, appreciates images' "*excess* meaning" (p. 68; italics in original), parts of which may be found in the surround. Indeed, the surround—or "ground" (in contrast to "figure") in MacDougall's terminology (p. 69)—"offer[s] a range of further details, not consciously intended, that may lead anywhere, challenging meaning because they are unexplained" (p. 69). If explained, these details no longer lead viewers anywhere but only to those places the explainer wishes viewers to visit. From a critical point of view, then, *anywhere* is an extremely fascinating place promising alternatives to either accepting or rejecting discursively established meanings. Like culture in general, then, images are best understood as "space[s] of multiple voices and forces" (Couldry 2000: 4), and some of these voices and forces operate in the surround. Identifying the spaces and forces that were hitherto marginalized is an important task of critical analysis, unearthing what has become sedimented in discourse and adding layers of meaning to established and taken-for-granted ways of seeing.

Scrutinizing the surround, i.e., that which does not appear in the image's center, means encountering "unwanted stuff" (Elkins 2011: 116).

Analyzing the surround requires some degree of interpretive stability because otherwise we would not know what qualifies as the image's center and what as its surround. However, such a lack of knowledge would not render impossible personal, first-person assumptions about center and surround, contributing to narrative plurality. Center and surround are not geographical terms locating image ingredients in the middle of an image or at its margins, respectively. As such, they are not to be taken literally. *The Falling Soldier*, for example, is asymmetric in terms of the relationship between the photograph's figure and its surround: the figure, appearing in the foreground, occupies the lower left quarter of the frame, while approximately 75% of the image comprises the sky and clouds (Susperregui 2016: 21). The photograph's main figure attracts our attention, while the surround does not. What happens and what can be seen in the surround is not the reason why the photograph was taken, nor is it the reason for our visual engagement with the photograph. The surround likens an accident; its appearance in the picture is not deliberate; if it were not represented, nobody would miss it.

Photojournalistic images possess a surround, but there is very little reflection upon it (except when a photograph is altered in the surround).[5] If the surround is at the image's margins, it can be cropped out of the picture (see below). Photojournalism considers cropping legitimate because by erasing hidden meanings and unintended connotations appearing in the surround, cropping prevents distraction from the author's purpose and may increase the image's aesthetic qualities. The surround is not identical to what Judith Butler (2010: 73) calls the "non-thematized background," i.e., "a set of contents and perspectives" ruled out as "impermissible to show" prior to the photographic act. The surround is *within* the frame; it is permissible and it is being shown. However, both Butler's background and Elkins's surround are characterized by non-thematization. Butler notes that "the field of representability … is constituted fundamentally by what is left out, maintained outside the frame within which representations appear" (Butler 2010: 73). However, also *within* this frame, there is a hierarchy of things observed and things

---

[5] That was the case when the Associated Press cut ties with the photographer Narciso Contreras who had removed a video camera from the surround of one of his images taken in Syria, thus allegedly manipulating the image in an unacceptable way (http://www.theguardian.com/media/2014/jan/23/photographer-dumped-altering-syria-image; accessed 5 January 2022).

disregarded, things singled out for attention and things ignored, things considered worthy and things considered unworthy of analysis. Thus, while it is still very important to reveal and analyze what is—systematically, ideology- and power-driven and/or habitually—excluded from representation, it is equally important to reveal and analyze what is *included in representation* but nevertheless *excluded from discourse* and, thus, politics. To be sure, to some extent, "the frame determines the limits of visibility/invisibility, and thus the limits of politics" (Callahan 2020: 22), but even within the frame, figures may be invisible or discursively assigned to oblivion; the limits of politics are more difficult to identify than merely by referring to an inside and an outside: the outside may be inside.[6] Thus, "get[ting] in the picture frame" is not sufficient (Callahan 2020: 25).[7]

The surround, as Elkins understands it, is not equivalent to a painting's background: background, in painting (and in many art photographs and studio portraits), is "always noticed, always intended" (Elkins 2011: 117), and background and foreground *together* create a compositional entity. In contrast, the surround is an accident; it is "often enough unwanted" (Elkins 2011: 117). It may, for example, reflect the working conditions of photojournalists in violent conflict determined by a lack of time for careful consideration of the image's composition. While photojournalists may succeed in identifying a photographic moment, the conditions in which they work may render it impossible for them to translate this identification immediately into a formally perfect image. Thus, for Elkins, the surround is irrelevant and

> only noticed when it helps identify the place the photograph was taken, or when it adds a general atmosphere. ... The surround only becomes an object of attention when the photograph is going to be used as an advertisement, in a publication, as a formal portrait, or as a scientific or technical illustration. Or when it is looked at oddly, for odd purposes. (2011: 117)

---

[6] Or elsewhere, "the visibility strategy's hermeneutic mode is useful for revealing who is left out of political debates: who is visible inside the frame, and who is invisible outside..." (Callahan 2020: 218). That's too mechanical an understanding: figures may be invisible inside the frame, thus excluded from politics despite visibility.

[7] Getting in the picture frame can also be dangerous (Callahan 2020: 25). This applies also to appearance in the surround but, perhaps, less so due to the lack of importance normally assigned to what happens and who appears in the surround.

This assessment underestimates the surround—unless what we are suggesting here is considered 'odd,' which, we think, it is not because it critically interrogates dichotomies routinely applied in photographic discourses such as inside/outside, inclusion/exclusion or visibility/invisibility, revealing the artificiality of such dichotomies, their limited explanatory potentialities and the existence of photographic ambiguities. Furthermore, "theory can be found in odd places"—such as the surround—"and practices" (Callahan 2020: 313)—such as revisiting images. Indeed, the surround may be unwanted, but serendipitously, it adds more than just a general atmosphere to the image. Even if unwanted and unplanned by the photographer, the image's center and its surround may communicate with each other and achieve something that they would not achieve independently. More importantly, the story (or stories) the surround tells may be different from, or even critical of, the image's main story. It is indeed arguable that center and surround, rather than showing the same story differently, often show different stories. The resulting tension can be productive for the viewing experience, changing the perceived story but also involving the viewer strongly in the process of interpretation, thus contributing to self-reflexivity.

Rather than having surrounds, art photographs (similar to paintings) are "said to have backgrounds, which means the photographer is supposed to have noticed what goes on around the figure, and taken it into account as part of the image as a whole" (Elkins 2011: 117). However, even if the photographer fails (or does not have sufficient time) to notice what goes on around the figure and, therefore, cannot deliberately take it into account as part of the image's overall composition, the surround is a part of the image; as such, it influences the meaning(s) viewers assign to the image—not necessarily the meaning(s) the photographer wanted to achieve but meaning(s) all the same.

We want to illustrate some of the above claims with reference, once again, to *The Falling Soldier*, Robert Capa's famous Spanish Civil War photograph formally titled *Death of a Loyalist Militiaman, Cerro Muriano, Córdoba Front, Spain*. José Manuel Susperregui has revisited this photograph, which, regardless of the huge amount of work spent by numerous people on deciphering the image, still poses obstacles that analysts such as Susperregui wish to conquer. As a pre-digital image, this photograph has remained the same while the meanings assigned to it have changed, reflecting controversy as to the photograph's authenticity. Rather than adding yet another image-immanent analysis to the existing, already quite substantial body of work on this photograph (see, among many others, Whelan 2007: 53–87), Susperregui decided to visit the location where this photograph supposedly had been taken. By analyzing those image ingredients that, while appearing in the original image, were ignored in earlier interpretations, he could reveal the limitations of earlier interpretations. While much has been written about those elements that condition the picture's iconic status—the person (alleged to be) depicted and what (seems to have) happened to him in the moment the photograph was taken—the photograph's surround (sky, clouds and mountains) has largely been ignored as irrelevant for the photograph's status. Indeed, the surround seems to offer "very little information in terms of location" (Susperregui 2016: 21). However, by analyzing the very little the surround does offer (e.g., the topography of the mountains appearing in the image), Susperregui could show that the photograph could not possibly have been taken where it was alleged to have been taken. He revealed where it had been taken in fact, as a result of which many assumptions revolving around and narratives derived from this photograph collapsed. (Whether such collapse damages or will damage the image's iconic status or not is a different question.) If analysis of even as inauspicious, unremarkable and nondescript a surround as *The Falling Soldier*'s can change the image's meaning, then it is a reasonable assumption that more spectacular or impressive surrounds are equally well or even more capable of contributing to meaning-making beyond the photographer's intentions.

"To recognize the *studium* is inevitably to encounter the photographer's intentions," Roland Barthes proclaims (2000: 27); to recognize the surround inevitably means disregarding these very intentions. However, critical analysis is not primarily interested in the photographer's intentions, and whereas Elkins notes that "[t]he surround does not advance our knowledge of the subject" (Elkins 2011: 124), this is precisely what it often does. Susperregui's analysis of *The Falling Soldier*'s surround, for example, *both* identifies the photograph's location—which is in accordance with Elkins—*and* provides new knowledge on the scene depicted—which is not. And, indeed, Elkins continues by suggesting that "in popular photography, photojournalism, and photography classes, what happens in the surround is a crucial guarantee of quality" (Elkins 2011: 124).[8]

---

[8] Elkins gives an example how to make the surround in one photojournalistic image published in the *New York Times appear* relevant through art historical interpretation and

However, it is not the surround's *quality* that interests us here primarily but rather its capability of adding narratives to the ones that emerge from reading only the picture's central figure. Indeed, in the surround, all sorts of things can and do happen, some of which provide new knowledge on a given scenario while others help problematize the operating procedures of photojournalism, as the following part, revisiting another famous photograph, will show.

Photographic Inclusions and Appearances, Exclusions and Disappearances

A photographer walks, somewhat casually, down a road toward the camera, inattentive to the little girl running in front of him who is screaming. Other children are moving in front of and behind the girl, and one boy's face is a mask of terror, but the photographer is the focal point of the picture, his posture so out-of-sync with what happens next to him. Rather than paying attention to the girl, stripped of her clothes, her arms held out from her sides, he is preoccupied with his camera, seemingly loading it. Behind him walk soldiers, equally casually. Behind them, roiling smoke indicates explosions in the surround of the scene depicted.

If you are familiar with the history of photojournalism and war reporting, you will probably recognize the photograph described above—and hesitate: there is something wrong here. Undoubtedly, the text describes Huynh Cong 'Nick' Ut's 8 June 1972 picture titled *Children fleeing South Vietnamese napalm strike near Trang Bang, Vietnam*, widely known as *Accidental Napalm*—another photojournalistic icon, the interpretation of which has also largely focused on the picture's main figure rather than the surround. However, the above text does not describe the image as it appears in most reproductions but as it appears before it was cropped. Our description paraphrases Robert Hariman and John Louis Lucaites's reading of the image's most famous incarnation, which is as follows:

> The naked girl is running down a road in Vietnam toward the camera, screaming from the napalm burns on her back and arm. Other Vietnamese children are moving in front of and behind her, and one boy's face is a

references. He dismisses the photograph's unusual elements as "insignificant, irrelevant, and illegible" (Elkins 2011: 126): a photojournalistic image posing as art.

11 EXPLORING THE SURROUND, APPRECIATING COMPLEXITY

mask of terror, but the naked girl is the focal point of the picture. Stripped of her clothes, her arms held out from her sides, she looks almost as if she has been flayed alive. Behind her walk soldiers, somewhat casually. Behind them, the roiling smoke from the napalm drop consumes the background of the scene. (Hariman and Lucaites 2003: 38–39)

This description is quite accurate (except that it includes elements that cannot be seen in the picture, thus requiring additional information), but it frames the photograph differently from our interpretation, thus inviting a different reading. Although both descriptions refer to the same image, this image has been presented to the public in two strikingly different ways: one unaltered (the first description, borrowing elements from the second one but changing focus) and one altered in such a way that photographers are cropped out of the image (the second description). Photographic representation has the capability of transforming any given occurrence into an event (see Linfield 2010), even when nothing else is depicted other than a mere routine. In the case of *Accidental Napalm*, the photograph shows such a routine,

> an everyday experience. ... The message is clear: what seems, from looking at the girl, to be a rare experience sure to evoke a compassionate response, is in fact, as evidenced by the soldiers, something that happens again and again, so much so that the adults involved ... can become indifferent, morally diminished, capable of routinely doing awful things to other people. (Hariman and Lucaites 2007: 180)

That this is routine—"something that happens again and again"—is not only evidenced by the soldiers but also, in the original photograph, by the photographers depicted who could not care less about what happened right next to them. For them, what is captured in the photograph is not "an unexpected event seized in mid-action by an alert photographer" (Sontag 2003: 55) but an expected event, or better: no event at all, missed by some of the photographers who were present on location because they have seen, and photographed, such occurrences in abundance. What is shown in the photograph is "repeated, and repeatable, behavior" (Hariman and Lucaites 2003: 43). Repeated behavior, everyday experience or routine do not qualify as events—except that they do, *if* photographically constructed as such (image operating in tandem with designations of meaning suggested by voices speaking with authority and shared by a significant number of people). In the context of Vietnam

War politics and photography, the photograph seemed an unlikely candidate for an icon, reproduced all over the world, as Hariman and Lucaites (2003) explain: "The photograph could not have been effective solely because of its news value, nor does it appear to be especially horrific" (p. 40).[9] That the girl is "screaming" can be seen in the image but not that she is screaming "from the napalm burns on her back and arm" (p. 39) as "[t]he burns themselves are not visible" in the image (p. 40), in part due to the low-resolution quality of the photograph, in part because the girl suffers from burns on her back.[10] The photograph's strength—its iconic character—emanates, among other things, from the girl "communicating the pain she feels" (p. 40).

Another reason why the picture became an icon is the way it was cropped. After cropping the picture,[11] the girl not only "faces the lens, which activates the demanding reciprocity of direct, face-to-face interaction, and she is aligned with the frontal angle of the viewer's perspective" (Hariman and Lucaites 2003: 40); she also appears in the center of the image—in the original, she does not. In the original, photographers appear at the right edge of the picture; in the icon, they do not. In the cropped version, the girl demands full attention; in the original, she shares the viewers' attention with the photographer: the picture radiates a tension between the screaming girl and the seemingly indifferent photographer. It is arguable, then, that *Accidental Napalm* is simultaneously one of the best-known photographs—the cropped one—and one of the least known photographs—the original—emerging from the war in Vietnam.

How does it affect the viewing experience if a picture is cropped in such a manner that the surround and, thus, the photographer disappears, and what does it mean, in contrast, when a photographer like Peress, although invisible in the pictures, insists on communicating his presence to the audience in written and spoken commentary? Photography, since its inception, has relied on "a seemingly tautological or self-affirming

---

[9] The girl's experience surely was horrific. As she explained later: "Napalm is the most terrible pain you can imagine. ... Water boils at 100 degrees Celsius (212°F). Napalm generates temperatures of 800 (1,500°F) to 1,200 degrees Celsius (2,200°F)" (quoted in Tucker et al. 2012: 466).

[10] Informed by the caption, the viewer 'sees' the burns all the same, visualizing what cannot be seen through what we, following Scott McCloud, called "closure" in chapter eight.

[11] See, for example, the photograph reproduced in *Life magazine* on 23 June 1972.

double truth about the world: the accuracy of the photograph confirmed that it was an objective trace, while the understanding that the photograph was an objective trace confirmed its accuracy" (Kelsey and Stimson 2008: xi–xii). The disappearance of the photographer from the cropped version of *Accidental Napalm* caters to photography's self-affirmation, its self-image and specifically to the photojournalistic notion of reality-as-is and its insistence on "resemblance between image and reality-as-seen" (Saugmann et al. 2020: 7). This notion includes the twin idea that the photographic image is "the duplicate of a thing" (Rancière 2009: 93)—which, according to Jacques Rancière (2009: 94), it is *not*: it "is always an alteration that occurs in a chain of images which alter it in turn"—and that in the absence of photographers, the scene depicted would have unfolded in an identical manner. As a general principle, this notion, supporting the understanding of photographers as neutral and accurate documentarians rather than participants, is misleading (although it may have been accurate in the case of *Accidental Napalm*): simply by being there, photographers change the social dynamics, as Radhika Chalasani acknowledges: "We're interfering with a situation by our very presence."[12] Photographers and photojournalists, thus, "are not flies on the wall that are neither seen nor heard" (Sacco 2012: xi), neutral documentarians who observe and only observe. Interference increases the photographer's responsibility—an issue much discussed in connection with Capa's *The Falling Soldier*. Understanding the connection between interference and responsibility helps non-photographers grasp what it *means* to experience politics visually, namely, that such representation could always be otherwise, constructing the world we see differently. Not only the surround but also photographers may lead viewers anywhere, not to mention commentators who, simply by changing the caption, may create a different image entirely. Thus, photography is politics, always and inevitably.

Every choice the photographer makes regarding inclusion and exclusion of subjects has political consequences, even if the choice itself was not made on the basis of political considerations; every choice a picture editor makes regarding exclusion of subjects visible in the original photograph has consequences as well, even if the choice was made on aesthetic or commercial rather than political grounds; every choice analysts make

---

[12] See http://www.guardian.co.uk/media/2012/jul/28/gutted-photographers-who-didnt-help (accessed 5 January 2022).

regarding inclusion in or exclusion from analysis of certain image ingredients has consequences: "to photograph"—and to edit photographs and even to comment on them—"is to frame, and to frame is to exclude" (Sontag 2003: 46). As noted above, cropping, i.e., cutting or trimming an image at the margins and thus reframing it and what can be seen in it, is considered legitimate practice in photojournalism. After cropping, the napalmed girl indisputably attracts the most attention (and rightly so), with arms outstretched. Much has been written about her (see Chong 2001; Miller 2004, 2012; Hariman and Lucaites 2003, 2007), but our attention here is directed to the surround, invisible after cropping: the photographer depicted at the right edge of the original photograph.[13] He does not seem to pay any attention to what is going on next to him—the naked girl, other children running and screaming, soldiers walking behind the children, fellow photographers, one of them looking back to the smoke signifying explosions. The photographer does not pay any attention to Nick Ut, either. Instead, he concentrates on his camera. Another photograph, "taken a few moments later," is said to be "even more damning" than the famous photograph with regard to the presence of photographers (Hariman and Lucaites 2003: 63 note 1).[14]

What, then, happens when we crop out the surround, 'disappearing' the photographer? With regard to Ut's photograph, cropping out a "photographer who is at least as professionally preoccupied as the soldiers on the road ... erases any sense of journalistic complicity in the war, while it also reduces the photo's reflexivity. We are to reflect on the war, but not on how it is photographed" (Hariman and Lucaites 2003: 63 note 1). What Hariman and Lucaites (2007: 180) note with regard to the soldiers appearing in the image—that they "are walking along slowly, oblivious to the horror surrounding them, almost nonchalantly, as if this were an everyday experience"—can also be said about the photographer: as noted above, for him, this *is* an everyday experience, not worthy of a photograph. To him, such a scene, witnessed many times, does not qualify as a photographic moment and surely not as the *decisive* moment—Henri Cartier-Bresson's catchy phrase for a photographer's recognition of a moment as worthy of a photograph and the instantaneous translation of

---

[13] There seem to be several photographers but we are interested here solely in the one in the foreground. Thus, even in the surround, there may be yet another surround.

[14] This photograph can be seen at http://www.vietnampix.com/fire9a2.htm (last accessed 17 June 2020; see also Ritchin 1999: 37).

this recognition into a formally perfect and aesthetically pleasing image (see Cartier-Bresson 2014). If *this* is routine, then we can be sure that in wars, many things happen that are much worse than those seen in this particular photograph.

The inclusion of the photographer in the photograph renders the scene depicted more complex, moving it away from a simple 'girl in pain' story to one acknowledging involvement beyond the picture's main figure, the girl. Such involvement concerns the soldiers and the photographers but, ultimately, the photograph's viewers, too. However, it does more. Photographers do not normally appear in photojournalistic images, at least not in their own images. Of course, in the frame of *Accidental Napalm*, the person who took this photograph, Ut, does not appear, either. Yet other photographers do appear, reminding viewers of the role of photographers in wars and crises: the photographer is the person who chose the frame, for whatever reasons, determining what we see and what we do not see. This is not just a visual intervention; it is an eminently political one. The inclusion in the photograph of other photographers shows and, thereby, reveals the photographic constructedness of the scene depicted and, by implication, of *any* scene—a constructedness that often disappears behind rhetoric, both visual and verbal, of documentation and objectivity. What we see is not reality but reality translated into a photograph. Photography and photographers are not external to the events depicted, and every event can be photographed in a variety of ways, inviting different interpretations. Interpretive openness, then, applies not only to photographs but also to the world as it appears in photographs.

Essentially, the above argument does not only concern *Accidental Napalm*. A similar argument can be made regarding some of the most famous and infamous photographs. The notorious *Hooded Man* photograph from Abu Ghraib, for example, is also often reproduced in such a manner that a person operating a camera at its right edge disappears (see Morris 2014: 72–119). Inclusion of the photographer would make abundantly clear that cameras, while documenting and potentially stopping violence, may also contribute to violence (see Sontag 1979), quite regardless of whether analysis focuses on the main figure or the surround—and this is nowhere clearer than in Abu Ghraib, where human beings were tortured for the purpose of the production of images (see Gourevitch and Morris 2009: 195). Eddie Adams's famous photograph of South Vietnamese National Police Chief Brigadier General Nguyen Ngoc Loan executing a Viet Cong suspect on 1 February 1968—a paradigmatic picture of an *event* (Sontag 2003: 55)—shows the scene without revealing the presence on location of other photographers, including a television crew (Perlmutter 1999: 203–204). The photograph cropped reality, including the uncomfortable question emerging from the suspect's death, whether or not Loan performed the execution, at least in part, for the photographers and for their audiences. Another example is Peter Leibing's 1961 photograph *Leap into Freedom* showing an East German soldier jumping over the barbed wire of what soon became the Berlin Wall. In some versions of this photograph, a photographer appears between the soldier and Leibing; in other versions, the photographer is cropped out of the picture or only his elbow can be seen.[15] While the soldier certainly did not jump in order to be photographed, photographs of his activity served an eminent political purpose in the heated atmosphere of the Cold War.

Seeing a photographer in the picture helps us understand that what we see is an *image*—a photographed version of reality: a particular scenario at a particular location at a given time involving selected, identifiable individuals operating specific and identifiable cameras in specific ways. Such understanding is important in a world where information is communicated largely by means of visual images. Should photographers appear in an image, they will most likely appear in the surround, as their presence was not the reason why the picture was taken (unless they are celebrity photographers). For this reason, if they can be seen in pictures, photographers will often be cropped out of them as both irrelevant to the image's meaning and problematic from the point of view of photography's self-image. Critical analysis must reappear the disappeared photographers or imagine them in order to raise awareness of the constructedness of photographic representation and the fact that such representation can always be otherwise.

Importantly, in *Bosnia: Uncertain Paths to Peace*, Peress reappears himself as a photographer—not by visually including himself in his images but by verbally and textually emphasizing the constructedness of his photographs and acknowledging the limitations of his insights. Reading his narrative or listening to his voice makes us think not only about the siege of Sarajevo but also about how it was photographed; and thinking about how the siege of Sarajevo was photographed invites reflections on

---

[15] See https://www.vintag.es/2016/09/leap-into-freedom-east-german-soldier.html (accessed 6 January 2022).

the role and function of journalists and photojournalists who inevitably were part of the siege economy (see Andreas 2008; Morrison and Lowe 2021).

Conclusion

In this chapter, we investigated the surround as an unplanned and accidental place, the analysis of which fosters new and potentially critical reading competences on the part of observers, thereby offering alternatives to either accepting or rejecting discursively established meanings and contributing to the plurality of meanings that images always carry with them. The surround has to be respected *as* surround; deliberately integrated, as a seemingly clever move, into the image, it will lose its surround-ness and become ordinary background, requiring different reading practices. The surround provides atmosphere (Elkins), but it also produces additional knowledge, and it does so either in conversation with the image's main figure as identified by the viewer (rather than planned by the image-maker) or as a subject of analysis in its own right. We referred to Susperregui's work on *The Falling Soldier* to exemplify analysis of the surround. Obviously, not every viewer will take such a great effort to analyze the surround (see also Morris 2014 for a particularly nerdy investigation), but even simpler reading practices will generate new insights. Ultimately, the knowledge that analysis of the surround produces cannot be anticipated. Nor can it be said beforehand where analysis of the surround may lead us: it may lead anywhere, guiding different observers to different places and fostering our understanding of images as spaces where multiple voices and forces meet and communicate with each other (see Couldry 2000).

As a special case of surround analysis, we discussed the surround of *Accidental Napalm*, from which photographers disappeared through cropping. Such disappearance supports the photojournalistic myth of photographers' non-involvement in that which they depict; their reappearance makes the constructedness of photographic images abundantly clear. The presence of photographers complicates our understanding of images, of that which they depict, and of how they operate within society, necessitating reflection upon the relationship between photographed and unphotographed reality. Regarding Ut's photograph, Hariman and Lucaites argue that after cropping, viewers "reflect on the war, but not on how it is photographed" (2003: 63 note 1). This is why Peress's reflections upon his role as a photographer in *Bosnia: Uncertain Paths to Peace* are so important. They do not appear in the surround but either as audio files or written comments associated with particular images. They are nevertheless important because it is through these comments that most viewers experience the ambiguous position of photographers in war and conflict—an experience that the photographs alone cannot communicate.

While *Accidental Napalm without* photographers offers a coherent, albeit rather simple narrative—the pain of an individual—the image *with* photographers invites a more complex, multilayered reading, including reflection on the role of photography in the scene depicted. What appears in the surround may appear there accidentally, but serendipitously, it may nonetheless increase our knowledge of the scenario depicted and the role of photography in and beyond it. We conclude this chapter with the eleventh of our Sarajevo photographs (Fig. 11.1) introduced in Chapter 2 in terms of photocomplexity.

Fig. 11.1 Sarajevo #11 (Photograph © Frank Möller)

References

Andreas, Peter. 2008. *Blue Helmets and Black Markets: The Business of Survival in the Siege of Sarajevo.* Ithaca and London: Cornell University Press.
Bal, Mieke. 2007. The Pain of Images. In *Beautiful Suffering: Photography and the Traffic in Pain*, ed. Mark Reinhardt, Holly Edwards, and Erina Duganne, 93–115. Williamstown: Williams College Museum of Art; Chicago: The University of Chicago Press.
Barthes, Roland. 2000. *Camera Lucida: Reflections on Photography*, trans. Richard Howard. London: Vintage.
Boudana, Sandrine, Paul Frosh, and Akiba A. Cohen. 2017. Reviving Icons to Death? When Historic Photographs Become Digital Memes. *Media, Culture & Society* 39 (8): 1210–1230.
Butler, Judith. 2010. *Frames of War: When Is Life Grievable?* London and New York: Verso.
Callahan, William A. 2020. *Sensible Politics: Visualizing International Relations.* New York: Oxford University Press.
Cartier-Bresson, Henri. 2014. *The Decisive Moment.* Göttingen: Steidl.
Chong, Denise. 2001. *The Girl in the Picture: The Story of Kim Phuc, the Photograph, and the Vietnam War.* London: Penguin.
Couldry, Nick. 2000. *Inside Culture: Re-imagining the Method of Cultural Studies.* London, Thousand Oaks, and New Delhi: Sage.
Danchev, Alex, and Debbie Lisle. 2009. Introduction: Art, Politics, Purpose. *Review of International Studies* 35 (4): 775–779.
Elkins, James. 2011. *What Photography Is.* London and New York: Routledge.
Fuller, Matthew, and Eyal Weizman. 2021. *Investigative Aesthetics: Conflicts and Commons in the Politics of Truth.* London and New York: Verso.
Gade, Solveig. 2020. Forensic (Im)Probabilities: Entering Schrödinger's Box with Rabih Mroué and Hito Steyerl. In *(W)Archives: Archival Imaginaries, War, and Contemporary Art*, ed. Daniela Agostinho, Solveig Gade, Nanna Bonde Thylstrup, and Kristin Veel, 365–384. Berlin: Sternberg Press.
Gourevitch, Phillip, and Errol Morris. 2009. *Standard Operating Procedure: A War Story.* London: Picador.
Hariman, Robert, and John Louis Lucaites. 2003. Public Identity and Collective Memory in U.S. Iconic Photography: The Image of 'Accidental Napalm.' *Critical Studies in Media Communication* 20 (1): 35–66.
Hariman, Robert, and John Louis Lucaites. 2007. *No Caption Needed: Iconic Photographs, Public Culture, and Liberal Democracy.* Chicago and London: The University of Chicago Press.
Kelsey, Robin, and Blake Stimson. 2008. Introduction: Photography's Double Index (A Short History in Three Parts). In *The Meaning of Photography*, ed. Robin Kelsey and Blake Stimson, vii–xxxi. Williamstown: Sterling and Francine Clark Art Institute; Yale and London: Yale University Press.

Linfield, Susie. 2010. *The Cruel Radiance: Photography and Political Violence*. Chicago and London: The University of Chicago Press.
Lister, Martin. 2013. Introduction. In *The Photographic Image in Digital Culture*, 2nd ed., ed. Martin Lister, 1–21. London and New York: Routledge.
MacDougall, David. 1998. *Transcultural Cinema*, ed. and with an introduction by Lucien Taylor. Princeton: Princeton University Press.
Mason, Jennifer, and Katherine Davies. 2009. Coming to Our Senses? A Critical Approach to Sensory Methodology. *Qualitative Research* 9 (5): 587–603.
Miller, Nancy K. 2004. The Girl in the Photograph: The Vietnam War and the Making of National Memory. *JAC* 24 (2): 261–290.
Miller, Nancy K. 2012. The Girl in the Photograph: The Visual Legacies of War. In *Picturing Atrocity: Photography in Crisis*, ed. Jay Prosser, Geoffrey Batchen, Mick Gidley, and Nancy K. Miller, 147–154. London: Reaktion Books.
Möller, Frank, Rasmus Bellmer, and Rune Saugmann. 2021. Visual Appropriation: A Self-Reflexive Qualitative Method for Visual Analysis of the International. *International Political Sociology* 16: 1. https://doi.org/10.1093/ips/olab029.
Morris, Errol. 2014. *Believing Is Seeing (Observations on the Mysteries of Photography)*. New York: Penguin.
Morrison, Kenneth, and Paul Lowe. 2021. *Reporting the Siege of Sarajevo*. London: Bloomsbury Academic.
Perlmutter, David D. 1999. *Visions of War: Picturing Warfare from the Stone Age to the Cyber Age*. New York: St. Martin's Griffin.
Phelan, Peggy. 2012. Atrocity and Action: The Performative Force of the Abu Ghraib Photographs. In *Picturing Atrocity: Photography in Crisis*, ed. Jay Prosser, Geoffrey Batchen, Mick Gidley, and Nancy K. Miller, 51–61. London: Reaktion Books.
Rancière, Jacques. 2009. *The Emancipated Spectator*, trans. Gregory Elliott. London and New York: Verso.
Ritchin, Fred. 1999. *In Our Own Image*. New York: Aperture.
Roberts, John. 2014. *Photography and Its Violations*. New York: Columbia University Press.
Sacco, Joe. 2012. *Journalism*. London: Jonathan Cape.
Saugmann, Rune, Frank Möller, and Rasmus Bellmer. 2020. Seeing Like a Surveillance Agency? Sensor Realism as Aesthetic Critique of Visual Data Governance. *Information, Communication & Society* 23 (14). https://doi.org/10.1080/1369118X.2020.1770315.
Shapiro, Michael J. 2008. Slow Looking: The Ethics and Politics of Aesthetics. *Millennium* 37 (1): 181–197.
Shapiro, Michael J. 2015. *War Crimes, Atrocity, and Justice*. Cambridge and Malden: Polity Press.

Smith, Shawn Michelle. 2013. *At the Edge of Sight: Photography and the Unseen*. Durham and London: Duke University Press.
Sontag, Susan. 1979. *On Photography*. London: Penguin.
Sontag, Susan. 2003. *Regarding the Pain of Others*. New York: Farrar, Straus & Giroux.
Stepanova, Maria. 2020. *Nach dem Gedächtnis*. Berlin: Suhrkamp.
Susperregui, José Manuel. 2016. The Location of Robert Capa's *Falling Soldier*. *Communication & Society* 29 (2): 17–43.
Sutherland, Ian, and Sophia Krzys Acord. 2007. Thinking with Art: From Situated Knowledge to Experiential Knowing. *Journal of Visual Art Practice* 6 (2): 125–140.
Tucker, Anne Wilkes, and Will Michels with Natalie Zelt. 2012. *War/Photography: Images of Armed Conflict and Its Aftermath*. Houston: The Museum of Fine Arts; New Haven and London: Yale University Press.
Whelan, Richard. 2007. *This Is War! Robert Capa at Work*. New York: International Center of Photography; Göttingen: Steidl.

CHAPTER 12

Active Looking: Images in Peace Mediation

Introduction

In this chapter, we explore how to apply visual research to conflict transformation and peace mediation. Similar to what we did in the preceding chapter when discussing the surround, we present our argument fairly detached from the case study explored in Part III of the book. Our purpose here is to increase our argument's applicability to peacebuilding in general and mediation in particular. We suggest that narrative approaches to peacebuilding can be strengthened and their effectiveness be enhanced by utilizing visual images and especially images' narrative openness and plurality of meaning—their non-coherence. We use insights generated in or epistemologically connected with visual peace research and consult visual and cultural studies to unearth those characteristic features of visual images that may help improve mediation. By taking one step back to the general literature on visuality, we put ourselves in a heuristic position from which we can traverse the path to peace which this literature, focusing on representations of violence, often ignores.

Many practitioners deem peace mediation in crisis, arguing that it is less effective today than it used to be (see Pentikäinen 2015; Dziatkowiec et al. 2016). While practitioners and academics call for innovative approaches, the study of international peace mediation has

© The Author(s), under exclusive license to Springer Nature Switzerland AG 2023
R. Bellmer and F. Möller, *Peace, Complexity, Visuality*, Rethinking Peace and Conflict Studies,
https://doi.org/10.1007/978-3-031-38218-5_12

hitherto ignored the challenges and opportunities of visual images—despite profound theoretical and conceptual knowledge produced in visual peace research. Mediation disregards a particularly promising path to innovation given the extent to which global politics is currently shaped by visual images and ignores one of the most powerful trends in current politics and societies, especially if thought of in connection with digitization, social media and the Internet. Therefore, we suggest starting a peace-politically fruitful dialog between academic discourses and the practical mediation level, which will help practitioners understand how images operate and academics increase their work's political relevance and social impact. It will especially speak to younger mediators who have grown up with and are accustomed to visual images in their daily communication and help them comprehend how images shape conflict perceptions, making some options possible while excluding others.

The chapter explores the relevance of visual peace research beyond theories and concepts by translating theoretical debates into more practical suggestions, thus serving as a starting point for a discussion among academic (visual) peace researchers and mediation practitioners. It clearly and deliberately focuses on the *opportunities* the visual offers for improving mediation (without disregarding challenges). Based on narrative approaches to peace mediation and inspired by the principle of active listening, we advance the concept of *active looking* in regard to conflict transformation involving a third party in general and peace mediation in particular. We understand active looking as a tool from which mediators in all sorts of conflict transformation processes can benefit (and not only those engaged in processes officially designated as mediation). By active looking, we mean a visual-discursive practice that includes images as a mode of expression and contribution to meaning-making capitalizing on specific characteristics of images, as specified below.

We first briefly review the existing mediation literature that is relevant in our context and elaborate on the narrative tradition in mediation with an emphasis on active listening. We then sketch the intricacies involved in trying to represent peace visually. Visual representations of peace are marginalized in mediation, photojournalism and the arts; we want to understand why this is so. Afterward, analyzing the word–image relationship, we proceed to active looking in peace mediation as both an approach to conflict mediation and a mediation skill derived from an understanding of conflict transformation that, rather than aiming at problem-solving based on sameness, appreciates openness, difference and ambiguity. Active looking does not necessitate peace images, but knowledge of peace images helps mediators instigate conversations among conflict parties with the aim of acknowledging difference rather than finding consensus. In sum, we develop preconditions for theoretically informed applied visual peace research relevant for peace researchers and mediation practitioners.

NARRATIVES IN MEDIATION: BEYOND CONSENSUS-AS-SAMENESS

The *United Nations Guidance for Effective Mediation* defines mediation as "a process whereby a third party assists two or more parties, with their consent, to prevent, manage or resolve a conflict by helping them to develop mutually acceptable agreements" (UNDPA 2012: 4). More broadly and detached from agreements, Marieke Kleiboer describes mediation as "a form of conflict management in which a third party assists two or more contending parties to find a solution without resorting to force" (1996: 360). Conflict transformation, as Louis Kriesberg and Kleiboer specify with regard to mediation, aspires to "help[] adversaries communicate with each other, even when they are engaged in deadly conflict" (Kriesberg 2015: 14) with the aim of "re-establishing social relationships" (Kleiboer 1996: 379). More modestly, it tries to prevent social relationships from collapsing totally. Peace mediation's effectiveness in today's conflicts is debated (see Pentikäinen 2015: 67; Dziatkowiec et al. 2016: 6). Mediation is accused of neglecting conflicts' complexity and disregarding diversity of cultural practices by, for instance, prioritizing the rational over the emotional (see Jones and Bodtker 2007; Brigg and Bleiker 2011; Cobb 2013: 75) as a result of which "not only the conflict ... becomes intractable, but also the mediation process itself" (Dziatkowiec et al. 2016: 24). Scholars and practitioners increasingly look for innovative ideas, concepts and methods to strengthen mediation's effectiveness and to refine understanding of what 'effectiveness' is supposed to mean in this context in the first place.

Said to be at the core of many mediation theories and practices, "consensus-as-sameness" refers to an understanding of conflict transformation as "a 'shared' experience, as though the sameness of experience, the reduction of differences, would be the venue for the evolution of relationships" (Cobb 2013: 235–236). Western peace mediation has "emphasised consensus, commonality, and unity rather than difference" (Brigg and Bleiker 2011: 23), which is why many mediation processes "presume that conflicts can be resolved via changes in attitudes or via meeting needs/interests as a function of negotiated settlements" (Cobb 2013: 11). Such approaches based on "resolution-as-agreement" (Cobb 2013: 72), however, might be counterproductive or even harmful, "reproduc[ing] the conflict rather than transform[ing] it because the parties discuss their 'interests' encased in narratives that delegitimize their Others" (Cobb 2013: 72)—or cultivate their Others as negative reference points to legitimize their own narratives. Either way, conflict transformation is unlikely.

In addition to interest-focused problem-solving approaches, a more transformative approach (see Harper 2006: 599–600; Stewart and Maxwell 2010: 38; Kelman and Fisher 2016) assumes that "people are concerned with their self-interests, but they are also simultaneously and pervasively concerned with their connection with others" (Folger and Simon 2017: 73). Several scholars analyze the process of meaning-making itself, particularly the *narratives* expressed by the conflict parties, usually by means of written or verbal accounts. Conflict transformation appears as "the poetic process of strengthening the narratives people tell, so that, paradoxically, they can be free to be human beings, being human" (Cobb 2013: 284). Transforming violent conflict toward peace requires engaging with narratives. A narrative is "a foundational building block for organizing meaning in life" (Winslade 2017: 87) both individually and collectively that tends to collapse in violent circumstances: "violence breaks not only relations, but it also breaks the narrative logic itself because persons are not able to make sense of the violence" (Cobb 2013: 26). Alternatively, they try to make sense of violence by simplifying their narrative such that it appears meaningful to them, although it often inadequately represents the overall patterns within which violence occurs. Such simplification frequently utilizes binaries such as victims versus perpetrators, which often hide more than they reveal and need to be disaggregated.

Importantly, "narratives are both productive of conflict and a resource for its resolution" (Cobb 2013: 155). Critical to conflict resolution is the "evolution of meaning" in Sara Cobb's or "plot evolution" in John Winslade and Gerald Monk's terms (Cobb 2013: 24; Winslade and Monk 2006). In conflicts, however, narratives tend to lose complexity and become simple and schematic, stressing what went wrong in a relationship—conflict—rather than what worked well—cooperation (see Winslade 2017). Complex narratives turn into "narrative 'short cuts' – events in the main plot line become 'dense' with meaning"—or even into narrative closure (Cobb 2013: 51 and 86).[1] This is why a narrative approach to mediation assumes that narratives must evolve, thus regaining complexity to allow people to move closer to a conflict's resolution. Trying to take advantage of all possibilities a narrative offers, a narrative approach "consider[s] the possibility of something different" (Winslade 2017: 89) inherent in every narrative. It emphasizes "the effort to re-author the relationship story first before facilitating the negotiation of resolution in the spirit of this relationship narrative" (Winslade 2017: 87).

To achieve such re-authoring, Cobb argues, presenting narratives to one another is necessary but insufficient, as the narrative's evolution "depends on the conditions under which it is told" (2013: 24). Furthermore, conflict-affected people might get "caught in narratives they did not make by themselves and cannot change by themselves" (p. 67). This is why "narrative transformation is unlikely from within the narrative structuration process" (p. 52), thus requiring "help in destabilizing the narrative structures (plots, characters, moral frames) that contribute to maintain their exclusion of the Other" (p. 222). Hence, regardless of sensitive issues pertaining to legitimacy, agency, power, self-interests and ethics, third party involvement is required to help the conflict parties complexify their narratives as a step toward conflict transformation.

Active Listening

In narrative-based mediation, different narratives coexist; they are presented such that they appear equally valuable (within a selected narrative frame; see below) instead of being hierarchically ordered. Such mediation requires a fundamental sense of narrative equality. Narrative-based approaches assume "that people are always situated within multiple story lines. [...] We do not have a bias in favor of integrating a person's multiple story lines into a singular or congruent whole" (Winslade and Monk 2008: 7). Narrative mediation, then, is interested in the relationship between different people (or different narratives) and their evolution; it focuses on "re-authoring the relationship story in order to address a problem issue, rather than addressing a problem issue in order to allow the relationship to go forward" (Winslade and Monk 2006:

---

[1] Note that 'closure' is referred to as it is in Chapter 2, thus narrative closure is different from closure as a reading technique in sequential art as explored in Chapter 8.

223). Successful mediation results in increasing complexity of the conflict parties' narratives (while it is difficult to establish beforehand at what point narratives are considered sufficiently complex).

An increase in narrative complexity and the evolution of meaning can be achieved through *active listening*, understood by mediation scholars and practitioners as one of a mediator's most crucial skills (Småberg 2009: 116; Fisher et al. 2012: 36; UNDPA 2012: 4; Kelly and Kaminskienė 2016: 57). Active—or careful, "reflective" (Småberg 2009: 116), "sensitive" (Rogers and Farson 1987: n/p) or "empathic" or, simply, "good" (Salem 1982)—listening refers to a high level of attentiveness to the interlocutors on the mediators' part, including priority given to listening to others rather than speaking themselves (Engel and Korf 2005: 7). Active listening includes double listening "assum[ing] that what a person says is selective and that there are multiple readings to be made of any conflict story" (Winslade 2017: 89). Mediators morph into acknowledgers, recognizing, accepting and making others accept the plurality of readings that every story suggests. In such situations, mediators need "sensuous perception" (Lederach 2005: 108)—"an aesthetic sensibility" enabling them to achieve "a state of receptivity, an appreciation of the many levels on which the words, sentences, images and metaphors convey meaning" (Cohen 1997: 288). Receptivity requires the capability of deciphering words, silences and dynamics of silencing, appreciating what is said straightforwardly, routinely, hesitantly, in metaphors, implicitly or not at all.

Active listeners want to learn *how* the conflict parties see things and *why* they do so, ideally establishing a non-hierarchical conversation among equals. This implies that active listeners must (learn to) cope with a plurality of narratives that may support, overlap, supplement, contradict or exist rather independently of one another. While the traditional mediation literature tends to treat positions, interests and needs (see, e.g., Fisher et al. 2012: 42 and 50) as manifestations of an essentialized character or identity, we understand them as developed through discourse, embedded in and constituted by narratives. Following a nonessentialist viewpoint, 'how' and 'why' are socially discursively constructed, and "there is no underlying essence that can be referenced as more trustworthy than its 'surface' manifestation" (Winslade and Monk 2006: 221).

Digital media facilitate speaking in one's own voice, but even today, "individuals are spoken *for*, much more than they speak in their own name – and they are not necessarily spoken for accurately" (Couldry 2000: 58; italics in original). The question of *accurateness* deserves some attention in our context, especially if one equates accuracy with the establishment of facts. Facts eliminate ambiguity. Such elimination may be desired in some but not in all contexts: the search for accurateness-as-facts may worsen the conditions in which mediation takes place, infringing upon the very mediation situation the negotiator seeks to improve. However, mediators and participants will always want to ensure that they understand the narratives presented as intended by the speaker. Thus, accuracy in the sense of 'This is the way I/we see things' differs from accuracy in the fact-oriented sense of 'This is the way things are.' In narrative-based approaches to mediation, the first dimension is more important than the second dimension, hence the focus on understanding divergent and potentially conflicting narratives. Even if the conflicting parties disagree on how social reality should best be narrated, it is important to understand why they disagree. Narrative openness can help achieve such understanding. It is probably painful for the participants (more so than for the mediator) being exposed to positions they reject or find insulting. Mediation reflects and follows conflict, occasionally violent conflict, but is itself also a conflict often including narrative incompatibility (see, e.g., Ross 2003). However, all conflicts have social functions to be identified by the mediator: conflict can be "positively functional for the relationship" (Coser 1956: 80), improving social relations if all participants accept "the basic assumptions upon which the relation is founded" (Coser 1956: 80). Mediators must establish these assumptions before or during mediation; the conflict parties must agree upon them.

Mediation based on active listening, while cultivating narrative openness within a certain frame, must define the borders of this frame. According to the UN, for example, mediators should "be clear that they cannot endorse peace agreements that provide for amnesties for genocide, crimes against humanity, war crimes or gross violations of human rights, including sexual and gender-based violence" (UNDPA 2012: 17). Thus, narratives denying or justifying war crimes cross the boundaries of the acceptable framework. Active listening, then, is a conversation technique that should be equated neither with moral judgment—that there is only one 'truth'—nor with moral indifference—accepting all narratives as equally valuable (see Bauer 2018). Evaluating narratives for their compliance with the established frame is a powerful, difficult and possibly dangerous task; it can be perceived as an act of silencing and censoring. Provided that the mediator and the parties succeed in defining such a frame, however, new spaces of possibility can emerge, diverging perspectives can stand side-by-side, and different narratives resulting from varying lifeworlds and reflecting different contexts—personal, regional, local or historically distant contexts—can coexist. Some narratives "are local in their sphere of circulation and some are pervasive discourses about, for example, gender, class, and race" (Winslade et al. 1998: 38).

As different participants are likely to interpret (what, from a neutral perspective, seems to be) the same context differently, mediators must treat the stories they are exposed to without assigning priority to any of them; they need to exhibit equal distance toward and equal empathy with all narrators, regardless of whether they agree or sympathize with individual stories and storytellers. Active listening, then, means enduring ambiguities and contradictions, at least for the duration of the mediation. Clear-cut categories based on binaries may help structure a conversation, but they regularly fail to adequately capture the dynamics of social reality and can be dangerous if mediators forget that they are socially constructed; if pre-formulated, guiding a conversation from the outset, they may even prevent a conversation from evolving.

Narrative-based mediations are highly convoluted scenarios. In what follows, we explore how they can be improved by including visual images so as to strengthen the characteristics of active listening, as sketched above. We refer to such inclusion of visual images as *active looking*, aiming at a visual-discursive re-complexification of narratives. We argue that active looking provides visual peace research with an *applied* dimension beyond conceptual and theoretical considerations, thus increasing the applicability of the knowledge produced in visual peace research to conflict transformation processes. We suspect that our approach appeals especially to the younger generation of mediators used to the operation of images in their daily lives. As noted above, we emphasize the opportunities that visual images present.

Active Looking

While having as yet little to say about images in mediation, visual peace research does include discussion of the peace potentialities of both images and discourses revolving around images, suggesting possible contributions to peace. While active looking need not be based on peace images, knowledge of peace images facilitates active looking. While some authors argue that the visual is inextricably linked with violence, their work nevertheless offers relevant starting points for an exploration of images' peace potentialities. Ariella Azoulay, for example, connects "the image, the artist/creator, the referent and the spectator" in order to "create a political space" within which civil imagination can evolve (2012: 55). Nicholas Mirzoeff, while regarding violence as "the standard operating procedure of visuality," explores how people insisting on the right to look can confront this violence (2012: 292). John Roberts identifies the photographic archive as a place for the discursive reconstruction of meaning assigned to photographs (2014: 93–119). Epistemologically more closely connected with visual peace research, Fred Ritchin explores how photojournalism, rather than merely documenting violence, can proactively help prevent it (2013: 122–141). Stuart Allan (2010) and Sharon Sliwinski (2011) analyze the contribution of visual images to human rights discourses and practices. Tiffany Fairey explores citizen photography as a contribution to community building and peace (2021). Other approaches look at images at the microlevel of peace, exploring peace conceptions at the individual and quotidian level of the international (Möller and Shim 2019), and suggest new ways of seeing peace that may—or may not—lead to new politics of peace (see Möller 2019). Visual peace research creates new visual perspectives on peace, thus exploring new ways of seeing peace and, ultimately, new politics of peace.

Images of peace, however, are "hard to sell" (Wenders and Zournazi 2013: 38). They are marginalized due to a powerful photojournalistic tradition emphasizing war, destruction and human suffering while referencing peace mainly by showing its absence (see, paradigmatically, Tucker and Michels with Zelt 2012). Consequently, the peace potentialities of images often remain unseen and unexplored, awaiting discursive rediscovery. "Ever since cameras were invented in 1839, photography has kept company with death" (Sontag 2003: 24, capitalization omitted; see also Barthes 2000), but photography—to the chagrin of photojournalists in search of 'great shots' (see Capa 1999: 141)[2]—has also always kept company with democracy, equality and—by implication—peace (see Brunet 2019). However, even books dedicated to the visualization of peace often confirm rather conventional visual narratives referencing peace negatively (see Hale and Turner 2020). It is almost impossible to make a career as a peace photographer—compare the media attention

---

[2] For Capa, peace appeared "as dull as apple pie."

devoted to the World Press Photo Award with the lack of such attention devoted to the Global Peace Photo Award—and peace *is* difficult to visualize: different kinds of peace require different forms of visual representation; competing understandings of peace condition whether observers see or do not see peace; different stages of a peace process and similar stages of different peace processes require different forms of visualization.

Images, as David MacDougall explains, "constantly reiterate the general forms in which the particular is contained" (1998: 246), alerting viewers to the general *and* the particular but also to the *relationship* between the general and the particular. As such, the visual gives us a sense of the complexity of the scene depicted—*any* scene, even a seemingly simple and obvious one. Complexity inherent in the visual and in its relation to the reality it (cl)aims to depict implies that different people interpret the same scene and the same image differently. Differences in interpretation may be so large that the very idea of the *same* image or the *same* scenario appears doubtful. In a narrative-based approach to mediation, it is the mediator's task to acknowledge and utilize images' plurality of meaning. Because mediation commonly revolves around language and because language is never politically neutral and often connected with violence, it is particularly important to reflect upon the word–image relationship in order to specify what we mean by active looking. We have already explored this relationship in earlier chapters and will therefore be brief.

While various peace visualizations and visual paths to peace (including mutually exclusive ones) coexist, visual documentation as such does not normally tell the mediator which interpretation of a given image is the 'correct' one. Photojournalism assigns the task of establishing truth to language, which reduces the plurality of meaning all images carry with them. "Normally", Susan Sontag acknowledges, "if there is any distance from the subject, what a photograph 'says' can be read in several ways." However, even if, initially, words are absent, "one day captions will be needed." That she adds "of course" tells us more about the power of photojournalistic conventions than about the potentialities of images (2003: 29). Susie Linfield, for example, strongly condemns photojournalistic work based on the segregation of text and pictures, as it allegedly inhibits understanding and action (2010: 217). However, Sontag knows (just as Linfield does) that "even an entirely accurate caption is only one interpretation, *necessarily a limiting one*, of the photograph to which it is attached" (Sontag 1979: 109, italics added). Despite the frequent use of a "positivist notion of evidence as indisputable facts" (Gade 2020: 380) in politico-aesthetic discourses on forensic photography, which is currently in vogue (see Fuller and Weizman 2021), the establishment of 'facts' by visual means alone is difficult indeed. Luckily, accuracy-as-facts is not what our approach to mediation is primarily about.

While we would not want to agree entirely with Jae Emerling that "[a]ll images ... require ... language as a necessary supplement of the visual" (2012: 134)—it is indeed one of our points below that such supplementation is neither always necessary nor possible—it is equally crucial to acknowledge, as W.J.T. Mitchell does, that "'language' (in some form) usually enters the experience of viewing photography or of viewing anything else" (1994: 282), including in the context of conflict transformation. Translating images into words and assigning meaning to images by means of language take place within established discursive patterns regulating what is permissible in a given context and what is not (Butler 2010: 71–74), in *"scopic regime[s]"* as "ensemble[s] of practices and discourses that establish the truth claims, typicality, and credibility of visual acts and objects and politically correct modes of seeing" (Feldman 2000: 49; italics in original). What is correct and permissible is, to a large extent, defined by what Jacques Rancière, rather vaguely, calls "the dominant media," removing from images "anything that might exceed the simple superfluous illustration of their meaning" (2009: 96). For example, the interpretation as an image of peace of the photograph showing the last US soldier stepping on board a transport plane to leave Afghanistan would hardly be permissible in Western media; instead, the photograph is said to show the "Last man out,"[3] anticipating disorder.

Converting the seeable into the sayable always means discussing images both in terms other than their own and in terms of what can be said in a given language and cultural context (see MacDougall 1998: 246). These are severe limitations. While it may be difficult to identify images' own terms (see Mitchell 2005), translating accounts of human existence produced by means of images into words reduces what images can tell us to what words can tell us about images. However, rather than only "tell[ing] us things differently," images and written texts "tell us different things" (MacDougall 1998: 257). It is the mediators' task to

---

[3] See https://www.theguardian.com/world/2021/aug/31/last-man-out-the-haunting-image-of-americas-final-moments-in-afghanistan, accessed 21 December 2021.

initiate conversations about images so that both the individual narratives and the overall story, i.e., the sum of the individual narratives, appear more complex than before. Some of the limitations involved in talking about images cannot be avoided entirely. Images, too, are—and serve—narratives; they cannot be completely separated from the language that supplements them, enters the experience of viewing them or operates in tandem with them. As argued in earlier chapters, words and images are always in association with each other. Thus, if mediators decide to use visual images, they must familiarize themselves with the intricacies of both images and the word–image relationship. Furthermore, mediators, too, operate within scopic regimes (see above) that, in turn, operate on them. However, the mediators' awareness of these intricacies helps them capitalize on images and their inherent "*excess* meaning" (MacDougall 1998: 68, italics in original), avoid visual-verbal pitfalls and develop active looking skills. Instead of suppressing some of the meaning images carry with them (e.g., in search of accurateness-as-facts), mediation could capitalize on images' plurality of meaning without establishing narrative hierarchies. In the remainder of the chapter, then, we engage with active looking as a mediation practice and a mediator's skill utilizing those characteristics of images that point toward appreciation of difference and ambiguity, thus contributing to the re-complexification of narratives. We suggest paying attention to four (partially overlapping) concepts: *ineffability* (of both situations and images), *approximation, elusiveness* and *commonalities*, all of which help us appreciate and, consequently, capitalize on narrative plurality, ambiguity and lack of assurance, thus complexifying the experience.[4]

Ineffability (as regards situations): As noted above (following Cobb), violent conflict tends to interrupt the narrative logic; such an interruption often results in an inability to speak. In a mediation process, participants will encounter situations where they cannot articulate in words what they want to describe or where words seem to be inadequate. Pain is a case in point, often said to be inexpressible or unrepresentable (see Scarry 1985), or anger, emotions, feelings, all of which emerge as consequences of violent conflict (see Pia 2013). An inability to speak renders active listening difficult. In such situations, images can help if participants, rather than addressing the image by means of words, address it visually, *taking it*

---

[4] Whether or not such re-complexification contributes, in the long term, to peace is an empirical question beyond the scope of this chapter.

in and letting it speak for itself. In such a situation, silence can be understood as agentive rather than passive.[5] Sensuous perception indeed refers to "the fuller range of senses, which includes but goes beyond the world of words" (Lederach 2005: 109). Refraining from talking, rather than signifying passivity, might indicate heightened awareness; taking an image in may lead to taking something out of the image—something other than that which words evoke. Allowing images to unfold their own narratives may also mobilize connotations that those participants who decided to show them were not themselves aware of, thus complexifying their experience. Images evoke different things in different people, the recognition of which is precisely what active looking wishes to establish.

Ineffability (as regards images): Images, at least some images, also possess something that we cannot grasp by means of words: How do we describe how an image affects us emotionally and how we feel when we regard an image, especially one triggering traumatic memories?[6] How do we express the importance we assign to a specific visual representation of (parts of) our or others' lives? There is something in images "that resists or eludes every effort to fix meaning through language" (Reinhardt 2007: 25). That this 'something' might invite misinterpretation does not bother us, as fixing meaning is *not* our aim. Indeed, the notion of misinterpretation is alien to active looking because it requires consensus on the correct interpretation of an image—consensus that we neither aspire nor absolutize. Here, again, establishing a frame from which certain (visual) positions are excluded is important—otherwise, an image's ineffability can threaten a peaceful conversation. This frame must deviate from the scopic regimes (see above) that the conflict parties bring with them to the negotiation lest active looking merely confirm them by reiterating established, exclusionary "'[t]elling' practices" (Feldman 2000: 54) often derived from or connected with violence serving as "organizer of the politically visible" (Feldman 2000: 54). This is one of the reasons why mediating active looking is so difficult and potentially risky.

---

[5] This is an intriguing suggestion by one of the reviewers of the original article. Limited space prevents us from exploring it in detail but see, in a slightly different context, Dingli and Cooke (2019), Parpart and Parashar (2019), and Mannergren Selimovic (2020).

[6] There is an emerging, fascinating literature on emotions and affect (suggested by the reviewer, too) which also goes beyond what we can do here. It is easy to understand that images trigger emotions but how to deal with these emotions in the context of mediation is a different question entirely. On emotions, see Bleiker and Hutchison (2008) and Hutchison and Bleiker (2013).

Approximation: Walter Benjamin interpreted Eugène Atget's photographs of deserted Paris streets approximately 1900 as "pieces of evidence in the historical process" to which "[f]ree-floating contemplation" would no longer be appropriate (1963a: 21, our translation). Instead, inscription was required to fix meaning and to prevent photographs from "getting stuck in the approximate" (1963b: 64, our translation). Equating Atget's photographs with photographs of crime scenes, Benjamin introduced a positivist understanding of photographs as evidence, but instead of locating evidence in the image, he found it in the accompanying inscription, which he elevated to a photograph's "most essential component" (1963b: 64, our translation). Benjamin thus anticipated today's standard approach to photojournalism as sketched in Chapter 4: images' plurality of meanings tamed by language eradicating the approximate and fixing meaning, thus not only informing spectators but also enabling action. In contrast, it is exactly the approximate that active looking wishes to capitalize on, recognizing that we never exactly know what a picture 'really' shows and that we can domesticate images' "instability of meaning" (Rubinstein 2010: 199) only at the peril of failing to take full advantage of what visuality offers to peace practitioners and mediators.

Writing about "an intellectual stereoscopic effect," Peter Gilgen presents a more sophisticated approach: "the image gains in profile through the verbal information conveyed in the caption; from the accompanying image this information gains persuasive power" (2003: 56). However, his approach also echoes Benjamin's skepticism of the approximate which must be eradicated by textual information. Furthermore, the image, merely accompanying the text, seems subordinated to text, thus confirming Ritchin's suspicion that picture editors "represent[ ] a medium which is almost everywhere considered secondary to the text" (1999: 99; see also Chapter 5 of the present book). Hence, the focus in the literature on discourses revolving around or meanings assigned to images. This focus reveals the uneasiness characteristic of Western approaches to visual culture (see Mitchell 1994: 24). Images' very visible ambiguity, interpretive openness and plurality of meanings often make Western audiences fear a loss of "*control* of meaning" (MacDougall 1998: 68, italics in original). Such uneasiness coexists with fascination bordering, in social media, upon obsession largely without reflection. In contrast, active looking as a mediation tool is *not* afraid of images, and it *does* reflect upon them: it appreciates the approximate, invigorates images' ambiguities and rediscovers discursively marginalized meanings such as peace.

Elusiveness: Images are elusive. As Wim Wenders and Mary Zournazi submit, they "don't 'mean' …! They'imply', 'suggest', 'hint' or whatever" (2013: 38). "It is not clear", Mitchell (2005: 140) assists, "that [images] actually 'say' anything" but rather "convey nondiscursive, nonverbal information that is often quite ambiguous with regard to any statement." Photography, thus, "allows for the existence of a multiplicity of narrations and storylines without privileging a single one by referring to some pre-defined notion of 'truth'" (Rubinstein and Sluis 2013a: 24). Instead of "superimposing an externally perceived image, it seeks to bring out multiplicities and ambiguities" (Bleiker 2001: 528). We appeal to images' plurality of meaning, including "unintended sites of connotation" (MacDougall 1998: 68), with its inherent "potential for political agency which depends on the possibility of a multitude of interpretations, ambiguities and differences" (Rubinstein and Sluis 2013b: 154).

In contrast to ineffability, then, elusiveness does not refer to verbal limitations but rather to the plurality of verbalizable and equally valuable interpretations that images always invite and that should not be reduced to one binding narrative. All of these interpretations, however, are approximations à la Benjamin. Exactly because of their inherent ambiguities and their surplus of meaning, images are apt vehicles to communicate diverse narratives, thus introducing new levels of complexity into mediation conversations. In sum, then, two components of the visual that are conventionally regarded as liabilities—first, that "the visual is too open to misinterpretation" and, secondly, "that it is too seductive" or "too engaging" (MacDougall 1998: 68, all quotations)—turn out to be merits in the context of narrative-based approaches to mediation. That the visual is seductive implies that "it draws the viewer into an interpretive relationship that bypasses professional mediation" (MacDougall 1998: 68). Ironically, then, it asks the mediator to dispense with mediation in search of consensus and to prioritize acknowledgment of differences. Knowledge on the visualization of peace facilitates this task.

Commonalities: In verbal language, we take the *general* for granted and emphasize the *particular*. Visual images also show the particular but often embedded within the general, co-representing the general and the particular, the central and the peripheral, differences and commonalities including "the commonalities of being human" that usually disappear from written accounts (MacDougall 1998: 246). Likewise, when talking about an image, people tend to emphasize the particular rather than the general: as "photographs manifestly contain visible images of people and their physical characteristics, people sometimes say *less* than they might otherwise do about those things, because there seems to be no real imperative to explain them" (Mason and Davies 2009: 594–595)—they are visible anyway. Consequently, the commonalities of being human escape attention (see Möller 2019: 255–257). In narrative mediation, however, acknowledging these commonalities is extremely important: it helps understand that although much seems to separate one group from another, there is always something that all groups have in common. Such understanding helps prevent the transformation of alterity into Otherness, the transformation of other people into the—ontological—Other with whom agreement is impossible. Mediators can use the display in images of human commonalities to bridge the gap between different groups and to work toward partial identification with one another. In this approach to mediation, groups of people do not have to identify with one another entirely but only partially; disagreement in some areas does not render impossible agreement in other areas, on the basis of which the contested areas can subsequently be reapproached.

We would neither expect the four above concepts to appear equally in all mediation conversations involving images nor would we expect all of them to appear in all conversations. The mediator decides which concept to prioritize in a given situation, and this depends, for example, on the degree of visual socialization the conflict parties bring with them to the conversation or the cultural context within which the conversation takes place. Active looking must be learned, and this applies to both the mediator and the conflict parties. However, the aim of active looking should be clear: rather than establishing consensus-as-sameness, active looking aims at *consensus-as-different-ness*, capitalizing on difference as articulated in complex, image-generated narratives without establishing narrative hierarchies. Individual narratives must be liberated from short-cuts and closure, and the overall story, i.e., the sum of all individual narratives, must be allowed a greater degree of complexity than could be observed at the beginning of the conversation. At the same time, complexity theory tells us that the overall story cannot be simply disaggregated into its constituent parts and subsequently reassembled as the parts interact with one another in unpredictable ways and some parts will be missed, no matter how hard mediators try to grasp all ingredients of a story. Ultimately and ideally, then, through image-generated evolution, re-complexification and re-authoring of narratives, the conflict parties, by means of active looking skills embodied in and promoted by the mediator, move closer to a conflict's transformation.

Conclusion

We ask peacebuilding practitioners to be open toward the inclusion of images in their work, to believe in the peace potentialities of images and to use images' inherent ambiguities to produce more complex narratives. Peace workers should enable people to tell their stories through and with images. How this should be done is context-specific and hardly generalizable. However, all mediators, being aware of the above discussion and possessing active looking skills, could invite participants in a narrative-based mediation setting to share images with the participants on a specific theme chosen by the mediator. Alternatively, participants may themselves decide what images they want to share with others because they deem them important in the context. Whole meetings can put images in the center; exhibitions or social media content on the subject matter discussed in the mediation process can be discursively engaged with. Rather than limiting such engagement to visual images in a narrow sense (photographs, paintings, or film), it should also include other means of visual representation, such as dance and performance. It is, however, important to note that participants and mediators can define images as *in*appropriate, thus establishing a frame within which narrative openness is appreciated and beyond which it is not. Normative judgments may be necessary, but norms such as decency and taste can also serve a limiting purpose, depending on the authority used to justify them (see Sontag 2003: 68).

While images have become increasingly present as important (f)actors in international politics, peace mediation, until now, has widely ignored them, thus also neglecting their potential contributions to peace processes. In this chapter, we argued that some of their qualities make images suitable to assist peace processes. We highlighted the role of ineffability, elusiveness and ambiguity, enabling individuals to express—and to deal with—complexity in both their and others' narratives. While images' ambiguity is an asset for those who want to emphasize a situation's openness, it is a liability for those who promote strict and rigid policies. We acknowledge "that any narrative, any model, must leave some things out, distort some things, privilege some things over others, and squeeze some things into categories where they fit uncomfortably, simply in order to maintain coherence" (Winslade and Monk 2008: 219). Our narrative is no exception. The way we emphasize complexity, narrative openness and difference reflects our current lifeworld, derived from which we suggest new mediation practices. Both these practices and our reflections are enmeshed in a variety of ontological and epistemological (and, occasionally, tacit) assumptions. While this chapter suggests a new perspective on mediation and the role of images in social processes that challenges currently common mediation conceptualizations, it also offers points of connection for practitioners to think about our ideas' value in their respective work. Thus, we wish to think of this chapter as a starting point, an open-ended contribution to an evolving repertoire of thinking about and conducting peace mediation through images. We conclude this chapter with the twelfth of our Sarajevo photographs (Fig. 12.1) introduced in Chapter 2 in terms of photocomplexity.

Fig. 12.1 Sarajevo #12 (Photograph © Frank Möller)

Acknowledgements This chapter appeared originally in *Peacebuilding* (https://doi.org/10.1080/21647259.2022.2152971) and is reproduced here with kind permission from Taylor and Francis, slightly adapted to the purpose of the book.

REFERENCES

Allan, Stuart. 2010a. Documenting War, Visualizing Peace: Towards Peace Photography. In *Expanding Peace Journalism: Comparative and Critical Approaches*, ed. Ibrahim Seaga Shaw, Jake Lynch, and Robert A. Hackett, 147–167. Sydney: University of Sidney Press.

Azoulay, Ariella. 2012. *Civil Imagination: A Political Ontology of Photography*, trans. Louise Bethlehem. London and New York: Verso.

Barthes, Roland. 2000. *Camera Lucida: Reflections on Photography*, trans. Richard Howard. London: Vintage Books.

Bauer, Thomas. 2018. *Die Vereindeutigung der Welt: Über den Verlust an Mehrdeutigkeit und Vielfalt*. Ditzingen: Reclam.

Benjamin, Walter. 1963a. Das Kunstwerk im Zeitalter seiner technischen Reproduzierbarkeit. In *Das Kunstwerk im Zeitalter seiner technischen Reproduzierbarkeit. Drei Studien zur Kunstsoziologie*, ed. Walter Benjamin, 7–44. Frankfurt: Suhrkamp.

Benjamin, Walter. 1963b. Kleine Geschichte der Photographie. In *Das Kunstwerk im Zeitalter seiner technischen Reproduzierbarkeit. Drei Studien zur Kunstsoziologie*, ed. Walter Benjamin, 45–64. Frankfurt: Suhrkamp.

Bleiker, Roland. 2001. The Aesthetic Turn in International Political Theory. *Millennium* 30 (3): 509–533.

Bleiker, Roland, and Emma Hutchison. 2008. Fear No More: Emotions and World Politics. *Review of International Studies* 34 (S1): 115–135.

Brigg, Morgan, and Roland Bleiker. 2011. Postcolonial Conflict Resolution. In *Mediating Across Difference: Oceanic and Asian Approaches to Conflict Resolution*, ed. Morgan Brigg and Roland Bleiker, 19–37. Honolulu: University of Hawai'i Press.

Brunet, François. 2019. *The Birth of the Idea of Photography*. Toronto: RIC Books.

Butler, Judith. 2010. *Frames of War: When Is Life Grievable?* London and New York: Verso.

Capa, Robert. 1999. A Legitimate Complaint. In *A Russian Journal. With Photographs by Robert Capa. With an Introduction by Susan Shillinglaw*, ed. John Steinbeck, 140–143. London: Penguin.

Cobb, Sara. 2013. *Speaking of Violence: The Politics and Poetics of Narrative in Conflict Resolution*. New York: Oxford University Press.

Cohen, Cynthia. 1997. *A Poetics of Reconciliation: The Aesthetic Mediation of Conflict*. PhD Dissertation. Durham: University of New Hampshire.

Coser, Lewis. 1956. *The Functions of Social Conflict*. New York: Free Press.

Couldry, Nick. 2000. *Inside Culture: Re-imagining the Method of Cultural Studies*. London, Thousand Oaks and New Delhi: Sage.

Dingli, Sophia, and Thomas N. Cooke. 2019. *Political Silence: Meanings, Functions, and Ambiguity*. London and New York: Routledge.

Dziatkowiec, Paul, Christina Buchhold, Elodie Convergne, Jonathan Harlander, and Tinahy Andriamasomanana. 2016. *Oslo Forum 2016 Report: Adapting to a New Conflict Landscape*. Geneva: Center for Humanitarian Dialogue.

Emerling, Jae. 2012. *Photography: History and Theory*. London and New York: Routledge.

Engel, Antonia, and Benedikt Korf. 2005. *Negotiation and Mediation Techniques for Natural Resource Management*. https://peacemaker.un.org/sites/peacemaker.un.org/files/NegotiationandMediationTechniquesforNaturalResourceManagement_FAO2005.pdf.

Fairey, Tiffany. 2021. Participatory, Community, and Citizen Photography as Peace Photography. *Image & Peace: Exploring Visual Culture and Peace* (2021). https://www.imageandpeace.com/2021/11/11/participatory-community-and-citizen-photography-as-peace-photography/.

Feldman, Allen. 2000. Violence and Vision: The Prosthetics and Aesthetics of Terror. In *Violence and Subjectivity*, ed. Veena Das, Arthur Kleinman, Mamphela Ramphele, and Pamela Reynolds, 46–78. Berkeley, Los Angeles, London: University of California Press.

Fisher, Roger, William Ury, and Bruce Patton. 2012. *Getting to YES: Negotiating an Agreement Without Giving In*. London: Random House Business Books.

Folger, Joseph P., and Dan Simon. 2017. Transformative Mediation: Illustrating a Relational View of Conflict Intervention. In *The Mediation Handbook: Research, Theory, and Practice*, ed. Alexia Georgakopoulos, 73–86. New York and London: Routledge.

Fuller, Matthew, and Eyal Weizman. 2021. *Investigative Aesthetics: Conflicts and Commons in the Politics of Truth*. London and New York: Verso.

Gade, Solveig. 2020. Forensic (Im)probabilities: Entering Schrödinger's Box with Rabih Mroué and Hito Steyerl. In *(W)archives: Archival Imaginaries, War, and Contemporary Art*, ed. Daniela Agostinho, Solveig Gade, Nanna Bonde Thylstrup, and Kristin Veel, 365–384. Berlin: Sternberg Press.

Gilgen, Peter. 2003. History After Film. In *Mapping Benjamin: The Work of Art in the Digital Age*, ed. Hans Ulrich Gumbrecht and Michael Marrinan, 53–62. Stanford: Stanford University Press.

Hale, Constance, and Fiona Turner, eds. 2020. *Imagine: Reflections on Peace*. Paris: Hemeria.

Harper, Christopher. 2006. Mediator as Peacemaker: The Case for Activist Transformative-Narrative Mediation. *Journal of Dispute Resolution* 2: 595–611.
Hutchison, Emma, and Roland Bleiker. 2013. Theorizing Emotions in World Politics. *International Theory* 6 (3): 491–514.
Jones, Tricia S., and Andrea Bodtker. 2007. Mediating with Heart in Mind: Addressing Emotion in Mediation Practice. *Negotiation Journal* 17 (3): 217–244.
Kelly, Edward J., and Natalija Kaminskienė. 2016. Importance of Emotional Intelligence in Negotiation and Mediation. *International Comparative Jurisprudence* 2 (1): 55–60.
Kelman, Herbert C., and Ronald J. Fisher, eds. 2016. *Herbert C. Kelman: A Pioneer in the Social Psychology of Conflict Analysis and Resolution*. Cham: Springer.
Kleiboer, Marieke. 1996. Understanding Success and Failure of International Mediation. *Journal of Conflict Resolution* 40 (2): 360–389.
Kriesberg, Louis. 2015. *Realizing Peace: A Constructive Conflict Approach*. Oxford and New York: Oxford University Press.
Lederach, John Paul. 2005. *The Moral Imagination: The Art and Soul of Building Peace*. Oxford: Oxford University Press.
Linfield, Susie. 2010. *The Cruel Radiance: Photography and Political Violence*. Chicago and London: The University of Chicago Press.
MacDougall, David. 1998. *Transcultural Cinema* (Edited and with an Introduction by Lucien Taylor). Princeton: Princeton University Press.
Mannergren Selimovic, Johanna. 2020. Gendered Silences in Post-conflict Societies: A Typology. *Peacebuilding* 8 (1). https://doi.org/10.1080/21647259.2018.1491681.
Mason, Jennifer, and Katherine Davies. 2009. Coming to Our Senses? A Critical Approach to Sensory Methodology. *Qualitative Research* 9 (5): 587–603.
Mirzoeff, Nicholas. 2012. *The Right to Look: A Counterhistory of Visuality*. Durham and London: Duke University Press.
Mitchell, W.J.T. 1994. *Picture Theory: Essays on Verbal and Visual Representation*. Chicago and London: The University of Chicago Press.
Mitchell, W.J.T. 2005. *What Do Pictures Want: The Lives and Loves of Images*. Chicago and London: University of Chicago Press.
Möller, Frank. 2019. *Peace Photography*. Houndmills: Palgrave Macmillan.
Möller, Frank, and David Shim. 2019. Visions of Peace in International Relations. *International Studies Perspectives* 20 (3): 246–264.
Parpart, Jane L., and Swati Parashar, eds. 2019. *Rethinking Silence, Voice and Agency in Contested Gendered Terrains*. London and New York: Routledge.
Pentikäinen, Antti. 2015. Reforming UN Mediation Through Inclusion of Traditional Peacemakers. *Development Dialogue* 63 (3): 67–76.

Pia, Emily. 2013. Narrative Therapy and Peacebuilding. *Journal of Intervention and Statebuilding* 7 (4): 476–491.
Rancière, Jacques. 2009. *The Emancipated Spectator*, trans. Gregory Elliott. London and Brooklyn: Verso.
Reinhardt, Mark. 2007. Picturing Violence: Aesthetics and the Anxiety of Critique. In *Beautiful Suffering: Photography and the Traffic in Pain*, ed. Mark Reinhardt, Holly Edwards, and Erina Duganne, 13–36. Chicago: The University of Chicago Press.
Ritchin, Fred. 1999. *In Our Own Image*. New York: Aperture.
Ritchin, Fred. 2013. *Bending the Frame: Photojournalism, Documentary, and the Citizen*. New York: Aperture.
Roberts, John. 2014. *Photography and Its Violations*. New York: Columbia University Press.
Rogers, Carl R., and Richard E. Farson. 1987. Active Listening. In *Communicating in Business Today*, ed. Ruth G. Newman, Marie A. Danziger, and Mark Cohen. Washington: Heath & Company.
Ross, Marc Howard. 2003. Competing Narratives and Escalation in Ethnic Conflicts: The Case of the Holy Sites in Jerusalem. *Sphera Publica* 3: 189–208.
Rubinstein, Daniel. 2010. Tag, Tagging. *Philosophy of Photography* 1 (2): 197–200.
Rubinstein, Daniel, and Katrina Sluis. 2013a. The Digital Image in Photographic Culture: Algorithmic Photography and the Crisis of Representation. In *The Photographic Image in Digital Culture*, 2nd ed., ed. Martin Lister, 22–40. London and New York: Routledge.
Rubinstein, Daniel, and Katrina Sluis. 2013b. Concerning the Undecidability of the Digital Image. *Photographies* 6 (1): 151–159.
Salem, Richard A. 1982. Community Dispute Resolution Through Outside Intervention. *Peace & Change* 8 (2–3): 91–104.
Scarry, Elaine. 1985. *The Body in Pain: The Making and Unmaking of the World*. Oxford: Oxford University Press.
Sliwinski, Sharon. 2011. *Human Rights in Camera*. Chicago and London: The University of Chicago Press.
Småberg, Maria. 2009. Witnessing the Unbearable: Alma Johansson and the Massacres of the Armenians 1915. In *War and Peace in Transition: Changing Roles of External Actors*, ed. Karin Aggestam and Annika Björkdahl, 107–127. Lund: Nordic Academic Press.
Sontag, Susan. 1979. *On Photography*. London: Penguin.
Sontag, Susan. 2003. *Regarding the Pain of Others*. New York: Farrar, Straus & Giroux.

Stewart, Katherine A., and Madeline M. Maxwell. 2010b. *Storied Conflict Talk: Narrative Construction in Mediation*. Amsterdam and Philadelphia: John Benjamin.

Tucker, Ann Wilkes, and Will Michels with Natalie Zelt. 2012. *War/Photography: Images of Armed Conflict and Its Aftermath*. New Haven: Yale University Press.

UNDPA. 2012. *United Nations Guidance for Effective Mediation*. https://peacemaker.un.org/sites/peacemaker.un.org/files/GuidanceEffectiveMediation_UNDPA2012%28english%29_0.pdf.

Wenders, Wim, and Mary Zournazi. 2013. *Inventing Peace: A Dialogue on Perception*. London and New York: I.B. Tauris.

Winslade, John. 2017. Narrative Mediation of Family Conflict. In *The Mediation Handbook: Research, Theory, and Practice*, ed. Alexia Georgakopoulos, 87–96. New York and London: Routledge.

Winslade, John M., and Gerald Monk. 2006. Does the Model Overarch the Narrative Stream? In *The Blackwell Handbook of Mediation: A Guide to Effective Negotiation*, ed. Margaret S. Herrman, 217–227. Malden, Oxford and Victoria: Blackwell.

Winslade, John, and Gerald Monk. 2008. *Practicing Narrative Mediation: Loosening the Grip of Conflict*. San Francisco: Jossey-Bass.

Winslade, John, Gerald Monk, and Alison Cotter. 1998. A Narrative Approach to the Practice of Mediation. *Negotiation Journal* 14 (1): 21–41.

CHAPTER 13

Concluding Reflections: Tolerance of Ambiguity and the Ambiguity of Tolerance

In this book, we suggest enhancing spaces of possibility for the performance of ambiguity. We are not primarily interested in methods with which to research ambiguity or to establish that our societies are in fact ambiguous or more ambiguous than they used to be. Our work is informed by complexity theory, which, following David Byrne and Gillian Callaghan (2023), we understand as a frame of reference or a way of thinking rather than a theory proper. Where there is complexity, there is also ambiguity. We wish to identify spaces where complexity and ambiguity can be embraced, performed and embodied, recognized, appreciated and capitalized on to improve the quality of social relations between and among individuals and groups of people. We found such spaces in visuality, conceived of in broad terms, and identified several characteristic features of images that, properly understood, can help us embrace ambiguity and difference. Rather than resorting to "dualistic polarities" (Lederach 2005: 35), embracing ambiguities facilitates constructive engagement with conflict. Which is another way of saying that relationships move "from those defined by fear, mutual recrimination, and violence toward those characterized by love, mutual respect, and proactive engagement" (Lederach 2005: 42). Tolerance of ambiguity, then, seems to deserve attention although, or because, like Bosnia's way to peace, paths to tolerance of ambiguity are uncertain.

Social conflict is a relationship. In our understanding, it is not a problem to be avoided or prevented but a normal and inevitable ingredient of social life reflecting limited resources, both intellectual and material. What should be prevented, however, is a violent escalation of conflicts; what should be strengthened is constructive engagement with conflict in a way "that respects complexity and refuses to fall into forced containers of dualism and either-or categories" (Lederach 2005: 36). Throughout the book, we explained our preference for tolerance of ambiguity in a complex and messy world and rejected disambiguation as the *default* response to complexity. Seemingly clearly describing what "is not itself very coherent," disambiguation "distort[s]" things "into clarity," as John Law would put it (2004: 2).

Conclusions are the place where a work's main arguments are summarized and some loose ends are tied up. We wish to do neither here. Summarizing a work's main arguments, while disrespecting and underestimating the readers' intellectual and mnemonic capabilities, does not add anything new to what has already been said. Writing and reading summaries offer little satisfaction (except for those who, for whatever reasons, wish to read *only* the summary). Furthermore, assuming that a work's contents can be neatly separated into its component parts and subsequently reassembled is problematic from a complexity point of view. A book isn't a car; its content comes to fruition through communication between authors and readers, and such communication is to some extent unpredictable. Individual readers may, for example, find what they regard as most interesting in the book's surround which is likely not to be included in an authorial summary. Like Gilles Peress in the book's case study, we are not afraid of corrections by the reader, but we would prefer to think about such interventions in terms of multiple permissible and equally valuable viewpoints. Rather than one point of view replacing another, these viewpoints should stand side-by-side, communicate with one another and endure tension when such communication is not possible. Failures to communicate are part of complex systems; they are also part of attempts at knowledge production. Likewise, tying up loose ends eradicates the invitation to the reader, implicit in loose ends, to think and develop the ideas presented in the book further in light of own experience and, by doing so, contribute to the book's contents. Reading a text is an interactive experience of actively engaging with it rather than merely passively consuming its contents; texts invite engagement in terms of reading, reflecting, changing, reflecting again and sharing. This is how we approached the texts informing this book, and this is how we hope our readers will approach our text. Indeed, social science is very much "the art of reframing other people's observations" (Collins 2008: 32), an appropriation, properly referenced. Such reframing is called knowledge production. It is an open-ended process. We need to say something on three issues, however, lest we be misunderstood.

What Are the Limits of Tolerance?

In this book, we suggest enhancing, by visual means, spaces of possibility for the performance of tolerance of ambiguity, but we have to ask: Are there limits to such spaces? What are the limits to tolerance of ambiguity? Tolerance, it may be argued, is the liberal mask for indifference,[1] a policy of not judging, a non-policy of accepting everything as equally valuable and permissible. We do not subscribe to this point of view. This is why we insist, throughout the book, on politico-discursive-visual frames within which tolerance of ambiguity may be performed while beyond which it may not. Ambiguity, as we argued in Chapter 3, is the space where "multiple permissible interpretations" (Sennet 2021) of an issue meet and where they are negotiated and re-negotiated—not with the aim of identifying and agreeing upon one correct interpretation thus othering deviating interpretations but, rather, with the aim of acknowledging that different interpretations of an issue are equally permissible in the circumstances. Such acknowledgment includes recognition that some interpretations are not permissible in the context. We wrote that focusing on *permissible* interpretations counteracts a reading of our argument in terms of 'anything goes,' i.e., lack of moral, political and other standards. Instead, we would like to think of our approach in terms of *engaged tolerance*. In complex systems, there is always more than one permissible interpretation, but from this, it does not follow that all interpretations are permissible. Engagement with the limits of tolerance is part of our approach. As Paul Cilliers writes when discussing the relationship between complexity and complex systems, on the one hand, and, on the other hand, postmodernism:

---

[1] Richard Sennett made this point in a lecture at Hamburg University a long time ago. Our apologies that this reference can't be more precise but it is simply too long ago.

> Instead of trying to analyze complex phenomena in terms of single or essential principles, these [postmodern; the authors] approaches acknowledge that it is not possible to tell a single and exclusive story about something that is really complex. The acknowledgement of complexity, however, certainly does *not* lead to the conclusion that anything goes. (1998: viii; italics in original)

The frontier where spaces of possibility meet spaces of impossibility is a space for politics, not a rigorous border but a meeting-place or at least a place for constant (re-)negotiation of what counts as permissible. The precise manifestation of such a frame distinguishing what is permissible from what is not is context dependent and always emerging. Such a frame will be defined by constitutions or laws, general frameworks or agreements regulating what can be said, done and shown in a given context, but it will also be influenced by the media as one of the most audible interpreters of social reality. It also has cultural-habitual elements such as the Bosnian way introduced in Chapter 10, one element of which is "bending the rules while accepting the game" (Markowitz 2010: 161). Culture often determines the extent to which the rules are being bent, while in the Bosnian context, the Constitution of Bosnia and Herzegovina, included as Annex 4 in the Dayton Accords, establishes "the game." As we noted in Chapter 9, despite its many flaws, the Dayton agreement is still the main formal arrangement within which the peace process in Bosnia evolves. With regard to the wars in the former Yugoslavia in the 1990s and current interpretations, the decisions of the International Criminal Tribunal for the Former Yugoslavia (ICTY) are also important, distinguishing permissible interpretations from inadequate ones. The ICTY decisions are especially relevant for the politics of memory, where different opinions and interpretations regularly clash. Spaces of possibility also have a historical dimension—"the game" comes from somewhere, it does not simply fall out of the sky—and a discursive one where not only the rules but also the game may change over time, reflecting discursive reconstructions, changing power relations in society and, indeed, conflict because conflict, as Lewis Coser (1956: 125) explains, "revitalizes existent norms and creates a new framework of norms within which the contenders can struggle."

Is Our Case Study Well Chosen?

Disaggregating a conflict does not imply relativizing pain and suffering or guilt and responsibility. The aim of disaggregation is a better, i.e., a more nuanced understanding of a conflict and of human behavior in conflict—in our case, in a conflict in which, as photojournalist Paul Lowe aptly observes, "one side was clearly the aggressor and the other the victim" (2015: 5). As a general description of the war in Bosnia and the siege of Sarajevo, Lowe's description seems appropriate; on a general level, disambiguation and the construction of binaries seem to adequately reflect social reality (within limits). At the same time, "the Sarajevo siege story provides a powerful illustration of the merits of disaggregating conflict and analytically embracing its messiness" (Andreas 2008: 165), grasped by Peter Andreas by, for example, distinguishing front-stage behavior from backstage behavior and by Fred Ritchin and Gilles Peress in our case study by visually paying attention to different locations within the city and to the residents' perceptions of social reality. Throughout the book, we emphasized that disaggregation, while being problematic from a complexity point of view, is unavoidable and useful for analysis as long as the analyst is aware of the limits of disaggregation and the resulting knowledge.

"Even in a conflict, the overall dimensions of which invited a simple binary reading, on the day-to-day level, things got murky: ambivalence ruled and alliances shifted; chaos and confusion dominated; and unpredictability and disorder prevailed" (Bellmer and Möller 2022: 2). Victims—or people socially constructed as victims—are never *only* (passive and helpless) victims, and aggressors—or people socially constructed as aggressors—are rarely *only* aggressors. People conventionally referred to as victims often exhibit profound agency in adverse conditions. Such agency is both extremely important and difficult to grasp in terms of passivity and dependence on help that are usually assigned to victims: everyday coping mechanisms with violence amount to forms of resistance including micro-resistance that are part and parcel of every conflict. Laughter, irony and sarcasm, dressing up, enjoying cultural events[2] and

---

[2] Silvija Jestrovic quotes Darko Diklić to the effect that from 1992 to 1995, "3,102 artistic and cultural events took place or on average 2.5 events per day … 263 books were published … 156 documentary and short films were produced during the war … In Sarajevo theatres, 182 performances premiered and over two thousand shows were

continuing everyday activities such as stubbornly going to work are all forms of everyday resistance, refusing both to accept the dynamics and logics of violence and to succumb to despair. Everyday resistance is a part of the Sarajevo siege story, just as is the experience of horror, gruesome violence and death at the barricades or on Sniper Avenue.[3]

Do such acts of (micro-)resistance mean that people are no longer victims? Certainly not as long as we stick to a basic definition of a victim as "one that is acted on and usually adversely affected by a force or agent," such as "one that is injured, destroyed, or sacrificed under any of various conditions" or "one that is subjected to oppression, hardship, or mistreatment."[4] However, it qualifies what we mean by victim, how we understand being a victim, and what agency we assign to a victim; it counteracts impressions of helplessness and passivity often implicit in definitions of victim[5] and directs our attention to everyday coping strategies in times of violence that earlier approaches in terms of generic victimhood tended either to disregard or to regard as irrelevant.[6] Acts of resistance can be photographed—and, indeed, they have been photographed in Sarajevo and elsewhere. Such photographs—see, for example, Tom Stoddart's famous photograph of Meliha Varešanović walking "proudly and defiantly to work during the siege"[7]—respond to accusations that photojournalism tends to freeze human beings in the subject position of a

performed that half a million people saw"—despite the fact that fifteen writers, eighteen visual artists and ten filmmakers were killed during the war (2013: 121–122).

[3] Such forms of micro-resistance can be performed in addition to or instead of armed resistance. One problem with armed resistance is that it is not always feasible. Another problem is that by resorting to armed resistance, victims copy and thereby confirm, the logic of violence that had triggered the attack on them in the first place.

[4] "Victim." *Merriam-Webster.com Dictionary*, Merriam-Webster, https://www.merriam-webster.com/dictionary/victim (accessed 3 April 2023).

[5] One definition of victim is indeed "a person who has come to feel helpless and passive in the face of misfortune or ill-treatment" (https://www.google.com/search?client=firefox-b-d&q=victim+meaning; accessed 3 April 2023) or a person who is represented as such.

[6] People who are victims in some situations may also become perpetrators in other situations (and vice versa) and they may be both at the same time. For example, a person can be targeted and attacked by someone while at the same targeting and attacking someone else.

[7] See https://www.theguardian.com/artanddesign/gallery/2020/oct/06/extraordinary-women-tom-stoddart-photographs (accessed 2 April 2023).

victim, helpless and without agency, appealing to and depending on pity on the part of viewers.

Similarly, "even those persons who are violent, are violent only a small part of the time" (Collins 2008: 2). Even during the siege of Sarajevo, "outside the periods of very heaving shelling and fighting, the city could be eerily still, with little to report" (Morrison and Lowe 2021: 119). During such periods of eerie stillness, 'aggressors' did something other than executing direct and physical violence. This does not mean that they stopped being aggressors, but it does mean that their subject positions cannot be adequately grasped in terms of aggressor only and that their behavior is more variegated than standard approaches in terms of aggressor or perpetrator tend to suggest. Disaggregation, thus, does not call into question the overall patterns of violence in the Bosnian war and the siege of Sarajevo, but it enables a more adequate and more comprehensive understanding of what human beings do—and are capable of doing, both constructively and destructively—in violent conflict. Finally, when applying social constructivist lines of thought in terms of identity, norms and culture to questions of national military security from which such lines of thought were routinely excluded, Peter Katzenstein argued for the merits of "hard cases":

> If the style of analysis and the illustrative case material can establish plausibility here, it should be relatively easy to apply this book's analytical perspective to broader conceptions of security that are not restricted to military issues or to the state. (1996: 11)

Bearing that in mind, we hope not only that the analysis and illustrative case material presented in our book succeed in establishing plausibility with regard to our "hard" case study, but also that the analysis we suggest can be fruitfully applied to broader conceptions and less obvious case studies where differentiation between victims and aggressors is more difficult than it used to be in the Bosnian war and the siege of Sarajevo.

Do We Establish New Binaries?

We would not want to think about and conceptualize tolerance of ambiguity or disambiguation and simplification or complexification in terms of strict binaries. Things are more complex. When discussing the original concept of tolerance of ambiguity in Chapter 3, we noted that such tolerance can be understood either in terms of a person's individual broader personality (in which case this person is either tolerant of ambiguity or not) or in relation to specific areas (in which case the degree of tolerance of ambiguity a person displays depends on the subject areas to which it is applied). Understood in relation to specific areas, a person may exhibit different degrees of tolerance of ambiguity in different subject areas: the more importance an individual assigns to a given subject, the less tolerant this person is likely to be vis-à-vis deviating opinions. The same person may display a huge degree of tolerance of ambiguity in subject areas that this person regards as insignificant or irrelevant. Thus, understood in relation to specific areas, a person may cultivate tolerance of ambiguity in some areas and disambiguation in other areas. Ultimately, however, the aim implied in our argument would be to make this person develop tolerance of ambiguity also in areas that this person considers important, acknowledging that even in important matters, there is always a variety of permissible interpretations. The ultimate aim, thus, would be to make this person move on the trajectory from disambiguation to tolerance of ambiguity in the direction of the latter.

This is a conflict, not least a conflict that this person has to fight with herself and her habits of making sense of her social situation; but conflict, we argued throughout the book, can be constructive as long as "the basic assumptions upon which the relation is founded"—including a person's relation with herself—are not contradicted (Coser 1956: 80). From this, it follows that there will be areas in which even the most tolerant person may stick to disambiguation. This is in accordance with what we wrote above about engaged tolerance, which implies the existence of some core norms and values that a person considers vital (e.g., for her individual and collective identity) and thus non-negotiable. The use of physical force, for example, might be such a norm: some people might make the use of force dependent on the objective that the use of force is meant to realize; others may regard it as the legitimate continuation of politics with other means. Other people, however, will accept it under no circumstances whatsoever. It is a part of tolerance of ambiguity to accept that for most people, some questions are non-negotiable.

We would not want to think about simplification and complexification in terms of duality, either. In Chapter 8, we noted that stories tend to become fixed in stereotypes connecting, in an idiosyncratic manner, simplification with complexification: some aspects of the story become simpler, while others become more complex. What is represented in simple terms and what in more complex terms depends to some extent on the audience: do I want to convince someone of my point of view or do I expect my audience to share my point of view anyway? Details may be given disproportional importance, while the commonalities of human appearance may be excluded from the narrative. Like visual narratives, then, storytelling consists of inclusions and exclusions as well as different degrees of saliency assigned to individual parts of the story. Views of conflict, however, are often articulated in simple terms of either-or reflecting a simplified interpretation of social reality neglecting spaces for complexification (even if such complexification would result in a more adequate representation of the conflict).

The academic discipline of International Relations in its Western form, for example, is constituted by such "core dualisms" as "inside/outside, order/disorder, the universal/the particular, the self/other, the civilised/the barbarian," all of which mask the "messiness of the world, its uncertainties and fragmentations" (Jabri 2007: 165). Furthermore, both Western politics and International Relations often make clear value judgments in favor of "the inside" rather than "the outside," "order" rather than "disorder," "the universal" rather than "the particular," "the self" rather than "the other" and "the civilized" rather than "the barbarian" and locate "the West" on the favorable side of its constituent dichotomies. In normal, routine circumstances, a certain relaxation of such clear dichotomies, inspired by interventions from critical peace and conflict studies, may be allowed based on "an often implicit acknowledgement, and fear, that the line (/) enabling the dualism is ever shifting, so that the outside is always already in, the other is the self-same, the universal has always been the particular, the civilised has always been the barbarian" (Jabri 2007: 165). In times of violent conflict, however, regression to strict categories can often be observed:

> We are right. They are wrong. We were violated. They are the violators. We are liberators. They are oppressors. Our intentions are good. Theirs are bad. History and the truth of history is most fully comprehended by our view. Their view of history is biased, incomplete, maliciously untruthful, and ideologically driven. You are with us or against us. (Lederach 2005: 35)

The same construction can currently be observed with regard to information and (what is called) misinformation: 'we' inform, 'they' misinform; 'we' engage in public diplomacy, 'they' in propaganda. Such patterns, assigning ontological superiority to one's own position and othering alternative ways of seeing things, are sadly familiar and incredibly unimaginative. In this book, we argue for the complexification of narratives, which implies moving from either-or to as-well-as even in times of conflict: we are right and they may be right, too; they are wrong but we may also be wrong. Such complexification also applies to such an extreme form of conflict as war, as Vivienne Jabri argues: "The account of any war must, by necessity, involve a number of narratives, some mutually conflicting, others mutually complementary, all told from some specific perspective on causation and consequence" (2007: 21). Even if every narrator's story remains relatively simple, the overall scenario loses its seeming simplicity by acknowledging that other, equally simple stories may be equally right or, in the terminology preferred in this book, *equally permissible in light of each individual's or group's own experience*. Such acknowledgment improves the quality of the conversation and, by showing respect for other people's experience, the quality of the social relation and, with it, the chance that social change will unfold constructively.

Finally, we wish to summarize the book after all, but we wish to do so visually, not textually (Fig. 13.1).

13 CONCLUDING REFLECTIONS: TOLERANCE OF AMBIGUITY ... 313

Fig. 13.1 Complexity grid (© Rasmus Bellmer and Frank Möller; photography © Frank Möller)

References

Andreas, Peter. 2008. *Blue Helmets and Black Markets: The Business of Survival in the Siege of Sarajevo*. Ithaca and London: Cornell University Press.

Bellmer, Rasmus, and Frank Möller. 2022. Messiness in Photography, War, and Transitions to Peace: Revisiting 'Bosnia: Uncertain Paths to Peace.' *Media, War, and Conflict* 16: 2. https://doi.org/10.1177/17506352211072463.

Byrne, David, and Gillian Callaghan. 2023. *Complexity Theory and the Social Sciences: The State of the Art*. London and New York: Routledge.

Cilliers, Paul. 1998. *Complexity and Postmodernism: Understanding Complex Systems*. London and New York: Routledge.

Collins, Randall. 2008. *Violence: A Micro-sociological Theory*. Princeton: Princeton University Press.

Coser, Lewis. 1956. *The Functions of Social Conflict*. New York: The Free Press.

Jabri, Vivienne. 2007. *War and the Transformation of Global Politics*. Houndmills: Palgrave Macmillan.

Jestrovic, Silvija. 2013. *Performance, Space, Utopia: Cities of War, Cities of Exile*. Houndmills: Palgrave Macmillan.

Katzenstein, Peter J. 1996. Introduction: Alternative Perspective on National Security. In *The Culture of National Security: Norms and Identity in World Politics*, ed. Peter J. Katzenstein, 1–32. New York: Columbia University Press.

Law, John. 2004. *After Method: Mess in Social Science Research*. London and New York: Routledge.

Lederach, John Paul. 2005. *The Moral Imagination: The Art and Soul of Building Peace*. Oxford: Oxford University Press.

Lowe, Paul. 2015. *Oziljak (Scar)*. Field Study 21.

Markowitz, Fran. 2010. *Sarajevo: A Bosnian Kaleidoscope*. Urbana, Chicago, and Springfield: University of Illinois Press.

Morrison, Kenneth, and Paul Lowe. 2021. *Reporting the Siege of Sarajevo*. London: Bloomsbury Academic.

Sennet, Adam. 2021. Ambiguity. In *The Stanford Encyclopedia of Philosophy*, ed. Edward Zalta (Fall 2021 Edition). https://plato.stanford.edu/archives/fall2021/entries/ambiguity/.

Bibliography

Abadžić, Amra. 2022. *Sarajevo: The Longest Siege*. Sarajevo: Scena MESS.
Adams, Robert. 1994. *Why People Photograph: Selected Essays and Reviews*. New York: Aperture.
Adler, Emanuel, and Michael Barnett, eds. 1998. *Security Communities*. Cambridge: Cambridge University Press.
Aggestam, Karin, and Annika Björkdahl. 2009. Introduction: War and Peace in Transition. In *War and Peace in Transition: Changing Roles of External Actors*, ed. Karin Aggestam and Annika Björkdahl, 15–31. Lund: Nordic Academic Press.
Aggestam, Karin, Fabio Cristiano, and Lisa Strömbom. 2015. Towards Agonistic Peacebuilding? Exploring the Antagonism–Agonism Nexus in the Middle East Peace Process. *Third World Quarterly* 36 (9): 1736–1753.
Albert, Mathias. 2019. Luhmann and Systems Theory. *Oxford Research Encyclopedias, Politics*. Available at: https://doi.org/10.1093/acrefore/9780190228637.013.7.
Allan, Stuart. 2011. Documenting War, Visualizing Peace: Towards Peace Photography. In *Expanding Peace Journalism: Comparative and Critical Approaches*, ed. Ibraham Seaga Shaw, Jake Lynch, and Robert A. Hackett, 147–167. Sydney: University of Sidney Press.
Allan, Stuart. 2013. Blurring Boundaries: Professional and Citizen Journalism in a Digital Age. In *The Photographic Image in Digital Culture*, 2nd ed., ed. Martin Lister, 183–200. London and New York: Routledge.
Amado, Jorge. 2005. *The War of the Saints*, trans. Gregory Rabassa. New York: Dial Press.

Andersen, Rune S., and Frank Möller. 2013. Engaging the Limits of Visibility: Photography, Security and Surveillance. *Security Dialogue* 44 (3): 203–221.

Andreas, Peter. 2008. *Blue Helmets and Black Markets: The Business of Survival in the Siege of Sarajevo*. Ithaca and London: Cornell University Press.

Apel, Dora. 2012. *War Culture and the Contest of Images*. New Brunswick and London: Rutgers University Press.

Aston, Judith, and Sandra Gaudenzi. 2012. Interactive Documentary: Setting the Field. *Studies in Documentary Film* 6 (2): 125–139.

Autesserre, Séverine. 2014. *Peaceland: Conflict Resolution and the Everyday Politics of International Intervention*. New York: Cambridge University Press.

Autesserre, Séverine. 2021. *The Frontlines of Peace: An Insider's Guide to Changing the World*. New York: Oxford University Press.

Azoulay, Ariella. 2012. *Civil Imagination: A Political Ontology of Photography*, trans. Louise Bethlehem. London and New York: Verso.

Bächtold, Stefan. 2021. Donor Love Will Tear Us Apart: How Complexity and Learning Marginalize Accountability in Peacebuilding Interventions. *International Political Sociology* 15 (4): 504–521. https://doi.org/10.1093/ips/olab022.

Baker, Simon, and Shoair Mavlian, eds. 2014. *Conflict · Time · Photography*. London: Tate Publishing.

Bal, Mieke. 2007. The Pain of Images. In *Beautiful Suffering: Photography and the Traffic in Pain*, ed. Mark Reinhardt, Holly Edwards, and Erina Duganne, 93–115.Chicago University of Chicago Press/Williamstown: Williams College Museum of Art.

Bargués, Pol. 2020. Peacebuilding Without Peace? On How Pragmatism Complicates the Practice of International Intervention. *Review of International Studies* 46 (2): 237–255.

Bargués-Pedreny, Pol. 2015. Realising the Post-modern Dream: Strengthening Post-conflict Resilience and the Promise of Peace. *Resilience* 3 (2): 113–132.

Bargués-Pedreny, Pol. 2019. Resilience Is "Always More" Than Our Practices: Limits, Critiques, and Skepticism About International Intervention. *Contemporary Security Policy* 41 (2): 1–24.

Bargués-Pedreny, Pol, and Elisa Randazzo. 2018. Hybrid Peace Revisited: An Opportunity for Considering Self-Governance? *Third World Quarterly* 39 (8): 1–18.

Barthes, Roland. 2000. *Camera Lucida: Reflections of Photography*, trans. Richard Howard. London: Vintage.

Bate, David. 2013. The Digital Condition of Photography: Cameras, Computers and Display. In *The Photographic Image in Digital Culture*, 2nd ed., ed. Martin Lister, 77–94. London and New York: Routledge.

Bauer, Thomas. 2018. *Die Vereindeutigung der Welt: Über den Verlust an Mehrdeutigkeit und Vielfalt*. Ditzingen: Reclam.

Beaumont, Paul, and Cedric de Coning. 2022. Coping with Complexity: Toward Epistemological Pluralism in Climate-Conflict Scholarship. *International Studies Review*. https://doi.org/10.1093/isr/viac055.

Bellmer, Rasmus, and Frank Möller. 2022a. Active Looking: Images in Peace Mediation. *Peacebuilding* 11: 2. https://doi.org/10.1080/21647259.2022.2152971.

Bellmer, Rasmus, and Frank Möller. 2022b. Messiness in Photography, War, and Transitions to Peace: Revisiting 'Bosnia: Uncertain Paths to Peace.' *Media, War, and Conflict* 16: 2. https://doi.org/10.1177/17506352211072463.

Bellmer, Rasmus, Tiffany Fairey, and Frank Möller. Forthcoming. Peace Photography, Visual Peacebuilding and Participatory Peace Photography. In *The Routledge Handbook of Conflict and Peacebuilding Communication*, ed. Stefanie Pukallus and Stacey Connaughton. New York: Routledge.

Benjamin, Walter. 1963a. Das Kunstwerk im Zeitalter seiner technischen Reproduzierbarkeit. Drei Studien zur Kunstsoziologie. Frankfurt: Suhrkamp.

Benjamin, Walter. 1963b. Das Kunstwerk im Zeitalter seiner technischen Reproduzierbarkeit. In *Das Kunstwerk im Zeitalter seiner technischen Reproduzierbarkeit. Drei Studien zur Kunstsoziologie*, ed. Walter Benjamin, 7–44. Frankfurt: Suhrkamp.

Benjamin, Walter. 1963c. Kleine Geschichte der Photographie. In *Das Kunstwerk im Zeitalter seiner technischen Reproduzierbarkeit. Drei Studien zur Kunstsoziologie*, ed. Walter Benjamin, 45–64. Frankfurt: Suhrkamp.

Bennett, Audrey G. 2012. *Engendering Interaction with Images*. Bristol: Intellect.

Bennett, Christopher. 2016. *Bosnia's Paralysed Peace*. London: Hurst & Company.

Bentwich, Miriam Ethel, and Peter Gilbey. 2017. More than Visual Literacy: Art and the Enhancement of Tolerance for Ambiguity and Empathy. *BMC Medical Education* 17 (1): 1–9.

Berger, John. 2013. *Understanding a Photograph*, ed. and introduced by Geoff Dyer. London: Penguin Classics.

Berger, Peter, and Thomas Luckmann. 1967. *The Social Construction of Reality: A Treatise in the Sociology of Knowledge*. London: Penguin.

Bishop, Claire. 2012. *Artificial Hells: Participatory Art and the Politics of Spectatorship*. London and New York: Verso.

Bleiker, Roland. 2001. The Aesthetic Turn in International Political Theory. *Millenium* 30 (3): 509–533.

Bleiker, Roland, ed. 2018. *Visual Global Politics*. London and New York: Routledge.

Bleiker, Roland, and Emma Hutchison. 2008. Fear No More: Emotions and World Politics. *Review of International Studies* 34 (S1): 115–135.

Boudana, Sandrine, Paul Frosh, and Akiba A. Cohen. 2017. Reviving Icons to Death? When Historic Photographs Become Digital Memes. *Media, Culture & Society* 39 (8): 1210–1230.

Bousquet, Antoine, and Robert Geyer. 2011. Introduction: Complexity and the International Arena. *Cambridge Review of International Affairs* 24 (1): 1–3.

Bousquet, Antoine, and Simon Curtis. 2011. Beyond Models and Metaphors: Complexity Theory, Systems Thinking and International Relations. *Cambridge Review of International Affairs* 24 (1): 43–62.

Bregman, Rutger. 2021. *Humankind: A Hopeful History*. London: Bloomsbury.

Brigg, Morgan, and Roland Bleiker. 2011. Postcolonial Conflict Resolution. In *Mediating across Difference: Oceanic and Asian Approaches to Conflict Resolution*, ed. Morgan Brigg and Roland Bleiker, 19–37. Honolulu: University of Hawai'i Press.

Brunet, François. 2019. *The Birth of the Idea of Photography*. Toronto: RIC Books.

Brusset, Emery, Cedric de Coning, and Bryn Hughes, eds. 2016. *Complexity Thinking for Peacebuilding Practice and Evaluation*. London: Palgrave Macmillan.

Bryan, Rebecca. 2016. Introduction: Everyday Coexistence in the Post-Ottoman Space. In *Post-Ottoman Coexistence: Sharing Space in the Shadow of Conflict*, ed. Rebecca Bryan, 1–38. New York and London: Berghahn Books.

Buckley, Bernadette. 2009. The Workshop of Filthy Creation: Or Do Not Be Alarmed, This Is Only a Test. *Review of International Studies* 35 (4): 835–857.

Budner, Stanley. 1962. Intolerance of Ambiguity as a Personality Variable. *Journal of Personality* 30 (1): 29–50.

Burgin, Victor, ed. 1982. *Thinking Photography*. Houndmills and London: Macmillan.

Burns, Danny. 2011. Facilitating Systemic Conflict Transformation Through Systemic Action Research. In *The Non-Linearity of Peace Processes: Theory and Practice of Systemic Conflict Transformation*, Daniela Körrpen, Norbert Ropers, and Hans J. Giessmann, 97–110. Opladen and Farmington Hills, MI: Barbara Budrich Publishers.

Butler, Judith. 2010. *Frames of War: When Is Life Grievable?* London and New York: Verso.

Byrne, David. 1998. *Complexity Theory and the Social Sciences*. London and New York: Routledge.

Byrne, David, and Gillian Callaghan. 2023. *Complexity Theory and the Social Sciences: The State of the Art*. London and New York: Routledge.

Callahan, William A. 2015. The Visual Turn in IR: Documentary Filmmaking as a Critical Method. *Millennium* 43: 891–910.

Callahan, William A. 2020. *Sensible Politics: Visualizing International Relations*. New York: Oxford University Press.
Campbell, David. 1998. *National Deconstruction: Violence, Identity, and Justice in Bosnia*. Minneapolis and London: University of Minnesota Press.
Capa, Robert. 1999. A Legitimate Complaint. In *A Russian Journal. With Photographs by Robert Capa*, ed. John Steinbeck, 140–143. With an introduction by Susan Shillinglaw. London: Penguin.
Cartier-Bresson, Henri. 2014. *The Decisive Moment*. Göttingen: Steidl.
Caspersen, Dana. 2018. A Persistent Mobility of Perspective. In *Can Art Aid in Resolving Conflicts?*, ed. Noam Lemelshtrich-Latar, Jerry Wind, and Ornat Lev-er, 42–43. Amsterdam: Frame Publishers.
Chandler, David. 2013. Peacebuilding and the Politics of Non-linearity: Rethinking 'Hidden' Agency and 'Resistance.' *Peacebuilding* 1 (1): 17–32.
Chandler, David. 2014. *Resilience: The Governance of Complexity*. New York: Routledge.
Chandler, David. 2017. *Peacebuilding: The Twenty Years' Crisis, 1997–2017*. Houndmills: Palgrave Macmillan.
Chong, Denise. 2001. *The Girl in the Picture: The Story of Kim Phuc, the Photograph, and the Vietnam War*. London: Penguin.
Chouliaraki, Lilie. 2018. The Humanity of War: Iconic Photojournalism of the Battlefield, 1914–2012. In *Visual Security Studies: Sights and Spectacles of Insecurity and War*, ed. Juha A. Vuori and Rune Saugmann Andersen, 71–90. London and New York: Routledge.
Cieplak, Piotr. 2017. *Death, Image, Memory: The Genocide in Rwanda and Its Aftermath in Photography and Documentary Film*. Houndmills: Palgrave Macmillan.
Cilliers, Paul. 1998. *Complexity and Postmodernism: Understanding Complex Systems*. London and New York: Routledge.
Cilliers, Paul. 2010. Difference, Identity and Complexity. In *Complexity, Difference and Identity, an Ethical Perspective*, ed. Paul Cilliers and Rika Preiser, 3–18. Dordrecht, Heidelberg, London, and New York: Springer.
Clemens, Walter, Jr. 2001. *The Baltic Transformed: Complexity Theory and European Security*. Lanham: Rowman and Littlefield.
Cobb, Sara. 2013. *Speaking of Violence: The Politics and Poetics of Narrative in Conflict Resolution*. New York: Oxford University Press.
Cohen, Cynthia. 1997. *A Poetics of Reconciliation: The Aesthetic Mediation of Conflict*. PhD Dissertation. Durham: University of New Hampshire.
Coleman, Peter T. 2006. Conflict, Complexity, and Change: A Meta-Framework for Addressing Protracted, Intractable Conflicts—III. *Peace and Conflict: Journal of Peace Psychology* 12 (4): 325–348.
Coleman, Peter T. 2011. *The Five Percent: Finding Solutions to Seemingly Impossible Conflicts*. New York: Public Affairs.

Collins, Randall. 2008. *Violence: A Micro-sociological Theory*. Princeton: Princeton University Press.

Coser, Lewis. 1956. *The Functions of Social Conflict*. New York: The Free Press.

Couldry, Nick. 2000. *Inside Culture: Re-imagining the Method of Cultural Studies*. London: Sage.

Danchev, Alex. 2009. *On Art and War and Terror*. Edinburgh: Edinburgh University Press.

Danchev, Alex, and Debbie Lisle. 2009. Introduction: Art, Politics, Purpose. *Review of International Studies* 35 (4): 775–779.

de Coning, Cedric. 2016a. From Peacebuilding to Sustaining Peace: Implications of Complexity for Resilience and Sustainability. *Resilience* 4 (3): 166–181.

de Coning, Cedric. 2016b. Implications of Complexity for Peacebuilding Policies and Practices. In *Complexity Thinking for Peacebuilding Practice and Evaluation*, ed. Emery Brusset, Cedric de Coning, and Bryn Hughes, 19–48. London: Palgrave Macmillan.

de Coning, Cedric. 2018. Adaptive Peacebuilding. *International Affairs* 94 (2): 301–317.

de Coning, Cedric. 2020. Insights from Complexity Theory for Peace and Conflict Studies. In *The Palgrave Encyclopedia of Peace and Conflict Studies*, ed. Oliver Richmond and Gëzim Visoka, 1–10. Cham: Palgrave Macmillan. https://doi.org/10.1007/978-3-030-11795-5_134-1.

Demick, Barbara. 2012. *Besieged: Life Under Fire on a Sarajevo Street*. London: Granta.

Deutsch, Karl W. 1954. *Political Community at the International Level: Problems of Definition and Measurement*. Garden City: Doubleday and Company.

Deutsch, Karl W., Sidney A. Burrell, Robert A. Khan, Maurice Lee, Jr., Martin Lichterman, Raymond E. Lindgren, Francis L. Loewenheim, and Richard W. Van Wagenen. 1957. *Political Community and the North Atlantic Area: International Organization in the Light of Historical Experience*. Princeton: Princeton University Press.

Deuze, Mark. 2007. Convergence Culture in the Creative Industries. *International Journal of Cultural Studies* 10 (2): 243–263.

Dingley, James. 2005. Constructive Ambiguity and the Peace Process in Northern Ireland. *Low Intensity Conflict & Law Enforcement* 13 (1): 1–23.

Dingli, Sophia, and Thomas N. Cooke, eds. 2022a. *Political Silence: Meanings, Functions, and Ambiguity*. London and New York: Routledge.

Dingli, Sophia, and Thomas N. Cooke. 2022b. Political Silence, an Introduction. In *Political Silence: Meanings, Functions, and Ambiguity*, ed. Sophia Dingli and Thomas N. Cooke, 1–19. London and New York: Routledge.

Donia, Robert J. 2009. *Sarajevo: A Biography*. London: Hurst & Company.

Dube, Saurabh. 2022. Decolonial Dissonance. *IWM Post*, No. 130: 18.

Dufour, Diane, ed. 2015. *Images of Conviction: The Construction of Visual Evidence*. Paris: LE BAL.

Durrheim, Kevin, and Don Foster. 1997. Tolerance of Ambiguity as a Content Specific Construct. *Personality and Individual Differences* 22 (5): 741–750.

Dziatkowiec, Paul, Christina Buchhold, Elodie Convergne, Jonathan Harlander, and Tinahy Andriamasomanana. 2016. *Oslo Forum 2016 Report: Adapting to a New Conflict Landscape*. Geneva: Center for Humanitarian Dialogue.

Emcke, Carolin. 2016. *Von den Kriegen. Briefe and Freunde*. Frankfurt: Fischer.

Elkins, James. 2011. *What Photography Is*. New York and London: Routledge.

Emerling, Jae. 2012. *Photography: History and Theory*. London and New York: Routledge.

Empson, William. 1949. *Seven Types of Ambiguity*. London: Chatto and Windus.

Engel, Antonia, and Benedikt Korf. 2005. *Negotiation and Mediation Techniques for Natural Resource Management*. https://peacemaker.un.org/sites/peacemaker.un.org/files/NegotiationandMediationTechniquesforNaturalResourceManagement_FAO2005.pdf.

Fairey, Tiffany. 2018. Whose Photo? Whose Voice? Who Listens? 'Giving', Silencing and Listening to Voice in Participatory Visual Projects. *Visual Studies* 33 (2): 111–126.

Fairey, Tiffany. 2021. Participatory, Community, and Citizen Photography as Peace Photography. *Image & Peace: Exploring Visual Culture and Peace*. https://www.imageandpeace.com/2021/11/11/participatory-community-and-citizen-photography-as-peace-photography/.

Fairey, Tiffany, and Rachel Kerr. 2020. What Works? Creative Approaches to Transitional Justice in Bosnia and Herzegovina. *International Journal of Transitional Justice* 14 (1): 142–164.

Favero, Paolo. 2013. Getting Our Hands Dirty (Again): Interactive Documentaries and the Meaning of Images in the Digital Age. *Journal of Material Culture* 18 (3): 259–277.

Favero, Paolo. 2014. Learning to Look beyond the Frame: Reflections on the Changing Meaning of Images in the Age of Digital Media Practices. *Visual Studies* 29 (2): 166–179.

Favero, Paolo S. H. 2018. *The Present Image: Visible Stories in a Digital Habitat*. Houndmills: Palgrave Macmillan.

Feldman, Allen. 2000. Violence and Vision: The Prosthetics and Aesthetics of Terror. In *Violence and Subjectivity*, ed. Veena Das, Arthur Kleinman, Mamphela Ramphele, and Pamela Reynolds, 46–78. Berkeley, Los Angeles, London: University of California Press.

Feldman, Allen. 2015. *Archives of the Insensible: Of War, Photopolitics, and Dead Memory*. Chicago and London: The University of Chicago Press.

Fisher, Roger, William Ury, and Bruce Patton. 2012. *Getting to YES: Negotiating an Agreement Without Giving In*. London: Random House Business Books.

Folger, Joseph P., and Dan Simon. 2017. Transformative Mediation: Illustrating a Relational View of Conflict Intervention. In *The Mediation Handbook: Research, Theory, and Practice*, ed. Alexia Georgakopoulos, 73–86. New York and London: Routledge.

Foucault, Michel. 1982. *This Is Not a Pipe*, trans. and ed. James Harkness. With illustrations and letters by René Magritte. Berkeley, Los Angeles, London: University of California Press.

Frenkel-Brunswick, Else. 1949. Intolerance of Ambiguity as an Emotional and Perceptual Personality Variable. *Journal of Personality* 18 (1): 108–143.

Fry, Douglas P. 2007. *Beyond War: The Human Potential for Peace*. Oxford: Oxford University Press.

Fuller, Matthew, and Eyal Weizman. 2021. *Investigative Aesthetics: Conflicts and Commons in the Politics of Truth*. London and New York: Verso.

Furnham, Adrian, and Joseph Marks. 2013. Tolerance of Ambiguity: A Review of the Recent Literature. *Psychology* 4 (9): 717–728.

Furnham, Adrian, and Tracy Ribchester. 1995. Tolerance of Ambiguity: A Review of the Concept, Its Measurement and Applications. *Current Psychology* 14 (3): 179–199.

Gade, Solveig. 2020. Forensic (Im)probabilities: Entering Schrödinger's Box with Rahib Mroué and Hito Steyerl. In *(W)ARCHIVES: Archival Imaginaries, War, and Contemporary Art*, ed. Daniela Agostinho, Solveig Gade, Nanna Bonde Thylstrup and Kristin Veel, 365–385. Berlin: Sternberg Press.

Gafić, Ziyah. 2015. *Quest for Identity*. Millbrook: de.Mo Design.

Gafić, Ziyah. 2016. *Heartland*. Sarajevo: Connectum.

Gallo, Giorgio. 2012. Conflict Theory, Complexity and Systems Approach. *Systems Research and Behavioral Science* 30 (2): 156–175.

Geller, Gail. 2013. Tolerance for Ambiguity. *Academic Medicine* 88 (5): 581–584.

George, Alice Rose, and Gilles Peress, eds. 2002. *Here Is New York*. Zurich, Berlin, New York: Scalo.

George, Jim, and David Campbell. 1990. Patterns of Dissent and the Celebration of Difference: Critical Social Theory and International Relations. *International Studies Quarterly* 34 (3): 269–293.

Gilgen, Peter. 2003. History After Film. In *Mapping Benjamin: The Work of Art in the Digital Age*, ed. Hans Ulrich Gumbrecht and Michael Marrinan, 53–62. Stanford: Stanford University Press.

Glenny, Misha. 1996. *The Fall of Yugoslavia: The Third Balkan War*. London: Penguin.

Goldstein, Donna M. 2003. *Laughter Out of Place: Race, Class, Violence, and Sexuality in a Rio Shantytown*. Berkeley, Los Angeles, London: University of California Press.

Golubović, Jelena. 2020. "To Me, You Are Not a Serb": Ethnicity, Ambiguity, and Anxiety in Post-war Sarajevo. *Ethnicities* 20 (3): 544–563.
Gordon, Sophie. 2017. *Shadows of War: Roger Fenton's Photographs of the Crimea, 1855*. London: Royal Collection Trust.
Gourevitch, Phillip, and Errol Morris. 2009. *Standard Operating Procedure: A War Story*. London: Picador.
Grønstad, Asbjørn, and Henrik Gustafsson, eds. 2012. *Ethics and Images of Pain*. New York: Routledge.
Gustafsson, Hendrik. 2019. *Crime Scenery in Postwar Film and Photography*. Houndmills: Palgrave Macmillan.
Habermas, Jürgen. 1985. *Die neue Unübersichtlichkeit. Kleine Politische Schriften V*. Frankfurt: Suhrkamp.
Hale, Constance, and Fiona Turner, eds. 2020. *Imagine: Reflections on Peace*. Paris: Hemeria.
Hancock, Jason, and Karen Mattick. 2020. Tolerance of Ambiguity and Psychological Well-Being in Medical Training: A Systematic Review. *Medical Education* 54 (2): 125–137.
Hariman, Robert, and John Louis Lucaites. 2003. Public Identity and Collective Memory in U.S. Iconic Photography: The Image of 'Accidental Napalm'. *Critical Studies in Media Communication* 20 (1): 35–66.
Hariman, Robert, and John Louis Lucaites. 2007. *No Caption Needed: Iconic Photographs, Public Culture, and Liberal Democracy*. Chicago and London: The University of Chicago Press.
Harman, Sophie. 2019. *Seeing Politics: Film, Visual Method, and International Relations*. Montreal: McGill Queens University Press.
Harper, Christopher. 2006. Mediator as Peacemaker: The Case for Activist Transformative-Narrative Mediation. *Journal of Dispute Resolution* 2: 595–611.
Haviv, Ron. 2020. Bosnia and Herzegovina Now. In *Imagine: Reflections on Peace*, ed. Constance Hale and Fiona Turner, 211–227. Paris: Hemeria.
Hirsch, Marianne. 1997. *Family Frames: Photography, Narrative, and Postmemory*. Cambridge and London: Harvard University Press.
Holbrooke, Richard. 1999. *To End a War*. New York: The Modern Library.
Holmes, Jamie. 2015. *Nonsense: The Power of Not Knowing*. New York: Crown Publishers.
Horn, Steve. 2005. *Pictures Without Borders: Bosnia Revisited*. Stockport: Dewi Lewis in association with the Bosnian Institute.
Hughes, Bryn. 2012. Peace Operations and the Political: A Pacific Reminder of What Really Matters. *Journal of International Peacekeeping* 16 (1–2): 99–118.
Hutchison, Emma, and Roland Bleiker. 2013. Theorizing Emotions in World Politics. *International Theory* 6 (3): 491–514.

Jabri, Vivienne. 2007. *War and the Transformation of Global Politics*. Houndmills: Palgrave Macmillan.
Jergović, Miljenko. 2015. *Vater*, trans. Brigitte Döbert. Frankfurt: Schöffling & Co.
Jestrovic, Silvija. 2013. *Performance, Space, Utopia: Cities of War, Cities of Exile*. Houndmills: Palgrave Macmillan.
Jones, Marc Owen. 2022. *Digital Authoritarianism in the Middle East: Deception, Disinformation and Social Media*. London: Hurst & Co.
Jones, Tricia S., and Andrea Bodtker. 2007. Mediating with Heart in Mind: Addressing Emotion in Mediation Practice. *Negotiation Journal* 17 (3): 217–244.
Jones, Wendell, and Scott H. Hughes. 2003. Complexity, Conflict Resolution, and How the Mind Works. *Conflict Resolution Quarterly* 20 (4): 485–494.
Juncos, Ana E. 2018. Resilience in Peacebuilding: Contesting Uncertainty, Ambiguity, and Complexity. *Contemporary Security Policy* 39 (4): 1–16.
Karahasan, Dževad. 1993. *Tagebuch der Aussiedlung*, trans. Klaus Detlef Olof. Klagenfurt: Wieser Verlag.
Karahasan, Dževad. 2014. *Sara und Serafina*, trans. Barbara Antkowiak. Frankfurt: Suhrkamp.
Karahasan, Dževad. 2023. *Einübung ins Schweben*, trans. Katharina Wolf-Grießhaber. Frankfurt: Suhrkamp.
Katzenstein, Peter J. 1996. Introduction: Alternative Perspective on National Security. In *The Culture of National Security: Norms and Identity in World Politics*, ed. Peter J. Katzenstein, 1–32. New York: Columbia University Press.
Kaufmann, Mareile. 2013. Emergent Self-Organisation in Emergencies: Resilience Rationales in Interconnected Societies. *Resilience* 1 (1): 53–68.
Kavalski, Emilian. 2007. The Fifth Debate and the Emergence of Complex International Relations Theory: Notes on the Application of Complexity Theory to the Study of International Life. *Cambridge Review of International Affairs* 20 (3): 435–454.
Kavalski, Emilian, ed. 2015. *World Politics at the Edge of Chaos: Reflections on Complexity and Global Life*. New York: State University of New York Press.
Kebo, Ozren. 2016. Looking into a Radical Wasteland. In *Heartland*, ed. Ziyah Gafić, 84–93. Sarajevo: Connectum.
Kelly, Edward J., and Natalija Kaminskienė. 2016. Importance of Emotional Intelligence in Negotiation and Mediation. *International Comparative Jurisprudence* 2 (1): 55–60.
Kelman, Herbert C., and Ronald J. Fisher, eds. 2016. *Herbert C. Kelman: A Pioneer in the Social Psychology of Conflict Analysis and Resolution*. Cham: Springer.
Kelsey, Robin, and Blake Stimson. 2008. Introduction: Photography's Double Index (A Short History in Three Points). In *The Meaning of Photography*, ed.

Robin Kelsey and Blake Stimson, vii–xxxi. Williamstown: Sterling and Francine Clark Art Institute/New Haven and London: Yale University Press.

Kelsey, Robin, and Blake Stimson, eds. 2008. *The Meaning of Photography*. Williamstown: Sterling and Francine Clark Art Institute/New Haven and London: Yale University Press.

Kennedy, Liam, and Caitlin Patrick, eds. 2014. *The Violence of the Image: Photography and International Conflict*. London and New York: I.B. Tauris.

Khanna, Parag. 2022. Ist eine Weltordnung möglich? *DIE ZEIT*, No. 33 (11 August): 47.

King, Barry. 2003. Über die Arbeit des Erinnerns. Die Suche nach dem perfekten Moment. In *Diskurse der Fotografie: Fotokritik am Ende des fotografischen Zeitalters*, ed. Herta Wolf, 173–214. Frankfurt: Suhrkamp.

Kleiboer, Marieke. 1996. Understanding Success and Failure of International Mediation. *Journal of Conflict Resolution* 40 (2): 360–389.

Knight, Gary. 2020. Preface: Out of War. In *Imagine: Reflections on Peace*, ed. Constance Hale and Fiona Turner, 7–11. Paris: Hemeria.

Korosteleva, Elena A., and Irina Petrova. 2022. What Makes Communities Resilient in Times of Complexity and Change? *Cambridge Review of International Affairs* 35 (2): 1–21.

Kriesberg, Louis. 2015. *Realizing Peace: A Constructive Conflict Approach*. Oxford and New York: Oxford University Press.

Krippendorff, Ekkehard. 2000. *Kritik der Außenpolitik*. Frankfurt: Suhrkamp.

Kromm, Jane, and Susan Benforado Bakewell, eds. 2010. *A History of Visual Culture: Western Civilization from the 18th to the 20th Century*. Oxford and New York: Berg.

Kruglanski, Arie W., and Donna M. Webster. 1996. Motivated Closing of the Mind: "Seizing" and "Freezing." *Psychological Review* 103 (2): 263–283.

Lange, Dorothea. 1982. *Photographs of a Lifetime. With an Essay by Robert Coles*. Afterword by Therese Heyman. New York: Aperture.

Law, John. 2004. *After Method: Mess in Social Science Research*. London and New York: Routledge.

Lederach, John Paul. 2005. *The Moral Imagination: The Art and Soul of Building Peace*. Oxford: Oxford University Press.

Levi, Primo. 1989. *The Drowned and the Saved*, trans. Raymond Rosenthal. New York: Vintage.

Linfield, Susie. 2010. *The Cruel Radiance: Photography and Political Violence*. Chicago and London: The University of Chicago Press.

Lisle, Debbie. 2011. The Surprising Detritus of Leisure: Encountering the Late Photography of War. *Environment and Planning D: Society and Space* 29: 873–890.

Lister, Martin. 2013. Introduction. In *The Photographic Image in Digital Culture*, 2nd ed., ed. Martin Lister, 1–21. London and New York: Routledge.

Loode, Serge. 2011. Peacebuilding in Complex Social Systems. *Journal of Peace, Conflict & Development* 18: 68–82.
Lowe, Paul. 2014. The Forensic Turn: Bearing Witness and the 'Thingness' of the Photograph. In *The Violence of the Image: Photography and International Conflict*, ed. Liam Kennedy and Caitlin Patrick, 211–234. London and New York: I.B. Tauris.
Lowe, Paul. 2015. *Ožiljak (Scar). Field Study* 21.
Loyd, Anthony. 2020. God Won't Have Forgotten. In *Imagine: Reflections on Peace*, ed. Constance Hale and Fiona Turner, 196–209. Paris: Hemeria.
Lyons, Robert, and Scott Straus. 2006. *Intimate Enemy: Images and Voices of the Rwandan Genocide*. New York: Zone Books.
MacDougall, David. 1998. *Transcultural Cinema*, ed. and with an introduction by Lucien Taylor. Princeton: Princeton University Press.
Mac Ginty, Roger. 2006. *No War, No Peace: The Rejuvenation of Stalled Peace Processes and Peace Accords*. Houndmills: Palgrave Macmillan.
Mac Ginty, Roger. 2014. Everyday Peace: Bottom-Up and Local Agency in Conflict-Affected Societies. *Security Dialogue* 45 (6): 548–564.
Mac Ginty, Roger. 2021. *Everyday Peace: How so-Called Ordinary People Can Disrupt Violent Conflict*. Oxford: Oxford University Press.
Mannergren Selimovic, Johanna. 2020. Gendered Silences in Post-conflict Societies: A Typology. *Peacebuilding* 8 (1). https://doi.org/10.1080/21647259.2018.1491681.
Margalit, Avishai. 2004. *The Ethics of Memory*. Cambridge: Harvard University Press.
Markowitz, Fran. 2010. *Sarajevo: A Bosnian Kaleidoscope*. Urbana, Chicago, and Springfield: University of Illinois Press.
Mason, Jennifer, and Katherine Davies. 2009. Coming to Our Senses? A Critical Approach to Sensory Methodology. *Qualitative Research* 9 (5): 587–603.
McCloud, Scott. 1994. *Understanding Comics: The Invisible Art*. New York: HarperCollins.
McLain, David L., Efstathios Kefallonitis, and Kimberly Armani. 2015. Ambiguity Tolerance in Organizations: Definitional Clarification and Perspectives on Future Research. *Frontiers in Psychology* 6: 344.
McQuire, Scott. 2013. Photography's Afterlife: Documentary Images and the Operational Archive. *Journal of Material Culture* 18 (3): 223–241.
Meadows, Donella H. 2009. *Thinking in Systems: A Primer*. London: Earthscan.
Millar, Gearoid. 2019. Toward a Trans-Scalar Peace System: Challenging Complex Global Conflict Systems. *Peacebuilding* 8 (3): 1–18.
Millar, Gearoid. 2021a. Ambition and Ambivalence: Reconsidering Positive Peace as a Trans-Scalar Peace System. *Journal of Peace Research* 58 (4): 640–654.

Millar, Gearoid. 2021b. Trans-Scalar Ethnographic Peace Research: Understanding the Invisible Drivers of Complex Conflict and Complex Peace. *Journal of Intervention and Statebuilding* 15 (3): 1–20.
Miller, Nancy K. 2004. The Girl in the Photograph: The Vietnam War and the Making of National Memory. *JAC* 24 (2): 261–290.
Miller, Nancy K. 2012. The Girl in the Photograph: The Visual Legacies of War. In *Picturing Atrocity: Photography in Crisis*, ed. Jay Prosser, Geoffrey Batchen, Mick Gidley, and Nancy K. Miller, 147–154. London: Reaktion Books.
Mirzoeff, Nicholas. 2005. *Watching Babylon: The War in Iraq and Global Visual Culture*. New and London: Routledge.
Mirzoeff, Nicholas. 2012. *The Right to Look: A Counterhistory of Visuality*. Durham and London: Duke University Press.
Mitchell, Jolyon. 2020. Peacebuilding Through the Visual Arts. In *Peacebuilding and the Arts*, ed. Jolyon Mitchell, Giselle Vincett, Theodora Hawksley, and Hal Culbertson, 35–70. Houndmills: Palgrave Macmillan.
Mitchell, Mitchell, and Tom Allbeson, eds. Forthcoming. *Picturing Peace: Photography, Conflict Transformation, and Peacebuilding*. London: Bloomsbury.
Mitchell, W.J.T. 1994. *Picture Theory: Essays on Verbal and Visual Representation*. Chicago and London: The University of Chicago Press.
Mitchell, W.J.T. 2005. *What Do Pictures Want: The Lives and Loves of Images*. Chicago and London: University of Chicago Press.
Mitchell, W.J.T. 2012. *Cloning Terror: The War of Images, 9/11 to the Present*. Chicago and London: The University of Chicago Press.
Moe, Louise Wiuff. 2015. The Strange Wars of Liberal Peace: Hybridity, Complexity and the Governing Rationalities of Counterinsurgency in Somalia. *Peacebuilding* 4 (1): 1–19.
Möller, Frank. 2007. *Thinking Peaceful Change: Baltic Security Policy and Security Community Building*. Syracuse: Syracuse University Press.
Möller, Frank. 2010. Rwanda Revisualized: Genocide, Photography, and the Era of the Witness. *Alternatives* 35 (2): 113–136.
Möller, Frank. 2012. Celebration and Concern: Digitization, Camera Phones and the Citizen-Photographer. In *Images in Mobile Communication: New Content, New Uses, New Perspectives*, ed. Corinne Martin and Thilo von Pape, 57–78. Wiesbaden: VS Research.
Möller, Frank. 2013. *Visual Peace: Images, Spectatorship, and the Politics of Violence*. Houndmills: Palgrave Macmillan.
Möller, Frank. 2017a. Witnessing Violence Through Photography. *Global Discourse: An Interdisciplinary Journal of Current Affairs and Contemporary Thought* 7 (2–3): 264–281.

Möller, Frank. 2017b. From Aftermath to Peace: Reflections on a Photography of Peace. *Global Society: Journal of Interdisciplinary International Relations* 31 (3): 315–335.

Möller, Frank. 2019. *Peace Photography*. Houndmills: Palgrave Macmillan.

Möller, Frank. 2020. Peace Aesthetics: A Patchwork. *Peace & Change: A Journal of Peace Research* 45 (1). https://doi.org/10.1111/pech.12385.

Möller, Frank, and David Shim. 2019. Visions of Peace in International Relations. *International Studies Perspectives* 20 (3): 246–264.

Möller, Frank, and Rasmus Bellmer. 2023. Interactive Peace Imagery: Integrating Visual Research and Peace Education. *Journal of Peace Education*. https://doi.org/10.1080/17400201.2023.2171374.

Möller, Frank, Rasmus Bellmer, and Rune Saugmann. 2021. Visual Appropriation: A Self-Reflexive Qualitative Method for Visual Analysis of the International. *International Political Sociology* 16: 1. https://doi.org/10.1093/ips/olab029.

Morris, Errol. 2014. *Believing Is Seeing (Observations on the Mysteries of Photography)*. New York: Penguin.

Morrison, Kenneth. 2016. *Sarajevo's Holiday Inn on the Frontline of Politics and War*. Houndmills: Palgrave Macmillan.

Morrison, Kenneth, and Paul Lowe. 2021. *Reporting the Siege of Sarajevo*. London: Bloomsbury Academic.

Moser, Benjamin. 2019. *Sontag: Her Life and Work*. New York: HarperCollins.

Mouffe, Chantal. 2013. *Agonistics: Thinking the World Politically*. London and New York: Verso.

Müller-Christ, Georg, and Gudrun Weßling. 2007. Widerspruchsbewältigung, Ambivalenz- und Ambiguitätstoleranz: Eine modellhafte Verknüpfung. In *Nachhaltigkeit und Widersprüche*, ed. Georg Müller-Christ, Lars Arndt, and Ina Ehnert, 180–197. Münster: LIT Verlag.

Nagle, John. 2014. From the Politics of Antagonistic Recognition to Agonistic Peace Building: An Exploration of Symbols and Rituals in Divided Societies. *Peace & Change* 39 (4): 468–494.

Nash, Kate. 2012. Modes of Interactivity: Analysing the Webdoc. *Media, Culture & Society* 34 (2): 195–210.

Nichols, Bill. 2001. Documentary Film and the Modernist Avant-Garde. *Critical Inquiry* 27 (4): 580–610.

Norton, Robert W. 1975. Measurement of Ambiguity Tolerance. *Journal of Personality Assessment* 39 (6): 607–619.

Oldfield, Pippa. 2019. *Photography and War*. London: Reaktion Books.

Orsini, Amandine, Philippe Le Prestre, Peter M. Haas, Malte Brosig, Philipp Pattberg, Oscar Widerberg, Laura Gomez-Mera, Jean-Frédéric. Morin, Neil E. Harrison, Robert Geyer, and David Chandler. 2019. Forum: Complex

Systems and International Governance. *International Studies Review* 22 (4): 1008–1038.
Paffenholz, Thania. 2021. Perpetual Peacebuilding: A New Paradigm to Move Beyond the Linearity of Liberal Peacebuilding. *Journal of Intervention and Statebuilding* 15 (3): 367–385.
Palu, Louie. 2017. Image Control in the Age of Terror. In *Art as a Political Witness*, ed. Kia Lindroos and Frank Möller, 57–64. Opladen, Berlin, Toronto: Barbara Budrich Publishers.
Parpart, Jane L., and Swati Parashar, eds. 2019. *Rethinking Silence, Voice and Agency in Contested Gendered Terrains*. London and New York: Routledge.
Patrick, Caitlin. 2014. Ruins and Traces: *Exhibiting Conflict in Guy Tillim's Leopold and Mobutu*. In *The Violence of the Image: Photography and International Conflict*, ed. Liam Kennedy and Caitlin Patrick, 235–255. London and New York: I.B. Tauris.
Perlmutter, David D. 1999. *Visions of War: Picturing Warfare from the Stone Age to the Cyber Age*. New York: St. Martin's Griffin.
Pentikäinen, Antti. 2015. Reforming UN Mediation Through Inclusion of Traditional Peacemakers. *Development Dialogue* 63 (3): 67–76.
Pfonner, Michael R., and Patrick James. 2020. The Visual International Relations Project. *International Studies Review*. https://doi.org/10.1093/isr/viaa014.
Phelan, Peggy. 2012. Atrocity and Action: The Performative Force of the Abu Ghraib Photographs. In *Picturing Atrocity: Photography in Crisis*, ed. Jay Prosser, Geoffrey Batchen, Mick Gidley, and Nancy K. Miller, 51–61. London: Reaktion Books.
Pia, Emily. 2013. Narrative Therapy and Peacebuilding. *Journal of Intervention and Statebuilding* 7 (4): 476–491.
Prosser, Jay, Geoffrey Batchen, Mick Gidley, and Nancy K. Miller, eds. 2012. *Picturing Atrocity: Photography in Crisis*. London: Reaktion Books.
Proulx, Travis, and Michael Inzlicht. 2012. The Five "A"s of Meaning Maintenance: Finding Meaning in the Theories of Sense-Making. *Psychological Inquiry* 23 (4): 317–335.
Pylyshyn, Zenon W. 2003. *Seeing and Visualizing: It's Not What You Think*. Cambridge and London: MIT Press.
Rancière, Jacques. 2009. *The Emancipated Spectator*, trans. Gregory Elliott. London: Verso.
Randazzo, Elisa. 2017. *Beyond Liberal Peacebuilding: A Critical Exploration of the Local Turn*. New York: Routledge.
Randazzo, Elisa, and Ignasi Torrent. 2021. Reframing Agency in Complexity-Sensitive Peacebuilding. *Security Dialogue* 52 (1): 3–20.
Reinhardt, Mark. 2007. Picturing Violence: Aesthetics and the Anxiety of Critique. In *Beautiful Suffering: Photography and the Traffic in Pain*, ed. Mark

Reinhardt, Holly Edwards and Erina Duganne, 13–36. Chicago University of Chicago Press/Williamstown: Williams College Museum of Art.

Reinhardt, Mark. 2018. Violence. In *Visual Global Politics*, ed. Roland Bleiker, 321–327. London and New York: Routledge.

Reinhardt, Mark, Holly Edwards, and Erina Duganne, eds. 2007. *Beautiful Suffering: Photography and the Traffic in Pain*. Williamstown: Williams College Museum of Art/Chicago: The University of Chicago Press.

Reis, Jack. 1997. *Ambiguitätstoleranz: Beiträge Zur Entwicklung Eines Persönlichkeitskonstruktes*. Heidelberg: Asanger.

Richmond, Oliver P. 2006. The Problem of Peace: Understanding the 'Liberal Peace.' *Conflict, Security & Development* 6 (3): 291–314.

Richmond, Oliver P. 2015. The Dilemmas of a Hybrid Peace: Negative or Positive? *Cooperation and Conflict* 50 (1): 50–68.

Ristic, Mirjana. 2018. *Architecture, Urban Space and War: The Destruction and Reconstruction of Sarajevo*. Houndmills: Palgrave Macmillan.

Ritchin, Fred. 1999. *In Our Own Image*. New York: Aperture.

Ritchin, Fred. 2009. *After Photography*. New York: Norton & Company.

Ritchin, Fred. 2013. *Bending the Frame: Photojournalism, Documentary, and the Citizen*. New York: Aperture.

Roberts, John. 2014. *Photography and Its Violations*. New York: Columbia University Press.

Rogers, Carl R., and Richard E. Farson. 1987. Active Listening. In *Communicating in Business Today*, ed. Ruth G. Newman, Marie A. Danziger and Mark Cohen. Washington: Heath & Company.

Rosler, Martha. 2006. *3 Works*. Halifax: The Press of the Nova Scotia College of Art and Design.

Ross, Marc Howard. 2003. Competing Narratives and Escalation in Ethnic Conflicts: The Case of the Holy Sites in Jerusalem. *Sphera Publica* 3: 189–208.

Rubinstein, Daniel. 2010. Tag, Tagging. *Philosophy of Photography* 1 (2): 197–200.

Rubinstein, Daniel, and Katrina Sluis. 2013a. Concerning the Undecidability of the Digital Image. *Photographies* 6 (1): 151–158.

Rubinstein, Daniel, and Katrina Sluis. 2013b. The Digital Image in Photographic Culture: Algorithmic Photography and the Crisis of Representation. In *The Photographic Image in Digital Culture*, ed. Martin Lister, 22–40. London and New York: Routledge.

Sacco, Joe. 2000. *Safe Area Goražde: The War in Eastern Bosnia 1992–95*. Seattle: Fantagraphics Books.

Sacco, Joe. 2004. *The Fixer: A Story from Sarajevo*. London: Jonathan Cape.

Sacco, Joe. 2005. *War's End: Profiles from Bosnia 1995–96*. Montreal: Drawn & Quarterly.

Sacco, Joe. 2012. *Journalism*. London: Jonathan Cape.
Salem, Richard A. 1982. Community Dispute Resolution Through Outside Intervention. *Peace & Change* 8 (2–3): 91–104.
Sánchez, Gervasio. 2011. *Desaparecidos—Disappeared*. Barcelona: Blume.
Saugmann, Rune, Frank Möller, and Rasmus Bellmer. 2020. Seeing Like a Surveillance Agency? Sensor Realism as Aesthetic Critique of Visual Data Governance. *Information, Communication & Society* 23 (14): 1996–2013. https://doi.org/10.1080/1369118X.2020.1770315.
Scarry, Elaine. 1985. *The Body in Pain: The Making and Unmaking of the World*. Oxford: Oxford University Press.
Sennet, Adam. 2021. Ambiguity. In *The Stanford Encyclopedia of Philosophy*, ed. Edward Zalta, Fall 2021 ed. https://plato.stanford.edu/archives/fall2021/entries/ambiguity/.
Shapiro, Michael J. 1988. *The Politics of Representation: Writing Practices in Biography, Photography, and Policy Analysis*. Madison: The University of Wisconsin Press.
Shapiro, Michael J. 2004. *Methods and Nations: Cultural Governance and the Indigenous Subject*. New York and London: Routledge.
Shapiro, Michael J. 2008. Slow Looking: The Ethics and Politics of Aesthetics. *Millennium* 37 (1): 181–197.
Shapiro, Michael J. 2015. *War Crimes, Atrocity, and Justice*. Cambridge and Malden: Polity.
Sheringham, Michael. 2006. *Everyday Life: Theories and Practices from Surrealism to the Present*. Oxford: Oxford University Press.
Shinko, Rosemary E. 2008. Agonistic Peace: A Postmodern Reading. *Millennium: Journal of International Studies* 36 (3): 473–491.
Short, Philip. 2014. *Mitterrand: A Study in Ambiguity*. London: Vintage.
Silber, Laura, and Allan Little. 1997. *Yugoslavia: Death of a Nation*. London: Penguin.
Sliwinski, Sharon. 2011. *Human Rights in Camera. Foreword by Lunn Hunt*. Chicago and London: The University of Chicago Press.
Småberg, Maria. 2009. Witnessing the Unbearable: Alma Johansson and the Massacres of the Armenians 1915. In *War and Peace in Transition: Changing Roles of External Actors*, ed. Karin Aggestam and Annika Björkdahl, 107–127. Lund: Nordic Academic Press.
Smith, Shawn Michelle. 2013. *At the Edge of Sight: Photography and the Unseen*. Durham and London: Duke University Press.
Solomon-Godeau, Abigail. 1991. *Photography at the Dock: Essays on Photographic History, Institutions, and Practices*. Foreword by Linda Nochlin. Minneapolis: University of Minnesota Press.
Sontag, Susan. 1979. *On Photography*. London: Penguin.

Sontag, Susan. 2003. *Regarding the Pain of Others*. New York: Farrar, Straus & Giroux.

Stepanova, Maria. 2020. *Nach dem Gedächtnis*. Berlin: Suhrkamp.

Stewart, Katherine A., and Madeline M. Maxwell. 2010. *Storied Conflict Talk: Narrative Construction in Mediation*. Amsterdam and Philadelphia: John Benjamin.

Stover, Eric, and Gilles Peress. 1998. *The Graves: Srebrenica and Vukovar*. Zurich: Scalo.

Strömbom, Lisa. 2019. Exploring Analytical Avenues for Agonistic Peace. *Journal of International Relations and Development* 23 (4): 947–969.

Susperregui, José Manuel. 2016. The Location of Robert Capa's *Falling Soldier*. *Communication & Society* 29 (2): 17–43.

Sutherland, Ian, and Sophia Krzys Acord. 2007. Thinking with Art: From Situated Knowledge to Experiential Knowing. *Journal of Visual Art Practice* 6 (2): 125–140.

Szubielska, Magdalena, Joanna Ganczarek, Karolina Pietras, and Anna Stolińska. 2021. The Impact of Ambiguity in the Image and Title on the Liking and Understanding of Contemporary Paintings. *Poetics* 87: 101537.

Telios, Thomas, Dieter Thomä, and Ulrich Schmid. 2020. Preface. In *The Russian Revolution as Ideal and Practice: Failures, Legacies, and the Future of Revolution*, ed. Thomas Telios, Dieter Thomä, and Ulrich Schmid, 1–16. Houndmills: Palgrave Macmillan.

Terry, Sara. 2005. *Aftermath: Bosnia's Long Road to Peace*. New York: Channel Photographics.

Terry, Sara, and Teun van der Heijden. 2018. *War Is Only Half the Story: Ten Years of The Aftermath Project*. Stockport: Dewi Lewis.

Thompson, Jerry L. 2003. *Truth and Photography: Notes on Looking and Photographing*. Chicago: Ivan R. Dee.

UNDPA. 2012. *United Nations Guidance for Effective Mediation*. https://peacemaker.un.org/sites/peacemaker.un.org/files/GuidanceEffectiveMediation_UNDPA2012%28english%29_0.pdf.

Urry, John. 2005. The Complexity Turn. *Theory, Culture & Society* 22 (5): 1–14.

van Alphen, Ernst. 2005. *Art in Mind: How Contemporary Images Shape Thought*. Chicago and London: The University of Chicago Press.

Vázquez-Herrero, Jorge, and Xosé López-García. 2019. When Media Allow the User to Interact, Play and Share: Recent Perspectives on Interactive Documentary. *New Review of Hypermedia and Multimedia* 25 (4): 1–23.

Visoka, Gëzim. 2016. *Peace Figuration after International Intervention: Intentions, Events and Consequences of Liberal Peacebuilding*. London and New York: Routledge.

Vuori, Juha A., and Rune Saugmann Andersen, eds. 2018. *Visual Security Studies: Sights and Spectacles of Insecurity and War*. London and New York: Routledge.
Walker, R.B.J. 1993. *Inside/Outside: International Relations as Political Theory*. Cambridge: Cambridge University Press.
Wallis, Brian. 2010. Recovering the Mexican Suitcase. In *The Mexican Suitcase: The Rediscovered Spanish Civil War Negatives of Capa, Chim, and Taro, Vol. 1: The History*, ed. Cynthia Young, 13–17. New York: International Center of Photography/Göttingen: Steidl.
Walsh, Lauren. 2019. *Conversations on Conflict Photography*. London and New York: Bloomsbury.
Watney, Simon. 1982. Making Strange: The Shattered Mirror. In *Thinking Photography*, ed. Victor Burgin, 154–176. Houndmills and London: Macmillan.
Wells, Liz, ed. 2003. *The Photography Reader*. London and New York: Routledge.
Wenders, Wim, and Mary Zournazi. 2013. *Inventing Peace: A Dialogue on Perception*. London and New York: I.B. Tauris.
Wendt, Alexander. 1999. *Social Theory of International Politics*. Cambridge: Cambridge University Press.
Whelan, Richard. 2007. *This Is War! Robert Capa at Work*. New York: International Center of Photography/Göttingen: Steidl.
Widmaier, Wesley W., and Luke Glanville. 2015. The Benefits of Norm Ambiguity: Constructing the Responsibility to Protect Across Rwanda, Iraq and Libya. *Contemporary Politics* 21 (4): 367–383.
Wilkes Tucker, Anne, and Will Michels with Natalie Zelt. 2012. *War/Photography: Images of Armed Conflict and Its Aftermath*. Houston: The Museum of Fine Arts.
Willasey-Wilsey, Tom. 2022. US Policy on Taiwan and the Perils of Strategic Ambiguity. 23 September 2022. https://rusi.org/explore-our-research/publications/commentary/us-policy-taiwan-and-perils-strategic-ambiguity.
Williams, Raymond. 1976. *Keywords: A Vocabulary of Culture and Society*. London: Fontana.
Williams, Val. 2015. What Happened Here: A Photographer in Sarajevo 1992–1996. *Field Study* 21: 2–3.
Winkler, Susanne. 2015. Exploring Ambiguity and the Ambiguity Model from a Transdisciplinary Perspective. In *Ambiguity: Language and Communication*, ed. Susanne Winkler. Berlin, Munich, Boston: de Gruyter.
Winslade, John. 2017. Narrative Mediation of Family Conflict. In *The Mediation Handbook: Research, Theory, and Practice*, ed. Alexia Georgakopoulos, 87–96. New York and London: Routledge.

Winslade, John M., and Gerald Monk. 2006. Does the Model Overarch the Narrative Stream? In *The Blackwell Handbook of Mediation: A Guide to Effective Negotiation*, ed. Margaret S. Herrman, 217–227. Malden, Oxford and Victoria: Blackwell.

Winslade, John, and Gerald Monk. 2008. *Practicing Narrative Mediation: Loosening the Grip of Conflict*. San Francisco: Jossey-Bass.

Winslade, John, Gerald Monk, and Alison Cotter. 1998. A Narrative Approach to the Practice of Mediation. *Negotiation Journal* 14 (1): 21–41.

Zabotkina, Vera, Didier Bottineau, and Elena Boyarskaya. 2021. Cognitive Mechanisms of Ambiguity Resolution. In *Advances in Cognitive Research, Artificial Intelligence and Neuroinformatics Proceedings of the 9th International Conference on Cognitive Sciences, Intercognsci-2020, October 10–16, 2020, Moscow, Russia*, ed. Boris M. Velichkovsky, Pavel M. Balaban and Vadim L. Ushakov, 201–212. Cham: Springer.

Zenasni, Franck, Maud Besançon, and Todd Lubart. 2008. Creativity and Tolerance of Ambiguity: An Empirical Study. *The Journal of Creative Behavior* 42 (1): 61–73.

INDEX

A
Abu Ghraib, 271
Accidental Napalm, 119, 266–269, 271, 273, 274
accurateness, 284, 285, 290
active listening, 280, 284–286, 290
active looking, 19, 236, 280, 286, 288, 290–292, 294, 295
Adams, Eddie, 91, 110, 119, 271
Adams, Robert, 113, 116
aftermath, 88, 96–99, 101, 143, 144, 175, 184, 210, 213, 237, 243
agonistic peace, 64, 246
Albert, Matthias, 32
Albright, Madeleine, 215
Allan, Stuart, 287
Alphen, Ernst van, 197, 199
Amanpour, Christiane, 138
ambiguity, 4, 9, 10, 12–17, 19, 20, 29, 45, 47, 107, 108, 114, 118, 122–124, 126, 280, 285, 290, 292, 295
    intolerance of ambiguity, 63, 65, 66

    strategic ambiguity, 55
    tolerance of, 4, 5, 10, 12–17, 20, 47, 62, 65, 71, 72, 81, 101, 107, 122, 126, 135–139, 152, 154, 161, 178, 179, 184, 193, 227, 228, 235, 237, 239, 241, 249, 250, 303–305, 309, 310
Andreas, Peter, 136–139, 151, 307
appropriation, 119, 121, 127, 260, 305
approximation, 19, 290
archives, 261
art photography, 197
Aston, Judith, 222, 223
as-well-as, 7, 161, 194, 197, 241, 312
Atget, Eugène, 292
audience interaction, 147
audio, 135, 139, 142, 148, 163, 175
Autesserre, Séverine, 58, 60
authenticity, 177
auto-ethnography, 18, 159
auto-navigation, 18, 159
Azoulay, Ariella, 287

B

Bächtold, Stefan, 30, 37
background, 262–264, 267, 273
Barthes, Roland, 192, 265
Baščaršija square (Sarajevo), 244
Bastašić, Lana, 243
Bauer, Thomas, 58, 62
Beaumont, Paul, 6, 14
Becher, Bernd and Hilla, 196
Bell, Martin, 84
Benjamin, Walter, 177, 292, 293
Bennett, Audrey, 123–126, 210–212, 217, 220, 221, 223
Bentwich, Miriam Ethel, 63, 71
Berger, John, 68
Besançon, Maud, 72
Bosnia(-Herzegovina), 5, 7, 9, 17, 72, 82, 85, 87, 96, 100, 107, 120, 162, 211, 244, 249, 306
Bosnian culture, 238, 239
Bosnian way, 5, 7, 240, 243, 248, 250, 306
Bosnia: Uncertain Paths to Peace, 8, 15–18, 72, 135, 138, 139, 141, 146, 148–152, 154, 159–162, 166, 174, 175, 178, 179, 183–186, 188, 189, 192, 195–203, 210–217, 219–223, 225, 226, 228, 235, 236, 243, 255, 256, 258, 261, 272, 274
Bousquet, Antoine, 31, 187
Brunet, François, 87
Buckley, Bernadette, 242
Budner, Stanley, 63
Burgin, Victor, 88
Burns, Danny, 36
Butler, Judith, 256, 257, 262
Byrne, David, 31–33, 35, 36, 44, 303

C

Callaghan, Gillian, 31–33, 35, 36, 44, 303
Campbell, David, 7, 8, 237, 238, 249
Capa, Robert, 84, 91, 97, 119, 264, 269
captions, 69, 83, 97, 101, 114–116, 128, 189
Cartier-Bresson, Henri, 270, 271
causality, 32, 33
center–surround dynamics, 257
Chalasani, Radhika, 85, 269
Chim (David Seymour), 84
Cieplak, Piotr, 144
Cilliers, Paul, 55, 187, 188, 305
citizen photography, 213, 227
closure, 185
closure (MCCloud), 200
co-author(ship), 17, 18, 135, 139, 147, 154, 161, 177, 192, 200, 202, 212, 216, 217, 223, 228
Cobb, Sara, 9, 40, 43, 64, 281–283, 290
cognitive closure, 27
coherence, 6, 25, 31, 38, 39, 41, 136, 221, 222, 225, 249, 259, 296
Coleman, Peter T., 27, 28, 32, 36–43
commonalities, 19, 239, 240, 248, 290, 293, 311
complexification, 9, 20, 28, 41, 137, 186, 236, 247, 309–312
complexity, 6, 8–16, 18, 20, 25–28, 30, 31, 33–47, 53, 54, 56–58, 60, 61, 64, 65, 67, 81, 87, 101, 107, 108, 114, 126, 135, 136, 139, 146, 154, 161, 162, 172, 179, 184, 185, 187, 193, 196, 197, 212, 222, 225, 228, 235, 236, 242, 247, 250, 255, 281, 282, 284, 288, 293–295, 303–307
complexity theory, 4, 15, 30, 31, 37, 44, 47, 57, 61, 108, 135, 154, 193, 196, 242, 294, 303

INDEX 337

conflict, 5, 8–10, 14–16, 18, 19, 26–30, 32–36, 38–43, 47, 56–60, 63, 64, 67, 72, 81, 82, 84, 90–92, 96, 98, 107, 112, 117, 119, 126, 135–137, 140, 143, 144, 151, 152, 162, 163, 165, 174, 175, 185, 187, 210, 212–214, 225–227, 236, 238, 246, 247, 263, 274, 279–286, 289–291, 294, 303, 306, 307, 309–312
conflict resolution, 9, 41, 43, 64, 136, 152, 163, 236, 247, 282
conflict transformation, 19, 136, 279–281, 283, 286, 289
consensus-as-sameness (Cobb, Sara), 281, 294
consistency, 5, 6, 12, 41
Contreras, Narciso, 262
cooperation, 282
Couldry, Nick, 9, 161, 178, 249, 250
Croatia, 237
cropping, 262, 270, 273
Curtis, Ben, 70, 83, 113
Curtis, Simon, 31

D
Danchev, Alex, 94, 97, 258
Davies, Katherine, 257
Dayton Peace Accords, 14, 141, 144, 147, 152, 162, 163, 210, 225, 240, 243, 306
de Coning, Cedric, 6, 14
Demick, Barbara, 185
Demnig, Gunter, 1
dichotomy, 235, 311
difference, 4, 6, 9, 10, 14, 17–19, 63, 64, 69, 70, 90, 101, 114, 124, 141, 188, 198, 236, 238, 239, 246, 247, 250, 280, 281, 290, 294, 296, 303

digitization, 18, 45, 69, 89, 118, 121–124, 126, 217, 228, 250, 280
Diklić, Darko, 307
DiNucci, Darcy, 214
disaggregation, 185, 213, 226, 243, 307, 309
disambiguation, 12, 15–17, 20, 45, 47, 62, 67, 69, 70, 81, 107, 108, 113, 115, 117, 118, 122, 123, 128, 135–137, 139, 152, 161, 227, 229, 235, 237, 250, 304, 307, 309, 310
discourse, 6, 8, 12, 17–19, 37, 44, 87, 88, 91, 98, 100, 108, 113, 136, 150, 237, 238, 248, 258, 261, 284
  photographic discourse, 71
discourse analysis, 12
discursive construction, 61
Donia, Robert, 151, 241, 249
dualism, 304, 311

E
East Sarajevo, 240
Eggleston, Williams, 111–114
either/or, 7, 161, 165, 194, 197, 200, 241, 304, 311, 312
Elkins, James, 111, 120, 236, 248, 255, 261–265, 273
elusiveness, 19, 290, 293, 295
Emerling, Jae, 196–198, 289
Empson, William, 56
engaged tolerance, 305, 310
European Union, 237
everyday peace, 92, 93, 174
excess meaning (MacDougall), 261, 290

F
Fairey, Tiffany, 94, 100, 287

Fako, Amela, 165
Farewell to Bosnia (Peress, Gilles), 143, 144, 209
Favero, Paolo, 216, 218, 219, 221, 223
feedback, 227
feelings, 219, 226
Fenton, Roger, 91, 119
Foucault, Michael, 195
frame, 257, 262, 263, 270, 271
Frenkel-Brunswick, Else, 62, 63, 65
Friedrich, Ernst, 92

G

Gafić, Ziyah, 95, 96
Galerija 11/07/95, 175
Gallo, Giorgio, 55, 60, 61
Gaudenzi, Sandra, 222, 223
Geyer, Robert, 187
Gilbey, Peter, 63, 71
Gilgen, Peter, 113, 166, 168, 177, 292
Global Peace Photo Award, 288
Golubović, Jelena, 185, 242
grid structure, 139, 148, 179, 184, 197, 198, 200, 203
Gutman, Roy, 86
Gwertzman, Bernard, 150

H

Habermas, Jürgen Habermas, 25, 26
Hariman, Robert, 119, 257–259, 266–268, 270, 273
Haviv, Ron, 86, 90, 99, 166, 218
Holbrooke, Richard, 140, 141, 144, 150, 210, 211, 215
Holmes, Jamie, 65, 67, 72
Horn, Steve, 97, 99, 120
Hughes, Scott, 30, 31, 36
human rights, 87, 88

I

identity, 1, 3, 5, 7, 18, 40, 64, 68, 93, 95, 96, 201, 236–238, 242, 249, 284, 309, 310
images
  ambiguity of, 68, 71
  dialectical images, 68
imagination, 238, 247, 248
incompatibility, 57, 63
ineffability, 19, 290, 291, 293, 295
inscription (Benjamin), 292
interaction, 19, 27, 28, 32, 35, 58, 67, 81, 118, 122–125, 147, 177, 213, 214, 217–219, 268
  active interaction, 17, 125–127, 184, 193, 220, 221, 223, 224, 227
  passive interaction, 127
interactive design, 135
interactive documentaries, 15, 213, 216, 218, 221, 222, 228
interactivity, 160, 212, 215, 217, 220, 221, 226, 229
International Criminal Tribunal for the Former Yugoslavia (ICTY), 306
International relations (IR), 9–12, 16, 30, 61, 136, 311
Internet, 138, 141, 146, 148, 150, 153, 184, 212, 214, 215, 227, 280
interpretive openness, 4, 12, 15, 97, 101, 149, 152, 165, 271, 292
intervention, 29, 33, 36
invisibility, 19, 111, 257–259, 263, 264
Inzlicht, Michael, 65, 72
Izetbegović, Alija, 211

J

Jabri, Vivienne, 311, 312
Jergović, Miljenko, 243

Jestrovic, Silvija, 82, 93, 100, 307
Jones, Wendell, 31, 36
journalism, 15, 141, 148, 183, 200, 219

K

Karahasan, Dževad, 137–139, 238
Katzenstein, Peter, 309
Kavalski, Emilian, 30, 31
Kebo, Ozren, 96
Kelsey, Robin, 88
Kerr, Rachel, 94, 100
Kleiboer, Marieke, 281
Knight, Gary, 144
knowledge, knowledge production, 7, 19, 69, 135, 147, 148, 153, 154, 159, 160, 175, 178, 179, 184, 188, 196, 214, 216, 236, 243, 259, 260, 262, 265, 266, 273, 274, 280, 281, 286, 304, 305
Kriesberg, Louis, 281
Krippendorff, Ekkehard, 110

L

language, 110, 113, 114, 116, 142, 288, 289, 291–293
Law, John, 5, 225, 304
Lederach, John Paul, 42, 143, 247
legitimacy, 244
Leibing, Peter, 272
Levi, Primo, 186
liberal peace, 34
limits of tolerance, 305
Linfield, Susie, 70, 87, 89, 94, 95, 109, 113, 142, 288
Lisle, Debbie, 97, 98, 101, 258
Lister, Martin, 121
local turn, 34, 35
Lowe, Paul, 82, 84–87, 89–93, 95–97, 137, 138, 140, 144, 146, 151, 209, 210, 307, 309

Lubart, Todd, 72
Lucaites, John Louis, 119, 257–259, 266–268, 270, 273
Lyons, Robert, 46, 47

M

MacDougall, David, 68, 69, 186, 187, 189, 256, 257, 261, 288–290, 292, 293
Margalit, Avishai, 144
Markowitz, Fran, 240, 241, 248, 250
Mason, Jennifer, 257
McCloud, Scott, 200–202, 268
McCullin, Don, 91, 92, 119
Meadows, Donella, 42, 47, 48
meaning, 3, 4, 7, 8, 12, 13, 17–19, 33, 40, 45, 108, 109, 115, 116, 135, 141–143, 149, 152, 153, 160, 161, 164, 166, 189, 195, 203, 215, 224, 228, 236, 250, 255, 257–259, 284, 287
  control of, 69, 109, 117, 118, 122
  designations of, 69
  excess meaning, 68
  meaning-making, 19, 45, 46, 72, 222, 224, 255, 265, 280, 282
  plurality of, 115, 123
  surplus of, 83
media, 146, 147, 149, 151
mediation, 279–281, 283–286, 288–295
Meiselas, Susan, 119
memory, memories, 1, 3, 4, 14, 59, 92, 95, 98, 99, 111, 118–120, 175, 186, 214, 244, 306
Mirzoeff, Nicholas, 287
Mitchell, W.J.T., 67–69, 110, 113, 289, 292, 293
Monk, Gerald, 43, 282–284, 286, 296
moral imagination (Lederach, John paul), 247

Morris, Chris, 83, 93
Morris, Errol, 152
Morrison, Kenneth, 84–87, 89, 91–93, 138, 140, 148, 151
Mouffe, Chantal, 246, 247
Müller-Christ, Georg, 63, 65, 66
multi-author perspective, 213
multiculturalism, 4, 7, 8, 151, 240, 248
multimedia, 218
multiplicity, 6, 7, 97, 166, 293
multi-sensory, 178, 216
multi-sensory narrative, 184

N
Nachtwey, James, 70, 87, 114
narrative, 4, 9, 11, 15, 18, 40, 41, 43, 72, 86, 96, 98, 112, 127, 128, 159–161, 163–165, 167–169, 175, 178, 235, 236, 243, 248, 255, 256, 260, 262, 272, 274, 279, 280, 282–285, 290, 293–295, 311, 312
narrative coherence, 221
narrative complexity, 284
narrative equality, 283
narrative openness, 213, 221, 222, 235, 279, 285, 295, 296
narrative plurality, 4, 154, 179, 184, 204, 228, 229, 236, 255, 290
narrative tradition, 280
narrative tradition in peacebuilding, 236
narrative transformation, 283
Nash, Kate, 218, 219, 221, 222, 226, 229
network, 188, 190, 192, 197
New York Times, 141, 149, 190, 222, 224, 227
New York Times on the Web, 15, 17, 135, 139, 159, 183
Nichols, Bill, 219

non-coherence, 6, 7, 10, 12, 13, 69, 117, 225, 242, 279
non-linearity, 6, 35, 141, 147, 165, 215, 222
Norfolk, Simon, 97, 98

O
Oldfield, Pippa, 175
open-ended narratives, 177
Orsini, Amandine, 29
Oslobodjenje, 241

P
Palalic, Edib, 97, 210
Palu, Louie, 83, 84, 89
panel-to-panel transitions/sequences, 192, 193, 201–203
patchwork, 242
peace, 5, 8, 9, 11, 15, 16, 19, 26, 28–30, 33, 35, 36, 39, 43, 47, 56, 58, 59, 63, 64, 67, 81, 88, 92, 93, 97–99, 107, 112, 118, 126, 135, 136, 139, 143, 146, 148–150, 152, 153, 160, 167, 175, 183, 184, 210, 213, 214, 220, 225, 227, 228, 236, 243–246, 279–282, 285–290, 292, 293, 295, 303, 306, 311
peace and conflict research/studies, 16, 136, 311
peacebuilding, 5, 6, 9, 18, 29, 33, 34, 36, 37, 39, 59, 143, 186, 211, 236, 247, 249, 279, 295
peace mediation, 64
peace photography, 98
peace research, 279–281, 286
Penfound, GIles, 94
Peress, Gilles, 8, 15, 17, 72, 94, 95, 120, 135, 138, 139, 141–144, 146–149, 153, 154, 159, 160, 163, 167–169, 172, 173, 175,

177, 183, 187, 203, 209–217, 219, 221, 222, 224, 226, 227, 255, 256, 268, 272, 274, 304, 307
photoambiguity, 16, 55, 67, 108, 112, 115, 126, 135, 139
photocomplexity, 16, 20, 43, 44, 48, 108, 126, 135, 139, 154
photographer–audience interaction, 212
photography, 70, 71, 107, 119, 122, 172, 175, 178, 184, 196, 258–261, 265, 268, 269, 272, 274
  aftermath photography, 15, 96, 98, 107, 112, 184, 213
  and ethics, 84
  as democratic art, 87
  documentary, 82, 212
  forensic photography, 15, 45, 93, 94, 107, 144, 213, 289
  participatory photography, 15, 99, 100, 213
  post-conflict photography, 15, 98–100, 213
  pro-active, 214
photojournalism, 13, 17, 18, 45, 68–70, 72, 81–85, 87–90, 92, 96, 98, 99, 101, 107, 108, 119, 123–125, 166, 169, 173, 178, 179, 189, 197, 209, 212, 213, 218, 219, 223–225, 228, 250, 257, 259, 265, 266, 270, 280, 287, 292, 308
plausibility, 309
plurality, 7, 12, 17, 18, 63, 70, 108, 112, 116, 118, 159, 172, 177, 179, 213, 222, 228, 229, 235, 236, 238, 250, 260, 262, 273
  of meaning, 6, 8, 12, 13, 15, 70, 101, 108, 112, 115, 116, 123, 135, 141, 149, 152, 161, 273, 279, 288, 290, 293
positive peace, 243
postmodernism, 305
poststructuralism, 45
pro-active documentation, 86
problem-solving, 19, 65, 280, 282
Proulx, Travis, 65, 72
punctum (Barthes, Roland), 192, 193

R
Rancière, Jacques, 109, 115, 123, 127, 128, 159, 160, 255, 269, 289
Randazzo, Elisa, 34–36
reconciliation, 3, 100, 162, 210, 225
representability, 19, 142, 257
representation, 257–259, 263, 267, 269, 272
resistance, 307, 308
Ristic, Mirjana, 1, 3, 188, 240
Ritchin, Fred, 8, 15, 17, 68, 70, 72, 98, 113, 117, 118, 121, 122, 135, 138–142, 146–152, 159–162, 164, 165, 171, 174, 177, 178, 183, 187, 189, 192, 197, 198, 202, 203, 210, 212–219, 221–226, 228, 229, 255, 256, 270, 287, 292, 307
Roberts, John, 243, 260, 287
Rosen, Jay, 223
Rosler, Martha, 88
Rubinstein, Daniel, 251

S
Sacco, Joe, 60, 249
sameness, 18, 19, 64, 236, 280, 281
Sánchez, Gervasio, 94
Sarajevo, 1, 3, 4, 7, 9, 10, 18, 20, 46, 48, 120, 127, 128, 183, 185,

188–190, 193, 195–197, 203, 204, 210, 211, 272, 274
  siege of, 1, 3, 7, 84, 87, 91, 137, 163, 174, 178, 185, 186, 216, 239, 244, 307, 309
Sarajevo Roses, 1, 3, 4
Schmid, Ulrich, 93
scopic regimes (Feldman), 290, 291
Sebilj (Sarajevo), 244, 245
Sennet, Adam, 57
Sennett, Richard, 305
sequential art, 192, 199, 201, 202
Serbia, 245
Shapiro, Michael, 14
simplification, 8, 16, 20, 39, 41, 42, 47, 96, 99, 101, 136, 137, 185, 186, 282, 309, 310
singularity, 7
Sliwinski, Sharon, 88, 99, 287
Slovenia, 237
Sluis, Katrina, 251
Smith, Shawn Michelle, 258
social construction of reality, 249
social media, 213, 228
sociology of knowledge, 109
Solomon-Godeau, Abigail, 88
Sontag, Susan, 69, 70, 88, 92, 95, 109, 111, 115, 116, 120, 122, 141, 148, 151, 287–289, 295
sovereignty, 7, 237, 238
space of architecture (Alpen), 198
space of landscape (Alpen), 198
space(s) of possibility, 33, 55, 82, 98, 101, 154, 303, 305, 306
Spanish Civil War, 84
speech act, 33, 38, 61
Spiegelman, Art, 199
Stimson, Blake, 88
Stoddart, Tom, 308
Stolpersteine, 1
Straus, Scott, 46, 47

suburbs (of Sarajevo), 151, 154, 164, 167, 168, 174, 183, 185, 189, 190, 197, 203, 204
surround, 19, 236, 255–258, 260–266, 268, 270–274, 304
Susperregui, José Manuel, 262, 264, 265, 273
system(s), 5, 6, 10, 13, 28–34, 36, 39, 43, 47, 48, 53–57, 61, 62, 65–67, 72, 107, 124, 304, 305
Sznaider, Natan, 136, 161
Szubielska, Magdalena, 71

T
Taro, Gerda, 84
Telios, Thomas, 93
Terry, Sara, 96–98, 210, 213
The Falling Soldier (Capa, Robert), 45, 118, 259, 262, 264, 265, 269, 273
Thomä, Dieter, 93
Thompson, Jerry, 44
Torrent, Ignasi, 34–36
trauma, 14, 98, 143, 175, 243, 246

U
uncertainty, 10, 14, 35, 36, 54, 235, 251
United Nations, 163, 215
Urry, John, 32
Ut, Nick, 119, 266, 270, 271, 273

V
Varešanović, Meliha, 308
victim(hood), 308
violence, 1, 3, 17, 19, 26, 28, 33, 34, 60, 64, 72, 87, 89, 92, 93, 96, 140, 143, 146, 151, 172, 174, 185, 210, 211, 214, 219, 227, 238, 242, 243, 245, 247, 248,

271, 279, 282, 285, 286, 288, 291, 303, 307–309
visibility, 19, 136, 151, 257, 260, 263, 264
Visoka, Gëzim, 33
visual analysis, 10, 12, 13, 260
visuality, 5, 7, 9, 10, 12, 13, 15, 43, 45, 55, 67, 69, 110, 126, 135, 279, 287, 292, 303

W

Walker, R.B.J., 26, 29
Walsh, Lauren, 99
Waltz, Christoph, 110
war photography, 258

Weßling, Gudrun, 63, 65, 66
Wenders, Wim, 116, 117, 166, 248, 287, 293
Wilkes Tucker, Anne, 143
Williams, Raymond, 109
Williams, Val, 82
Winslade, John M., 43, 282–284, 286, 296
word–image relationship, 113–115, 118, 280, 288, 290
World Press Photo Award, 288

Z

Zenasni, Franck, 72
Zournazi, Mary, 287, 293